LONG ISLAND MODERNISM
1930–1980

LONG ISLAND MODERNISM

1930–1980 | CAROLINE ROB ZALESKI

SOCIETY FOR THE PRESERVATION OF LONG ISLAND ANTIQUITIES

IN ASSOCIATION WITH

W. W. NORTON & COMPANY

NEW YORK • LONDON

Furthermore:
a program of the J.M. Kaplan Fund

This book was produced with support from Furthermore: a program of the J. M. Kaplan Fund

Copyright © 2012 by Caroline Rob Zaleski

All rights reserved
Printed in Canada
First Edition

For information about permission to reproduce
selections from this book, write to Permissions,
W. W. Norton & Company, Inc., 500 Fifth Avenue,
New York, NY 10110

For information about special discounts for bulk
purchases, please contact W. W. Norton Special Sales
at specialsales@wwnorton.com or 800-233-4830

Manufacturing by Friesens
Book design by Abigail Sturges
Digital production by Joe Lops
Production manager: Leeann Graham

Library of Congress Cataloging-in-Publication Data

Zaleski, Caroline Rob.
 Long Island modernism : 1930-1980 / Caroline Rob Zaleski. —
First Edition.
      pages cm
Includes bibliographical references and index.
ISBN 978-0-393-73315-0 (hardcover)
1. Modern movement (Architecture)—New York (State)—
Long Island. 2. Architecture—New York (State)—Long Island—
History—20th century. I. Title.
NA730.N42L669 2012
720.9747'210904—dc23
                          2012011619

ISBN: 978-0-393-73315-0

W. W. Norton & Company, Inc., 500 Fifth Avenue,
New York, N.Y. 10110
www.wwnorton.com
W. W. Norton & Company Ltd., Castle House,
75/76 Wells Street, London W1T 3QT

0 9 8 7 6 5 4 3 2 1

CONTENTS

FOREWORD / 6
PREFACE AND ACKNOWLEDGMENTS / 6

1. WALLACE HARRISON / 26
2. A. LAWRENCE KOCHER AND THE FORT SALONGA COLONY / 36
3. FRANK LLOYD WRIGHT / 52
4. ANTONIN RAYMOND / 58
5. DAVID L. LEAVITT / 64
6. MARCEL BREUER / 70
7. JANE YU / 82
8. WILLIAM LANDSBERG / 86
9. HAMILTON P. SMITH / 94
10. JOSEP LLUÍS SERT / 98
11. HERMANN HERREY / 106
12. BENJAMIN THOMPSON WITH THE ARCHITECTS COLLABORATIVE AND SHOGO MYAIDA / 112
13. EDWARD DURELL STONE / 126
14. PERCIVAL GOODMAN / 152
15. RICHARD NEUTRA / 164
16. WILLIAM LESCAZE / 180
17. GORDON CHADWICK WITH GEORGE NELSON / 194
18. LUDWIG MIES VAN DER ROHE / 216
19. PHILIP JOHNSON / 224
20. I. M. PEI / 238
21. DAMAZ, POKORNY & WEIGEL, GRUZEN & PARTNERS, ET AL. / 252
22. JOHN JOHANSEN, ALEXANDER KOUZMANOFF, AND VICTOR CHRIST-JANER / 268
23. PAUL RUDOLPH / 276
24. JOHN W. STEDMAN JR. / 292
25. RICHARD MEIER / 300

NOTES / 314
INVENTORY OF ARCHITECTS AND THEIR LONG ISLAND PROJECTS / 318
SELECTED BIBLIOGRAPHY / 325
PHOTO CREDITS / 333
INDEX / 334

FOREWORD

This project began as a New York State Council on the Arts–funded field survey in Nassau County, but through her vigorous efforts, Caroline Rob Zaleski greatly expanded it into the first comprehensive record of the radically inventive Modern period on all of Long Island. Following up on every lead and making innumerable visits to far-flung archives, she has unearthed a wealth of new material about architects and their clients, added to our knowledge of the period, and helped us understand what is worth preserving. A compelling storyteller, Caroline guides us to an understanding of how modern architectural principles from abroad entered the Long Island context, in part as a result of exhibitions at the Museum of Modern Art and the refashioning of American architecture schools. She also shows us how various architects' aesthetic and programmatic expressions changed along with conventions and the rise of post–World War II prosperity.

An informed preservation advocate, Caroline's work on the project enabled her to influence outcomes. Her discovery, along with the staff at Esto Photographics, for example, of Ezra Stoller's 1941 photographs of the Edward Durell Stone–designed A. Conger Goodyear House in Old Westbury played an important part in the efforts to preserve that modern landmark. For SPLIA, *Long Island Modernism 1930–1980* is the latest title in a publication program dating back to 1960 that focuses on salient aspects of Long island's remarkable past with particular reference to architecture, landscape design, and the decorative arts. This project was made possible with funding from the New York State Council on the Arts and the Gerry Charitable Trust,Furthermore . Our hats are off to Huyler C. Held, Chair of SPLIA's Publications Committee, and Nancy Green, Senior Editor at W. W. Norton, who recognized the possibilities of this publication when it was still only an outline.

ROBERT B. MACKAY, PH.D.
Director
Society for the Preservation
of Long Island Antiquities

PREFACE AND ACKNOWLEDGMENTS

The starting point for *Long Island Modernism 1930–1980* came in 2002, when Robert MacKay asked me to undertake a field survey of modern buildings for the Society for the Preservation of Long Island Antiquities (SPLIA). As its executive director and chair of the New York State Preservation Board, he felt strongly that historical societies around the state needed to take stock of the more recent past. *Long Island Country Houses and Their Architects, 1860–1940*, the book he coauthored with Anthony Baker, Carol A. Traynor, and Brendan Gill, also published in association with W. W. Norton, documents the architecture of the great estates. This book is a kind of sequel to theirs, as it examines the period when the majority of the great estates and much of Long Island's farmland were subdivided, making way for a tidal wave of suburbanization.

Not as encyclopedic as its distinguished older cousin, this book presents a series of essays on the Long Island projects of a representative selection of important modern architects. The appendix, "Inventory of Architects and Their Long Island Projects," provides a more comprehensive list, proof positive that important architecture was built on the island by architects of regional, national, and international renown. The list is not exhaustive, however. No doubt others will make new discoveries, and I imagine that I will too. But it does indicate that Long Island—the largest and longest island in the contiguous United States and today more populated than Ireland—was a testing ground for the new architecture, which had its preliminary showing in the U.S. at the Museum of Modern Art's *Modern Architecture: International Exhibition* in 1932. A surprising number of the torch-bearing European and American-based architects whose work was represented in the now-famous exhibition built projects on Long Island, as did a rebellious generation of their students and protégés.

Modernism was never monolithic, as the variety of projects in the book makes clear. Yet, by 1980, the end date of this study, it had fallen completely out of favor, its artifacts often neglected and in danger. Postmodernism, the pastiche-driven antidote to modernism, took off on Long Island after the time frame that the book covers. With its penchant for classical and "ye olde" ornamentation, the movement put modernism at risk by reviling it.

Many of the projects featured in the book were designed in response to the 1939 and 1940 World's Fairs in Flushing Meadows, Queens, whose organizers promoted a futuristic "World of Tomorrow" that envisioned a vast regional plan incorporating modern architecture. World War II put a temporary halt to carrying out the fairs' vision on the domestic front, but it was resumed at war's end, particularly on Long Island. The generation that won the war embraced modernity and aesthetic risk, and many looked to architecturally progressive idioms to show off the American way of life as practical and bursting with ingenuity. Most people wanted suburban lifestyles and chose to move out of the city, taking advantage of the economic incentives to do so.

Further study is needed about a number of the architects listed in the appendix who could not be included in the body of the book because of limited space. The practice of Frederick and Maria Bentel, for instance, merits greater attention. Out of their Locust Valley studio, they built residences and what they called "community architecture" out of strong materials and minimalist forms for a number of commercial and institutional clients. George Nemeny, an architect of daring shapes and rugged materials, also deserves renewed recognition. Out of offices in Manhattan and Great Neck, he designed bold residences in partnership with Abraham W. Geller and others. A third example is the husband-and-wife team of Julian and Barbara Neski. Most of their production is found out on the East End, where they designed houses that were paeans to convenience and cozy domesticity, often complex multilevel spaces with a powerful structural presence, but never out of place.

Before I began this project, my view of Long Island was telescoped directly from the East River to the East End, in the manner of Saul Steinberg's famous *New Yorker* cover from 1976, "The World as Seen from 9th Avenue," in which he depicted a view from Manhattan to China, with not much of importance in between. Arriving in Manhattan in the mid-1970s, I quickly learned to appreciate invitations from friends to spend summer weekends in East End beach villages, where it was cool . In those days there was a feeling of open space on the East End, with sweeping vistas of flat fields and the ocean and bays from the roadways. The traffic-clogged drive out on the Long Island Expressway made it seem as if there were little of interest between Manhattan and the Manorville exit, just exit-ramp architecture and suburban sprawl. Myopic no longer, I know that the entire island is a wonderful place for the exploration of historic architecture, gardens, parks, and museums, as well as the most beautiful beaches and scenic locations anywhere.

I feel privileged to have been welcomed by so many to see their buildings, gardens, and views and to listen to their stories. I am enormously grateful to Bob MacKay for his guidance and to the board of SPLIA for providing me with the opportunity to work on the book under their aegis. In my telephone calls to introduce myself to building owners and archivists, the time-honored SPLIA name, either the long or the short of it, always got me in the door.

Field-survey work, follow-up research, and interviews are social activities, whereas writing requires steely discipline and uninterrupted time. What helped me through the isolated writing process was my knowledge that the project had support from foundations whose discerning officers were willing to provide financial assistance. I am honored to thank Huyler C. Held from the Gerry Charitable Trust for his encouragement and belief in the project from the start. I also want to thank Anne Van Ingen, formerly director of the Architecture Planning and Design Program at the New York State Council on the Arts, whose committees provided two grants, including one in the Independent Scholars category.

A special thank you to Erica Stoller at Esto for allowing me to spend several days going through

Ezra Stoller's photographic archive in search of forgotten Long Island, and to Christine Cordazzo at Esto, who processed a large order.

I am deeply grateful to archivists and librarians: Bob Allard, Westhampton Free Library; Jonathan Aubrey, Reference Librarian, Great Neck Library; Wendy Hurlock Baker, Rights and Reproductions Coordinator, Archives of American Art, Smithsonian Institution; Indira Berndtson, Administrator Historic Studies, Frank Lloyd Wright Archive; Melanie Bower, Manager of Collections Access, Museum of the City of New York; Dr. Edward Chappell, Director of Architectural Research, Colonial Williamsburg Foundation; Gail Cooke, Archivist, Garden Club of America; Mary Daniels, Special Collections Librarian, Loeb Library, Harvard University Graduate School of Design; Nicolette A. Dobrowolski, Head of Public Services and Reference and Access Librarian, Syracuse University, Special Collections Research Center; Elaine Engst, Director, Division of Rare and Manuscript Collections, Kroch Library, Cornell University; Russell Flinchum, Archivist, Century Association Archives Foundation; Laura Galvanek, Director of Archives and Exhibitions, Richard Meier & Partners Architects LLP; Cecelia Gibson, Exhibition Registrar, National Building Museum; Teresa Harris, Project Coordinator, Marcel Breuer Digital Archive, Syracuse University; Lilace Hatayama, Literary Manuscripts Specialist, Manuscripts Division, Department of Special Collections, Charles E. Young Research Library, UCLA; Jarron Jewell, Special Collections Librarian, Rare Books Archivist, and Conrad Schoeffling, Department Head, Special Collections Librarian, C. W. Post Campus, Long Island University; Sean Khorsandi, Co-Director, Paul Rudolph Foundation; Stephen Kirkpatrick, Library Director, SUNY Old Westbury; H. Kevin Miserocchi, Executive Director, Tee and Charles Addams Foundation; Gary Monti, Director of Visitor Services, Cradle of Aviation Museum, Garden City; Jane Nakasako, Reference Assistant and Project Manager, Japanese American National Museum; Eugene Neely, University Archivist and Special Collections Librarian, , Adelphi University Library; Kristen Nyitray, University Archivist and Head, Special Collections and University Archives, Stony Brook University; Janet Parks, Curator of Drawings & Archives, Avery Architectural and Fine Arts Library, Columbia University; C. Ford Peatross, Curator, Center for Architecture, Design and Engineering, Library of Congress; Amy Rule, Archivist and former Head of Research Services, Center for Creative Photography at the University of Arizona; Jennifer Santo, Librarian, Locust Valley Library; Geoffrey Stark, Special Collections Reading Room Supervisor, University of Arkansas Library Special Collections; Joshua Stoff, Curator, Cradle of Aviation Museum, Garden City; Jennifer Tobias, Librarian, Reader Services, Museum of Modern Art; William Whitaker, Collections Manager, Architectural Archives, Fisher Fine Arts Library, University of Pennsylvania; the staff of the Queens Public Library, Long Island Division.

For sharing precious information and memories, I thank: Kathryn Abbe; Julius and Anne Abeles; Earl Anderson; Frederick Ayer II; Elizabeth Barker; Saretta Barnet; Roger Bartels; Adam Bartos; Elizabeth Bassine; Bjorg Bastiansen; Frederick Bentel; Paul Bentel; Patsy Nemeny Berman; Nina Bernstein; Theodore Bindrim; Peter Blake; Cornelius Bliss; Leslie Blum; Walter Blum; Beth Bogie; Charla Bolton; Pete and Sandy Bourdelle; Fran Bourquet; Norman L. Brickell; Jean-Luc Brouillaud; Ann Brower; Peter Brower; Patricia Rosen Burgman; Maria S. Calderone; Francesca Calderone-Steichen; Marcia Cantoni; Peter Capone; Oleg Cassini; Mrs. Russell Chadwick; Karey Christ-Janer; Katherine Christ-Janer; Barbara Comfort; Jane and John Comfort; Bryant Conant; William Condon; Jane White Cooke; Dave Corner; Thaddeus Crapster; Matthew A. Cuomo; Godfrey Dallek; Hubert Damisch; Barbara Deane; Maurice Deane; Elizabeth de Cuevas; Bill Degennaro; Michael de Havenon; Hester Diamond; Ruth Eckstein; Elsa Edmonds; Claude Engle; Laurie Nemeny Estep; Phyllis Rothschild Farley; Frances Fennebresque; Sarah Fletcher; Susan Grossi Forsyth; Jean France; Paul Friedberg; Debra Miller Gates; Amy Geller; Andrew Geller; Joseph Geller; Michael Geller; Philip George; Craig Gibson; Nina Gibson; John Lawrence Githens; Sharon F. Goldwyn; Joel Goodman; Rabbi Linda Henry Goodman; Rachel Goodman; Zachary Goodyear; William H. Grover; Lee Gruzen; Molly Goodyear Gurney; Bea Hanson; Blake Hanson; Margaret M. Hargraves; Irving Harper; Virginia Harrison; Antony Herrey; Peter and Mary Hirdt; Anita Hoffman; David Hoffman, Jr.; Pamela Howard; Margaret

(TEXT CONTINUES ON PAGE 25)

MARCEL BREUER

Bert and Phyllis Geller House I, Lawrence, 1945. Combining a Russian Constructivist aesthetic with traditional New England wood-based construction techniques, Breuer designed a prize-winning house.

Bert and Phyllis Geller House I, Lawrence, 1945. The main entrance door, painted Breuer's signature blue. The two wings of his binuclear plan for the modern family are clearly seen in this view.

OVERLEAF
Map from "Long Island: The Sunrise Homeland," a booklet published for the Long Island Regional Exhibit, New York World's Fair, Flushing Meadows, Queens, 1940. The Fair promoted Nassau County as an enterprinsing modern suburb, and Suffolk County as where "Vacation Land Begins."

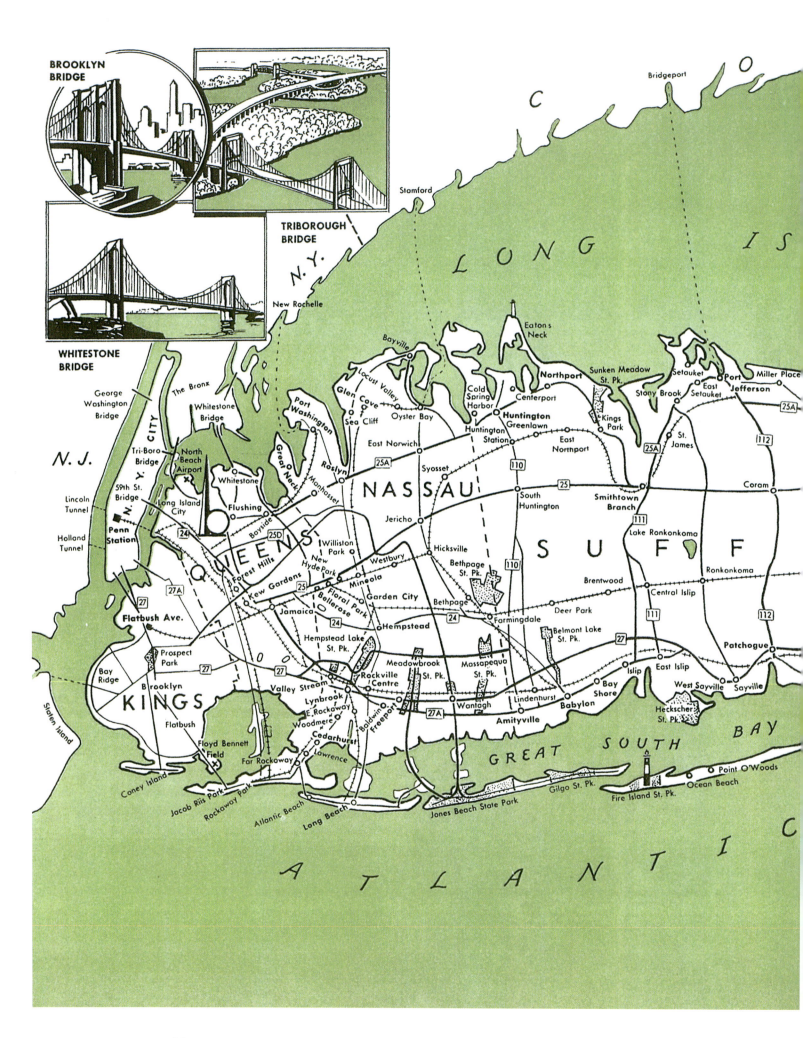

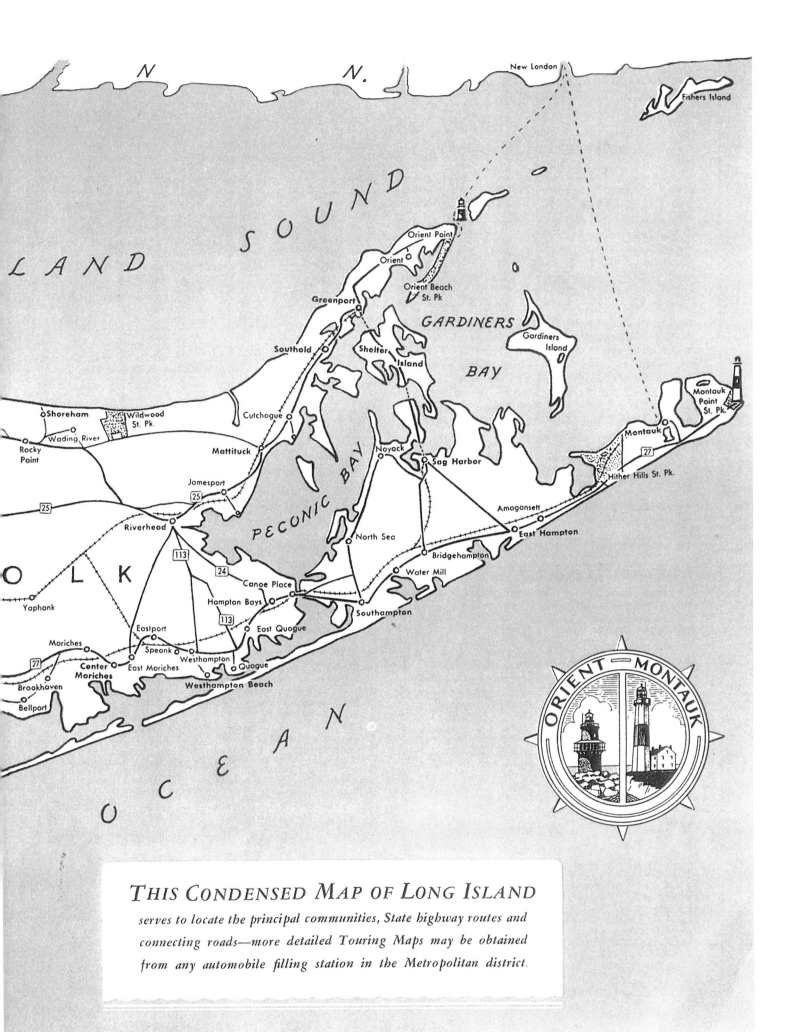

THIS CONDENSED MAP OF LONG ISLAND

serves to locate the principal communities, State highway routes and connecting roads—more detailed Touring Maps may be obtained from any automobile filling station in the Metropolitan district.

ANTONIN RAYMOND

Charles Briggs and Raoul Carrerà House, Montauk, 1941–42. The newly built house in an indigenous dunescape, before nursery plantings encroached on the oceanside terrain along Montauk Highway.

Charles Briggs and Raoul Carrerà House, Montauk, 1941-1942. View of the living and dining room from the den. The interior elevations and furniture were designed by Noémi Raymond and fabricated at the Raymonds' New Hope Workshop.

ANTONIN RAYMOND

Daniel and Rose Krakauer House, Great Neck, 1946. Living/dining room, 2003. By the mid-1950s the Krakauers had turned to living room furniture by Hans Wegner and other modern designers. George Nakashima, who worked with the Raymonds at their New Hope Workshop, designed furniture for the master bedroom.

Daniel and Rose Krakauer House, Great Neck, 1946. Bedroom hallway, 2003. The Raymonds used low-cost building materials from local building-supply houses for this house, just as they did for the Charles Briggs and Raoul Carrerà house. Note the cork flooring, which is used throughout the house.

EDWARD DURELL STONE

Levitt and Sons Executive Office Building, Lake Success, 1968. Developer William Levitt relished relocating his company to a place called Lake Success. And he chose Stone to design the new building because he knew that a signature design by the then world-renowned architect would generate a great deal of publicity.

RIGHT
Levitt and Sons Executive Office Building, Lake Success, 1968. Interior atrium, reminiscent of Stone's United States Embassy in New Delhi.

OPPOSITE
Gabriele Lagerwall House (Villa Rielle), Lloyd Harbor, 1963. The dining room, at the opposite end of the atrium from where Stone placed the living room.

JOSEP LLUÍS SERT

Marian Willard and Dan Johnson House, Locust Valley, 1947. South façade of "Meudon sur Lac", as Marion Willard named their house on the pond, 2011.

BENJAMIN THOMPSON WITH TAC

Mary Griggs and Jackson Burke House, Centre Island, 1953–61. Japanese-style pencil-and-ink presentation drawing of the south façade and entrance court garden. Draftsman and date unknown.

RICHARD NEUTRA

John Nicholas and Anne Brown Windshield House, Fishers Island, 1938. Presentation drawing, selected as the final version for the northeast façades of the house. As seen here, Richard Neutra typically drew in the style of Gustav Klimt and Egon Schiele, contemporaries of his in Vienna, where he grew up.

LEFT
John Nicholas and Anne Brown Windshield House, Fishers Island, 1938. Presentation drawing, final version, view from the southwest. Neutra specified aluminum paint for the wood siding to give the exterior a decidedly machine-age appearance.

17

RICHARD NEUTRA

Adelphi University, Garden City, 1957–67. Color crayon drawing, The Institute of Communication Arts. This early proposal features a three-story library building and an adjacent tear-drop-shaped "World in Focus Auditorium." Neutra incorporated red brick into his design to echo the six existing brick campus buildings by McKim, Mead & White.

RICHARD NEUTRA

Adelphi University, Garden City, 1957–67. Color crayon perspective drawing by Neutra showing the final version of Neutra and Alexander's as-built master plan with Swirbul Communications Center, left; Institute of Business and Commerce, center; Institute of Science and Industry, right.

THE CROSSAXIS of the QUADRANGLE
ADELPHI UNIVERSITY

TOP
GORDON CHADWICK WITH GEORGE NELSON

Julius and Anne Abeles House, Roslyn, 1954. The living room, with its original color scheme and furniture designed by George Nelson & Associates. Taking the place of curtains, sliding shoji screens provide light filtration and privacy.

ABOVE
PHILIP JOHNSON

Eugene and Margaret Farney House, Sagaponack, 1945–46. The living and dining space opens out onto a deck that overlooks the dunes and the ocean.

RIGHT
PHILIP JOHNSON

Robert and Mary Leonhardt House, Lloyd Neck, 1954–56. The living space, viewed from the waterside lawn.

OPPOSTITE TOP

PAUL RUDOLPH

Endo Laboratories, Garden City, 1964. View of the cafeteria from the roof garden.

OPPOSTITE BOTTOM

PAUL RUDOLPH

Maurice and Barbara Deane House, Kings Point, 1970. Viewed from uphill, the house appears nestled into the land.

ABOVE

PAUL RUDOLPH

Maurice and Barbara Deane House, Kings Point, 1970. The living room is the core of the interior. Several of the hexagonal modules converge here. Note the different floor levels, the planter running beneath the ceiling, and the reflection of the curtain of plants in the mirrored bands on the ceiling above the entryway.

23

PAUL RUDOLPH

Daniel Siegel Beach House, Westhampton Beach, 1978. Front façade. Note the stairway crossing the front of the house to the main entrance.

RICHARD MEIER

Richard Maidman House, Kings Point, 1971–76. Meier splashed the living room with color. Flame-red velvet covers the seating he designed, vivid emerald green paint coats the metal HVAC duct beneath the balcony wall, and an intense purple can be glimpsed on the wall of an adjacent stairwell.

(TEXT CONTINUED FROM PAGE 8)

Luce Howe; Morris Hylton III; Anthony Jackson; Huson Jackson; Oliver James Janney; Stover Jenkins; Phyllis Krakauer Jeswald; Hope Johnson; Miani Johnson; Richard Johnson; John F. Johnston; Mildred Joseph; James Kantor; Jill Kaplan; Phyllis Karasov; Kevin Keim; Joan Kent; Ann Kirschner; Lawrence Kocher, Jr.; Sandra Kocher; Jan Kouzmanoff; Alice Krakauer; Gladys Kruh; Sally Stedman Kuhn; Ed Labaton; Muriel Landsberg; William Landsberg; June Noble Larkin; Jack Lenor Larsen; Ronald and Karyl Lemberger; Cliff Leonhardt; Rebecca Lescaze; Kyna Leski; Simone Levitt; Matthys Levy; Douglas Libby; Mary Lindsay; Jan Locketz; Janet Loewy; Hilda Longinotti; Andreas Lowenfeld; Ira Lubin; Donald Luckenbill; Teri Lynam; Jack Macey; Malcolm MacKay; Richard Maidman; James S. Marcus; Andrew Marglin; Peter Marino; Bart Marksohn; Katherine Marshall; Nora Spivak Marvullo; Angus McIntyre; Randall McIntyre; Edward Messina; Debra Rae Miller; Ron Mitchne, Jr.; George Mittendorf; Carol Morrison; Robert Motzkin; Miyeko Murase; Michael Muserlian; Theodore Musho; Jacqueline Nelson; Barbara Neski; Doris Novick; Eugene Oberdorfer; Rolf Ohlhausen; Abby Milton O'Neill; Ken T. Oshima; Don Page; Diana B. Perron; Mary Petrie; Vincent Polimeni; Florine Polner; Lorin Price; Mary Purcell; Terry Rankine; Christopher Rawlins; Ron Rebhuhn; Debora Reiser; Ken Resen; Edward Resor; Donald Richardson; Phillip and Edna Ritzenberg; Connie Legakis Robinson; Robert Rohrich; Harvey Rosen; Shirley Rosen; Peter Samton; Robert Sargent; Pat Davison Savadove; Andrew Scharf; Melvin Schnall; Katie Schwab; Michael Schwarting; Der Scutt; Bette Segal; Laura Dumper Seitz; William Shopsin; Dani Siegel; Jeff Siegel; Ernest and Arlene Silva; Mark Simon; Melaine D. Small; Hamilton and Caroline Smith; Peter Sobel; Tony Spaeth; Mike Spector; Erwin and Freddie Staller; Bill Stedman; Mary Stedman; Edward Stein; Barbara Sullivan; Edgar Tafel; Susan Tamulevich; Dana Tang; Katrina Thomas; David and Julie Tobey; Terry Townsend; Audrey Troy; Mark Twersky; Hans Van de Bovenkamp; Jim Venturi; Gabriele Viereck; Barbara Von Dehmlein; Edwina von Gal; Ernst Wagner; Helene Wainston; Tom Walton; Mrs. Bradford Weekes; Farley Welch; Laura Welch; Margaret Welch; Judge Leonard Wexler; Gill White; Sandy Williams; Tom Williams; Rabbi Bernard Zlotowitz; Thomas Zung.

Most of all, thank you to Nancy Green, Senior Editor at W. W. Norton, for being a real pro and a pleasure to work with. A special thank you to Brendan Shera for his superb handling of the seemingly relentless photography permissions process. Thanks to Justin Bracanto for helping me organize my collection of photographs on the computer. I am also grateful to Eric Anderson and Lauren Racusin for working with me on this project while they were graduate students at Columbia University.

1

WALLACE HARRISON 1895–1981

Wallace K. and Ellen Harrison House, Huntington, 1932–62

During the Depression, when many architects were out of work, Wallace K. Harrison was a principal partner at Allied Architects, the firm behind the design of Rockefeller Center. In 1931, he and his wife, Ellen, purchased eighty-five acres of farmland in West Hills, outside the town of Huntington, Long Island, to seek respite from his hectic schedule. The property consisted of a number of old buildings, including two barns and a large potato shed near the property line on Round Swamp Road. The couple became land rich but cash poor, and they proceeded to sell off parcels of the land to friends, a practice they continued until the mid-1960s, when they were left with eleven acres.

Wallace Harrison's career was protean and prolific. In addition to overseeing the planning and building of the United Nations (1947–52) and Lincoln Center (1961–65) in Manhattan and Empire State Plaza (1964–75), New York State's government complex, in Albany, he served as master planner and supervising architect for a number of important Long Island–based projects, including the World's Fairs of 1939 and 1964 in Flushing, Queens, and LaGuardia and Idlewild (now John F. Kennedy) airports. In partnership with Max Abramovitz,[1] he designed some specific buildings for these ensembles, as well as scores of university and corporate buildings, including the Time & Life (1959) and Socony-Mobil (1956) buildings, designated New York City landmarks. The New York Hall of Science from the 1964 World's Fair is still in use today; a towering, eighty-foot-high space,

New York Hall of Science, World's Fair, Flushing Meadows, Queens, 1964–65. Schoolchildren approaching the building soon after its opening. Harrison's design for a space-age educational center and museum is still in use today.

its walls are composed of concrete coffers glazed with thin panels of concrete that are studded with shards of cobalt glass. The walls undulate like an Alvar Aalto vase or screen, though Harrison proposed to his colleagues that the shape represented an organic cell.

Harrison was widely admired for his commanding yet unpretentious manner, ability to work out the politics in order to accomplish a job, and robust enthusiasm for architecture and art. But his work was often excoriated by members of the architectural establishment for being derivative—a charge he proudly accepted. People also claimed that Harrison had all the advantages of access to the Rockefeller family because his wife was sister-in-law to Nelson Rockefeller's only sister, Abigail.

Today, however, criticisms have faded, and Harrison's buildings have come to be appreciated as noteworthy American interpretations of the work of the twentieth century's most radical trailblazers in modern architecture, including the Europeans Le Corbusier, Alvar Aalto, Marcel Breuer, and Ludwig Mies van der Rohe, and the Brazilian Oscar Niemeyer.

In 1931, shortly after purchasing their country property, the Harrisons came upon an inexpensive but decidedly futuristic way to live on their land until they could raise the funds to build a suitable house. They bought the Aluminaire House, a compact, ready-to-assemble steel-and-aluminum structure that had caused a stir when it was exhibited in April at the Allied Arts and Building

OPPOSTIE
Wallace K. and Ellen Harrison House, Huntington, 1932–62. The Harrisons lived in Kocher and Frey's Aluminaire House, seen here attached to the round dining room, the first built volume of their new house, late 1930s. This makeshift arrangement worked until they could afford to build a kitchen, living room, and bedrooms.

Wallace K. and Ellen Harrison House, Huntington, 1932–62. Amorphous skylight designed by Wallace Harrison in the paneled breakfast nook.

Products Exhibition in the Grand Central Palace in New York. Albert Frey, the Swiss architect who in 1928–29 had worked in Le Corbusier's Paris studio, designing cabinetry and window details for the Villa Savoye, created the diminutive machine for living with architect Lawrence Kocher, then managing editor of *Architectural Record* (see pages 38–39).

Harrison had a difficult time reconstructing the house on his land, as Kocher's and Frey's system of numbers, chalked onto the parts, had been washed off by a heavy rainstorm. The final construction failed to reproduce the original tight, seamless look of the structure. Dubbed the "Tin House" by the Harrisons, it provided the couple with shelter for eight years, until Wallace Harrison finished the main house. Throughout the 1930s photographs of the Aluminaire House were featured in several exhibitions, including the seminal Modern Architecture: International Exhibition, curated by Henry-Russell Hitchcock and Philip Johnson, at the Museum of Modern Art in 1932. The photographs depicted it at its pristine best, not as the ramshackle Tin House that the Harrisons were in the end delighted to give up as a residence.

The Harrisons' permanent house got off to a start in 1932, when Wallace Harrison designed a round dining room volume to adjoin the Aluminaire kitchen. He soon added a large, circular, white concrete and steel-frame living room, double the size of the dining room and most likely inspired by his involvement with the design of the Rainbow Room at Rockefeller Center. Like that dramatic space, the Huntington house living room had two-story-high steel-frame windows and a parquet dance floor set over black-and-white terrazzo tiles. The tiles are just like those that originally paved the hallways around the Rainbow Room's revolving parquet floor. The two circular volumes were linked by a curved corridor that flowed from the front entry hall and was outfitted with built-in shelves and a desk—a library of sorts.

By 1940 Harrison had finished a kitchen and bedroom wing west of the living room, as well as a wing incorporating stables and a garage to the east, adjacent to the dining room and attached to the main house by a glass-walled passageway. At that point, the Tin House was moved down the hill away from the main house, to be used over the years as a bunkhouse and as storage space. According to Thaddeus Crapster, an architect for many years in Harrison's office who sometimes slept in the Tin House when visiting the Harrisons, it "was the last place people from the office chose to sleep in, as it was hot in the summer and cold in the winter, besides being a ramshackle version of its original design."[2]

In the mid-1930s Harrison converted the large, pitched-roof potato shed on Round Swamp Road

Wallace K. and Ellen Harrison House, Huntington, 1932–62. From the left, the round living room, kitchen wing, and greenhouse hallway to the bedrooms, mid 1950's.

into a drafting studio, so that architects from his Manhattan office could come out on weekends and during the summer to work on drawings and models related to the forthcoming 1939 World's Fair. Thaddeus Crapster remembers it being busier than the Manhattan studio in July and August.³

Throughout World War II, Ellen Harrison remained with their daughter, Sarah, born in 1931, on Long Island. Her husband spent the war years in Washington, D.C., working for Nelson Rockefeller's Office of Inter-American Affairs and traveling to Latin America. To supplement their modest income, Ellen Harrison had potato fields planted, cultivated a two-acre vegetable garden, and raised chickens, which she sold along with vegetables. The potato shed became a guesthouse for long-term visitors who wanted to help with the farm work and otherwise spend time out of the city. As Ellen's niece Abby Rockefeller Milton O'Neill recalled, "During the war, people needed to stay put, what with gas coupons and rations. Aunt Ellen was relatively self-sufficient out there and she always took the train, if she had to go into the city."⁴

After the war and into the 1950s, Harrison continued to invite architects to live on the property and work in the potato-shed studio and in a series of offices he created out of the stable wing. The concept of working at the feet of the master

Wallace K. and Ellen Harrison House, Huntington, 1932–62. The swimming pool at night, with Ellen Harrison's painting inspired by Fernand Léger's *Divers* series illuminated, mid-1950s.

had been perfected by Frank Lloyd Wright at his Taliesin and Taliesin West studios, but for Harrison it never took hold. Only Tadeusz Leski, the firm's key designer and the man who put Harrison's ideas into working drawings, was willing to live near the Harrisons. Leski built a small, elegant house on land given to him by them. In 1962, while Wallace Harrison was overseeing the planning of Lincoln Center and designing the Metropolitan Opera House, he built another studio space, this time a large, round, white, windowless structure in a circular clearing north of the house, reached along a path through the woods. The interior featured an undulating ceiling with two cloud-shaped skylights and a cavelike corner sound studio, where the architect worked with acoustical engineers. The use of cloud-shaped motifs in his architecture began in the late 1920s and continued throughout his career, seemingly influenced by his admiration for the forms of Jean Arp, Isamu Noguchi, and other sculptor friends.

By the 1950s, the house and grounds had become a study of circles in play with sweeping arcs and rectangles. A key component of this theme was a circular swimming pool, the bottom of which was originally augmented with images of swimmers painted in black outline by the Harrisons in the manner of Fernand Léger's *Divers*

31

Wallace K. and Ellen Harrison House, Huntington, 1932–62. View of the house from the swimming pool, mid-1950s.

series;[5] unfortunately, the chlorine in the water obliterated the painting by the 1960s. Situated at the base of the hill, the pool is reached via a grassy rectangular ramp that descends from the living room patio. Round and undulating beds of low-to-the-ground pachysandra, Harrison's plant of choice for its large, flat leaves, dotted the lawns and outlined buildings and walls in abstract shapes of vivid green.

The eclectically modern house and its grounds can be seen as a metaphor for Wallace Harrison and the working methods of his long career. Like the man, the main house was large in scale, modern in expression, and adaptable, changing according to the projects the architect was working on at any given time.

Ellen Harrison used to say that the Huntington house was less a country house in the traditional sense than a workshop and a place of retreat for her husband. Although a fixture on the New York social scene of the time—boasting genuine friendships with the region's two great power brokers, Robert Moses and Nelson Rockefeller—Harrison had a serious brooding side and a need to be alone. He relieved his dark moods by drawing and making models while blasting the symphonic music and operas he loved throughout the house and grounds. For hours on end, in just about any room or building on the property, he drew with large felt-tip pens on rolls of drafting paper or tinkered with spray paint and bits of paper to make ad hoc collages or models. Doors and even entire walls became canvases for his drawing and painting. On a more practical level, he often tried out colors for architectural projects by painting walls of the house. He also experimented with new building materials by installing them at home. He integrated artists' maquettes and casts into the décor of the house. The working plaster casts for Alfred Janniot's *Beauté* and *Poésie* (1933), now in gilded bronze on La Maison Française at Rockefeller Center, and a large cartouche of Marianne,

RIGHT
Wallace K. and Ellen Harrison House, Huntington, 1932–62. Wallace Harrison at work on a collage in the greenhouse hallway, mid-1950s.

BELOW RIGHT
Wallace K. Harrison and Ellen House, Huntington, 1932–62. A sculpture from Mary Callery's *Acrobats* series adorns a courtyard wall.

BELOW
Wallace K. and Ellen Harrison House, Huntington, 1932–62. Outdoors the Harrisons installed a maquette of Alfred Janniot's *Poésie*, part of the gilded-bronze relief *Friendship between America and France* that now graces the main entrance to La Maison Française, Rockefeller Center.

a symbol of the French Republic (1936), were set right into the walls.

The house was furnished eclectically; there were traditional pieces that Ellen Harrison had inherited from her family, furniture that he had designed for exhibitions, and anything not used in the end for the interiors of his many buildings. The upholstered living room furniture that can be seen in photographs taken in the mid-1950s includes sofas and chairs designed for the Rainbow Room lounge in 1934 by Elena Schmidt. Wallace Harrison was not a proponent of residential interior

Wallace K. and Ellen Harrison House, Huntington, 1932–62. In the entry hall, a maquette of Alfred Janniot's *Elégance*, also part of *Friendship Between America and France*.

design as a total work of art, in which every element must conform to the architect's aesthetic. As Ellen's niece reported, "They were very casual in the way they lived and they did not stand on ceremony or appearances. A dinner visit to their house made for enormous fun with him wanting to show everyone around the property, perhaps even a session shooting clay pigeons, while she took care of preparing a wonderful meal."[6]

In addition to the Modern movement in architecture, much of Harrison's inspiration came from the work of artists such as Fernand Léger, Jean Arp, and Alexander Calder. Well acquainted with the art world, Harrison asked many of these artists to lecture in the classes he taught at Columbia and Yale in the late 1930s and 1940s. Artist friends often returned Harrison's favors with gifts of their work.

Both Harrisons were unabashed copyists of paintings they admired. Only the cognoscenti knew whether the painting on the wall was a real Miró or Léger. Even the large canvas above the living room fireplace cannot be attributed directly to Léger. Ellen Harrison and her daughter produced the large work from a graphite, ink, and gouache cartoon on graph paper that Léger had given them—a colorful study for *La Danse*, his 1942 painting of free-floating dancing figures. Working from the cartoon, the women made scaled drawings on paper and then reproduced them on the rectangular canvas, first in pencil and then in black paint, standing on ladders to reach the upper portion of the canvas.[7] [ill. 01-09] Ellen Harrison donated Léger's cartoon to the Portland Museum of Art in 1985.

The Harrisons sold the house to their neighbors, interior designer Hester Diamond and her husband, Harold, an art dealer, in 1974. The Harrisons had not been using the place regularly for several years, as they had been spending their summers, at Nelson Rockefeller's invitation, in a barn converted by Harrison within the Rockefeller family compound in Deer Isle, Maine. The Diamonds found vines growing into the masonry and the grounds in disarray. They restored the house and made a number of alterations, including replacing the original steel-frame windows and converting the office wing into large bedrooms. Every corner of the round studio was stuffed to the ceiling with sketches and drawings and the potato shed was piled high with copies of important works of modern art. Selected architectural renderings were picked up by former colleagues and the rest were thrown out, while the canvases were cut up with an axe, so there was no chance whatsoever that any could inadvertently end up in the art market as originals.[8]

Wallace K. and Ellen Harrison House, Huntington, 1932–62. Robert Moses, left, and Wallace Harrison, conferring in the living room. Over the fireplace is the partially finished painting on canvas, executed by Ellen Harrison and her daughter, from a site-specific cartoon by Fernand Léger.

2

A. LAWRENCE KOCHER 1885–1969
AND THE FORT SALONGA COLONY

ALBERT FREY, 1903–98, with A. Lawrence Kocher, Aluminaire House, 1931;
Kocher Canvas Weekend House, 1934;
ROBERT LEAVITT DAVISON, 1890–1982, Robert L. and Constance Davison Prefabricated House, 1936;
JOHN HANCOCK CALLENDER, 1908–1995, Davison House, 1936;
Subhi M. Sadi House, 1936;
with Huson Jackson, 1913–2006, Bogie House addition, 1946;
WIILLIAM BOGIE, 1908–94, with A. Lawrence Kocher, Colonel William P. and Betty Bogie House, 1938;
addition with Larry Vita, 1954

THE BAUHAUS ON LONG ISLAND IDEA

It was A. Lawrence Kocher's national role as managing editor of *Architectural Record* and his advocacy of affordable housing that led to his collegial friendship with Walter Gropius, pioneer of modern architecture and founder of the German Bauhaus school. Kocher and Gropius met, at the German architect's insistence, in the spring of 1928, when he and his wife Ise were staying at the Plaza Hotel in Manhattan, at the end of their first visit to the United States. The Gropiuses had come to fulfill a long-standing desire to see the New World and to temporarily escape the increasingly menacing political situation in Germany, which had caused him to resign his leadership of the Bauhaus.

With Gropius back in Germany, the two colleagues engaged in a lively transatlantic correspondence. At first the letters concerned cooperative publishing and collaboration on research about prefabricated houses using machine-age materials and modern design. But by 1934, even before the Gropiuses reluctantly moved to London to escape certain persecution in Germany, Kocher wrote to encourage them to move to America permanently.

Determined to gain American acceptance of the modern architecture being built in Europe, Kocher's hope was to establish an American Bauhaus on twenty acres of hilly land he had purchased above the old British Fort Salonga and adjacent to Sunken Meadow State Park, near Northport. He knew that if Gropius joined him in forming a school, others would follow suit and together they could reignite the Bauhaus flame, which had been snuffed out in 1933, when then director Ludwig Mies van der Rohe closed it, following a Nazi raid.

For Gropius, leaving Europe, where he had built his pioneering body of work and established the architectural practice associated with his famous name, was an agonizing decision. But he wrote back to Kocher, saying that he liked the idea of joining forces on a new school and agreed to come if Kocher could arrange for him to lecture at American universities, with his and Ise's expenses paid. Kocher set to work writing to deans of American universities on Gropius's behalf, a seemingly futile task at the height of the Great Depression. Nevertheless, given Gropius's eminence as an architect and experience as a visionary educator, Kocher remained optimistic.

In one reply to a letter from Kocher, Gropius described his vision for a new school in America: "[R]unning the Bauhaus taught me that it would be best to try to start workshops as laboratories which are paid directly by the industry, filled with the best skilled workmen, but headed by independent architects gifted for both design and for technik. So the students of Architecture could be taught in a creative sense as well in the offices for design as in the laboratory workshops of the school, always sticking to the very practice instead of a platonic curriculum."[1]

Further on in the same letter he wrote, "It could then be possible for the leaders to work successfully toward machine-made houses, in which you are interested, as I am. . . . I think the only country to accomplish that immense task, to erect machine-made dwellings in substantial fireproof construction—to work out on a large scale the toy building blocks [*den Baukasten*] of children—will be in America. In no other country do people seem prepared to accept houses from stock, as the long record of Sears Roebuck and Montgomery Ward in selling [prefabricated] wooden country houses would show. I would like very much to work with you and others in your school for the realization of this idea."[2]

Architect Antonin Raymond and his wife, designer Noémi Pernessin Raymond, also expressed interest in joining the effort to start the school, as their own flurry of letters to each other and to Kocher indicates. In November 1935, Antonin Raymond wrote to his wife that he had bought five acres of Kocher's Fort Salonga land, so that they could build a house near the school grounds. The Raymonds had wanted a country home close to Manhattan to live in between their trips to Tokyo, where they had established a successful practice in the 1920s, after working with Frank Lloyd Wright on the city's Imperial Hotel. Antonin Raymond introduced concrete construction to Japan, and the couple had a superb ability to cross International Style design with traditional Japanese methods and aesthetics (see pages 58–59).

But the Raymonds did not build on their Fort Salonga land or take part in the school. Instead, in 1940 they set up their own workshop on a farm in New Hope, Pennsylvania, with a coterie of young people eager to learn from them. At the New Hope workshop, the Raymonds designed the Charles Briggs and Raoul Carrerà house (1940) on the cliffs along the main highway into Montauk. In 1956–57, they designed two houses in Great Neck, in a parklike setting for the Rosen and Krakauer families (see pages 60–63).

The Raymonds' desire to participate in a Long Island–based Bauhaus waned in part because Kocher's efforts to gain Gropius employment at an American university succeeded far beyond anyone's expectations, thus making it impossible for him to take part in Kocher's plans for a school. Kocher's letters to Dean Joseph Hudnut at Columbia University resulted in Gropius's appointment as a professor at (and eventually as chairman of) Harvard's Graduate School of Design in 1937, shortly after Hudnut became dean of the school.

Gropius's arrangement with Harvard permitted him to set up a private practice, and he soon established a firm in Cambridge with Marcel Breuer, after encouraging Hudnut to hire Breuer as a professor at Harvard. Formerly director of the Furniture Workshop at the Bauhaus, Breuer became a much-liked professor at the school, and one of several former Bauhaus teachers to join the Harvard faculty and help Gropius shape the only long-lasting attempt to reestablish the Bauhaus in America. Under Gropius's leadership, the Harvard Graduate School of Design program had a huge influence on architectural education and practice everywhere in the country, to the extent that the old Paris-based Beaux-Arts manner of designing began to be replaced with inventive modern architecture.

All the while Kocher was trying to solicit others to join with him in forming a school, he was busy transforming *Architectural Record* from a journal that promoted decidedly new architecture in European historic styles into one that espoused an architecture of uncompromised association with modern building methods. Kocher led broad journalistic investigations into how industry's approach to mass production could be applied to the building trades and practice of architecture. Although he was a scholar of architectural history, and his first contact with *Architectural Record* had been as the author of several articles on the architecture of the early American colonies, he became critical of copying historical styles when modernity had surely arrived in America, but without its own expression in architecture.

ALUMINAIRE HOUSE

Kocher's partnership with the young Swiss architect Albert Frey put him at the forefront of architectural practice, as theirs was one of the few firms working in the International Style idiom. During their four years together, they produced four experimental buildings and several visionary city-planning projects and co-authored a number of journal articles. Frey had worked for the influential Swiss architect Le Corbusier during the pivotal year 1928–29, when teams of acolytes helped him at his Paris atelier with the design of radically modern built commissions—the Centrosoyuz Building in Moscow, the Salvation Army Hostel in Paris, and what became an iconic twentieth-century modern house, the Villa Savoye, built in Poissy, a village near Paris.

Kocher and Frey's steel-and-aluminum Aluminaire House, exhibited in 1931 at the Grand Central Palace and later moved to Wallace and Ellen Harrison's house near Huntington, Long Island (see pages 27–29), was their first building. The job came to them when Kocher was asked to produce a crowd pleaser of a modern building prototype by the curator of the annual Allied Arts and Building Products Exhibition, organized in conjunction with the Architectural League. Frey designed the showhouse, working out of a room in Kocher's Forest Hills Gardens house that served as the firm's architecture office. In general, Frey was responsible for most of the designing and drafting for the firm, while Kocher offered critiques when he returned home in the evening from *Architectural Record*'s office in Manhattan.

The Aluminaire House was the first American building designed by an architect who had worked for Le Corbusier. It was based on Corbusier's "Five Points Towards a New Architecture," a formula elaborated in a 1926 article and in a pavilion for a Paris exposition. A building incorporating the five points started with a steel frame supported by pilotis, or steel posts, and thus raised above the ground; a free façade, which meant that the walls were not load bearing and could be arranged at will; an open floor plan, with easily moved wall planes; horizontal ribbon windows; and a roof terrace for enjoyment of the outdoors and what in those days everyone thought was healthy, sunbathing.

The popular press was unimpressed by the Corbusier influences and dubbed the small, all-metal building the "Zipper House," as it was erected in less than ten days. It had prefabricated walls and built-ins, including a retractable table and beds, as well as inflatable furniture. All the attention, even a mention in *Time* magazine, helped attract more than 100,000 visitors, who eagerly lined up to enter the house. Soon after the show closed, the house was moved to the Harrisons' property. Despite Harrison's difficulties re-erecting it, Kocher and Harrison remained friends, and Harrison was best man at Lawrence Kocher's marriage to Margaret Taylor in 1932.

In 1934, the Kochers decided to erect a Le Corbusier–inspired weekend house for themselves on the Fort Salonga land, incorporating Kocher and Frey's experiments with materials donated by various companies that were trying to expand their business into architecture and the construction trades by finding new applications for their materials. On the drawing board, the house was named the Canvas Weekend House, as its exterior walls were clad in cotton canvas provided by the Cotton Textile Institute.

THE FORT SALONGA COLONY

While their country house was being designed and built, Lawrence and Margaret Kocher tried to persuade friends to buy lots nearby for their own equally experimental modern houses. Three other families—the Robert L. Davisons, the William P. Bogies, and a bachelor friend, Subhi M. Sadi—bought land from Kocher, and a colony of experimental modern houses was born, a kind of diminutive version of the housing exhibitions that the German Werkbund had organized in Germany, such as the Weissenhof Estate in Stuttgart in 1927, to demonstrate its commitment to minimal functional design and experimentation with low-cost materials and methods.

In 1940, the Kochers moved to Asheville, North Carolina, where he became an architecture professor and architect of several buildings at Black Mountain College. The family returned to their Long Island country house for summer vacations until they sold it in 1951. By then, they had settled in Williamsburg, Virginia, where Lawrence Kocher served as editor of Colonial Williamsburg's Architectural Records and chief preservation architect and advisor for the monumental task of reconstructing the near derelict first capital of the United States.

The Bogies remained in their modern house long after the others had sold theirs and moved away from the colony, which by the 1960s was becoming surrounded by new development and forgotten as a place of experimentation and a potential locale for an American Bauhaus. The Bogies' house was sold in 2010 by their daughter, Beth Bogie, who took care of it as an artifact of a historic time when the intensely practical, straight-lined modern buildings of Gropius's and other European pioneers' pre–World War II architecture were just beginning to exert influence in America. Before Beth Bogie moved out of state, the Museum of Modern Art purchased a steel chaise longue covered in aluminum-based paint for its permanent exhibition. These were included in the temporary exhibit Shaping Modernity: Design 1880–1980. Lawrence Kocher gave the chaise to the Bogies, along with other metal terrace furniture he had designed, when the Kochers left Fort Salonga for Williamsburg. Created for a Manhattan photography school building that was not completed, the simple metal furniture was as much a part of the strikingly modern look of the Bogie house porch as its architectural elements.

CANVAS WEEKEND HOUSE

Like the Aluminaire House, the Kocher Canvas Weekend House was designed by Albert Frey, with Kocher weighing in for the final analysis. Kocher supervised the construction quickly and economically without Frey, who was busy overseeing their

Colonel William P. and Betty Bogie House, Fort Salonga, 1938. Chaise longue designed by Laurence Kocher, seen next to the Bogie house porch, 2004.

design for a mixed-use building in Palm Springs, California, for Kocher's brother, the first medical doctor to live and practice there. Kocher and Frey had explored using cotton canvas in design plans and small, to-scale models—the Experimental Five-Room House and the Experimental Weekend House—as part of their arrangement with the Cotton Textile Institute to conduct research and generate publicity. Facing competition from new synthetic fabric manufacturers and overseas cotton producers, the institute's public relations people were doing all they could to find new uses for American-produced cotton. Kocher and Frey's house models demonstrated how thick cotton canvas could be used to clad wall surfaces and floors and provide awnings for sun protection over outdoor rooms and windows, as well as ceiling-to-floor curtains to delineate interior spaces.. Canvas had for centuries been part and parcel of marine decks and roofs but had never before been promoted as a material for house cladding.

Kocher and Frey did not succeed in getting

Kocher Canvas Weekend House, Fort Salonga, 1934. The house was a celebrity in the world of modern architecture, yet, few understood how the Kochers managed without basic amenities such as electricity. The water pump in the right foreground was the only water source for the house.

their prototypes mass produced; the only one actually built and lived in was Kocher's own house. Their aspiration had been to collaborate with other industries to mass-produce steel-framed rectangular houses raised several feet above the ground on steel pilotis, with interchangeable prefabricated steel components for staircases, deck railings, and plumbing. Aluminum foil, a relatively new material then being used primarily for packaging in the food industry, was their innovative choice for wall insulation. Wood framing proved far less expensive than steel, so they ended up using it for the Canvas Weekend House.

The Canvas Weekend House got plenty of press both at home and overseas; articles and books about it were published in Europe and as far away as Japan. The *Texaco Star*, an oil industry magazine, reported, "Things haven't quite reached the stage where you can run up a 10-room house on the family sewing machine, but the practicality of cotton in house construction has been amply demonstrated."[3] As the article further elaborated, "The entire exposed face of the house sides and roof deck is of canvas duck stretched over tongue and groove redwood flooring. The canvas is No. 8 duck, 42 inches wide, which was applied in a horizontal direction starting at the base of the wall and overlapping each strip on the one below."[4]

Kocher placed an illustrated article in *Architectural Record* that made the house seem quick and easy to build and maintain. The caption for an image of a swatch of canvas duck material declares, "It takes paint admirably."[5] What Kocher's writer

Kocher Canvas Weekend House, Fort Salonga, 1934. Stanley Walker, city editor of the *Herald Tribune*, posing with female colleagues during a photography shoot. On the left, the 1936 addition, a room for an ice box, storage, and occasionally guests.

neglected to mention, however, was the painstaking process of weatherproofing the cotton with layers of paint. First, a primer of lead paint had to be applied, then a gluey adhesive, followed by two coats of deck paint, and finally, a coat of silvery aluminum paint, so that the façade of the house on stilts would appear metallic and machinelike, as if an engineer with no knowledge of architectural styles had designed it.

The Kochers' precise little house got attention from architectural cognoscenti everywhere primarily because it seemed to be a simplified incarnation of Le Corbusier's Villa Savoye, which by the mid-1930s was as famous as its architect. In fact, Kocher's fanciful little box of a house in the air bore a closer resemblance to the Villa Savoye's gatekeeper house, a lodge on pilotis that was consistent in style with the main house.

The Museum of Modern Art's *Guide to Modern Architecture: Northeast States*, published in 1940 with a mission to encourage appreciation of the new modern architecture, included Kocher's house in its Long Island section. Curiously, the description of the house makes no mention of the obvious Le Corbusier associations: "One of the first modern houses built in the US, this is an excellent example of the 'International Style' in its severe rationalism, stringently utilitarian forms, rejection of tradition and traditional materials and its uncompromising 'machine age' esthetics."[6]

Ironically, as modern as the house looked, it had no modern appurtenances whatsoever; it was essentially a one-room primitive cabin in the woods. Most people, who knew the house from its publicity, had no idea that it had cost only $1,500 to build, because it was basically shelter.

In a letter to architectural historian Mary Mix Foley in 1968, Kocher wrote, " In our age of pressures of city life (1930–on) there has been a need for relief in the nature of a contrast in living, such as is afforded by a close contact with the sea-shore and the mountains. The weekend house was conceived as an answer to such a need, and the site on Long Island was convenient for our family (parents and two small children living at Forest Hills Gardens) within a short distance from the Long Island parkways."[7]

The Kochers' children, Larry and Sandra, have fond memories of the house, and as for its lack of modern amenities, Sandra Kocher said, "We liked it that way!"[8] How the family lived is described best in her own words:

> At the weekend, we'd arrive at night and take what we needed out of the car, with the headlights left on, to show the way to the spiral staircase up to the house entrance. Once inside, the only light was from kerosene lamps. If my mother needed to cook inside, it was on a two-burner kerosene stove, which she typically used when it rained. They almost always cooked at an outdoor grill, near a picnic table and clearing, which we got to along a path through beautiful sycamore trees with honeysuckle vines around them. Before a simple icebox refrigerator was put into what we called the guesthouse addition, built in 1936, food was kept in the trunk of the car, usually parked in the shade under the house. We would get our water from a pump near the road. If we needed water in the house, usually for flushing what were perfectly good toilets and taking quick showers, we would carry it up the spiral stair in galvanized buckets.[9]

Time and effort were required to get the house ready for the summer season. Every spring, the Kochers had scaffolding erected around the house so the bright red cotton awnings could be reinstalled or replaced and new layers of paint added to the canvas surfaces of the exterior. Once the family

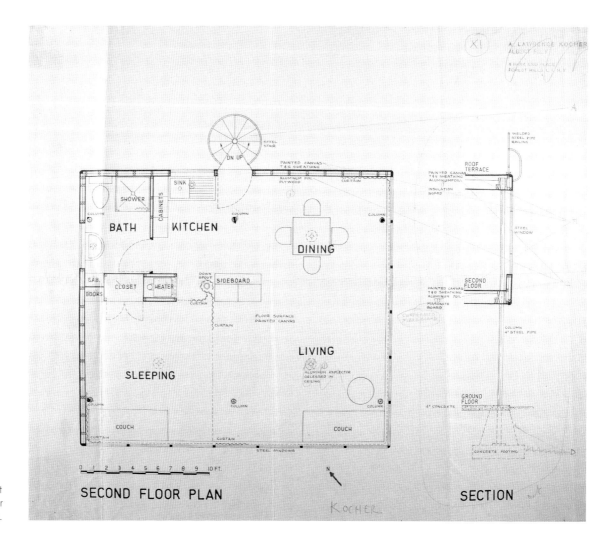

Kocher Canvas Weekend House, Fort Salonga, 1934. Floor plan for flexible living.

Kocher Canvas Weekend House, Fort Salonga, 1934. Spiral stair to the entrance of the one-room house.

had moved back in, the one-room living space in the air served as a living and dining room during the day; beds were used as lounging furniture, and there was a square, glass-topped metal table and four metal chairs. At night, for privacy and sleeping, thick, aluminum-painted cotton curtains could be pulled along a track system to divide the space into three bedrooms. The house did not need curtains on the windows, as it was up high and sufficiently private. However, adjustable awnings were necessary to keep the house from heating up in the sun. The interior walls were plywood, and only the bathroom was enclosed by a wall.

A true Renaissance man, as his son, Larry, called him, Kocher was interested in a number of fields besides architecture, including botany, American literature, and rare books. An obsessive bibliophile, he would start the day at home in Forest Hills Gardens leafing through rare-book catalogues before heading off to the *Architectural Record* office. At the house in the country, which had no telephone, communication with his office was limited, so it was there that he found the peace to read his favorite books, enjoy the outdoors with his family, and visit with his neighbors, the likeminded people who had been invited to build their own modern houses in the colony.

DAVISON HOUSE

Robert Leavitt Davison joined the *Architectural Record* staff as director of technical news and research in 1928, and proved to be an enormous help to Kocher, writing articles and generating ideas for new research about building methods.

Gropius was responsible for introducing Davison to Kocher, having taken him along to the pivotal meeting with Kocher at the Plaza Hotel, three days before the Gropiuses sailed back to Germany. Davison wrote in his unpublished autobiography, "Gropius said that I was the only man he had met in the United States who was trying to do what he was doing in Germany."[10] Davison, E. P. Goodrich, Henry Wright, and others founded the Research Institute of Economic Housing to advance construction technology and new ways of thinking about building houses practically and economically. When Gropius, Kocher, and Davison met in New York that day, the inventive Davison was the country's preeminent researcher on improving construction methods, materials, and mechanical systems to use space more efficiently and lower costs.

Davison wanted to study how housing could be built affordably when he was a student at Harvard in 1913–14, but there were no courses on the subject. James Ford, a professor of social ethics, took Davison under his wing and encouraged him to research, on an independent-study basis, what Ford deemed to be the gross inefficiencies of the housing industry. In 1936, Ford published *Slums and Housing*, a definitive two-volume work on the history and future prospects of the housing reform movement. By that time, the student had become as important in the field as his professor.

Davison left *Architectural Record* in 1931 to set up a housing division for the John B. Pierce Foundation, which had been endowed by the founder of the hugely profitable American Radiator Company. At the Pierce Foundation, Davison collaborated with architect John Hancock Callender on developing prefabricated housing systems.

Davison, Callender, and others built a number of test houses in their search for materials and structures to yield housing at the lowest possible cost. One of their aims was to find a single material that could serve as both the structure and the enclosure of building units and that could be manufactured in modular panels for floors, walls, and ceilings. In the early twentieth century, Grosvenor Atterbury had experimented with standardized precast concrete panels, which he eventually fabricated off site and positioned by crane to assemble houses on Park End Place in Forest Hills Gardens, including the Kochers' Tudor-style house.

Pierce Foundation teams continued Atterbury's experimentation with concrete and also explored a wide variety of materials, including plywood, composition board, stabilized earth, and a hydro-calcium silicate composition known as Microporite. In their search for inexpensive, lightweight insulation they looked at using tin foil. Interestingly, John Hancock Callender published an article entitled "Aluminum Foil for Insulation" in *Architectural Forum* in January 1934, shortly before Kocher used aluminum foil to insulate the walls of the Canvas Weekend House.[11]

The Davison House in the Fort Salonga colony was a combination of two Pierce Foundation test houses, one on top of the other. The look of the finished house seemed strikingly influenced by the flat-roofed, boxy, predominantly white stucco houses that Henry-Russell Hitchcock and Philip Johnson had included in their 1932 Modern Architecture exhibition at the Museum of Modern Art. On editorial business during his first year at *Architectural Record*, Davison traveled to meet Gropius in Germany in 1929. There Gropius showed the young American the Dessau Bauhaus, and its three International Style, semidetached masters' houses, which Gropius had designed three years earlier in a grove of pine trees using building-block construction methods.

Davison entitled a series of articles that he edited for the Pierce Foundation *The Engineered Dwelling*,[12] an apt term for the house he erected in a grove of sycamore trees down the hill from the Kochers' Canvas Weekend House. Davison's engineered house consisted of two seemingly identical four-room prefabricated test houses that had been disassembled and trucked to the site. One was made of plywood panels and had been shown at an exhibition in the Grand Central Palace; the other was made of Microporite panels and had been seen only by a few Pierce Foundation employees when it was being produced at a Long Island City factory. Callender and Davison placed the plywood house on top of only a quarter of the Microporite house, thereby creating space for a covered terrace at the entrance and a garage. *Architectural Record* commented on the uniqueness of this configuration: "The prefabricated units in this house differ from those generally found in prefabricated houses in that the units are placed horizontally, transferring the loads as a load bearing wall unit. The horizontal wall units are, in effect, a deep girder which carries the floor-roof load, much the same way as a steel girder in a skyscraper transmits the load to a steel column."[13] Clips were used to fasten the horizontal

Robert L. and Constance Davison Prefabricated House, Fort Salonga, 1936. Front of Davison House, comprising two test houses funded by the Pierce Foundation, one atop another and wrapped in canvas.

panel units to widely spaced columns. Each panel was two and a half feet wide, with twelve and a half feet being the largest structural dimension for the floor and roof spans and therefore for most of the rooms. For the foundation, Davison used his solution to what he called "the foundation problem" of prefabricated systems.[14] First the floor plate was installed on top of wooden posts embedded in iron shoes and then, after the walls and floor sections had been built and the house had settled, the concrete foundation was poured in under the ground floor.

Like the Canvas Weekend House, the Davison House was clad in cotton duck, as the plywood second floor had no adequate weather protection. The canvas was attached with latex cement to the exterior walls and decks when the house was already in situ, and painted stark white with Tornisite, a chlorinated rubber paint used customarily for the hulls of ships. The family lived in the house year round until they moved to Upper Manhattan in 1944. According to the Davison daughters, Anita Davison Engelman and Pat Davison Savadove, it held up very well in all kinds of weather, including the devastating hurricane of 1938.[15]

Davison was not a professional architect, so John Callender was responsible for the house's interior plan and elevations, which had all the requirements of a modern house, according to Callender's "scientific studies." He led numerous

Robert L. and Constance Davison Prefabricated House, Fort Salonga, 1936. Living/dining room, designed for a casual, modern way of living based on Pierce Foundation "scientific studies." This photograph was taken just before the family moved in.

studies at the Pierce Foundation to determine how families most efficiently used space and spent their time doing everyday activities. In the second article in *The Engineered Dwelling* he wrote that a whole new terminology was needed to avoid all previous conceptions about designing for families. For example, he suggested that designers use terms such as "space for eating" and "space for sleeping," and refer to a chair as a "surface for supporting a body in a seated position, which is cumbersome, but it is an excellent corrective to methods of thinking that are so traditional that they are ingrained in our everyday language."[16] A photograph of the Davisons' open kitchen-dining arrangement was reproduced in this article, showing the buffet ledge between the kitchen and living spaces and a rectangular dining table abutting the ledge. This so-called kitchen pass-through was featured in a number of popular magazines as a thoroughly modern and efficient innovation for the housewife. The built-in cabinets and seating ledges added throughout the house over time were also conceptually modern. The first built-ins were installed in the master bedroom, which functioned as an upstairs living room for the whole family, as it had a fireplace and access to a large sunbathing deck with views of Long Island Sound.

Davison wrote proudly about technical aspects of his family's first house in his unpublished autobiography: "The second floor was heated by my

Robert L. and Constance Davison Prefabricated House, Fort Salonga, 1936. Master bedroom, with view of fireplace. In conjunction with the ground-floor fireplace, it provided experimental central heating.

modernized version of a Franklin Stove. With the doors to the fireplace closed (the coal fire in the grate of the fireplace) the fuel efficiency was 87%. It had ducts going from it to the bathroom and two other bedrooms."[17] The downstairs "living space" fireplace worked similarly to heat the first floor through flues. The all-metal kitchen and two bathrooms in the house had been prefabricated in a factory and installed in large sections. Davison had considered installing back-to-back kitchen and bathroom stacks, as Buckminster Fuller had done in his all-metal Dymaxion House. However, a back-to-back system was impossible in the Davison House because the two test houses that comprised it were offset from one another.

SADI HOUSE

Subhi Sadi, a friend of Robert Davison's, purchased five acres from the Kochers and in 1936, while the Davison House was being erected, engaged John Callender to design another modern house in the colony. The Museum of Modern Art's *Guide to Modern Architecture: Northeast States* attributes the house design to S. M. Sadi, which provoked Callender to write to the museum, "The summer house for S. M. Sadi listed under Northport, Long Island, was designed by me, not by Mr. Sadi. (. . . oh, yes, we designed it ourselves . . . of course, we hired a young draftsman to draw up the plans . . .)"[18] Born in Beirut, Lebanon, Sadi came to

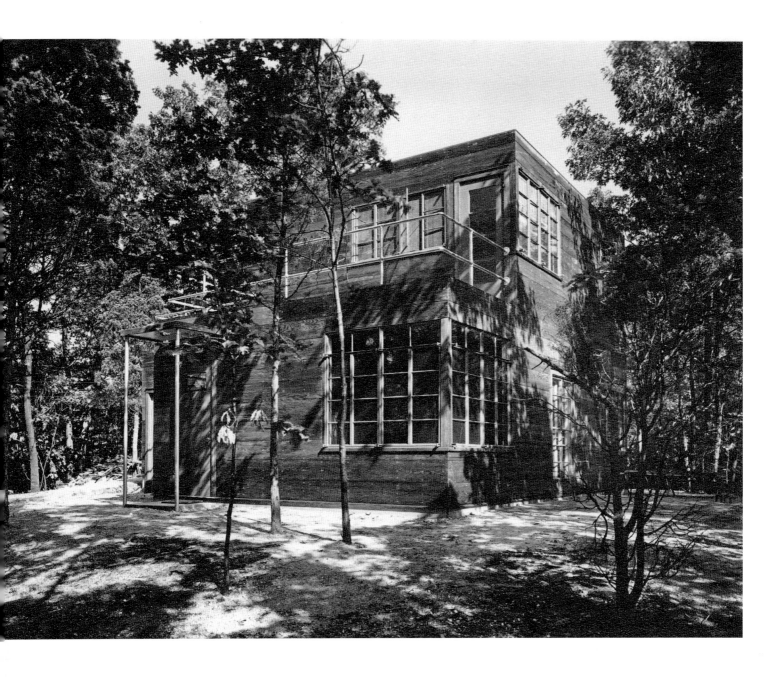

Subhi M. Sadi House, Fort Salonga, 1936. A test house designed by John Callender to demonstrate the merits of redwood for the building trade.

the United States in the mid-1920s to study business at Columbia University and then attend law school at New York University. He practiced as a lawyer in Manhattan before serving as a captain in the U.S. Armed Forces in Cairo during World War II.

Callender was able to convince the forestry industry trade group to provide him with redwood so that he could make Sadi's house a test house. The result was a two-level house similar to the Davisons' but clad in vertical boards of redwood, a material so resilient and rot resistant that it was the number one choice in the 1930s for decking if not for house cladding. The house was featured in a book published in 1938 by the California Redwood Association[19] that touts redwood as a modern, economical, and long-lasting material.

BOGIE HOUSE

William and Betty Bogie, neighbors and friends of Larry and Margaret Kocher in Forest Hills Gardens, purchased eight acres of woods adjacent to the Kochers' property in Fort Salonga. In spring 1938, Lawrence Kocher drew up a set of drawings for a small split-level, rectangular weekend house for them. It had a basement with a large workroom, a dark room, and subgrade space for a carport. On the ground floor, a covered semicircular porch supported by a central concrete column led to a living space that could be divided into separate living and dining areas by a ceiling-to-floor curtain like the one in the Canvas Weekend House. A steel spiral stair, repeating the circular motif of the porch, began in the basement and ended at a third-level landing for the master bedroom with a fireplace. Within a deeply recessed hallway, the stair turned around and up through a curved casing of translucent glass blocks, popular in the 1930s as a practical, modern way to define space yet not block illumination.

In May 1938, Kocher billed the Bogies $100 for the set of drawings, and his estimate for getting the house built, including his fees, was $6,000. William Bogie decided to draw up his own plans for a simpler, less expensive house and to be his own general contractor. This arrangement must have suited the Kochers, as the Bogies slept in the Kochers' guest room, which was built on the land adjacent to the Canvas Weekend House in the summer of 1936, so they could clear their property and work on the house. According to Beth Bogie, Lawrence Kocher must have provided some architectural advice.[20]

William Bogie's keen amateur interest in modern architecture culminated in a small, rectangular, flat-roofed one-level box similar in appearance to one of Robert Davision's "engineered" houses assembled nearby. Not structurally inventive, the

BELOW
Colonel William P. and Betty Bogie House, Fort Salonga, 1938. Beth Bogie, standing at the front entrance of her parents' modernist version of a cabin in the woods.

BOTTOM
Colonel William P. and Betty Bogie House, Fort Salonga, 1938. The 1946 addition is to the right of the original rectangular building, and the 1954 addition is to the left.

Bogie House was made from traditional building materials—stucco over concrete block walls—and had a basement. The windows were steel-frame casements, a typical architectural feature of modern buildings of the 1930s, and similar to the windows of the Davison House.

Reached via a winding dirt driveway, the compact house was just what the Bogie family needed for their version of a cabin in the woods. It had an open-plan living and dining area, a separate kitchen, and a small study adjacent to the living space and the hall to the master bedroom, off of which there was a bathroom and a small nursery. Like the Kochers' house, the Bogie house provided basic shelter, but it had electricity, modern plumbing, and a small modern kitchen.

At the end of World War II, the Bogies decided to add on to their Fort Salonga house and settle there year round. In spring 1945 they called upon John Hancock Callender to design the addition. Callender had spent the war years with the National Housing Agency, Staff Army Engineers, supervising the building of laboratories at Los Alamos, New Mexico, for the Manhattan Project, which developed the atomic bomb. Upon his return to New York after the war, he formed a partnership with architect Huson Jackson, and the two men designed a few houses on Long Island and in the region before Jackson moved on to other partnerships.

Although there had been drives for scrap metal during the war for use in the munitions industry, Callender had access to stored steel components for the Starrett-Lehigh House, a test house that the Pierce Foundation's Research Housing Division had erected in 1932 on the roof of the Starrett-Lehigh Building, on the lower West Side of Manhattan.[21] Apparently never shown to the public, the inventive house had steel truss framing, horizontally aligned steel wall panels, and a prefabricated mechanical utility core, as well as a spiral stair. In a letter to William Bogie Callender wrote, "I look forward with a great deal of interest to the re-erection of the Starrett-Lehigh House, since I worked on it from its birth to its death about 1939. In many

Colonel William P. and Betty Bogie House, Fort Salonga, 1938. Children from the Salonga Colony in front of the Bogie House. From left, Barbara Taylor, Patsy Davison, A. Lawrence Kocher, Jr., and Beth Bogie.

Colonel William P. and Betty Bogie House, Fort Salonga, 1938. The original structure, a modernist version of a cabin in the woods, before later additions allowed the family to live in the house year round.

respects it was a more advanced design than those we did much later at the Pierce Foundation, and far in advance of most prefabricated houses even today."[22] The Starrett-Lehigh House was not re-erected for the Bogies, but its steel trusses and girders were used as the support skeleton for a small study and living room perpendicular to the original house, and the steel spiral staircase with its thick airplane propeller–shaped steps was installed to provide access to a roof terrace from a new front porch, the roof of which was held up with steel pilotis, also from the Starrett-Lehigh House trove.

John Callender and Huson Jackson's living room addition featured large picture windows that frame the landscape. Below them, at William Bogie's insistence, the architects designed countertops to display his archive of magazines and journals, as well as benches. The addition gave the house a sophisticated, decidedly International Style look at a time, ironically, when modern architects were turning to softer, less machine-inspired versions of modernism. The architects used the style's basic tropes: white stucco exterior walls, horizontal windows, a flat roof with a steel pipe railing to create a sundeck, and of course steel pilotis to hold up the new covered porch and a carport. The Bogies maintained all of the metal elements from the Starrett-Lehigh House with aluminum paint. When their contractor, Larry Vita, an inventor with patents for numerous devices, worked with William Bogie in 1954 to design and build two bedrooms and a bathroom above the original house and the carport, Vita installed four wide, steel-frame windows, which, in combination with their mesh metal screens, could slide down into the walls electrically. These steel window frames were also painted with aluminum paint, signaling the Bogies' continued allegiance to the earlier International Style elements of the house and to the colony that Lawrence Kocher founded in the 1930s.

3

FRANK LLOYD WRIGHT 1867–1959

Ben and Anne Rebhuhn House, Great Neck, 1938

In 1937 Frank Lloyd Wright was asked to design a residence for civil libertarian and small-press publisher and bibliophile Ben Rebhuhn and his wife, Anne, in Great Neck. It was Wright's only Long Island commission and the first house he built east of the Great Lakes. An elegantly detailed, formal house, it is a small masterpiece in the grammar of his early-twentieth-century Prairie Style houses. The design was a decidedly conservative gesture, as in the late 1930s Wright was at work on two radically modern buildings that reshaped the principles he had expounded in the Prairie Style architecture. Each was a tour de force: Fallingwater (1936–39), distinguished by the enormous concrete terraces that cantilevered out over a waterfall at the site of the house on the Bear Run mountain stream, outside Pittsburgh, and an outstanding, light-filled brick office complex with streamlined curved corners for the Johnson Wax Company (1939) in Racine, Wisconsin. By the mid-1930s, Wright was in his sixties and experiencing a renewed respect around the world. The rebirth of his career was astounding, as during the boom times of the 1920s it had almost ceased because of major scandals attached to his name and a consensus that his architecture was passé.

According to Edgar Tafel, who worked with Wright as an apprentice architect on the Rebhuhn House, Ben and Anne Rebhuhn had read an article in *Coronet*, then an esoteric art magazine, about

Ben and Anne Rebhuhn House, Great Neck, 1938. Frank Lloyd Wright's presentation drawing of a two-story Prairie Style house.

Wright and a small house he had designed in the Midwest when work for him was sparse. The article prompted Ben to pen a long, admiring letter in November 1937, beseeching Wright to design the couple's house. Rebhuhn wrote, "For some time now, I've considered you the choicest master spirit to be found in the world today. A supreme artist; a creative thinker of a new modern kind; the greatest dreamer of dreams that are steering the modern world to Utopias of reality. . . . At the moment, too, we were going about having a small house built. . . . We're just two of us, Anne and myself, two dogs, a parrot, two love-birds and loads of books. We have the lot out here in Great Neck—15,000 sq. ft. Above that we wanted to spend about $10,000—It seems too great a dream to expect to come true, but if Frank Lloyd Wright could create it we could stretch our funds to $12,000 or even a thousand or two more."[1]

Within a few days Wright wrote back and agreed to meet the couple the following week at the Hotel Lafayette in New York City. Rebhuhn sent a telegram: "Your letter is a rejoicing to us, an unearthly dream coming true. Though we can't believe it. Could you stay with us over coming weekend?"[2] The meeting went well, and on his next trip to New York Wright stayed with the Rebhuhns at their apartment in Russell Gardens, Queens. A genuine friendship developed between architect and clients over the course of the many meetings and train rides to visit the site in Great Neck—a friendship that the Rebhuhns continued to cultivate with visits through the years to Wright's apartment at the Plaza Hotel in Manhattan and to his Taliesin West workshop in Scottsdale, Arizona.

Anne Rebhuhn—a hat and clothing designer in New York City, who, according to the Rebhuhns' only son, Ronald, designed and sewed the red cape that Wright often wore—kept up a lively correspondence with the architect while the house was being built. In one letter she wrote, "I must tell you that your loving nature shows itself to me in almost every line, your kindliness, the overhanging roof, the shelter so to speak of the arteast [sic]. I think I can judge your very nature by your work."[3]

Though the Rebhuhn House has sometimes been referred to as Usonian, it is much more formal, elegant, and expensively built than the low-cost houses that Wright built across the country after the success of the Herbert and Katherine Jacobs First House of 1937, in Madison, Wisconsin. These houses, which Wright called "Usonian" (the term he preferred for "American") and envisioned as prototypes for a middle-class lifestyle, were one-story structures with carports instead of garages and open-plan living and dining rooms set around a central kitchen and laundry core. Like the Prairie Style houses that Wright had designed in the first two decades of the century, the Great Neck house, with its overhanging roof, strong horizontal planes of brick, and elongated lines, appears to hover above the earth, while being perfectly integrated with its garden and the surrounding wooded landscape. The interior plan has a dynamic asymmetry and a sense of continuity and a flow of space through rooms of various heights and proportions. In signature Wright fashion, the house is entered through a small, dark vestibule. From there, a transitional space curves around the double-height fireplace—which serves the living and dining rooms and the master bedroom on the floor above—to provide access to the

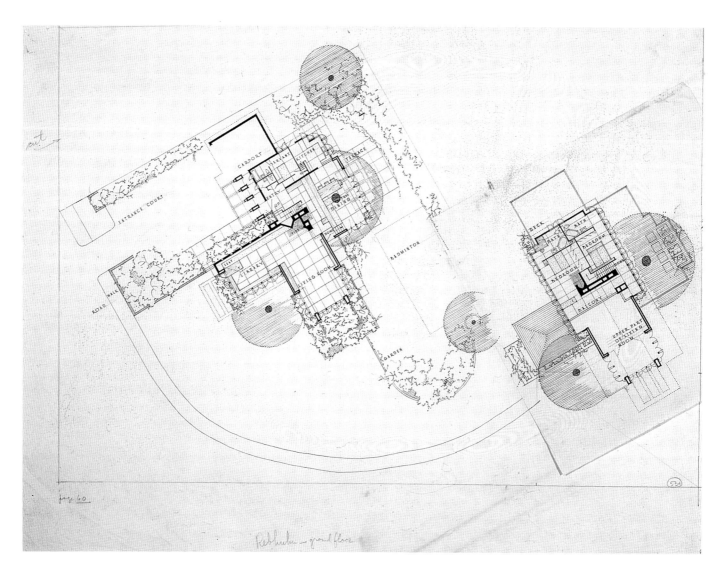

Ben and Anne Rebhuhn House, Great Neck, 1938. Presentation drawing of the floor plan and landscaping. Wright's landscaping plan incorporated several existing tall trees. Note that all the ground-floor rooms have access to terraces.

54 FRANK LLOYD WRIGHT

Ben and Anne Rebhuhn House, Great Neck, 1938. View of the living room from the garden. The sculpture on the right is by Anne Rebhuhn, who was a professional sculptor, as well as a hat and clothing designer.

dining room, living room, and library. The master bedroom is accessed from the stair hallway, which leads to an interior cypress balcony that projects into the double-height living room, with its high-pitched ceilings and banks of tall vertical windows, which Wright called light screens.

Like the exterior of the house, the interior exhibits a harmony with the outdoors, which can be reached from all of the downstairs rooms, except for a maid's room adjacent to the kitchen. Wright frequently used the metaphor of the tree in his designs, but in this case he incorporated an actual tree, which he left standing in the skylit dining room. Though Wright would never admit to being influenced by other architects, the incorporation of a tree had been a modernist trope ever since Le Corbusier included one in an interior patio of the Pavillon de l'Esprit Nouveau, the minimalist house he showed at the 1925 International Exposition of Decorative Arts in Paris.

Edgar Tafel remembers how surprised, even miffed, he and the other apprentices at Taliesin were when Wright told them to bring out one of the plans of his two-story Prairie houses soon after he returned from his visit to the Great Neck site. "[H]e proceeded to design their house, based upon his earlier period . . . in the drafting room [where] we apprentices had worked on Fallingwater, the Johnson Building . . . and we thought he was doing a "throwback" design. . . . We felt it wasn't looking

Ben and Anne Rebhuhn House, Great Neck, 1938. The library, viewed from the main entrance; above the built-in seat on the right is the balcony corridor to the bedrooms.

OPPOSITE
Ben and Anne Rebhuhn House, Great Neck, 1938. The library, looking toward the main entrance hall; the entrance to the living room is on the right.

ahead, and several just wouldn't work on it—but I did . . . for Christmas was coming along, I would go home to NYC to visit my folks, and maybe I would become involved . . . and, I was!"[4] According to Tafel, the reason Wright chose a Prairie Style design was that he felt he had a better chance of getting one of his classic designs built than a modern house.[5] There was a six-week battle to get a permit, and Wright started building without one. As Anne Rebhuhn said, "I always tell everyone that admires the house that the wonderful mayor of the town laughed as the building was going up, but later showed the house proudly as the Best in Great Neck."[6]

Wright, who was a frequent visitor to New York during the 1940s and 1950s—the city he loved, but loved to hate, particularly in press interviews—would often find respite by taking the train out to Great Neck to visit the Rebhuhns at the house he had designed for them. He also used the house for meetings with his New York–based clients. A major commission occupying him at this time was the Guggenheim Museum, which was put on hold during World War II but eventually built in 1956–59. The architect would spend countless hours at the Rebhuhns' going over schemes with Baroness Hilla Rebay, the museum's first director and the guiding force behind Guggenheim's hiring of Wright. During the years 1945–47 the Rebhuhns hosted repeated visits from the progressive founders of Usonia, the community of low-cost houses developed by Wright in Westchester, New York.

Wright greatly admired those who stood up for their ideals, as he did. Much of his friendship with the Rebhuhns was based on their mutual enjoyment of music and the great works of literature, especially books by D. H. Lawrence, George Bernard Shaw, William Blake, Ralph Waldo Emerson, and Walt Whitman—writers who challenged established conventions and social mores. The friendship was put to the test in 1939, when Ben and his nephew Ben Raeburn were convicted of distributing obscene books through the mail and sent to Lewisburg Prison, in Pennsylvania, for eighteen months. Wright wrote to the federal judge to plead for a dismissal of the case, but when Rebhuhn was not granted a reprieve, he visited him in prison.

In 1951 the Rebhuhns established Horizon Press with Ben Raeburn. Though Ben and Anne Rebhuhn eventually parted ways with this venture, Horizon went on to publish seven books by Wright and nine about him after the architect's death.

4

ANTONIN RAYMOND 1888–1976

Charles Briggs and Raoul Carrerà House, Montauk, 1941–42;
Daniel and Rose Krakauer House, Great Neck, 1946;
Sidney and Shirley Rosen House, Great Neck, 1947

By the late 1930s, Antonin Raymond had become a key proponent of the modernist movement in Japan, where the Czech-born architect had a busy practice with his American wife, Noémi. Through their Tokyo office, established in 1923, he introduced stylistic principles of the European modernist avant-garde and advanced building technologies, including reinforced-concrete construction, which he knew about from working in the office of architect Cass Gilbert when the firm was designing the structurally modern Neo-Gothic Woolworth Building (1913) in downtown Manhattan. From 1916 to 1920 the Raymonds were valuable assistants to Frank Lloyd Wright on his design of the Imperial Hotel in Tokyo. The couple's subsequent collaboration was guided by Wright's concept of the total work of art, whereby a building's exterior and interior architecture, as well as its furnishings, were conceived to relate harmoniously to each other and to the surrounding landscape. But, what influenced the couple's aesthetic more profoundly than anything else was their exposure to Japanese culture and its design and architecture, particularly Japanese vernacular farmhouses.

Increased militarism and anti-American fervor in Japan during the late 1930s made it decidedly dangerous for foreigners, so the Raymonds reluctantly closed the Tokyo office and made their way back to the United States. In 1939, they opened an architecture practice on a 150-acre farm, formerly owned by

Charles Briggs and Raoul Carrerà House, Montauk, 1941-1942. View of the Atlantic Ocean from the living room.

a Quaker community, in New Hope Pennsylvania. One of their first commissions was to design a beach house in Montauk, the easternmost hamlet on Long Island. They landed the job when Noémi Raymond befriended the Midwesterner Charles Briggs at a meeting in Manhattan of the American Theosophical Society. Briggs and his friend Raoul Carrerà, the son of a Cuban sugar magnate, had just bought land atop a bluff overlooking the Atlantic Ocean in Hither Hills near Montauk. Soon the Raymonds and the New Hope workshop staff were busy drawing up plans so that the house could be built by the end of the following summer (1942).

At the farm, the Raymonds, their associates, and their apprentices worked and lived communally in the manner of Frank Lloyd Wright's Fellowship at Taliesin. Among the group was a trusted Japanese associate, Junzo Yoshimura (1908–97), who worked on the design of the Briggs Carrerà House up until he returned to Japan in the fall of 1941, just months before the attack on Pearl Harbor. David Leavitt, later the architect of Russel Wright's Dragon Rock house in Garrison, New York, became intrigued by the Raymonds' architecture when he read Antonin Raymond's book *Architectural Details* (1938) during his senior year at the University of Nebraska.[1] In 1940, he hitchhiked from his family's home in Lincoln, Nebraska, to the New Hope farm with the hope of spending the summer there, before starting at Princeton University's School of Architecture in the fall. After being put to a character test picking cherries for a week, Leavitt was invited to stay on that summer as an apprentice architect, and they put him to work on the complex drawings of cabinetry and interior elevations for the Briggs Carrerà House in Montauk.

BRIGGS CARRERÀ HOUSE

The Briggs Carrerà House had to be built with basic, low-cost materials culled from the domestic market because building materials were being diverted to military use as America mobilized for possible involvement in the war. But the limitations on materials did not deter the Raymonds and Yoshimura from designing a beautifully crafted modern house in harmony with its natural setting. Square modular panels of light plywood were used for the walls and tray ceilings and off-the-shelf planks of inexpensive woods for the built-in furniture, which was manufactured at the New Hope carpentry shop. Rough-hewn cedar trunks held up the structure and framed the views beyond the sliding glass doors leading to the decks. According to age-old Japanese practice, the house was divided into three distinct but connected building volumes, each incorporating the column-and-beam construction and hipped roofs used in traditional Japanese architecture and also employed by Wright for his Prairie houses. The construction budget of $75,000, a large one for the time, did permit some extravagance. Large, rough-hewn stones for a fireplace retaining wall, floors, and outdoor paths were trucked in from the fields of New Hope, and the interior floors were made from oak boards.

The house plan was designed to take full advantage of a sublime panoramic view of the Atlantic and the dunescape, which included indigenous beach plum shrubs and grasses blown by the ocean breezes. Today this native landscape no longer exists, replaced by thick bushes, vines and pine trees. The house is still there, however, though now decidedly private and hidden from view, and meticulously cared for by fashion designer Ralph Lauren and his wife, Ricky.

Each building volume's split-level layout steps down to the dunes, and in site plan the house resembles a fanned-out deck of cards. The largest volume is a combination living/dining room, opening through sliding glass doors to an expansive deck, which appears to reach out to the ocean with the same drop-away effect as a classic infinity pool on the edge of a cliff. This volume's massive, stone-clad chimney wall extends into the western dune behind the house, as a declarative aesthetic statement. The wall also anchors the living/dining room to the adjoining service wing, which branches out toward the road. The main bedroom wing is to the east and can be reached by steps leading up from the dunes. Throughout the house the architects used screens (shoji) to alter the sizes of the various rooms, sliding doors between rooms, and horizontal wood-framed windows that slid along tracks, as well as solid wooden shutters (amado), which could also be moved in and out of the walls along parallel tracks and quickly deployed to protect the house against stormy weather.

Noémi Raymond supervised the design of the interior built-ins, furniture, and fabrics. Although trained as a graphic designer—and, like her husband, an artist at heart—she was interested in architecture and worked alongside him as a full-time partner on all of their important projects. Even light fixtures, hardware, and the fireplace andirons for the Montauk house were designed and manufactured at the New Hope workshop and studio. The house fit the concept of the total work of art in all respects.

TWO GREAT NECK HOUSES

Six years later, the Raymonds were commissioned to design for another Long Island site, this time with their partner, Ladislav Rado, with whom they practiced from 1945 until their retirement in 1971. Their clients were two young couples, the Rosens and the Krakauers, who knew each other from Brooklyn and decided to buy adjoining lots from a dairy farmer in then mostly rural Kings Point, an incorporated village within Great Neck. This was the area that F. Scott Fitzgerald dubbed West Egg in *The Great Gatsby*, although by the 1950s most of the land on which the grand Gatsby-esque houses stood was being subdivided for development. It is unclear how the two couples came to select the Raymonds as architects, and it seems neither had a strong interest in Japanese culture before they encountered the Raymond firm.[2]

Sidney Rosen was an engineer and contractor on Long Island and had inherited a

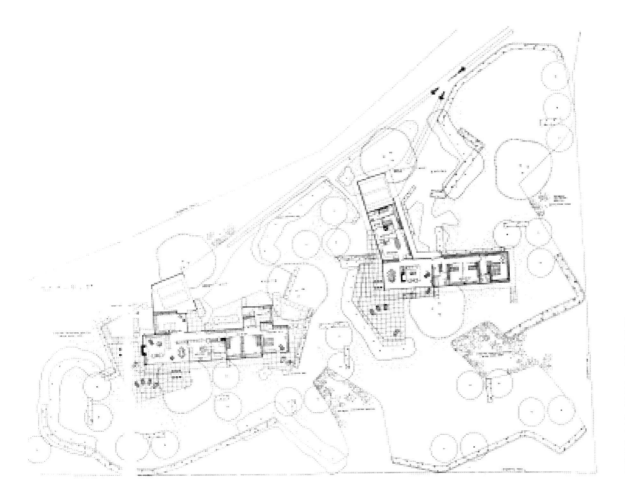

Daniel and Rose Krakauer and Sidney and Shirley Rosen Houses, Great Neck, 1946-47. Plot plan by landscape architect James Rose, with Antonin Raymond and Ladislav Rado. It shows a coordinated, parklike landscape for the two houses.

window-manufacturing plant based in Queens. Perhaps Antonin Raymond's reputation as an expert in the use of sliding horizontal sash windows caught Rosen's attention. His factory was under contract to produce the windows for Long Island's Levittown, so he was well versed in modern building techniques and the use of windows to control sun, light, and heat. In fact, Rosen served as the general contractor for both his house and the Krakauers'.[3]

Dan Krakauer was owner and president of his family business, Inner Springs Constructions, a manufacturer of mattress springs. A scientifically oriented intellectual, he took great pleasure in the houses' passive solar heating aspects and in-floor radiant heating system, which conducted water heated by oil through wrought-iron pipes. His wife, Rose, had an artistic flair and over the years she purchased an eclectic mix of objects for the house, including modern pottery and folk-art pieces, as well as furniture by George Nakashima and Hans Wegner, among others.

The Rosen and Krakauer houses were similar in design and shared the same driveway, yet they were intentionally sited in a carefully contrived landscape so that their proximity was not obvious. James Rose (1913–91), a pioneering designer of modernist landscapes, created a unified outdoor scheme that took into account the existing tall trees and imparted a sense that the two houses were built in a parklike setting. Rose worked with the Raymond firm on a number of jobs and shared the Raymonds' affinities for Japanese aesthetics, Frank Lloyd Wright's design philosophy, and the notion of the experiential naturalistic garden, which was deliberately informal and somewhat antithetical to Beaux-Arts concepts. Rose typically incorporated outdoor terraces and garden rooms away from the house and below grade within leafy surrounds. Both the design of the Great Neck houses and their site planning, featuring discreet barrier trees and bushes, were inspired by the middle-class residences the Raymond firm had designed in Japan during the country's post–World War II reconstruction period. The architects created passive solar heating to supplement the in-floor heating systems by adopting the Japanese method of orienting the

OPPOSTITE TOP
Daniel and Rose Krakauer House, Great Neck, 1946. View of the newly installed entrance garden, photographed from the drive that the Rosen and Krakauer houses shared.

OPPOSTITE BOTTOM
Daniel and Rose Krakauer House, Great Neck, 1946. The steel structure on the back lawn is by Isamu Noguchi.

TOP
Daniel and Rose Krakauer House, Great Neck, 1946. Installation of the radiant heating system in the floor.

ABOVE
Daniel and Rose Krakauer House, Great Neck, 1946. Installation of one of the outdoor terraces that were a feature of both the Rosen and Krakauer houses.

houses to the south to take maximum advantage of the winter sun. The houses' hipped roofs derive from traditional Japanese farmhouses and Frank Lloyd Wright's Prairie houses. Plans of each house show two rectangular volumes set at an angle to each other, as in the Briggs Carrerà House.

The Rosen House was furnished with modern pieces that the couple acquired on a buying trip to Denmark,[4] while the Krakauer House was appointed with Noémi Raymond's designs, including built-in cabinetry, desks, pull-out storage bins, dining and living room furniture, and even the fireplace andirons.[5] Noémi's bold, abstract fabric designs turned up on curtains and pillows throughout the house. Until sometime in the 1980s, the Krakauers' view of the lawn from their living room included a sculpture of a large steel cage, by Isamu Noguchi overgrown with wisteria. This piece, from a set design for a Martha Graham dance, was probably given to the Raymonds soon after the house was built to provide a point of reference in the newly landscaped, still barren area near the living room patio. Noguchi was part of their circle of artist friends, as was the artist Ben Shahn, which perhaps explains why the Krakauers hung a large Shahn lithograph in a wood frame designed by Noémi above the living room hearth. Like Charles Briggs and Raoul Carrerà, the Krakauers put their trust in the Raymonds' approach to design, which strove to unify the architecture and everything contained within it through a single aesthetic.

5

DAVID L. LEAVITT b.1919

Ernest M. and Arlene Silva House, Lloyd Neck, 1956
Bill Miller "Box Kite" House, Fire Island, 1956

In 1954, David Leavitt arrived in New York after three years spent working in Antonin and Noémi Raymond's busy Tokyo office, which the pair had established when they returned to Japan to participate in the post–World War II rebuilding of the country. Over the next six years, as a principal in Leavitt, Henshell and Kawai in Manhattan, Leavitt designed several commissions, including two houses on Long Island—one for photographer Ernest Silva and his wife, Arlene, and the other, a summer house on Fire Island, for advertising executive Bill Miller. The Silva House revealed the architect's keen understanding of Antonin Raymond's Frank Lloyd Wright– and Japanese-inspired aesthetic. The other was a departure from this well-defined aesthetic and decidedly an experiment for Leavitt.

On the flight back to Idlewild Airport from their honeymoon in the Bahamas in 1953, Ernest and Arlene Silva, owners of a prosperous photography studio in Manhattan, spotted a relatively uninhabited peninsula, Lloyd Neck, jutting out into the waters of Long Island Sound near Huntington. They soon procured a two-acre lot on Lloyd Neck in a grove of tall oaks with access to the nearby sandy beach. In 1954, the Silvas joined the throngs visiting both the Japanese Exhibition House at the Museum of Modern Art and Frank Lloyd Wright's Usonian Exhibition House at the future site of the Guggenheim Museum. With their minds made up

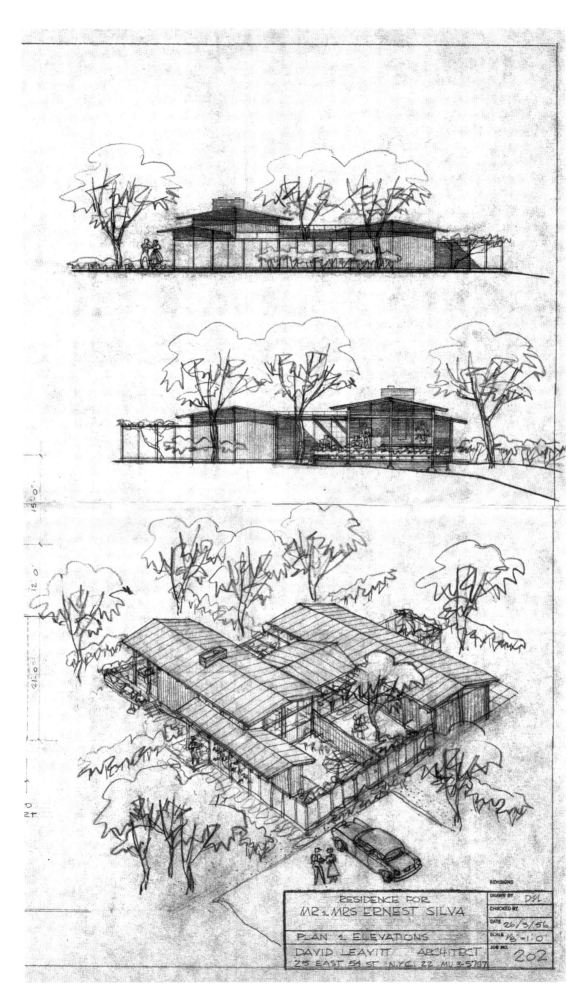

Ernest M. and Arlene Silva House, Lloyd Neck, 1956. Plan and elevations, drawn by David Leavitt.

Earnest M. and Arlene Silva House, Lloyd Neck, 1956. The distinctly Japanese lines of the front façade; the garden courtyard is on the right.

OPPOSITE TOP
Ernest M. and Arlene Silva House, Lloyd Neck, 1956. The house at night. From left, the master bedroom wing, dining area, center, and living room under an extending roof, including an outdoors porch. Shoji screens lead from the living room to the porch.

OPPOSITE BOTTOM
Ernest M. and Arlene Silva House, Lloyd Neck, 1956. View of the kitchen from the courtyard garden.

to find someone who could design in the manner of Wright and with a Japanese vocabulary, the Silvas stumbled upon Leavitt's work through a small Japanese model room he had designed for a Midtown art gallery. The couple contacted Leavitt and soon commissioned him to design their new house. "It was a pleasure to work with David Leavitt," Ernest Silva recalls. "He gave us exactly what we wanted at a time when we wanted to learn all we could about Japanese house design."[1]

Leavitt designed a compact but seemingly spacious, light-filled, one-story house with a garden courtyard that functioned as an outdoor room—an enclosed world of nature. An overhanging roof covered with white pebbles and vertical redwood framing and siding gave the house distinctly Japanese lines. The walls of the courtyard garden were composed of "gray-white panels" of "asbestos cement" framed in contrasting redwood strips. Leavitt located the main entrance to the house between the living room and the kitchen, but the Silvas wanted to enter through a Shinto-inspired gate into the garden courtyard. Ernest Silva had the gate made and Leavitt installed it, but reluctantly, as he knew

that this type of gate (torii) was traditionally the entrance to a Shinto shrine, not to a residence. The gate disappeared when a subsequent owner added a garage that extended out from the garden wall. This was the only significant change ever made to the house, however. Its interior plan—the original oak floors and Dutch elm paneling in almost every room, and Japanese architectural elements such as sliding paper-screen doors (*shoji*), interior partitions (*fusama*), and alcoves (*tokonoma*)—and outdoor walkways are still intact. Only a few basic pieces of furniture were needed, according to Leavitt, who observed: "For a Japanese house the structure is the design and it doesn't need an interior designer."[2]

The house did not need a landscape designer either, as Ernest Silva, working with Leavitt, came up with a scheme for the garden. Once, long after the house was built, when the Silvas were about to leave for Japan, they were asked if the house could be included in a garden tour and if their Japanese gardener could show the garden while they were traveling. Arlene Silva said, "I had to say my Japanese gardener was going on the trip

to Japan with me."³ Ernest Silva not only selected and tended to the plantings but also enjoyed making the Japanese-inspired fencing and gates that surrounded the house. The couple often went to exhibitions and attended lectures at Japan House in Manhattan.

The house brought Leavitt what he called the commission of a lifetime—Russel Wright's Dragon Rock, 1956,⁴ the noted designer's Japanese-inspired house overlooking a waterfall and pond on the site of an abandoned granite quarry in Garrison, New York. Unfortunately, as the years went by, Wright did not credit Leavitt's significant role in the project, yet any comparison of drawings and photographs of the Silva House with those of Dragon Rock provides unmistakable evidence of Leavitt's pronounced hand in the architecture of both buildings.

The Box Kite House, as Leavitt dubbed it, in Cherry Grove, Fire Island, overlooking the Great South Bay, was an entirely different kind of house.⁵ The ultimate summer getaway, with running water and indoor plumbing but no electricity, it was whimsical and low cost, yet technologically

LEFT
Box Kite House, Fire Island, 1956. When open, the shutters functioned as balconies.

BELOW LEFT
Box Kite House, Fire Island, 1956. View of the outrigger cables, which had to be adjusted daily to keep the structure stable.

radical. There was no direct access to it by road, so all of the building materials were shipped in by boat or seaplane. The client, advertising executive Bill Miller, wanted the house to be raised up in the air and have views of the bay, so Leavitt designed a square box on stilts, with adjustable folding balconies that served as shutters during the winter. A spiral staircase inside extended through three levels, somewhat like a lighthouse stair.

The house did indeed resemble a high-quality box kite. Its steel-and-wood structural frame held walls of translucent Mylar plastic sheeting run through with chicken wire. The wood-framed sliding windows were also made of Mylar. If it had not been for the outrigger cables attached to turnbuckles all around the structure it could have easily broken and blown away. The house structure sat on a ten-inch-thick concrete slab at grade, held up by three-and-a-half-foot-deep wooden posts that were secured underground with anchor bolts. Because of constantly varying wind conditions, Miller had to climb onto plank platforms around the house almost every day and adjust the turnbuckles on the guy-wire rigging to stabilize the frame. Leavitt instructed Miller that the house was less likely to collapse if he let the wind blow through it leeward, with the shutters closed in the windward direction. During the off-season all the shutters were pulled down around the box. Ironically, it was not wind but a stove fire that destroyed the house in the early 1960s.

RIGHT
Box Kite House, Fire Island, 1956. Interior stair soon after construction. Note the kerosene lamp, one of several used to light the house.

BELOW
Box Kite House, Fire Island, 1956. Corner of the house, with view of the Great South Bay, toward Sayville, Long Island.

6

MARCEL BREUER 1902–1981

Bert and Phyllis Geller House I, Lawrence, 1945;
Gilbert Tompkins House, Hewlett Harbor, 1946;
John and Bea Hanson House, Lloyd Harbor, 1951;
Bert and Phyllis Geller House II, Lawrence, 1969

arcel Breuer had just dissolved his partnership with Walter Gropius and set up a solo practice in Cambridge near the Harvard campus when he was introduced to Bertram Geller. Recently graduated from Dartmouth College and living in Cambridge, Geller had gone into his family's shoe business instead of fulfilling an ambition to become an architect or pursue city planning, which he had studied. Yet, with an avid interest in what was going on at Harvard's Graduate School of Design, Geller sat in on workshops and classes there with his former college roommate Joseph Stein, who was enrolled in the school. Geller became taken with Breuer's engaging personality and his approach to teaching design and architecture, and visited the architect's house in Lincoln, Massachusetts, as well as houses Breuer had designed in collaboration with Gropius. Soon after returning to New York to work in the Andrew Geller Shoes headquarters, Geller and his wife, Phyllis, asked Breuer to design a house on a flat, eleven-acre site in Lawrence that would accommodate their family of four growing boys.

Though today Marcel Breuer is recognized as one of the giants of twentieth-century architecture, in the mid-1940s he was known and admired by a narrow circle of architecture and design insiders for his association with the Bauhaus in Germany, where he studied art and design (he did not have a degree in architecture) and became head of the carpentry workshop. His renown rested primarily

Bert and Phyllis Geller House I, Lawrence, 1945. Back of the house, showing its vertical cedar siding, fieldstone cladding, custom-made wood-frame windows, and butterfly roof.

on his radically modern furniture models for mass production such as the famous Wassily chair from 1925, still sold throughout the world. In 1937, he arrived in Boston to teach at Harvard at the invitation of his former teacher Walter Gropius. Four years later, Breuer stepped away from the architectural partnership they had formed, having become dissatisfied with sharing credit on a number of house commissions that were predominantly of his own design.

The strikingly modern house that Breuer produced for the Gellers shocked other residents in Lawrence, a neighborhood of grand old traditional houses near the Rockaway Hunting Club, and was a target for local slurs and protestations. However, it was applauded by the popular and architectural press nationwide, which considered the design spectacular and an entirely new house type for the modern American family. *Progressive Architecture* named it House of the Year for 1947, putting Breuer on the architectural map as an innovative designer. He was hailed for his binuclear plan, in which living spaces were combined with the master bedroom in one wing and children's play and sleeping quarters were consigned to another. The wings were joined by a connecting entry hall. The house, with its detached guest suite, to which a garage was attached, became synonymous with glamorous mid-twentieth-century living. It showcased Breuer's highly original architecture, with its

Bert and Phyllis Geller House I, Lawrence, 1945. View of the living room toward the fieldstone fireplace. All of the furniture was designed by Breuer.

references to the abstract sculptural forms of Russian Constructivism and traditional New England wood-based construction, as well as the designer's penchant for saturated primary colors and appreciation of diverse buildings materials, both natural and manmade. Besides providing Breuer with a substantial commission at the close of World War II, when work was hard to come by, the Geller House (Geller House I) enabled him to shake off his reputation among architects as being strictly a disciple of Gropius.

Geller gave Breuer several more commissions over the years, including a second house on Long Island and his company's executive offices and showrooms. Geller not only had the means to be Breuer's patron-client but also had complete trust in and commitment to Breuer as an artist, and gave him carte blanche to design both the buildings and furnishings for all of his commissions. Breuer designed Geller House I from his Cambridge office but by 1946 had moved to New York to set up practice there so he could take full advantage of the attention the house had generated.

During the time the Gellers owned their first Breuer house—they sold it in the late 1960s—it was situated on eleven acres of cleared land along the floodplain of bays and inlets on Long Island's South Shore. The original site offered Breuer a field—clearly reminiscent of the Great Hungarian Plain near Pécs, where Breuer had grown up—on which he could splay the house and divide it into three distinct volumes (the two wings of the binuclear plan and the freestanding guest quarters and garage), which were amply extended by low courtyard walls and outdoor spaces. Vertical cedar siding, custom-designed wood-frame windows with wooden louvers, and large fieldstones were used for the outer façades and the butterfly-shaped roofs, sloped inward in defiance of the omnipresent pitched roofs in the neighborhood. Large, rugged fieldstones clad the immense living room fireplace and echoed the fieldstone-clad low wainscoting in some of the bedrooms. The wainscoting appeared to extend out to the landscape as stone walls that formed semi-enclosed outdoor courtyards. The interior of the house had flagstone floors. The rooms were defined by party walls with glass windows at the ceiling level to let in light and featured built-in closets and drawers. Ironically, despite the aim of the binuclear plan, which was to separate the activities of two generations living under the same roof, the house offered very little privacy. The Gellers' son Joe, who grew up in the house, recounts, "My mother was a fastidious housekeeper and she taught us to put everything away in all those built-in drawers and bins throughout the house, but she didn't mind us as young children running throughout the expansive house indoors to outdoors and from room to room all day with our friends. My parents enjoyed living there and they certainly didn't deliberately design the house as a showcase to make a declarative statement about architecture and themselves."[1]

Over the years, the Gellers introduced works of art to the house, particularly three-dimensional art, including a stabile by Alexander Calder, as

Bert and Phyllis Geller House I, Lawrence, 1945. A bedroom in the guest quarters overlooks a wall that appears to be a continuation of the room's fieldstone wainscoting. Breuer designed the furniture and a curtained-off sleeping loft above.

well as drawings and prints by artists influenced by Breuer's teachers at the Bauhaus, such as Josef Albers, Wassily Kandinsky, and Paul Klee. Breuer thought of himself as an artist, and according to another Geller son, Michael, the house felt as much like art as architecture. "The doors and walls and even the radiator covers were painted in supremely bright colors. Breuer supervised the paint job himself and we all knew that the paint marks on the garage wall were put there by Breuer when he was working out what colors to use."[2] In 1950, Phyllis Geller asked Breuer if he could recommend a way to hang art in the living room, which had no wall space, to liven it up. The standing-shelf room divider between the kitchen and dining room had a plywood back, and Breuer decided to ask Jackson Pollock to come by and measure the divider so that he could create a site-specific painting for this surface.[3] The result was a magnificent 72- x 96-inch painting of rusty reds and spirals of thick, dripped paint—one of the earliest examples of the artist's drip paintings and of Abstract Expressionism. He

OPPOSITE
Bert and Phyllis Geller House I, Lawrence, 1945. The entrance hall connects the adults' wing (living spaces and the master bedroom) with the children's wing on the far side of the wall on the right.

ABOVE
Bert and Phyllis Geller House I, Lawrence, 1945. The kitchen and dining area. Note the pass-through counter.

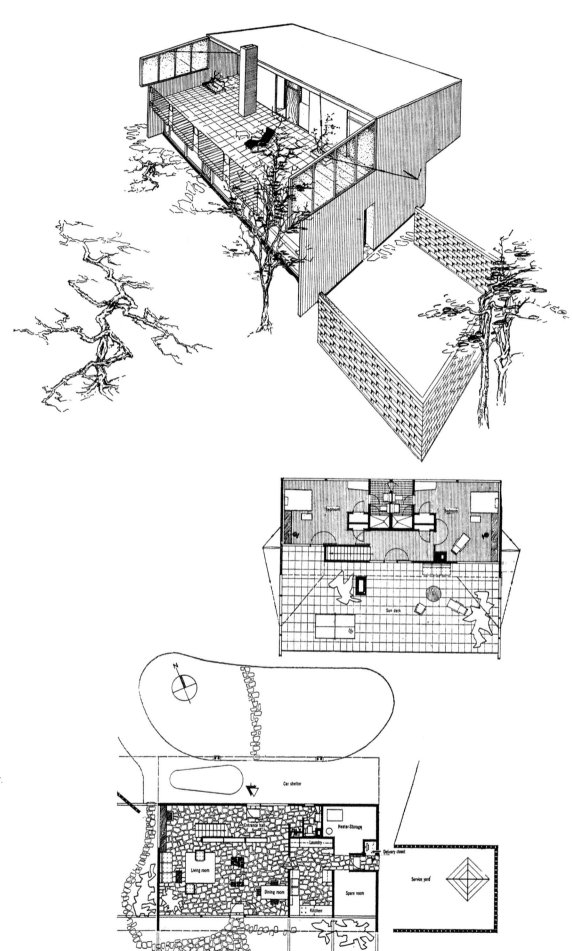

Gilbert Tompkins House, Hewlett Harbor, 1946.
Top: Perspective drawing, southeast view.
Center: plan, upper level.
Bottom: plan, ground floor.

titled it *Mural on Indian Red Ground*. "We used to prop bikes and sports gear up against the painting during the daytime," Michael Geller recalls.[4]

In 1945, Gilbert Tompkins, an agent for graphic designers who worked for art-book publishers and museums, found out about the Geller house, and he and his wife asked Breuer to design a house for their waterfront property in Hewlett Harbor, a town neighboring Lawrence. The Tompkins House harked back to the structures Breuer had designed with Gropius in Cambridge: flat-roofed, cantilevered two story-houses in which the living areas are on the ground floor and the bedrooms on the second, with an offset balcony along one façade. Yet the Tompkins House diverged from this type in two ways: its exterior stucco walls were painted in daringly bright colors and it had a stark, sculptural silhouette that created a strong presence on the flat, sandy ground overlooking the Atlantic bays. The house was ground based at the entry façade and cantilevered to hold a large sundeck on the façade overlooking the water. The cool modernity of the house's structure and exterior belied the warm atmosphere of the interior. In the open-plan living area Breuer introduced wood cabinetry and bookshelves and a hung stairway. A fieldstone fireplace served to divide the space. A sculptural tour de force, it clearly drew on the folk tradition of the

Gilbert Tompkins House, Hewlett Harbor, 1946. A fieldstone fireplace divides the living and dining areas of the open-plan interior. Its warm atmosphere is belied by the stark modernity of the exterior.

TOP
John and Bea Hanson House, Lloyd Harbor, 1951. View from the back yard, a former apple orchard.

ABOVE
John and Bea Hanson House, Lloyd Harbor, 1951. The carport at left later became a bedroom wing. The front door and entrance hallway are between the carport and the house itself, at right.

countryside surrounding Pécs. Sadly, the Tompkins House was destroyed in a storm that whipped over Hewlett Harbor sometime in the 1970s.

In the late 1940s, the Museum of Modern Art, in an effort to further its mission of showing the public the "art of our time," took an interest in Breuer as an architect. Staff members suggested to the board of trustees that he design an exhibition house in the museum's courtyard. After learning of the prospect, Breuer invited Philip Johnson, Alfred Barr Jr., A. Conger Goodyear, Mrs. John D. Rockefeller, and others on the museum's board to visit both the Geller and Tompkins houses in the spring of 1948.

The exhibition job became his and he decided to build a prototype of an affordable modern house for a family with a middle-class budget and a willingness to discard conventional trappings, including inherited furniture and china. The show house was furnished and equipped entirely by Breuer. Like Geller House I, the exhibition house had a butterfly roof, wood siding, and stone walls. Perceived by the public as radically modern, it projected a new sense of optimism and domesticity to the generation that had endured World War II.

The House in the Museum Garden at the Museum of Modern Art fetched Breuer numerous new clients, among them John and Bea Hanson, who joined the viewing crowds at the Modern in their search to find an architect to design a house for land they had purchased in Lloyd Harbor. The young couple had been living in a brownstone apartment in Brooklyn Heights, New York, and they wanted a modern house with open spaces and views of the outdoors. Despite a small budget, they considered contacting a number of leading architects, including Walter Gropius, Ludwig Mies van der Rohe, Richard Neutra, and even Frank Lloyd Wright. Breuer was the first on the Hansons' list to visit. After meeting him, they decided to go no further, as he was engaging, listened to their needs respectfully, and speedily incorporated their ideas into a proposal. Bea Hanson recalls, "We told him how we wanted to live and he immediately pulled out a yellow legal pad and drew circles to show us where he suggested we have different rooms and areas of the house. He really understood our budgetary concerns and drew in a carport that we could eventually adapt into more bedroom space as our family grew."[5]

The Hanson House is set on a two-acre site surrounded by apple trees that, like the site of Geller House I, recalls the Great Hungarian Plain. It includes many features of both the museum exhibition house and Geller House I: it is binuclear in plan and has a butterfly roof; its interior is focused toward the outdoors; and fieldstone garden walls extend from the house into the landscape. Over the years, Breuer's original plan has proved as adaptable as architect and client intended it to be. In 1966, a local architect converted the carport into a separate apartment for the Hanson children and later for Bea's guests. In 2005, the Hansons' son moved back into the house with his own young family, and Bea Hanson took over the apartment. She says of the architect, "Breuer was interested in people and how they live, as well as how they could enjoy his particular beautifully crafted architecture."[6]

Breuer's house commissions were his bread and butter during the 1940s and 1950s, but by the 1960s he was turning them down for larger, more lucrative commissions from universities and corporations. Yet, for his old friends the Gellers, Breuer was glad to make an exception. With their children now parents themselves, Bert and Phyllis Geller wanted to build a new house on a six-acre site with a superb view of the Atlantic bays, down the road from their first Breuer-designed house. In 1968, Breuer and his partner Herbert Beckhard, who for a number of years had been in charge of the Breuer firm's house commissions, showed the Gellers plans for the Paepcke Vacation Ski House in Aspen, Colorado, which was not built because of the client's unexpected death soon after working drawings were completed. One look at the plans

John and Bea Hanson House, Lloyd Harbor, 1951. A bookshelf and entertainment center designed by Breuer separates the living room from the entrance hall.

LEFT
Bert and Phyllis Geller House II, Lawrence, 1969. The Japanese-inspired rock garden in the entrance courtyard. The concrete walls surrounding the courtyard are textured to suggest board-and-batten formed siding.

BELOW LEFT
Bert and Phyllis Geller House II, Lawrence, 1969. The bayside façade and poured-concrete, parabolic arch–shaped roof.

persuaded the Gellers that it was the house for them, with a few adjustments to suit their needs and the site.

Geller House II is a feat of concrete engineering and, with its parabolic arch–shaped roof soaring over a square of concrete and stucco walls, stands in complete contrast to the Gellers' first earthbound, asymmetrical wood- and stone-clad house, which had caused a sensation twenty years earlier. By the 1960s, Breuer was acknowledged to be at the forefront of concrete construction, producing massively sculptural architecture that emphasized the texture of the concrete surfaces. For Geller House II, a masterpiece of Brutalist architecture, Breuer designed a powerfully sculptural concrete shell, treating its surfaces so that it became a collage of textures and planes interrupted by shadows and light. Neither hard nor cold, as its material might imply, the house is inviting and integrated into its wooded site.

The entrance façade faces north and is fronted by a courtyard made to look like a Japanese-inspired rock garden surrounded by concrete walls that are textured to suggest board-and-batten siding. The visitor approaches the house along a flagstone path. The mossy ground at the front entrance is adorned with two of sculptor Costantino ("Tino") Nivola's giant concrete apples, specially commissioned by Breuer for the Gellers. The concrete entrance façade is restrained; the front door punches it in the center and horizontal windows pierce it high off the ground.

The patio side to the south is set above a grassy slope leading down to the marshes. A wall of windows under the arched roof brings views of the marshlands into the main living space. The horizontal and vertical window openings provide a sculptural visual contrast to the arch of the roof. A large concrete terrace reaches out from this façade and is defined as an outdoor room by board-and-batten-textured concrete walls, similar to those defining the front courtyard.

The Gellers wanted to live casually in an open space, and Breuer accommodated them with a large, two-story-high living and dining area. Guest bedrooms are located off the front entry hallway, where there is also a stair to the master bedroom, which overlooks the main living space. Breuer achieved a sense of intimacy in the interior, emphasizing standard features of domestic architecture—the entry hall, an enclosed stair, the hearth—that make people feel at home. The entire curved roof of the house interior is crafted from the cork mold used to form the concrete exterior roof. The cork ceiling is painted white, except in the bedrooms, where it was left in its natural brown color. As was typical of Breuer's domestic architecture, the house included a mixture of natural earthy materials—flagstone floors and warm-toned woods—and brightly colored walls for a planar effect.

Most of the Gellers' Breuer-designed plywood furniture from Geller House I was either donated to a local charity or irreparably damaged by their boisterous young family, so the couple asked Breuer to provide furniture for the new house. He designed the sofas for the sunken conversation and seating area, and a version of his signature Pécs desk and a storage cabinet to flank the fireplace. For the open kitchen and dining space, he designed a thick, granite-topped rectangular dining table, around which he placed his Cesca chairs.

Bert and Phyllis Geller House II, Lawrence, 1969. With its large, two-story-high, open-plan living and dining space, the house is of a markedly different type than Geller I. The table, chairs, and sunken seating were all designed by Breuer. The ceiling fixtures are by Achille and Pier Giacomo Castiglioni.

7
JANE YU b.1938

Bert and Phyllis Geller House III, Lawrence, 1978

In 1978, two years after Bert Geller retired, he and his wife, Phyllis, commissioned a third modern house in Lawrence. The first two were designed by Marcel Breuer (see pages 70–81). The Gellers turned to architect Jane Yu, an interior designer who worked in Breuer's office from 1954 to 1980, with several interruptions to take jobs elsewhere. Among her interiors were those for Lincoln Center's Avery Fisher Hall (1962) by Wallace Harrison and Max Abramovitz and New York University's Bobst Library (1972) by Philip Johnson and Richard Foster. Yu got to know the Gellers, who had a high regard for her work, when she oversaw the design, with Breuer's firm, of the Andrew Geller Shoes showroom in Manhattan.

Contemplating Bert's retirement, the Gellers initially decided to move out of Lawrence and into Manhattan—to 800 Fifth Avenue, an enormous apartment building designed by Ulrich Franzen. They asked Yu to design the renovation of an entire floor in the building, but the management balked when they saw Yu's preliminary drawings, which featured an open-plan, loftlike space with no doors except to the bathroom. As a result, the Gellers opted to stay in Lawrence, acquiring a four-acre wedge-shaped piece of land overlooking Reynolds Channel.

Yu's mandate from the Gellers was to design a simple two-bedroom house quickly and inexpensively, with a minimum of deliberation. Rather similar in its exterior structure to Breuer's Tompkins

House of 1946 in nearby Hewlett Harbor (see pages 76-78), Geller House III is a small, elegant, and beautifully sited two-story structure. Unlike the Tompkins House, which featured pure white stucco over its wood framing and was designed as a singular sculptural object, this house, with its palette of soft colors that blended in with the reeds and marsh grasses beyond it, exuded warmth. The Gellers enjoyed the marshland view from a large roof deck that cantilevered out from the upstairs bedroom, in the manner of the Tompkins House and Walter Gropius's own house, which Breuer had had a hand in designing.

The exterior of Geller House III is fabricated from a combination of stock vertical cedar siding, beige concrete blocks, and Anderson windows— a departure from Breuer's penchant for custom windows. These inexpensive materials were part of the solution to the challenge of building the house at low cost and expeditiously. Toward this end there were few drawings, and decisions were often made on site with contractor Ed Stein, who enjoyed a prolific thirty-year practice on Long Island constructing high-quality modern buildings for various architects. In keeping with the architect's serious interest in alternative energy sources in the late 1970s, Yu included a solar-powered hot-water heater on the flat roof of the house.

The light-filled interior of the house is open in plan, with the kitchen as the linchpin between the

Bert and Phyllis Geller House III, Lawrence, 1978. Jane Yu designed the Gellers' third house economically, using split-face concrete blocks to suggest stone, stock vertical cedar siding, and large factory-made windows. Note the solar panels on the roof.

Bert and Phyllis Geller House III, Lawrence, 1978. View of the living space and the bedroom loft above.

dining area and a small, comfortable, sunken sitting room overlooking the lawn and marshland. Instead of Breuer's standard flagstone, Yu chose waxed red brick for the downstairs floors, except in the lounge area of the living space, where the brick forms a wide border running around the perimeter, but the area itself is covered with beige carpeting.

The brick is in striking contrast to the split concrete blocks used for both the interior and exterior walls. A small bedroom is tucked into the area left of the entrance to the downstairs space. A simple ladder stair with a chrome tube rail ascends to a catwalk that leads to the master bedroom, which is completely open to the first-floor living space. Yu notes,

"The Gellers didn't like doors, not even for their closets, which were faced with hanging textiles."[1] The openness of the house allowed for maximum appreciation of *Proportions*, the magnificent, large, silk-weave tapestry that Breuer originally designed in 1977 for the Andrew Geller Shoes showroom. At Geller III the tapestry was hung upstairs on the wall along the catwalk, so the large rectangular piece depicting three squares in Breuer blue, white, and flame orange on a heather green field, framed in a border of light brown, could be seen from the first-floor living areas.[2]

Geller House III received no recognition from the architectural profession. As Yu recalls, "The Gellers asked me to keep quiet about the commission, as they didn't want to offend the others in the [Breuer] office. I did the job on my own, off the firm's books. The principals in the office had pegged me as an interior designer and they never would have allowed me to do the job through the office. In fact, when the house was finished, the mayor of Lawrence encouraged me to put in an application for an AIA Long Island award. But Herbert Beckhard, who usually took charge of house commissions in the Breuer office, was on the committee and he would not consider the application."[3] Nonetheless, the Gellers were delighted with the house; Yu remembers Phyllis Geller saying that it was her favorite of all their houses—easy to take care of, compact, and intimate.

Bert and Phyllis Geller House III, Lawrence, 1978. The lounge area of the living space.

8
WILLIAM LANDSBERG b.1915

William and Muriel Landsberg House, Port Washington, 1951;
Rudolph and Mildred Joseph House I, Freeport, 1953;
Rudolph and Mildred Joseph House II, Freeport, 1956;
O. E. McIntyre Plant, Westbury, 1954;
Randall and Helen McIntyre House, Deer Park, 1957;
Angus and Bobbie McIntyre House, Deer Park, 1957

In 1948, after establishing his practice in Manhattan, Marcel Breuer asked William (Bill) Landsberg, an architect who had been his student at Harvard's Graduate School of Design and had worked as chief draftsman in Breuer's fledgling practice in Cambridge in the late 1930s, to join him in designing the exhibition house for the House in the Museum Garden series at the Museum of Modern Art. At the time Landsberg was working for Gordon Bunshaft at Skidmore, Owings and Merrill. Landsberg executed all the drawings for the Modern's project, giving him the opportunity to again immerse himself in Breuer's architectural language. As he explained, "Breuer would give me a sketch of his concept for a building and I would do the drawings. He was not schooled as an architect and so he did not know how to produce drawings. I would also write his letters, in the terse manner that I had learned with the Army, as his command of English was not so good."[1]

As director of design for Breuer's firm, Marcel Breuer Architect, from 1948 to 1956, Landsberg was Breuer's most trusted associate. He worked on a number of the house commissions that sprang from design concepts first explored in the house for the Museum of Modern Art exhibition. Two were on Long Island—the Hanson House in Lloyd Harbor and the Witalis House in Kings Point, both built in 1951, the same year Landsberg designed a house for his own family in Port Washington.

William and Muriel Landsberg House, Port Washington, 1951. Front façade. Built at low cost out of locally sourced materials, this Breuer-esque house is beautifully situated in its wooded site.

In 1950, William and Muriel Landsberg purchased an acre of land for $2,500 in an unused swampy area within an established neighborhood of traditional houses below Port Washington's historic old Main Street. The hilly site was considered unfit for a building, but Landsberg had it bulldozed so that he could tuck into it a typologically Breuer-esque house—long and with two stories. The first-floor slab, which rests on piles driven into the swampy land, houses a garage, an adjacent entry hall, and two rooms, which became Landsberg's home drafting studio and office. The wood-frame second story features an open-plan living and dining room, approached by an elegantly simple switchback stair enclosed by plain wood studs. The entire second story cantilevers over the site, affording a grand sense of space and connection with the surrounding tall old beech and oak trees. Although constructed with minimal means out of basic building materials, the house is compact, elegant, and perfectly in keeping with its wooded site. All of the windows, sliding doors, and built-in cabinets and shelves were custom designed and fabricated at a nearby mill, and the stone front façade was made from Manhattan schist—rock blasted away to make room for the city's subways—which was available until the mid-1950s at a stone yard in nearby Glen Cove.

In 1952, Rudolph and Mildred Joseph asked Breuer to design a family house with a small

William and Muriel Landsberg House, Port Washington, 1951. Across from the architect's first-floor drafting studio and office is a switchback stair, fabricated from plain wooden studs.

medical office near the entrance, so Dr. Joseph, a general practitioner, could see patients during off-hours from his practice in downtown Freeport. They, too, had been impressed with Breuer's exhibition house at the Modern. Breuer met with the Josephs initially, but he turned over the entire job to Landsberg. Indeed, a 1955 article in *Architectural Record* cites William W. Landsberg as the architect of the two-volume L-shaped house, with a courtyard.[2] The Josephs liked working with Landsberg, as evidenced by the larger, but similar house he designed for them nearby only three years later.

In 1954, with Breuer out of the country working on the UNESCO headquarters in Paris, France, Landsberg also took complete charge of the design and production of the O. E. McIntyre Plant in Westbury, Long Island.[3] Randall McIntyre and his brother, Angus, had decided to approach

Breuer after visiting their friends the Hansons at their Breuer-designed house in Lloyd Harbor (see pages 78–79). Randall recalled telephoning Marcel Breuer's office to commission the architect to design the plant, but a secretary referred him to William Landsberg, and McIntyre never did meet Breuer.

The McIntyre family business, a pioneer in direct-mail marketing, was growing fast, with major contracts from magazines such as *Time*, *Life*, *McCall's*, and *House & Garden*. Both Randall and Angus admired modern architecture and were ready to embrace it for their corporate headquarters in New York, as well as for a new production plant. The McIntyres were the first tenants in Mies van der Rohe's Seagram Building on Park Avenue, where they leased the twenty-seventh and twenty-eighth floors as business headquarters. Randall was involved in the decision to select Richard Neutra for the design of the Swirbul Library at Adelphi University (see pages 171–79), where he sat on the board of trustees.

The plant's design riled other factory owners in the Westbury industrial park, where the McIntyres chose to build. The neighboring factories were built in traditional styles and their main entrances all faced west, overlooking the street that led into the development from West John Street. The entrance of the McIntyre building was on the east, facing a parking lot set in a grove of tall oak trees. A petition was circulated to stop the McIntyres from building a long strip of windows and the outdoor dining porch along the southern façade overlooking West John Street and a plain façade to the west. But according to Randall McIntyre, "Our point of view was to design a modern building and make the best possible environment for our employees with a pleasant arrival into the building, views to the trees outdoors and the best use of light conditions, especially the southern sun."[4] The result was an elegant rectangular building with an open-plan workspace that included a small area for offices divided by glass partitions and a company canteen with southern exposure and an outdoor terrace.

O. E. McIntyre Plant, Westbury, 1954. The main entrance from the east parking lot. The soffit of the marquee was painted bright red.

O. E. McIntyre Plant, Westbury, 1954. South façade. In front of the glass-walled canteen is the employees' dining terrace, which overlooks a lawn on the John Street side.

The interior walls were painted in Breuer's signature blue, red, and yellow, with background whites and grays. The marquee over the main entrance had a bright red soffit and Y-shaped supports, which Landsberg added in homage to the scissor arches he had admired at Wells Cathedral in southern England, near the area where he was stationed during World War II.

After setting up his own independent practice in Port Washington in 1956, Landsberg built a number of Breuer-esque houses and office buildings in various communities along Long Island's North Shore. He later remarked, "I knew how to design like Breuer, and his approach to architecture became mine. His was the only one that captured my imagination, even though I worked for several New York–based architects during the 1940s, including Gordon Bunshaft, Edward Durell Stone, Josep Lluís Sert, and Paul Lester Wiener."[5]

Both Randall and Angus McIntyre asked Landsberg to design Breuer-inspired houses on a seventy-five-acre tract of hilly land in Deer Park that they had inherited, along with their parents' summer-house compound.[6] The Angus McIntyre House was eventually altered by the addition of a traditional-style wing. Randall and Helen McIntyre's house was a much more elaborate and expensive version of Landsberg's own house, and like his, was custom made. It won an *Architectural Record* 1957 House-of-the-Year award and was featured in the magazine. Set into the slope of a hill, the bilevel rectangular structure was built with simple wood framing, expansive windows, and cinder block, which was used on the lower

Randall and Helen McIntyre House, Deer Park, 1957. Front façade. The panels beneath windows and above the garage, bedroom, and kitchen are colored white, lemon yellow, red, and Breuer's favorite cerulean blue.

exterior and for retaining walls. The exterior was enlivened with Breuer-esque vertical cedar siding and panels of stark white, lemon yellow, cerulean blue, and bright red. The first-floor entrance hall was located below grade. On the first floor were a carport, service elements—including a dumbwaiter to the kitchen—and two maid's bedrooms, which were reached by a spiral staircase from near the kitchen. From the entrance hall, stairs led to the upper floor, which contained the living room, kitchen space, and the family's bedrooms. A large brick fireplace with exposed tubular chimneys divided the living room. Both McIntyre houses were demolished after a developer purchased the land from the brothers in 2000 with a quickly broken pledge to appropriately market and sell the houses.[7] Fifty-eight houses were subsequently built on the site, now a gated community called Hunting Hollow Farm.

By the late 1960s, Landsberg was having difficulty bringing in commissions, so he closed his practice and for the next twenty years worked primarily as a project manager for a succession of firms: Edward Durell Stone, Kahn & Jacobs, and Welton Becket. He never returned to designing buildings under his name in the Breuer idiom. By the late 1970s, interest in such versions of modern architecture began to wane, with the onset of Postmodernism and the public's desire for traditional forms and devices. Several Landsberg buildings have been demolished or drastically altered; likewise, Breuer's designs on Long Island have been subjected to alterations and lack of appreciation from new owners.

Randall and Helen McIntyre House, Deer Park, 1957. A Breuer-esque exposed-brick fireplace, with yellow and red cylindrical chimneys, separates the dining and sitting areas.

Randall and Helen McIntyre House, Deer Park, 1957. The living room's sitting area.

9
HAMILTON P. SMITH b.1925

Hamilton and Caroline Smith House, Springs, 1972

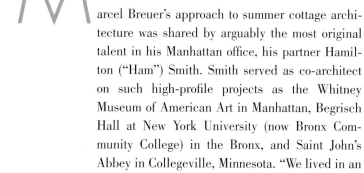

Marcel Breuer's approach to summer cottage architecture was shared by arguably the most original talent in his Manhattan office, his partner Hamilton ("Ham") Smith. Smith served as co-architect on such high-profile projects as the Whitney Museum of American Art in Manhattan, Begrisch Hall at New York University (now Bronx Community College) in the Bronx, and Saint John's Abbey in Collegeville, Minnesota. "We lived in an apostle's house," Smith observed of the summer getaway that he built for himself and his wife, Caroline, overlooking Accabonac Harbor in Springs.[1] Indeed, the Smith house appears to be a nod to the flat-roofed, single-story, boxlike wood cottages set on wood posts that Breuer had designed, first for himself and later for friends Rufus and Leslie Stillman and György and Juliet Kepes in Wellfleet, on Cape Cod, beginning in 1948. But in its design details, there is much that is different and innovative about the Springs house.

For one, the house stands noticeably taller on its posts and is more horizontal in configuration than Breuer's Cape Cod houses. And whereas Breuer's own rustic cottage is sited on a rise of wood and brush above William's Pond, the Smith House is located in a clearing. When the Smiths lived there, the approach to the house was a long, gravel driveway flanked by a deep thicket of bushes and vines that obscured it from view until the drive took a sharp turn into the grassy clearing. And there,

off in the distance, loomed the bargelike structure, a freestanding sculptural object with water and wetland views on either side and through the open spaces beneath it. The house was obviously designed to capitalize on its astounding views, facilitated by a stairway that recalled the stair adjacent to the original entrance of the Whitney Museum, as well as by protruding decks and large, screened, sliding windows

The Smiths bought the property, with a promise to donate easements to the Nature Conservancy, from landscape architect M. Paul Friedberg, who was selling subdivided parcels of land formerly owned by the Miller family, which had farmed much of the Springs for generations.[2] "After the sale, on a freezing cold day, we took a ladder to the site and took turns climbing it. Once I decided to build up, a certain clarity took over in my head, similar to what it takes to design a dining table."[3]

The basic structure is, in effect, that of a dining room table, with the wood posts connected to the house volume from roof to floor and anchored in below-ground concrete footings, thereby creating an essentially rigid frame. Structural engineer Matthys Levy of Weidlinger Associates, the company that worked with Breuer's firm on structurally challenging projects, was enlisted to help ensure that the house could withstand gale-force Nor'easters, as well as cocktail gatherings on the rectangular decks, with their spectacular views

Hamilton and Caroline Smith House, Springs, 1972. North façade. The entrance is in the tower structure, which contains the stairway. Accabonac Harbor is visible in the background.

Hamilton and Caroline Smith House, Springs, 1972. On the south façade, balconies offer panoramic views of the harbor and wetlands.

of the harbor. Levy worked out the engineering for an upside-down U-shaped tower to house the entrance stair. As he said, "The strong side walls of the tower were designed to brace the rectangular house against lateral movement, as the rigid frame would have been insufficient while high winds hit against the house's long faces."[4] Smith enumerated other benefits of the structure: "No mosquitoes. If it rained, we could put the dogs under the house. If it was sunny, we could put the car under the house. And of course, the views in different lights, winds and weather."[5]

Like Breuer's cottage, which the Smiths knew well from their visits, the Smith House is a celebration of the basic building techniques of American wood-frame construction, which had so impressed Breuer when he first came to the United States, for its expeditiousness and economy as compared to the standard brick-and-mortar methods used in Europe. Smith learned of a quantity of reasonably priced cypress that had been held in a storage facility under the Manhattan Bridge and used it for the exterior cladding, giving the house a more substantial and imposing appearance than the Wellfleet houses, which were clad in humbler New England pine planks.

Inside the rectangular house, the living, dining, and kitchen areas occupy a combined space on one side, and three bedrooms open off a hallway on the other. A large, white-painted brick fireplace heats the common area and also functions as a dividing wall between the living area, the entry space, and the bedroom wing.

In addition to its "floating" structure and its harbor-view wall of windows, the house is distinguished by the quality of its interior woodworking. Smith's drawings for the kitchen and living room built-ins and a large, blocky, L-shaped seating and table unit were realized by Naftaly Weiss, an Israeli immigrant who had perfected the craft of cabinet making on a kibbutz, where he had grown up. Smith and others at Marcel Breuer and Associates had relied on Weiss to do the woodworking for such projects as the Whitney Museum and an exhibition of Breuer's furniture and architectural designs at the Metropolitan Museum of Art in 1972. After spending a good part of the summer of 1972 in the house with no interior insulation or wall finishes, Smith installed wall paneling himself the following spring and Caroline painted the brick fireplace, among other tasks. All of the wall and ceiling surfaces in the living area were clad with unpainted cypress, echoing the exterior. Smith executed his design for a plain, windowless wall behind the living room seating arrangement, with a view of the water opposite. The wall accommodated a display of Smith family memorabilia, including a collection of nautical shadow boxes and a tall case clock, complementing the interior's otherwise modern idiom, grounded in the aesthetic vocabulary of Marcel Breuer.

10
JOSEP LLUÍS SERT 1902–1983

Marian Willard and Dan Johnson House, Locust Valley, former Guthrie Estate, 1947;
Josep Lluís and Moncha Sert House, Locust Valley, former Guthrie Estate, 1947

In 1947, on the subdivided grounds of Meudon—the 300-acre Locust Valley estate of William Guthrie designed by C. P. H. Gilbert—two abandoned structures were converted into weekend residences by the Barcelona-born modernist architect Josep Lluís Sert. One was a picturesque icehouse on a pond, which the architect transformed into a radical modern statement and home for Guthrie's granddaughter, Marian Willard. The other was an enormous abandoned Beaux-Arts–style carriage house and stable manager's quarters, which Sert made habitable for himself and his wife, Moncha.

The two projects were quite different in design and purpose. The house on the pond served as a manageable country house for Marian Willard and her husband, Dan Johnson, where they could raise their children in close proximity to Willard's mother, who lived in the grand Italianate mansion on the estate's highest ground until her death in 1957. The carriage house, on the other hand, was meant as a spacious getaway, a welcome respite for the Serts from their small loft in Manhattan and from the tight quarters of Town Planning Associates, the architecture and planning firm Sert had started in 1941 with partner Paul Lester Wiener. Above all, Sert's carriage house was intended as a built metaphor for the Spain the Serts had left behind as refugees from the Spanish Civil War and as a place for them to host their European-exile friends during and after World War II.

As different as they were from each other, the two projects at Meudon were both opportunities for Sert to build, after a long period of not seeing his designs realized, and further develop his own idiosyncratic version of Le Corbusier–derived modernism, which he had adopted in the early 1930s in his native Barcelona. There, during the brief artistic flowering of Catalonia's quasi-independence from Spain's central government, Sert and an active group of young architects had founded the Catalonian branch of the Congrès International d'Architecture Modern (International Congress of Modern Architecture), the umbrella organization promoting planning and design in the modernist mold of Le Corbusier. In 1937, Sert had been responsible for Republican Spain's pavilion at the international exposition in Paris; his contribution was a functionalist modern courtyard building designed to show artworks, film, and objects as propaganda for the Spanish democratic republic against the rising fascist tide of Generalissimo Francisco Franco. The pavilion included Pablo Picasso's large antiwar painting *Guernica*, another large painting by Joan Miró, and a fountain by Alexander Calder, as well as numerous examples of Catalonian folk art. The artists were from Sert's circle of close friends, and the art itself—modernist, surrealist, and regionalist, as opposed to classical and nationalist—reflected Sert's own cultural and political sympathies.

Marian Willard and Dan Johnson House, Locust Valley, 1947. On the porch at "Meudon sur Lac," Marian Willard, holding daughter Miani; seated in the background, Dan Rhodes Johnson and daughter Danna.

Arriving in the United States in 1938 as a refugee after the fall of Catalonia to Franco, Sert spent the war years homesick for the world he had left behind. He tried hard to reconnect with friends and fellow refugees, many of them artists whom he had originally met through his uncle, the renowned muralist Josep Maria Sert, and his wife Misia, both café society fixtures. The Serts came from a noble old Catalonian family of great wealth, little of which could be accessed by Josep Lluís until after Franco's death in 1975. Sert kept busy writing and lecturing at universities, and—after the founding of Town Planning Associates—with numerous urban planning proposals for Latin American cities.

Josep Lluís Sert most likely met Marian Willard in Paris shortly before his emigration. At the time, he was working on his design for the Spanish Pavilion, and she was there to acquire artworks for her newly founded East River Gallery on East 57th Street in Manhattan. While a part-time student at Barnard College, Willard had quickly tired of the role her family expected her to fulfill: a proper marriage, prominence in society, and the eventual inheritance of Meudon. Traveling to Europe several times, she befriended numerous figures in the modernist avant-garde and was one of only a few American women who got to know the inner circle of CIAM architects, including Le Corbusier, Walter Gropius, Alvar Aalto, and Sert, as well as artists associated with the Bauhaus such as Lyonel Feininger, Paul Klee, and Josef and Anni Albers. Realizing that her place was in the art world, Willard used her inheritance to open her Manhattan gallery, becoming a doyenne of what was then a small world of contemporary art supporters, well before Peggy Guggenheim or Betty Parsons opened their galleries.

With her grandfather's death in 1939, Marian Willard assumed disposition rights to Meudon. She made it into a haven for her architecture, literary, and artistic friends, many of them exiled Europeans, including Sert. In 1944, the artist Fernand Léger visited Meudon, and it seems likely that during this visit he, Sert, and historian Sigfried Giedion wrote the tract called "Nine Points on Monumentality." This essay, which called for a civic-minded modernism, integrating architecture, art, and planning for an enhanced community life, became key to the subsequent work of both Town Planning Associates and of Sert, Jackson & Associates, the office Sert founded with Huson Jackson and Joseph Zalewski in Cambridge in 1956, after Sert took over from Walter Gropius as dean of the faculty of the Harvard Graduate School of Design.

The days of Meudon as Willard's artist-friendly compound began to draw to a close after the war, however, when she and her mother arranged to subdivide the compound. But even as most of the sale went through, Willard—now married to Dan Rhodes Johnson—reserved the old icehouse in the western sector of the estate for herself, and in 1947 she asked her friend Sert to convert it into a house for herself and her new family. The architect set to work immediately on what the unpretentiously wry Willard liked to call "Meudon sur Lac."[1]

Meudon Estate Icehouse, Locust Valley, 1912. Ice cutters in front of the building that Sert adapted into a country house for Marian Willard and Dan Johnson in 1947.

Oscar Niemeyer Small Hillside House, Rio de Janeiro, 1947. This photograph in *Architectural Forum*, November 19, 1947, no doubt influenced Sert's design for the icehouse adaptation.

WILLARD JOHNSON HOUSE

Sert converted Meudon's picturesque icehouse into a bracingly modern piece of architecture. It was originally a rustic-looking, granite-walled cottage with a pond-side, semi-enclosed porch; in the days before refrigeration, hired ice cutters lived there in bedrooms beneath a deep-pitched roof with dormer windows. These rooms were ruined in a fire, providing the architect with an excuse to demolish the upstairs level, even as he retained the stone walls of the ground floor as a base for a new steel-framed wooden upper floor extending beyond the original walls. Around the perimeter, fourteen slender gray iron pilotis supported the projecting extension, and on the pond side a new porch was built beyond the old porch walls.

Beneath the bright yellow undercroft of the new upper floor, the house was entered through a red wooden door, partially surrounded by glass transoms framed in white wood casing. A hallway, as well as the icehouse's original stairway, went off to the left. Behind a wood-paneled wall, the entire first floor appeared—an open-plan dining and living space with an expansive view of the pond through plate-glass windows set between what had been the thick stone walls of the outdoor porch. On the projecting upper level, the bedrooms and a second living room also afforded splendid views of the water. The sense of openness to the views and to light was enhanced in the master bedroom by a glass wall separating it from the second living room.

Seen from across the fields in the years before it was sold for development, the house gave the impression of a great ship, the second floor cantilevering out over the pond, reminiscent of Le Corbusier's Villa Savoye, only here enlivened by broad swaths of color on panels applied to the exterior walls and a row of deep balconies on the south façade. The house's overall shape also displayed a pronounced abstract, even surrealist quality, and its rustic stone base was essentially in tune with the more elastic, imaginative, and vernacular modernism that had begun to slip into the work of architects like Le Corbusier and Gropius by the late 1930s.

The design's abstract play with color was recognized by *Architectural Forum* in its issue of July 1950:

> Viewed head on from the south across the pond, the colored squares of the upstairs balconies create the effect of a Mondrian in architecture. As the viewer walks by this façade and the colored sides of the various separating panels come into view,

the effect is that of a changing abstraction—a dark gray panel appears next to the red square, light gray beside yellow, yellow beside gray, light blue beside dark blue.[2]

Sert knew Mondrian well, especially after the Dutch artist moved into a loft above the Serts' in New York. Yet, Sert's use of saturated color squares was not influenced by Mondrian. Works from Sert's Barcelona years, like the Casa Bloc apartments and the Dispensario (both of the mid-1930s), displayed a comparable polychromy, with a special affinity for the blue, yellow, and fire red of the Catalonian flag—the same colors that appear in the Willard Johnson House.

What may have influenced Sert more than anything else in his design for the icehouse was his visit to Rio de Janeiro the year before, where he had encountered the architecture of the Brazilian modernists Lucio Costa and Oscar Niemeyer. Paul Lester Wiener had worked with the two architects on the stunningly modern Brazilian Pavilion for the 1939 World's Fair in Flushing Meadows, and Sert accompanied his Town Planning partner to Brazil in 1946 on an assignment from the General Motors Company. While there, he likely visited several houses by the same architects, and saw another by Niemeyer that appeared in an *Architectural Forum* article in 1947. These, as well as many other Brazilian modernist houses of the period, bears an unmistakable resemblance to the Willard project, whose prismlike massing and piloti-supported balconies had already emerged as distinctive features of Brazilian modernism.

THE HOUSE AS PIAZZA

In the years when the Serts were frequent guests at Meudon prior to its subdivision, Marian Willard usually put them up in a wing of an enormous Beaux-Arts carriage house on the eastern end of the property. At the same time as she decided to take the old icehouse as her own residence, Willard consented to sell the carriage house to the Serts and to Sert's partner Paul Lester Wiener and his wife Alma Morgenthau to use as their own Long Island retreats. The foursome purchased the huge structure in 1947 with the intention of dividing and modernizing it for their separate residences.

Sert's preliminary sketches show that he was thinking of different schemes to transform the entire complex. Thwarted by its restrictions and enormous size, the group decided to demolish the entire western piece of the building quadrangle. This was the highest, most massive wing, with maisonettes—one for the chauffeur and one for the stable manager—on either flank and a central clock tower above the livery and harness rooms. The architects were left with two massive, parallel wings flanking the courtyard, which was entered through high iron gates at the east. Sert took the southern wing of the U-shaped complex as his own house; Wiener, the northern one. Soon after the demolition of the western wing, Wiener and Morgenthau dissolved their marriage, and architect Hermann Herrey stepped in to work out a design for what became Morgenthau's house (see pages 106–8).

Sert's piece was now the 75- x 36- x 16-foot carriage hall, which he transformed into an all-purpose living space for cooking, dining, and socializing, modifying the exterior by replacing the former double doorway with large plate-glass windows. In place of the demolished stable manager's house on the western side of the carriage hall, Sert erected a two-story, wood-framed bedroom wing on brick supports and connected it to the old building by a glass-walled hallway with a front door arrangement similar to the one at the Willard Johnson House. Thus, all the private areas were relegated to one side of the plan, leaving the whole interior of the huge hall undivided and unencumbered by columns, walls, or floors, save for a sectioned-off area at the eastern end, which housed the garage and a second-level office and guest bedroom.

The yellow Dutch brick floor in the carriage hall space, laid in a herringbone pattern, continued out to the courtyard. Sert closed off views to the courtyard by installing a wall of pine boards along the northern façade, except where the original barn doors opened onto a red brick loggia under the base of the elevated bedroom addition. He installed central heating in the roof loft, rather than disrupt the beautiful brick floor, which was pitched slightly toward drains so housecleaning could be done with a hose.

Vivid color was part of the interior design—an uncluttered living space with simple wood shelves as room dividers and long wood benches that Sert had used for earlier projects. All of the furniture and picture frames were painted white to sharpen

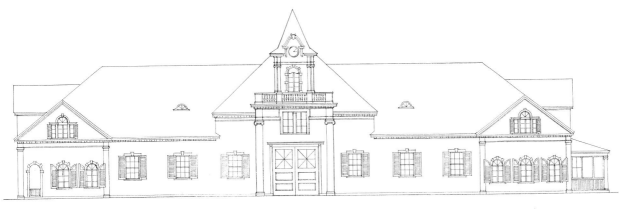

Guthrie Estate Barn Complex, Locust Valley, 1912. Soon after drawing these elevations of the west and south elevations of the huge barn complex at Meudon, Sert demolished the west wing entirely, including the stable manager's maisonette.

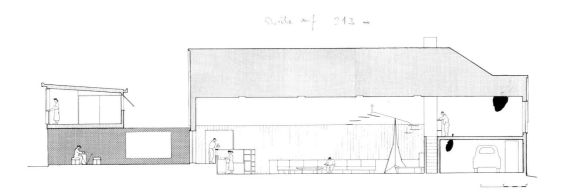

Plans for Sert Renovation of Guthrie Estate Barn Complex, Locust Valley, 1947. Longitudinal section of Sert house from the south. The two-story bedroom addition, at left, replaced the stable manager's maisonette. Note the inclusion of Alexander Calder's large stabile in the plan.

colors. As Sert said, "I really learned a lot about color from Miró—and from the South American Indians."[3] Most of the color—shocking pink, purplish blue, yellow, black, and some touches of green—appeared in upholstered panels on the benches. The red-and-black floor rugs were woven by Colombian Indians. Paintings by friends such as Léger and Miró were either hung on the walls or propped up on narrow wall shelves. Long curtains at the windows were of white linen, offset by the deep window recesses, which Sert painted azure blue, in line with a Spanish folk superstition that this color in window frames would ward off flies.

The new wing provided a contrast in form to the original pitched-roof building, and an opportunity for Sert to design according to Le Corbusier's "modular" system of rationally idealized proportions. Upstairs, two bedrooms were accessed from a hallway along the western outer wall of white, wood-framed vertical windows, with views of the

LEFT
Josep Lluís and Moncha Sert House, Locust Valley, 1947. West façade of the two-story addition. Bright yellow panels lent the second-level and the ground-level patio façades a bit of Spanish flair.

BELOW LEFT
Josep Lluís and Moncha Sert House, Locust Valley, 1947. Josep Lluís Sert looks out at the all-purpose room from his second-level office space. Calder's stabile dominates this area of the room, providing vertical thrust like a bell tower in a village square, as visitors often remarked.

curvilinear beds and rock formations that the Serts had installed in the manner of Brazilian landscape architect Roberto Burle Marx. Wall-to-wall sliding doors, clad in red linoleum, closed off the bedrooms, which were kept spare with built-in closets and drawers. Midway down the hall, near the bathroom, Sert interrupted the outer window wall with a rectangular panel of bright yellow, angled wooden studs. A similar panel was installed on the wall adjacent to the doorway leading to the brick patio below, and together the yellow panels introduced an element of Spanish flair, or perhaps Dutch Rationalist design, to what otherwise would have been a banal façade.

An invitation to one of the Serts' parties in the main living space was highly coveted, whether it was to fete a visiting dignitary, such as Le Corbusier, or Sert's graduating students from the Harvard Graduate School of Design. The Serts considered the gathering together of architects, artists, and other friends a kind of vocation, with the house as a metaphor for the idea of community in a changing world, where traditional gathering places had been lost to ill-conceived suburbanization and the disintegration of town centers. The couple entertained in typically Spanish style; lively Catalonian music filled the air and Moncha served her version of paella out of a large pan that she had had shipped over from Barcelona. As in Sert's architecture, there was a Catalonian mood in how he and Moncha lived—a pride as much political as personal, reflecting both committed opposition to the fascist Franco government and nostalgia for their homeland. As Giedion said in 1969, "Sert is one of the strongest proponents of the Mediterranean mentality in his contemporary architecture. It lives

Josep Lluís and Moncha Sert House, Locust Valley, 1947. This view of the all-purpose room looks toward the dining area. The kitchen area is located behind the bookcase. Moncha Sert is relaxing on a signature Sert bench. Derived from Catalonian vernacular interiors, theyse benches were included in all of Sert's projects.

in him, just as Ireland lived in James Joyce after a nearly life long existence abroad."[4]

As one frequent visitor, the artist Saul Steinberg, observed, the interior of the large hall was like "a town square in Catalonia,"[5] a public space charged with a civic spirit. Likewise, critic Peter Blake wrote, "Once you think of the living room as a piazza, all the elements assume a special meaning."[6] Indeed, the bridgelike wooden pathway that led visitors past the kitchen, the Calder stabile standing like a campanile in the middle of the floor, and the herringbone-patterned brick floors all suggested a kind of urban composition, like the bustling plazas of Sert's native Barcelona. In his own Long Island house, as in his building designs, Sert sought to foster a sense of openness, joy, and community.

11
HERMANN HERREY 1904–1968

Alma Morgenthau House, later Richard Lippold Studio and House, Locust Valley, 1950;
Robert and Lola Mautner House, Massapequa, 1950–51

In 1947, when Josep Lluís Sert's conversion of the southern wing of the huge stable complex at Meudon into an architectural homage to Catalonia was well under way, Paul Lester Wiener (1895–1967) began to adapt the northern wing into a residence for himself and his wife Alma Morgenthau. Only months into the process, however, his marriage ended, and with it went his plan.

The north building—or what remained of it, after the initial demolitions and preparatory work carried out by Wiener—went to Morgenthau. She decided to complete the building project with the help of another architect, Hermann Herrey, an Austrian émigré like her husband. The Alma Morgenthau House, like the Serts', was to become a setting for artists to mingle and perform in, but with a rather different cast of characters.

Alma Morgenthau (1887–1953) was the daughter of Henry Morgenthau Sr., businessman, diplomat, and founder of an American political dynasty that would include a treasury secretary and a Manhattan district attorney. A talented vocalist and dedicated patron of new American music, she found herself perfectly at home in the Meudon milieu. Aaron Copeland, the "Dean of American Composers," was supported by Morgenthau in his early career and was a frequent guest of hers in Locust Valley.[1]

With the completion of her country house in 1950, she began dividing her time between Locust

Alma Morgenthau House, Locust Valley, 1950. View of the south-facing back terrace of Hermann Herrey's adaptation of the Meudon barn complex's northern wing.

Valley and her Park Avenue Manhattan apartment, where she had been holding musical evenings to benefit young composers and musicians since the 1920s. In 1950, she launched the Locust Valley Music Festival, a series of all-day music events, using her large terrace and lawn as an auditorium for some 250 ticket holders and featured performers.

The new Herrey-designed building that was the setting for this activity was as boldly modernist as the Sert residence that faced it across the yellow brick courtyard, yet it was altogether distinct from that in tone and intent. In Berlin, Herrey had studied with influential German designer Hans Poelzig. After he graduated, Herrey quickly found a place with Gruppe Junger Architekten, a Berlin-based firm of progressive young designers. Herrey had considerable success getting important commissions for theaters, stores, and residences; he also worked as a stage and costume designer. A 1929 concrete-and-glass curtain-wall garage, still standing in Berlin, is listed on the German National Register under the name Hermann Zweigenthal—his birth name, which he anglicized to Herrey after moving his family to London in 1935. Five years after that, the Herrey family emigrated to the United States with the help of Walter Gropius, who offered Herrey a temporary position in his Cambridge-based practice.

By 1942, the Herreys had relocated to Manhattan, where Herrey opened a solo practice as an

107

Alma Morgenthau House, Massapequa, 1950. The upstairs landing, with view of entrance to the master bedroom.

architect and urban planner. He continued to keep in touch with European émigré friends, including Breuer and Mies van der Rohe, the latter a friend from their professional associations in pre-war Berlin. Yet Herrey, like so many established professionals from the European diaspora, found it difficult to reestablish the level of professional prestige that he had enjoyed before World War II. He did, however, find commissions to sustain his career as an architect, along with teaching positions at East Coast colleges and universities.

The house he created for Morgenthau was a pitched-roof, cedar-clad structure that retained some elements of the ornate Beaux-Arts building it had replaced, including the main hall of the original stable, which he preserved in its entirety. Herrey also kept the ground floor's original stuccoed masonry façade, which provided a plain contrast to the vertical cedar cladding with its random widths and subtle variations in color. The wood was appropriately chosen to blend with the older building; in an article in *Architectural Record*, the architect stated that he and Morgenthau agreed that "a composite of age, weather, wear and patina can go far in compensating for architectural deficiencies in an old house."[2] The house they created was intended to mellow with time and become a natural part of the wooded landscape, "a fresh design that should not have to depend on a state of newness for effect."[3]

The foundation and footprint of the northern wing of the old carriage house complex, its sloping roofline, interior stairway, and fireplace were all retained, as was Wiener's rectangular plan for the east–west axis and the addition of a second level on the western end. The upper floor housed three bedrooms, a maid's room, and a guest room, each with partitioned, sliding glass windows. The lower floor contained the main public spaces: a combined living and dining room connecting to a south-facing porch, and a "music shed"—the former stable itself—in the single-floor eastern wing. Here Morgenthau planned to host her music festival, with the audience in the "music shed" spilling out onto the adjoining terrace to the north, as the guests and musicians enjoyed what she hoped would become an important yearly staple of Long Island's cultural calendar.

Sadly, it was not to be. In 1953, after only two seasons, the Locust Valley Music Festival came to end when its sponsor died at the age of sixty-six.

Her house, however, had a second life when another major cultural figure, sculptor Richard Lippold (1915–2002), acquired it two years later as a place for him and his wife, Louise Greuel, to raise their family, with space allotted for his art studio and her dance practice.

Lippold found out about the property's availability through Marian Willard Johnson, his dealer. In the early postwar years, she had helped make Lippold a well-known figure in the New York art world and beyond. His elaborate kinetic constructions, typically comprising hundreds of tense wire strands suspended in air and woven into beguiling configurations, were often mounted in public spaces or as abstract ornaments on building façades. Lippold viewed his art as a kind of para-architectural practice, and it proved congruent with the brand of modern design that Hermann Herrey himself espoused. Lippold created the sculptures *World Tree* for a Harvard dormitory courtyard designed by Gropius with The Architects' Collaborative (TAC) and *Flight* for Gropius's Pan Am Building (now MetLife Building) on New York's Park Avenue in 1963.

Lippold's work required a great deal of space to design and build, and the Locust Valley house provided it. The artist turned Morgenthau's music shed and the courtyard into his studio, and by 1955 it was his primary workspace. Numerous building models, including to-scale versions of his sculptures, occupied one corner of the studio and at the east wall he installed a wood pipe organ, custom made in Denmark to his specifications in the Baroque manner. An accomplished organ player, he tried to practice daily when he was at the house.

Lippold made certain changes to Herrey's original interior that reflected his own aesthetic preferences; always keen on high-finish metals, he replaced the stainless-steel and wood stair rail leading to the second floor with one of shiny brass, and applied gold leaf to the living room walls. Between Lippold's added layer of artistic spectacle and Herrey's underlying Bauhaus-inflected design, the Lippold house stood as an interesting counterpoint to Sert's Mediterranean, Le Corbusier–derived house across the courtyard.

Herrey designed one more house on Long Island, also in 1950. The client, Robert Mautner, a television engineer employed by RCA, commissioned a beach house in Massapequa, on the South Shore. Like the Morgenthau project, the house featured

Robert and Lola Mautner House, Massapequa, 1950–51. The glass-walled living room afforded unimpeded views of the Great South Bay.

cedar siding, except that it was set horizontally instead of vertically. But in form it is altogether different: U-shaped in plan, most of the building is a low, single-story structure, with exterior walls of fieldstone masonry extending into the landscape, in a Breuer-like manner. At its southern end, the main house adjoins a sloped-roof segment containing the kitchen and a glassed-in living room with views of the Great South Bay. The kitchen was particularly elaborate in design, featuring wooden, double-sided cabinetry with sliding doors and a collapsible table that could be hidden away. The expansive southern window, only partially sheltered by a piloti-supported awning, was buffeted by high winds coming off the water. The wind was so strong at times that the client feared that the roof of the house might blow off. It never did, but the house suffered a sadder fate: it was completely reclad in aluminum siding and given an asphalt-tiled pitched roof.

Robert and Lola Mautner House, Massapequa, 1950–51. Herrey was a master of multipurpose cabinetry design. The kitchen features double-sided cabinetry and a retractable dining table. In this photo, the kitchen is open to the living space and the table is out of sight.

Robert and Lola Mautner House, Massapequa, 1950–51. In this photo, the kitchen is closed off from the living space and the dining table is set up.

12

BENJAMIN THOMPSON 1918–2002 WITH THE ARCHITECTS COLLABORATIVE (TAC) AND SHOGO MYAIDA 1897–1989

Mary Griggs and Jackson Burke House, Centre Island, 1953–61;
Pool House, co-architect Paul Dietrich, 1925–2001;
Chase Manhattan Bank, Great Neck Plaza, 1960 (without Myaida); co-architerct Paul Dietrich

Mary Griggs and Benjamin Thompson grew up in the same neighborhood, along scenic Summit Avenue in St. Paul, Minnesota, in the decades between the world wars. Their two families were from a tight-knit sphere of wealthy industrialists, professionals, and civic leaders, many with strong ties back East. Both Griggs and Thompson would take the educational route out of the Midwest—he to Yale University to study architecture, she to Sarah Lawrence College to study art—and their paths would cross again on Long Island, where together they created a house and garden that would be important to their respective future careers in the worlds of art and design.

The two met again in New York around 1950, each having decided to stay in the East. Thompson had served in World War II. The year after the war ended, he and six other young architects prevailed upon Walter Gropius to form a new joint practice. The Architects' Collaborative (TAC) was to be modeled on the innovative group-design process that the émigré Harvard dean had pioneered at the Bauhaus school in Germany in the 1920s. Hierarchy was, in theory, anathema to the firm, but Gropius was its eminence grise, acting more as critic than designer, with all the young partners eager to curry favor with the master.[1] Thompson took the role of team leader in the new firm, heading up several projects, including his own house at the partners' Six Moon Hill residential development

in Lexington, outside Boston. By 1953, he had embarked on a parallel track as a design entrepreneur, launching Design Research's first retail store, which would allow the partners to furnish their building commissions with good modern design.

Mary Griggs, in the meantime, had set up residence in Manhattan, where she collected abstract art and entered a period of uncertainty over what to do for a vocation. Years later she remarked, "The war years made such pursuits as collecting art seem frivolous."[2] But what began to put her on a determined course of cultural exploration was her purchase of seven hilly beachfront acres on the grounds of Applegarth, a demolished estate on Centre Island. "It was not until the 1950s," she claimed, "when I first gave expression to my own taste by building a house in a wooded area facing Long Island Sound . . . that my interest in things of an artistic nature revived."[3]

She asked Ben Thompson and TAC to design a simple modern beach house with an open-plan living space and two guest bedrooms downstairs, and a bedroom and study for herself upstairs. It was unusual for a single woman in her mid-thirties to build a house for occasional use, but Griggs was an independent spirit, and she missed the proximity to nature that had been so much a part of her upbringing in the Midwest. And to live in the kind of thoroughly modern house that she had in mind would be in itself a mark of independence, proof

Mary Griggs and Jackson Burke House, Centre Island, 1953–61. The south-facing dining room looks out on the entrance court's Japanese-style garden by Shogo Myaida. Weeping willows provide the room with shade.

positive of her own venturesome originality.

The type of houses that TAC had become known for were perfect for the kind of statement Griggs wanted to make. The office's residential projects of the early 1950s were typically flat-roofed, clad in vertical redwood and white brick, and composed of two or three boxes attached together, often with steel stilts on the outside as structural supports. Other common features were asymmetrical placement of building members and interior elements like spiral stairs, large interior spaces of one and a half or two stories, and Plexiglas domed skylights resembling bomber ball turrets. Yet each TAC project was fine tuned to suit its own natural setting and enhance appreciation of the outdoors, and for Griggs, both the universality and the particularity of TAC's design strategy had great appeal.

For Thompson, Griggs had equal appeal as a prospective client. The lumber and utilities fortune she had inherited made her just the kind of individual that Thompson wanted to attract, and a commission from her was bound to enhance his own position in the firm at a time when commissions were scarce and low-budget. The enterprising Thompson took the nominal lead on the new project, and the credit he received for it was, in the main, deserved. But the final design was not the work of Thompson alone, not only because of TAC's collaborative design approach, but also because of the unique client that Mary Griggs proved to be.

GRIGGS-BURKE HOUSE

The final drawings were finished in 1953, and by early spring 1954 the house was under construction. The design is a composition of rectangles spread out in three directions, with semi-enclosed

Mary Griggs and Jackson Burke House, Centre Island, 1953–61. The Japanese-inspired guest bedroom wing overlooks a courtyard garden designed by Shogo Myaida, featuring locust trees and a typically Japanese combination of gravel and grass.

Mary Griggs and Jackson Burke House, Centre Island, 1953–61. The Japanese-inspired guest bedroom wing, before the second-story addition.

courtyards, decks, and walkways. A south-facing courtyard leads to the front door, which opens into a hall in the middle of the plan, with the dining room, topped by TAC's signature Plexiglas skylight, to the right and a two-story living room, featuring a sliding-glass window wall facing Long Island Sound, straight ahead. The southern guest wing, accessed by a hallway to the left, is largely unseen by the entrant; Griggs's bedroom and study suite was reached by a switchback stair with a landing overlooking the living room, and was effectively sequestered from the public areas of the house.

At the opposite end of the residence, on the far side of the dining room to the right of the entrance, were the kitchen and two maid's rooms with a screened porch.

The courtyards arrayed around the three-story building were visible from the decks that project from the northern, western, and eastern bays of the house. Because the hillside house is entered on what is in fact the second floor, the decks on the Long Island Sound side hover a full story above the sloping ground, projecting over the lowest floor, where recreation and utilities rooms were located, and affording views of tall trees, lawn, bushes, and tall grasses to the west. The natural surroundings are complemented by the house's clearly defined geometries of red cedar and white-painted brick façades, wood trim, white-painted steel deck rails and looped-wire balustrades.

Soon after Mary Griggs moved into the house in 1954, she became engaged to book designer and typographer Jackson Burke. They shared enthusiasm for modern art, among other urbane pursuits, and appreciation of nature. The couple married in 1955, and that same year TAC designed a study and bedroom for his use above the guest bedrooms. His suite was accessed by a spiral stair that was easily inserted into the hallway space.

In 1954, before any final decisions had been made about how to landscape the grounds and courtyards, Walter Gropius insisted that Mary Griggs go to Japan to study their gardens. Gropius had returned earlier that year from his first journey there—a lecture tour that drew packed audiences of architects wanting to hear what the founding father of modern architecture had to say—and he had been deeply impressed with the beauty of traditional Japanese architecture. He gave Griggs letters of introduction before she left and arranged for her to tour the country in the company of architect Junzo Yoshimura, who had designed the Museum

Mary Griggs and Jackson Burke House, Centre Island, 1953–61. The study in Mary Burke's bedroom suite, furnished with pieces from Design Research.

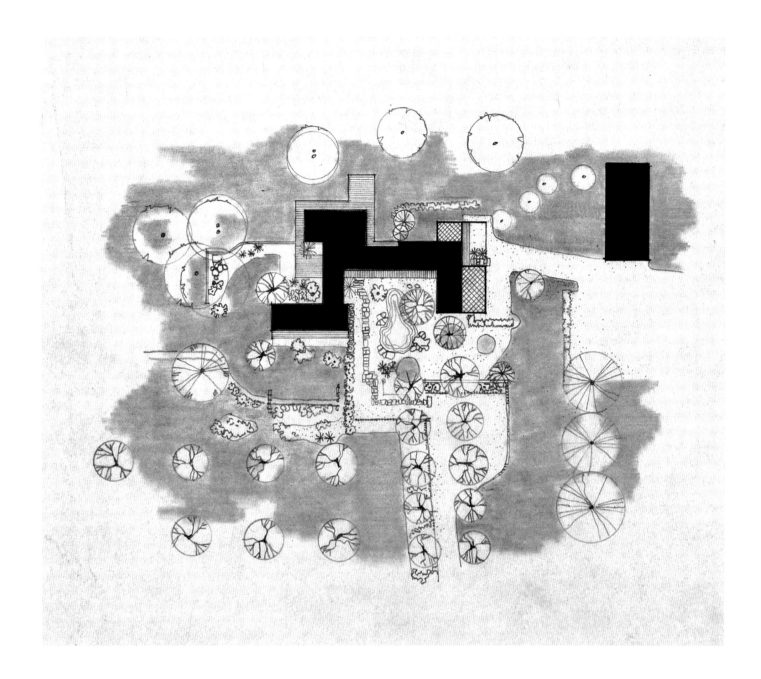

Mary Griggs and Jackson Burke House, Centre Island, 1953–61. The Architects Collaborative's plot plan showing a service wing addition, on the east, 1961.

of Modern Art's Japanese Exhibition House of 1954. Together they visited many of Japan's important gardens, both public and private. As Griggs recalled in 1985, "Mr. Yoshimura, a warm and gracious man and one of the best modern architects of his country, was of tremendous help to me in my understanding of Japanese aesthetics and architecture. Together we sat on the bamboo moon viewing platform of Katsura Imperial Villa and looked out over the garden with its lakes, winding paths and tea houses with intense pleasure."[4]

The trip had a profound effect on Mary Griggs Burke, and over the next half century she returned to Japan more than thirty times. After tentatively collecting what she called "souvenirs,"[5] she honed her taste and eye with the help of Japan's pre-eminent dealers and American-based scholars. In time, she became a formidable expert in her own right; her collection is among the most important outside of Japan and the largest and most outstanding private collection in the United States—over nine hundred pieces in all, including Buddhist and Shinto sculpture and painting, calligraphy, Muromachi ink painting, and ceramics.

Despite their passion for Japanese art and customs, the Burkes lived in the Centre Island house as Mary had always intended, leading a casual, modern style of life with a focus on indoor and outdoor entertaining. In 1956, she purchased at auction a rectangular Edo-period Genki screen,

117

Mary Griggs and Jackson Burke House, Centre Island, 1953–61. View of the house from the back lawn. The decks overlook Cold Spring Harbor and an elaborate strolling garden near the beach.

Mary Griggs and Jackson Burke House, Centre Island, 1953–61. Presentation drawing by The Architects Collaborative of the spiral stair to the guest wing's second-story addition.

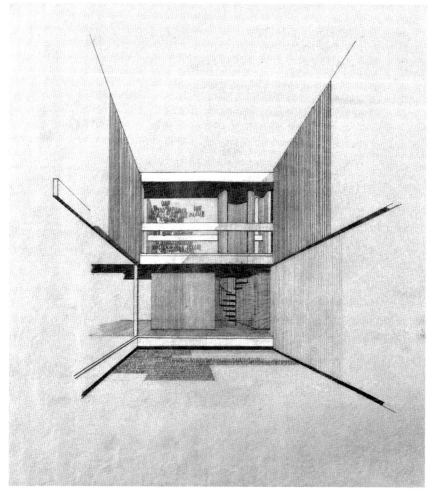

Mary Griggs and Jackson Burke House, Centre Island, 1953–61. The double-height living room, soon after Mary Griggs moved in and before it was furnished with upholstery pieces designed by Ben Thompson. The mate to the Edo-period Japanese screen was purchased by Frank Lloyd Wright for Taliesin in Spring Green, Wisconsin.

which hung in the living room for a season. Frank Lloyd Wright purchased its mate, which he hung in his Taliesin house at Spring Green, Wisconsin.[6] The screen was the first important work she acquired and the last work of that caliber to be shown in the Centre Island house. She quickly realized that she could not display important art, particularly works on paper, in the house because the abundant natural light posed a threat to conservation of the work.

Eventually, the Burkes built what they called their "Mini Museum," designed by Jasuo Kabaski, in an apartment adjacent to their New York apartment. It was designed to be a Japanese enframement, a flexible space that could be adapted to the specific needs and character of the various exhibitions they mounted. For the three decades that Miyeko Murase was a professor of Japanese art history at Columbia University, the Mini Museum was part and parcel of her teaching program. Mary Burke studied with Murase as a Columbia graduate school student. In the mid-1980s, the Burkes engaged Junzo Yoshimura to design a museum to house and exhibit their collection on the Centre Island property. The local planning authority nixed the idea as inappropriate.

Furniture for the house was chosen with Ben Thompson and the interior design staff at Design Research from its newly opened store next door to the TAC offices in Cambridge. Hans Wegner chairs and a table for the dining room, Noguchi lamps, and Alvar Aalto pieces made the house a paean to Design Research's mission to bring Americans affordable modern furniture and household goods. A down-filled sofa that Thompson designed especially for the Burkes' living room, titled the DR Down Sofa, became a major seller for the retailer. Throughout the house, oak floors were covered with rush matting, a nod, perhaps, toward Japanese tatamis.

SHOGO MYAIDA AND THE GARDEN

The landscape at Holly Pond, as Mary Griggs Burke named the property, was created in several phases. In the first phase, begun soon after her return from her pivotal journey, a general scheme

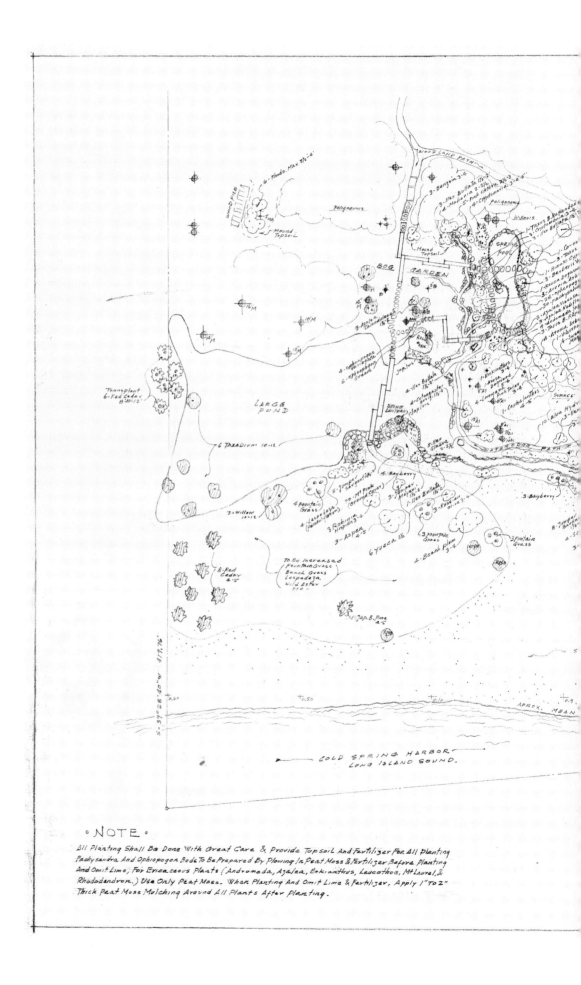

Mary Griggs and Jackson Burke House, Centre Island, 1953–61. Planting Detail of the Landscape Improvement Plan—Beach and Pond Area. Designed and drawn by Shogo J. Myaida, October 1956.

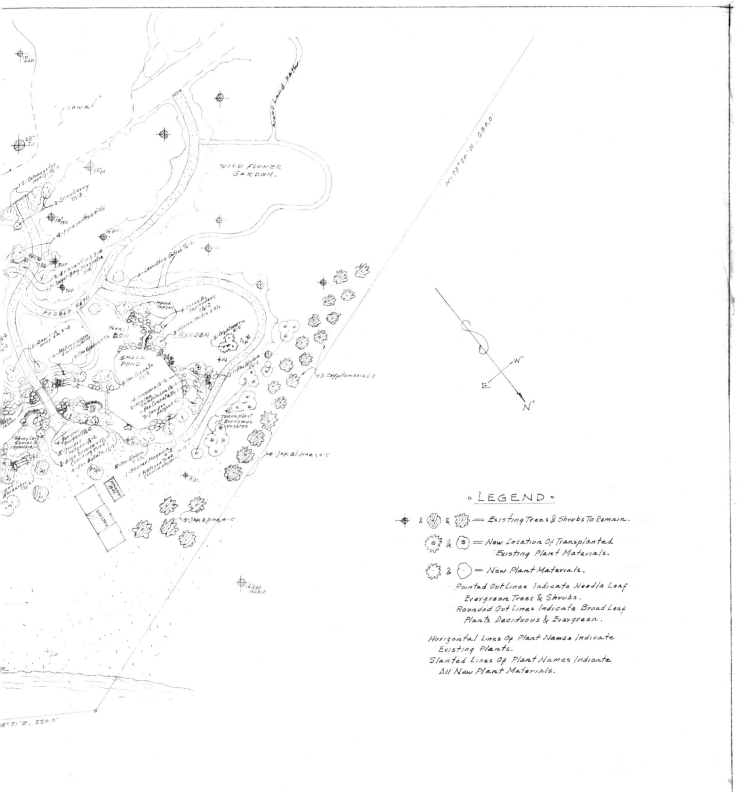

Mary Griggs and Jackson Burke House, Centre Island, 1953–61. A section of the Bog Garden, probably mid-1960s.

was devised for the semi-enclosed courtyards. The front entrance courtyard is picturesquely Japanese: an irregular path of flat stones in the pebble landscape leads past a lily pond—a habitat for goldfish—near the front door. Large rocks surround the pond, and flat circles of trimmed grass are placed at intervals in the pebblescape—inspired, evidently, by the famous circles of moss set in white sand at Samboin Temple in Kyoto. A canopy of weeping willows hovers over the pond and provides shade to the dining room. A holly hedge separates the front courtyard from the more private courtyard of the guest-bedroom wing. Here the garden is more informal, a rectangle of grass and locust trees, bounded along its long end by a brook with birch trees bordering its bank.

TAC is credited with the landscape plan in an illustrated 1956 *Architectural Record* article titled "Informal Landscaping Keynotes a New House."[7] Yet it seems unlikely that Thompson and his team at TAC had the expertise to design gardens of such superb sensitivity toward traditional Japanese devices and methods. A landscape architect of considerable experience would have had to work with TAC and the Burkes to achieve the distinguished garden design so evident in the magazine photographs. The irrigation systems alone, as well as the choice of plantings, point to an exceptionally well-qualified expert in Japanese garden design. Kiyoshi Seike (1918–2005), one of the best known of Japan's modern architects, arrived in January 1955 to work in the TAC offices, at Gropius's invitation.[8] It seems quite plausible that he would have weighed in on discussions about the design of the garden, but it's improbable that he was its designer, as he was not a landscape architect by training.

Shogo Myaida is the figure most likely to have taken the lead in collaborating with TAC and the Burkes on the first phase of the landscape's Japonification, as he is known to have been the landscape architect for all subsequent phases of the garden's development. The drawings he made for the Burkes, dating to 1956, 1960, and 1971, were drafted in the small landscape architecture and nursery business he operated out of his house in nearby Albertson.[9] Myaida was well suited for the job, as he had been trained as an architect and horticulturist in Japan, where he helped the Imperial University in Tokyo establish a Landscape Studies program. By 1925, he was established in Florida working for architect Addison Mizner on his firm's most important projects.[10]

By the time Myaida started working with the Burkes, much of the wartime prejudice toward Japanese Americans had dissipated and there was a revival of American interest in Japanese culture.

Myaida had moved to Albertson around the time he was commissioned to design two gardens for the Nippon Pavilion at the 1939 World's Fair in Flushing. He managed to avoid internment during the war years, which he spent working as a low-paid plantsman in an Albertson nursery.[11] His practice picked up after the war and included site and landscape planning for Levitt and Sons on Long Island and in Pennsylvania. By the 1950s, Myaida was again in high demand as a landscape architect of Japanese gardens. In 1957, he designed the quite formal Japanese garden at Hillwood, Marjorie Merriweather Post's estate in Washington, D.C., now a museum.[12]

Myaida's 1956 master plan for the Burke property in the area beyond the house indicates that he encouraged the Burkes to retain specimen trees from the Applegarth estate landscape, while allowing others to be replanted elsewhere, thus creating more open views from the house and an elaborate, if informal, strolling garden near the beach. Before damage occurred from storm flooding, the strolling garden paths circumnavigated a system of two ponds, a spring with a pool, and the banks of a small stream. An essential feature of the entire strolling experience was what Myaida called a Bog Garden, where he installed an asymmetrical series of wooden plank bridges over the wetlands. Long rows of rocks defined the edges of the ponds, the stream, and turns in the paths, which were punctuated by occasional Japanese stone lanterns.

THE POOL HOUSE

In 1961, Ben Thompson and TAC's Paul Dietrich designed a summer pavilion to accommodate the Burkes' guests and large gatherings. Sited to the west of the main house at the bottom of the hill, it overlooks a swimming pool. Heavy, exposed timber framing supports the steel sliding walls, which enclose a huge room with an ochre tile floor. The architecture feels earthbound and weighty, very different from that of the aerie up the hill, reflecting

Mary Griggs and Jackson Burke Pool House, Centre Island, 1961. The all-purpose pavilion designed by Ben Thompson with Paul Dietrich features a heavy, exposed timber frame.

Chase Manhattan Bank, Great Neck Plaza, 1960. The banking hall features a concrete "waffle" ceiling. The brick walls, butcher-block counters and desks, and ochre clay floor tiles lent a Scandinavian atmosphere to the interior.

OPPOSITE
Chase Manhattan Bank, Great Neck Plaza, 1960. The banking-transactions counter.

the distinctly heavy and rusticated modern idiom that Thompson and his team had developed by the 1960s. From the back-door entrance, a hallway accesses four small bedrooms with slider doors and a galley kitchen that is open to the living area.

Adjacent to the low-lying pavilion, Myaida designed a combination of Japanese and American gardens to soften the effect of the new building. A rhododendron garden sits to the north beyond a terraced garden, designed for enjoyment of views of the Sound and sculpture. South of the pool house, the Burkes installed a row of Korean ancestor figures to lead the way to an upper lilac garden.

CHASE MANHATTAN BANK

Thompson headed up one more TAC project on Long Island, again with Paul Dietrich a branch of the Chase Manhattan Bank in Great Neck Plaza. The almost perfectly square plan had deep roof overhangs, a "waffle" roof system, and a grid of exposed-concrete support piers. The design was a prototypical "building module," an example of the universal building system that Thompson and his team had developed for a number of New England institutions, including Phillips Academy in Andover and Tufts University near Boston.

Like the Burke pool house, the elegant building had a Scandinavian feel, probably derived from Thompson's furniture-buying trips to northern Europe for Design Research. The bank interior had an eclectic palette of wall surfaces: common red brick, steel-framed glass, oak and birch millwork, and raw concrete to match the exterior support columns. These vertical surfaces were offset by long butcher-block counters and desks, which resembled tables Thompson had made popular through Design Research.

In 1963, Thompson left TAC to start his own firm, Benjamin Thompson & Associates (BTA), a pioneer in the adaptive reuse of old factories, warehouses, and entire historic districts. He became an impresario of festival marketplaces, designing buildings and spaces of huge scale. Many of the concepts that he had perfected with TAC in the design of the Griggs-Burke House and the bank in Great Neck became apparent in this new phase of his career.

13

EDWARD DURELL STONE 1902–78

A. Conger Goodyear House, Old Westbury, 1939;
Eleanore Potter Ayer Harris House, Locust Valley, 1941;
Jacques and Therese Makowsky House, Great Neck, 1946;
Bernard Tomson House, Kings Point, Great Neck, 1946;
Joseph S. and Ronnie Wohl House, Lawrence, 1946;
Walter C., Jr., and Helen James Janney, House, Cold Spring Harbor, 1947;
Frederick L. and Ethel Maduro House, Great Neck, 1954;
Barrett F. and Mary Scott Welch House, Oyster Bay Cove, 1955;
Murray Gordon House, Hewlitt Bay Park, 1963;
Levitt and Sons Executive Office Building, Lake Success, 1968;
Gabriele Lagerwall House (Villa Rielle), Lloyd Harbor, 1963

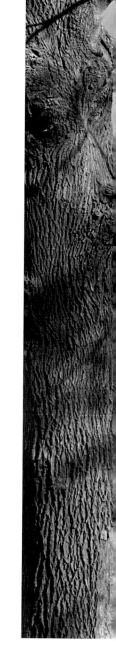

In 2002, architect Edward Durell Stone, who had been renowned the world over in the 1950s and 1960s, returned to the public eye when the A. Conger Goodyear House in Old Westbury was saved from demolition by the Society for the Preservation of Long Island Antiquities with the World Monuments Fund. Stone's idiosyncratic career had long been overlooked, nowhere more so than on Long Island, but it experienced a revival of interest with the media attention surrounding the last-minute rescue of the International Style residence, a project that had signaled a turning point in Stone's career and that he had described as "my best work to date."[1]

In 1938, industrialist A. Conger Goodyear (1877–1964), marking a late-life arrival in the established world of the North Shore, decided to build on the highest point of 110 acres of rolling hills. He chose the site for its proximity to the mansion and gardens of Zaidee and Cornelius ("Neil") Bliss, who shared his enjoyment of Anglophile pursuits like hunting to hounds, beagling, and long walks along the riding trails linking the estates.

Fifty-two years old when he left his wife and four children in Buffalo, Goodyear—the heir to a timber and railroad fortune—was a complex figure, a self-declared Futurist, a general in the two world wars, an art collector, and a patron of the avant-garde. Within a week of setting up residence in Manhattan in 1929, he was having lunch

A. Conger Goodyear House, Old Westbury, 1939. View from Wheatley Road of the south and west façades, freestanding garage, and chauffeur's house to north, 1941.

with the three women who founded the Museum of Modern Art. They asked him to be its first president, in part because he was dapper and sociable, but primarily because he was someone who would keep tabs on funds.

Goodyear and Stone became well acquainted through the give and take of completing a signature building for the Museum of Modern Art. Goodyear was in charge of the building committee, and Stone, one of the first architects to enter the museum's orbit, seemed a perfect candidate to design it. Ed Stone, as he was known then, was a charmingly genteel Southerner, born into a prosperous merchant and political family in Fayetteville, Arkansas. A sometime student (though never a graduate) at Harvard University, Massachusetts Institute of Technology, and the University of Arkansas, he journeyed to Europe in 1929 on a Rotch Travelling Scholarship. There he was exposed to the early work of pioneering modernist architects. Especially meaningful for his future development were Dutch designer J. J. P. Oud and other Dutch Rationalists, as well as Ludwig Mies van der Rohe, whose luxurious yet abstract Pavilion for his native Germany at the 1929 Barcelona International Exposition Stone saw firsthand.

Returning to America a full-fledged adherent of the emerging Modern movement in architecture, Stone found work in large firms on projects like the Art Moderne redo of the Waldorf=Astoria Hotel and Rockefeller Center's Radio City Music Hall and Center Theatre. That same year he launched his own practice with a house in Westchester for Richard Mandel. It was a Le Corbusier–derived modernist house, with all kinds of Jazz Age interior design references. In 1937, Stone was selected, at Goodyear's urging, to work with Philip Goodwin on the new Museum of Modern Art building on 53rd Street. Goodyear insisted on Stone because he wanted an American to get the job and he knew Stone was one of only a few Americans who understood the new modern architecture.

While the construction of the museum was under way, Goodyear began to discuss the prospect of a country house in Old Westbury with Stone. Goodyear later said that what he most wanted for this home-away-from-home was "a long gallery in which to hang my pictures, a large living room with steps leading down to it, a circular dining room and a swimming pool next to the house."[2] Stone was happy

A. Conger Goodyear House, Old Westbury, 1939. South façade and swimming pool in disrepair, prior to the house's rescue from demolition, 2001.

A. Conger Goodyear and Mrs. Cornelius N. Bliss Jr. (first two on left) at retriever trials, Lloyd Neck, 1935. Goodyear and Bliss married fifteen years later.

Oak Hill, Cornelius N. Bliss Jr. Residence, Wheatley Heights. Living room, November 3, 1950, just prior to the Goodyear-Bliss marriage.

to oblige. The house received the New York Architectural League's silver medal in 1950, the same year that the Museum of Modern Art won the gold.

A. CONGER GOODYEAR HOUSE

Stone later cited Goodyear's practical, modern taste as evidence of his good judgment: "He was a wise man [because] . . . he asked for only two master bedrooms; all his neighbors were saddled with forty-room relics of a former era—and no household help."[3] Indeed, Stone's original proposal—a larger scheme that included an elaborate greenhouse and a system of motorized, retractable, vertical steel-framed windows for the curved window walls in the dining room—was deemed too extravagant by Goodyear. Client and architect settled instead on a more modest plan of five main rooms, all on one level and connected by a wide corridor, or (in Stone's phrase) "spinal column."[4]

The house had an L-shaped configuration, sheltering a garden courtyard—a bow to Mies's courtyard houses of the mid-1930s—circumscribed by an undulating brick wall. From the steps of a covered brick walkway leading up to the house, the interior could be seen through a glass wall directly ahead. Walking along toward the front door, at the middle point of the L, one passed the courtyard to the left and a rectangular linoleum cutout painting with a lacquered surface, *The African Hunt*, by Pierre Bourdelle, on the exterior wall of the kitchen and pantry to the right. The red brick path continued inside the front door, where one found oneself in Goodyear's art gallery, the "spinal column" of the house, which was hung with works by Pablo Picasso, Paul Gauguin, Vincent van Gogh, Salvador Dalí, and other first-rate artists.

The view to the south was the most expansive, so Stone oriented all of the main rooms in that direction. In the manner of Frank Lloyd Wright, deep roof overhangs along the fully glazed southern

Axonometric projection of the A. Conger Goodyear House, Old Westbury, 1939.

1. Maid's Room
2. Kitchen
3. Pantry
4. Dining Room
5. Study
6. Living Room
7. Guest Room
8. Bed Room
9. Dressing Room
10. Gallery
11. 1952 extension space

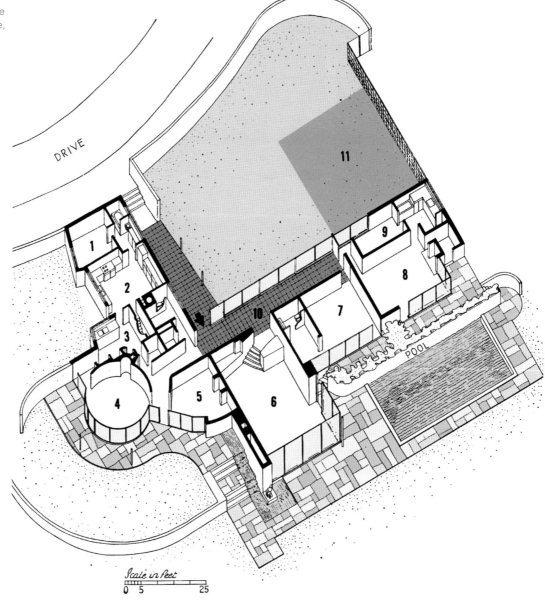

A. Conger Goodyear House, Old Westbury, 1939. Presentation etching on scratchboard of Pierre Bourdelle's *The African Hunt*, probably late 1940s. The work itself, a rectangular linoleum cutout painting with a lacquered surface, was displayed, from the early 1950s on, on the wall along the walkway to the front door.

OPPOSITE
A. Conger Goodyear House, Old Westbury, 1939. Skylit west end of "the long gallery." An Aristide Maillol torso stands against the hallway side of the curved dining room wall.

130 EDWARD DURELL STONE

A. Conger Goodyear House, Old Westbury, 1939. Entrance hall, "the long gallery," seen through steel-framed glass curtain wall. Pablo Picasso's *Guitar* (1919) is at east end. On the adjacent wall, from the left, are Henri Matisse's *Music* (Sketch) (1907) and André Dunoyer de Segonzac's *Village on the Marne* (mid-1920s). Paul Cézanne's *Peasant in a Blue Smock* (1892 or 1897) is inside living room entrance. Salvador Dalí's *The Transparent Simulacrum* of the Feigned Image (1938) is partially visible at far right.

façade modulated the sunlight that passed through the glazing, ensuring that the rooms "were shaded during the summer months, and . . . during the winter months, [the sun's] welcoming rays penetrated the house."[5]

Throughout the residence, Goodyear's own peculiar mix of pragmatism, eclecticism, and proclivity for the avant-garde were everywhere in evidence. In the bedroom, rare tiles made by Hopi Indians for tourists in the late nineteenth century (the tiles were acquired on a visit to Arizona) faced

the fireplace surround; directly opposite stood an old Colonial Revival single bed that appears to have been Goodyear's since childhood. Specimens of modern design—chairs by Alvar Aalto, a rosewood coffee table made especially for Goodyear by his friend Isamu Noguchi in 1939, and bold modern fabrics by Dan Cooper—were interspersed with traditional furniture and antiques. Sumptuous wood veneer finishes for paneling and cabinetry, monk's-cloth wallpaper in the gallery and living room, and silver-gray textured-plaster walls and a pale blue ceiling in the round dining room lent each room a singular atmosphere. Custom-crafted stone surfaces, such as the colorful polished Italian marble counters of the sinks in the bathrooms and the black Swedish granite fireplace in the dining room, gave the interior a hard-edged refinement. Still another unique feature designed by Stone was the circular dining room rug, depicting an abstracted plan of the house on a yellow-green background. It fit neatly under a round, wood-veneered tabletop set on a single nickel-plated steel column

A. Conger Goodyear House, Old Westbury, 1939. Sunken living room, facing south. Vincent van Gogh's *La Maison de la Crau* (1888) hangs to the left of the fireplace.

A. Conger Goodyear House, Old Westbury, 1939. Guest room. Giacomo Balla's *Dynamism of a Dog on a Leash* (1912) is displayed on the wall.

A. Conger Goodyear House, Old Westbury, 1939. Goodyear's bedroom.

A. Conger Goodyear House, Old Westbury, 1939. Goodyear's bathroom.

A. Conger Goodyear House, Old Westbury, 1939. The dining room. The circularity of the glass-walled room is echoed in the domed light well in the ceiling and the round dining room table and rug that Stone designed. The rug depicts an abstracted plan of the house.

piercing the floor. The column retracted into the floor through a hydraulic cylinder, so that the room could be used for dancing parties when inclement weather prevented them from being held outdoors on the wide elliptical terrace. The terrace rests on a plinth atop built-up ground. Its supporting wall functioned as a ha-ha, affording Goodyear unobstructed panoramic views of the surrounding landscape, including his many sheep and a donkey grazing in his fields.

Evidence of Stone's European influences was pervasive. Taking a page from Le Corbusier's Villa Savoye, Stone designed the building to accommodate the chauffeured automobile. The long drive uphill to the walled house ended in a turnaround sheltered by the building's cantilevered roof, thereby removing "automobiles and services . . . from the house proper."[6] A separate flat-roofed garage and chauffeur's quarters stood opposite the house on the turnaround. The metal muntins and floor-to-ceiling glass panels were nearly identical to those Stone was incorporating into the Museum of Modern Art design and may, in fact, have been manufactured simultaneously. Ingenious modulations of the interior volumes, wall placements, and floor levels give the house a spatial complexity that recalls Mies's Barcelona Pavilion, as do the two pools, one a rectangular swimming pool and the other a smaller pool in front of the southern façade. The thick, curved white planter wall fronting the walkway to the bedrooms, which overlook the small pool, references Willem Dudok's public buildings in Holland, and the slender black steel pilotis around the perimeter supporting the overhanging roof hark back to the early houses of Le Corbusier.

Goodyear engaged Stone again in 1954 to make a final addition to the house: an east-facing new bedroom projecting into the courtyard and connecting to Goodyear's own. It was for Zaidee Bliss, who married Goodyear, her longtime admirer, in 1950, within a year of her first husband's death. The new room was executed in much the same mode as the original structure, a restrained and refined International Style modernism relying heavily on European precedent. But by the time the expansion was complete, Stone's work elsewhere on Long Island had evolved considerably.

A. Conger Goodyear House, Old Westbury, 1939. South façade. The two pools and the extension of the roofline beyond the steel-framed window walls recall Mies van der Rohe's Barcelona Pavilion, 1929. The sculpture on a plinth in the pool on the left is by Aristide Maillol, and visible in the living room is Isamu Noguchi's sculptural, rosewood-based and glass-topped coffee table.

Walter C. Janney, Jr. and Helen James Janney House, Cold Spring Harbor, 1947. A brick-floored loggia leads into the entrance hall. In the use of brick flooring and steel pilotis, it is similar to the entrance to the A. Conger Goodyear House.

THE "HAIR SHIRT" YEARS

"Toward the end of the thirties," Stone wrote years later, "I was beginning to question the International Style approach to the design of residential architecture."[7] Earlier perhaps than any of his contemporaries, Stone started to turn away from the reductive modernism exemplified by the Goodyear House. Influential in this development was Stone's visit in 1940 to Taliesin, the Wisconsin home and studio of Frank Lloyd Wright. There, Stone said, "the architecture was attuned to the natural beauty of site."[8] This discovery would send Stone in search of his own more expressive organicism, which he tried to work out on unbuilt projects and built commissions for clients in the coastal villages of Long Island.

Signaling this new trend in Stone's work was the Eleanore Potter Ayer Harris House of 1941. Located in what was at the time a sparsely settled area of cornfields between Locust Valley and Oyster Bay, the house was built for the divorced Mrs. Ayer and her two sons, who were soon joined by her new husband, John W. Harris, founder of Hegeman-Harris Company, the main contractor for Rockefeller Center. In the Harris House design, Stone jettisoned the flat roof of his earlier houses for a pitched one, bringing the eaves down low over the windows. Rough-hewn wooden siding took the place of the smooth white contours of the Goodyear House, and the master bath featured a projecting timber-frame solarium that brought sunlight and lush greenery right into the house, an element that would become a favorite of Stone's.

The Harris House was not the first Stone building to manifest this slightly rustic tendency. Intimations of what Stone later referred to as his "Hair Shirt Period" were evident in a small, redwood-clad pavilion built atop a terrace at Rockefeller Center in 1940. A promotional expo for *Collier's* magazine called the "*Collier's* Idea House," the pavilion was just one example of Stone's emerging

flair for public relations. He used it to prevail upon Mrs. Ayer and her husband-to-be to build a house along similar lines. Indeed, interest in Stone's woodsy pavilion spread farther afield than Locust Valley. The Idea House plans could be bought for three dollars, and there were a number of takers.

Another example of Stone's new naturalism is the 1946 house in Great Neck for Jacques and Therese Makowsky, who had amassed a considerable fortune breeding and popularizing the Rock Cornish game hen. The large, two-story house, clad in wooden siding and brick with a flagstone chimney, bears the mark of another leg of Stone's trip west in 1940. Reaching the Pacific, Stone was moved by the "West Coast prophets," architects like Greene & Greene and Bernard Maybeck who had started a Bay Area tradition of informal architecture employing Oriental wood techniques and flexible space planning. The project for the Makowsky family had a decidedly Californian airiness to it, with Craftsmanlike eaves projecting over a first-floor balcony. The couple were plant lovers, and Stone indulged them in the entrance hall, installing an innovative planter that could water some two thousand tropical flowers in ten minutes via a hidden piping system. Flora also took center stage in a specially built garden room, with bushes and shrubs growing from perforations in the floor.

One last iteration in the "Hair Shirt" idiom was the Walter Janney House of 1947 in nearby Cold Spring Harbor. Mrs. Janney had grown up at Eagle's Beak and Burrwood, the estates of her grandparents on either side of her family. Her decision to build a thoroughly modern house on the grounds of Burrwood was a declaration of her interest, as a young bride, in a manageable, modern lifestyle. A long, low, one-story structure, the house is arranged around a central brick-floored corridor, with the primary rooms facing the same direction, as at the Goodyear House. [ill. 13-16] The similarities, however, end there. The exterior finishes of the Janney House forgo stucco and glass for brick

Walter C. Janney, Jr. and Helen James Janney House, Cold Spring Harbor, 1947. Built on the grounds of Burrwood, Mrs. Janney's family estate.

Joseph S. and Ronnie Wohl House, Lawrence, 1946. Looking through the "long gallery" toward the "sunroom."

OPPOSITE
Joseph S. and Ronnie Wohl House, Lawrence, 1946. View of the staircase through the wood-framed hall window from the entrance loggia.

cladding and wooden window sashes. At the center of the plan, taking pride of place in the spacious living room, a large fireplace faced in brick seems an homage to Wright's commanding hearths, and clerestory windows replace Goodyear's floor-to-ceiling window walls, creating a more private, subdued atmosphere.

Stone's choice of materials for the Harris and Janney projects was in part a consequence of supply shortages and strict restrictions on the use and transport of metals during World War II. Following Pearl Harbor, Stone was stationed first in Washington, D.C., then in Florida, but he returned to New York by war's end and settled with his family for a time in Great Neck. Practicing out of his house, he garnered a number of showhouses from the women's magazines, in the mold of the *Collier's* Idea House, as well as new commissions. The Harris, Janney, and Makowsky projects proved to be only the beginning of a burgeoning regional practice and a new mode of modern design.

POSTWAR LUXURY

After the war, Stone turned out a string of residential projects across the New York suburbs, as well as in his native Arkansas and elsewhere. These new projects marked the culmination of earlier developments in his progress toward an ever-greater sense of novelty and spectacle.

What might be described as a decorative impulse in Stone's work began to emerge even during his earlier, more austere period. Shifting for the first time from the North Shore to the South Shore town of Lawrence, Stone designed a new residence in 1946 for the family of Joseph S. Wohl, a lawyer and real estate developer who aspired to amass an

important art collection to display there. As in the earlier houses, a long, brick-floored entrance loggia leads past an enclosed courtyard into a central gallery, which features not just an airy corridor but a dramatic, sinuously curving staircase of gleaming white plaster, its high-gloss banisters supported by Plexiglas sheets that follow the contours of the curve. Glass makes a comeback throughout the house, and almost every room has a fully glazed wall; the circular dining room in particular harks back to Goodyear House, but with conventional parquet floors and wooden window mullions instead of steel.

The same year, Stone completed another large house, the Bernard Tomson House, on the water's edge at Kings Point in Great Neck. With its brick-floored corridor, wide staircase, and open-plan living space, which could be modulated with sliding screens, on the first floor, this thirteen-room residence was similarly sumptuous. Mr. Tomson, a jurist and sometime neighbor of Stone's, was so pleased with the result that he spent years thereafter writing legal articles and briefs in support of architects' contractual rights.

In the immediate postwar period, Stone also received large institutional commissions outside the United States. His travel to these places lent his subsequent architecture a distinctly exotic flavor. Especially significant was Stone's design for the three-hundred-room El Panama Hotel in Panama City, begun in 1946 and finished in 1951. A collaboration with landscape architect Thomas Church, the building eschewed internal corridors for extensive balconies overlooking lush enclosed gardens. In 1954, Stone visited Japan on his honeymoon with his new wife, Maria. Japan had long served as an inspiration to his friend Frank Lloyd Wright and to Walter Gropius, who happened to be there with his wife Ise at the same time as the Stones. The two architects met on this trip.

The year after his first visit to Panama, Stone oversaw the completion of a project for Panamanian clients. The Frederick and Ethel Maduro House in Great Neck bears the traces of Stone's recent peregrinations. The clients, unaccustomed to the inclement weather of wintertime New York, wanted something to remind them of their balmy homeland, and Stone delivered a design replete with tropical references. The walled courtyard and walkway to the front door and the wide overhang of the roof—a single angled slab rather than a gabled

OPPOSITE
Joseph S. and Ronnie Wohl House, Lawrence, 1946. The dramatic curvilinear staircase in the "long gallery."

ABOVE
Bernard Tomson House, Kings Point, Great Neck, 1946. Entrance gallery. The loggia connecting the garage to the residence is visible through the window.

Barrett F. and Mary Scott Welch House, Oyster Bay Cove, 1955. View of the kitchen, on the right, from the children's play area. Sliding screens can close off the children's wing from the living room.

pitch—imparted a Central American character to the architecture. Inside, latticed screens and plantings were intended to invoke a tropical ambience, retooled for a northern climate. For the outdoors, landscape architect Daniel Rose designed paved patios above grass terraces that stepped down to a copse of tall trees.

The plan of the house exhibits the architect's ongoing effort to move away from his familiar hallway scheme toward a more natural and flowing spatial arrangement. The entrance foyer communicates directly with the dining room, eliminating the running gallery that had long been Stone's hallmark (no pun intended).

The Welch House (1955), located in Oyster Bay Cove, is the strongest example of the influence of Stone's sojourn in Japan on his architectural thinking. Indeed, the design is part and parcel of the Katsura effect—a fascination with the seventeenth-century Katsura Imperial Villa in Kyoto, first promulgated by Walter Gropius after his visit to Japan. A simple rectilinear pavilion in white wood punctuated by black window frames and yellow paneled doors, the Welch House is surrounded by an *engawa*, the traditional Japanese outdoor walkway under extended rooflines. The house is perched atop the highest hill of the former Louis Comfort Tiffany estate on land that its landscape designers from the Olmsted firm had designated as a sheep-grazing meadow.

The initial house drawings demonstrate Stone's continuing development away from the long central corridor as a unifying device toward a more open plan. Inside, floor-to-ceiling sliding windows brought views of the Syosset Hills and waters of Oyster Bay into the brick-floored living spaces. In typical Japanese style, translucent sliding paper screens served as room dividers and could close off the kitchen and the children's playroom from the living and dining spaces. Also in the manner of traditional Japanese house construction, the post-and-beam support system was exposed. The Welch family ate at a round dining table designed by George Nakashima in the brick-floored garden room, which was also an entry hall, and the living room was furnished with other pieces by Nakashima.

Barrett and Mary Scott Welch purchased their five-acre plot at a time when the great estates were being subdivided into affordable parcels for middle-class budgets. The couple were not wealthy, but they had the imagination and trust in their architect to let him design an eccentric modern house. Their four children apparently derived the most enjoyment from the stable on the property and the riding trails through the surrounding woods. Mary Scott Welch, a prolific writer and a leader in the feminist movement, worked in her own enclave, a room and patio on the ground floor, adjacent to an efficiency apartment for a nanny. Her husband commuted to his job at an advertising firm in the city.

The theatricality of these comfortable postwar houses was to be even more ramped up in the years to come, as a series of marquee projects around the world significantly increased Stone's public profile and interested other Long Islanders in his new brand of modernism.

MONUMENTS IN MINIATURE

The name William J. Levitt is synonymous with the conversion of Long Island's vast farmlands into sprawling automobile suburbs. By 1963, Levitt's greatest achievements as a developer, notably the eponymous Levittown, were behind him. Yet his company, Levitt and Sons, was still a major force in residential construction, with large-scale projects from France to Puerto Rico. The extravagant Levitt decided to relocate the firm's headquarters and its large staff from northern New Jersey to Long Island, within commuting distance of his Mill Neck estate, La Colline, and his Manhattan pied-à-terre. He purchased a fourteen-acre site in Lake Success and started to look for an architect to design the new headquarters as the first of three monumental buildings around a plaza, echoing Lincoln Center, which was then going up on the West Side of Manhattan.

It was only appropriate for the cachet-seeking Levitt to hire Stone, as he had catapulted from well-regarded architect to international phenomenon in 1959, with the opening of the United States Embassy in New Delhi, India. This ambassadorial pavilion became fixed in the public mind as the prototypical Stone project. It is a monumental glass-walled rectangle raised on a ceremonial *socle*, its projecting roof supported by slender, shiny gold steel columns, behind which a grill of perforated handcrafted ceramic tiles shields offices that overlook a large central atrium with elaborate water features and plantings. Stone's, and the embassy's, considerable exposure in the global press, including a *Time* magazine cover, increased demand for his services and expanded his office tenfold. It was as the architect of the embassy that Stone came to be known to prospective high-profile clients like Levitt.

Maria—whom Stone had met in 1954 on a flight to Europe and proposed to within hours of landing—was an active influence on her husband's architecture, encouraging him to pursue an increasingly sensational, ornamental vision of modern design based on classical precedents. It was she who encouraged him to abjure "Ed Stone" for the more orotund "Edward Durell Stone." She also made him give up drinking and his routine of meeting colleagues and even clients at the bar across the street from his office. The phrase "Ed has gone from the bar to the grill" began to flit through design circles.

The 72,000-square-foot Levitt and Sons Executive Office Building Stone designed in late 1963 and completed in 1968 evoked the "Taj Maria," as Frank Lloyd Wright dubbed the embassy, in tribute to Mrs. Stone's sway. New Delhi came to Lake Success with a similar flat, projecting roof and central quadrangle on a raised podium encircled by a colonnaded walkway. Yet, the Levitt project differed from its subcontinental forebear; in the absence of cheap labor and craftsmen to make screen walls, and taking climatic conditions into consideration, the exterior walls of the Levitt building consist of two-story white slatted aluminum jalousies flanked by panels of white glazed brick.

The rooftop apertures of the embassy's central two-story atrium were replaced in the Levitt

Levitt and Sons Executive Office Building, Lake Success, 1968. Reception area.

OPPOSITE
Levitt and Sons Executive Office Building, Lake Success, 1968. Entrance façade. Note the two-story aluminum jalousies and panels of white-glazed brick.

headquarters by geodesic domes to keep out the weather. The courtyard was a showplace; four sets of corner stairs led to second-floor open walkways, from which employees had a view of gleaming white terrazzo floors, towering plants in rectangular beds, and octagonal fountains with concealed lighting playing host to lily pads. For the plaza in front of the building, Levitt commissioned Dutch artists Gerrit and Hans van de Bovenkamp to design a rectangular water garden that would attract attention to the site from the main road and provide office workers with a place to enjoy their breaks.

Just across the plaza from the Levitt headquarters, an architectural twin with almost identical exterior features sprang up in 1971. The architect was not Stone, but Anthony J. DePace, who copied the Levitt building at the insistence of the company's new owners after Levitt succumbed to bankruptcy. The new building was for the Medical Society of the State of New York, which like so many Manhattan-based institutions in the 1970s wanted a suburban location adjacent to an expressway.

During this period, Stone's work found favor with general audiences, but the architectural community increasingly viewed his projects as empty gestures in fashionable excess. A pair of Bloomingdale's department stores in Garden City and Manhasset that also referenced the New Delhi embassy looked cobbled together, rather than carefully conceived, as the Levitt building had been.

In 1959, Stone received another high-profile commission, the performing-arts complex known at the time as the National Cultural Center in Washington, D.C. The original congressional plan had called for a rather modest structure, budgeted at about $25 million, but with the selection of Stone's proposal, the cost of the John F. Kennedy Center—renamed in 1964 for the assassinated president—ended up exceeding $70 million. With its enormous hallways, thousands of tons of Carrara marble, the world's largest and most elaborate crystal chandeliers, and miles of plush red carpeting, the oversize white citadel did not (to put it mildly) endear itself to the design press. Yet the center would influence, in muted form, two of Stone's Long Island residences of the 1960s.

The waterfront Gordon House in Hewlett Bay Park (1963) was built for Murray Gordon, a prosperous executive who had made his fortune, in part, as a manufacturer of covers for folk and rock 'n' roll albums. Mr. Gordon did not, by most accounts, enjoy popular music himself; his tastes inclined more toward classical music, the paintings of Marc Chagall, and the sculptures of Chaim Gross—precisely the educated-yet-popular tastes to which Stone's Kennedy Center style (and the Kennedy Center itself) was directed. The Gordon House design is a paragon of a certain mid-century luxe and sophistication. Japanese screens like those in the Welch House reappear, reoriented here around a central marble-clad atrium with a small circular pool and Levitt-esque dome. The dome's construction is plainly derived from the geodesics of Stone's friend Buckminster Fuller; it adds a touch of sheer '60s grooviness. A lawn sloped gently down to the water, where Gordon kept his boats, and courtyards and gardens designed by Stone's son, landscape architect Edward Stone, Jr., were adorned with sculptures.

That same year, Stone designed another lavish, atrium-centered house, this time in Lloyd Harbor overlooking the water, for a female client then at the peak of her career as a somewhat atypical fixture of the international café-society scene.

Murray Gordon House, Hewlitt Bay Park, 1963. Designed concurrently with the National Cultural Center, renamed the Kennedy Center for the Performing Arts, Washington, D.C.

Gabriele Lagerwall was the sometime companion of numerous very rich men, including Baron Walter Langer von Langendorff, whose claim to fame was as the creator of the immensely successful White Shoulders perfume,[9] and she eventually became his second wife. In 1961, a decade before her marriage to the baron, she purchased a thirty-two-acre wooded parcel from the Colgate family, and subsequently gave Stone the commission to build a house on it. The architect was intimately familiar with the baroness's social milieu, being a sought-after member of it himself, and he designed the house as the perfect gilded getaway for a high-toned, insouciant crowd. With its rectangular plan and surrounding colonnade, formal interiors, and white marble floors, the Villa Rielle, as the house became known, bears a resemblance to the Kennedy Center and the New Delhi embassy. The requisite interior water feature—embellished with tropical trees in the corners and lit by a rooftop

Murray Gordon House, Hewlitt Bay Park, 1963. View, from entrance, of, clockwise from left, the dining room, living room, and den.

149

Gabriele Lagerwall House (Villa Rielle), Lloyd Harbor, 1963. Back of the house, photographed from the beach, showing the two-story loggia and the covered terraces at either end.

OPPOSITE
Gabriele Lagerwall House (Villa Rielle), Lloyd Harbor, 1963. The double-height, skylit atrium and the living room beyond.

dome—took on a somewhat different role here: the baroness turned the atrium into a sort of Roman *natatorium*, and often took a swim in the ovoid pool along with guests before or during cocktail hour.

LOOKING BACK

So many of the projects Stone executed on Long Island demonstrated a greater or lesser degree of deviation from modernist orthodoxy. The architect never regretted that deviation, though he suffered for it at the hands of his critics. But he does seem to have come to rue another aspect of his Long Island work. Years later, speaking of what he called the American "sentimentality about a single dwelling with land all around it," Stone questioned the whole culture of the automobile and the subdivision that his houses in the region had been a part of. Alluding, perhaps, to the romance of Old Europe that drew him to historical architectural detail in his mature work, he said:

> I wish to hell Long Island had been built like [European cities], instead of just paving the countryside.... If you take a Long Island development and put row houses or attached houses on fingers penetrating a park, you'd be amazed how big that park would be.[10]

Consciously or not, these words constitute a critique of himself and of a process he was very much engaged in: the ushering out of the old Long Island of farms, villages, and great estates.

14

PERCIVAL GOODMAN 1904–1989

Model house for H. Arthur Colen, Hempstead State Park Homes, Hempstead, 1934;
Nassau Community Temple, West Hempstead, 1948;
Temple Beth Sholom, Roslyn Heights, 1954 and 1960;
Union Reform Temple, Freeport, 1957;
Jewish Community Center, Franklin Square, 1958;
Temple Beth Israel, Port Washington, 1960;
Great Neck Synagogue, Great Neck, 1962;
East End Synagogue of Long Beach, Congregation Beth Sholom, Long Beach, 1963;
Reform Jewish Congregation of Merrick, Merrick, 1963;
Unitarian Universalist Congregation of Central Nassau, Garden City, 1964;
Percival and Naomi Goodman House (additions to a prefabricated structure), Springs, 1974.

Architect, teacher, and author Percival Goodman executed numerous architectural commissions on Long Island that put his theories of community building into practice. Goodman, a gregarious, affable figure known as Percy to his friends, viewed architecture and planning as tools for strengthening bonds within social groups and improving the well-being of society as a whole. *Communitas*, the landmark planning text that he wrote with his brother, Paul, had a profound influence on a generation of American architects and on the reshaping of cities and suburbs in the 1950s and 1960s. Among the most ambitious of his early housing projects was Hempstead State Park Homes, a middle-class community near Hempstead Lake in southwestern Nassau County. The design dates to 1934, when residential development was just beginning in the rural areas south of the village of Hempstead and when modernist architecture was gaining recognition in the United States. Tied to the Garden City movement, the largely unbuilt project emphasized harmonious community planning in an idyllic setting, all within commuting distance of New York City. Only one of the Hempstead buildings was constructed, which, as one of the first wave of modernist houses built in the United States, ranks among Goodman's most important realized house designs.

After World War II, Goodman remained focused on housing issues as a professor at Columbia University's architecture school, but also established

Philip Batchker House project, Long Beach, 1931. Presentation drawing for a Bauhaus-style house in Long Beach, known then as "The Riviera of the East," probably not built.

himself as a prolific designer of synagogues. New Jewish enclaves were forming all over western Long Island, as populations migrated from city to suburb. For Goodman, designing synagogues was a way of binding together these nascent communities. By 1980, "the synagogue architect," as he came to think of himself, had built more than fifty across the United States, with the greatest concentration of them in Nassau County. His spare, modernist designs, defined by their humble materials, bold geometry, and incorporation of abstract art, were revolutionary, helping to transform Jewish religious architecture, as well as that of churches.

Goodman's concern with creating strong communities and his bent toward non-conformity may have been a response, in part, to the lack of stability that he experienced as a child. He was born into a cultured, well-established German-Jewish family in Manhattan, but after his father abandoned them to run off to Argentina with his mistress in 1911, his mother, he, and his three siblings were forced into near poverty. At thirteen, Goodman left school to live on his own in a boarding house and support himself as a draftsman in his uncle's architectural practice. He went on to work for various reputable firms, where he became an expert draftsman and renderer. In 1925, his intellect and facility as a renderer won him the extremely competitive Paris Prize, which awarded the recipient four years of study, all expenses paid, at the École des Beaux-Arts in the French capital.

Goodman excelled in the École's rigorous classical training program but ranged widely outside the confines of the tradition-bound Parisian institution, which taught students how to draw and understand the great buildings of history. With his friend Alexander (Sandy) Calder, he mingled with the avant-garde and café society, got to know the eccentric writer and composer Erik Satie, and attended exhibitions of Pablo Picasso and André Derain. Goodman also frequently went to services at the great Catholic churches, as he enjoyed the architecture, ceremony, and music. He immersed himself in the writings of Le Corbusier, well beyond the prescribed École curriculum.

Upon his return to New York in 1929, he quickly established a successful practice in high-end commercial and residential design. His interiors for department stores, including Saks Fifth Avenue and Henri Bendel, were superb, as were his apartment interiors for fashionable and wealthy clients. Though he was able to support himself designing these French-influenced, Art Moderne–style interiors, he nurtured more radical ambitions. In an effort to find a socially relevant path, he joined groups like the leftist New Day association and Buckminster Fuller's Structural Study Associates and cofounded the Design Laboratory in Greenwich Village, a short-lived school modeled on the German Bauhaus. He also turned his attention to the problem of lower- and middle-income housing reform, which, with New Deal funding, was becoming a coveted source of work for architects.

In an essay of 1931, Goodman declared his commitment to houses that are "good to live in . . . honest, expressive of their function, and logical."[1] With a dry, occasionally caustic wit that echoed the tone of Le Corbusier's anti-establishment essays of the 1920s, Goodman took swipes at the contemporary architectural scene. He was especially critical of what he saw as a vacuously novel kind of "modernistic" architecture for wealthy clients who "will do anything to be conspicuously wasteful."[2] He called instead for a more rigorous modernism based on attention to practical necessity and the inhabitant's well-being. He advocated ridding houses of superfluous, outmoded features such as attics and cellars, which he considered nothing more than "places for the family ghost or cat to wander in."[3] Especially important, in his view, was to design individual dwellings with attention to their role in a wider urban and social framework. "The end and rationale of all construction is the happiness of the individual, but the beginning and instrument of all construction is the planning of the community," he concluded.[4]

In the early 1930s, he produced several unrealized housing schemes, which he modeled directly on International Style modernism. His Community Service Homes project of 1932 reflected the social utopian aims of workers' housing built in Germany by Walter Gropius and others. In the basic style of the Bauhaus, Goodman designed a never-built white-walled concrete house for Philip A. Batchker in Long Beach, Long Island, then an upscale beach resort with large hotels. In a different vein, his 1932 Week-End beach house for an unspecified site in Montauk consisted of prefabricated aluminum parts. The design echoed Lawrence Kocher and Albert Frey's Aluminaire House (see page 38), which he had seen the year before at the Allied Architects exhibition in New York. Goodman's lightweight, prefab house was meant to provide an affordable way to escape the overcrowded city. As he wrote of the project, "It is a means by which the city-dweller can escape the inevitable claustrophobia brought on by unnatural compactness. It is the proper housing for the health and sport cult, and it is a compromise with economic conditions."[5]

HEMPSTEAD STATE PARK HOMES

In the early 1930s, Nassau County had not yet begun to experience the great building boom that would soon transform its farm fields into endless suburbs. But changes had begun to arrive in 1925 with Robert Moses's development of the Southern State Parkway, which provided efficient automobile transit from Brooklyn through Hempstead Lake State Park (also initiated by Moses) and all the way across the county. New infrastructure spurred new development. A May 1931 headline in the *New York Times* read, "Builders Active on Long Island. Many New Homes Being Erected to Meet the Increased Spring Demand."[6] The article noted that the bucolic area around Hempstead Lake in particular had become a magnet for house construction.

Around 1933, the developer H. Arthur Colen approached Goodman about designing a group

FIRST FLOOR   SECOND FLOOR

PERCIVAL GOODMAN: Hempstead House
Courtesy of Architectural Forum

Model house for H. Arthur Colen, built, Hempstead, 1934. This photograph of the model house appeared in the article "Modernity's First Sub-Division," *Architectural Forum*, January 1935.

Model house for H. Arthur Colen, built, Hempstead, 1934. Percival Goodman's final presentation drawing of the prototype house for the Hempstead State Park Homes development site.

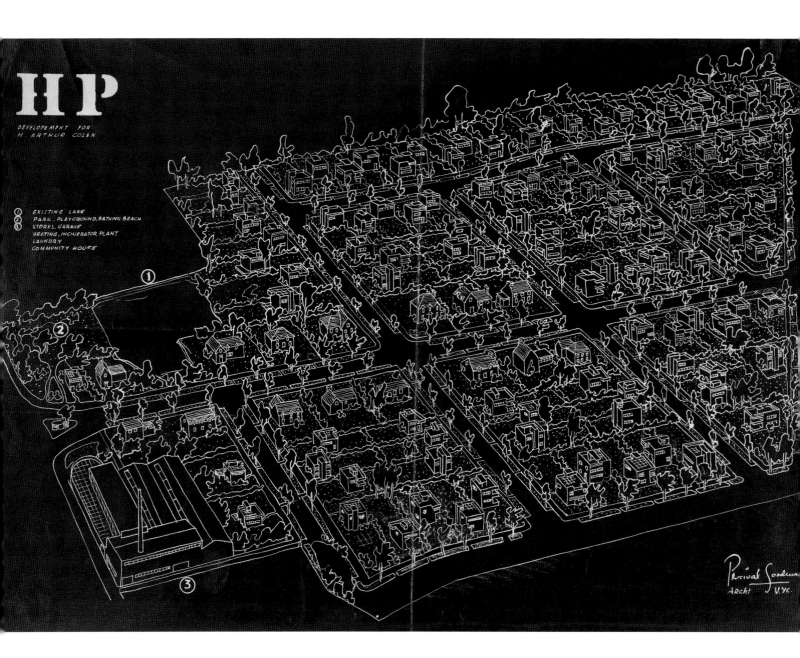

Modern House Development for H. Arthur Colen, Hempstead, 1935. Presentation drawing for Hempstead State Park Homes, showing 140 modern houses within an already existing street grid. The architect incorporated a playground and park (2), Hempstead Lake (1), shopping and laundry facilities, a community house, and even an incinerator (3).

of houses in a modernist manner on a site near Hempstead Lake. At the time, only a select few European-trained architects, including William Lescaze and Richard Neutra, had built International Style residential projects in the United States. But in the wake of the Museum of Modern Art's 1932 exhibition on International Style architecture, the new modern architecture had attracted enough popular attention that developers like Colen became intrigued by its commercial appeal. An article in *Architectural Forum* describing the Hempstead Lake project stated that Colen first encountered Goodman's work at an exhibition in New York in October 1933. According to the article, the developer was not an enthusiast of Goodman's architecture per se, but was intrigued by the untapped market potential of modernism.

Apparently he was not the only developer at the time to hold this view. As the article reported, "It has become a commonplace in New York City real estate circles to say that the first man to promote a modern home subdivision within commuting distance of the city will make a pot of money."[7]

Ironically, Goodman himself was an enthusiastic city dweller who never learned to drive a car.[8] But in the early 1930s he was intrigued by the urban reforms proposed by two heroes of the Modern movement, Le Corbusier and Frank Lloyd Wright, both of whom advocated a variation on the Garden City concept of dispersed, architecturally harmonious residential planning.[9] Writing in the pages of the journal *Architectural Progress* in 1932, Goodman argued for a planning strategy akin to Wright's Broadacre City. "Work should be centralized—living quarters should be decentralized," Goodman stated. "This means a greater density of buildings used for business purposes and garden cities for living."[10]

Following the Garden City model, Goodman arranged 140 single-family houses on an approximately ten-square-block swath just to the west of Hempstead Lake. In his rendering of the Hempstead Lake development, Goodman depicted a community of small houses set on 40-foot-square lots with trees and ample garden areas. The layout of the plan was determined by the preexisting street grid, but rather than lining up the houses in even rows, he set them at varying distances from the road, softening the grid somewhat and giving the plan an element of picturesque freedom. He incorporated shared amenities, including green space, a playground, a beach, a "community house," and a shopping area, to encourage gathering among residents. He designed several types and sizes of dwellings, but gave them all the same formal vocabulary of white walls, cubic volumes, flat roofs, and bright yellow and red trim for windows and doors.

Although only a single prototype house was constructed, it was an important achievement, placing Goodman in a small group of American architects who had built modernist houses. He was one of an even smaller number who had built a middle-income version, rather than fulfilling a commission for a wealthy client. Goodman's architecture stuck closely to European models. Drawing on Le Corbusier's 1924 Pessac houses and Gropius's Bauhaus faculty residences of 1926, Goodman incorporated upper-level terraces with tubular-steel railings, long windows that reveal the structural independence of the façade, and red and yellow accents to relieve the monotony of white walls. Inside, the house featured an open plan. Following Le Corbusier, Goodman employed a structural grid of slender pilotis to allow for the flexible placement of walls and creative arrangement of spaces, which included a large sunken living room and a "dining balcony."

The most experimental, and ultimately most risky, aspect of Goodman's Hempstead prototype house was his use of poured-in-place reinforced concrete as the primary building material. Although the architect managed to convince his developer that concrete would provide an economical and elegant means of realizing his designs, Goodman encountered intractable construction difficulties. The biggest problem was the workers' hesitancy: "The fact that a cantilever could be built was a great shock and surprise to the concrete men. . . . The plumber . . . was completely at a loss. He had only installed plumbing in wooden houses and did not have the vaguest idea of what should be done in this type of house."[11] Amid mounting tensions and several months behind schedule, the first story was erected. Immediately, however, the whole thing had to be torn down after it was deemed structurally unsound. Construction started anew and the house was eventually finished. It should have attracted substantial attention as the promising work of a young American modernist. But by that time Goodman had become so frustrated that he dissociated himself from Colen, who abandoned the development before attracting a single buyer. Despite the ambition and promise that had accompanied its beginnings, Goodman's white concrete cube bore the taint of failure. Its historical significance was not enough to keep it from soon being forgotten. In fact, it was long thought to have been demolished. But the solid concrete walls have stood the test of time and the house lives on—somewhat faded but largely unaltered. Situated today in a tidy neighborhood of more traditional houses, the distinctive, flat-roofed structure testifies to Goodman's ambitious vision of a different kind of house and community.

LONG ISLAND SYNAGOGUES

1944 marked a critical juncture in Goodman's personal and professional life. "Hitler reconverted me to Judaism" was his way of describing the crisis of identity that he experienced following the Holocaust.[12] Born into a secular family and having held Marxist convictions during the 1930s, Goodman had never been religious nor had he identified strongly with his Jewish heritage. In the aftermath of World War II, however, he began to think of how, as an architect, he might not only play a role in Jewish life but also gain commissions. His first opportunity came in 1944 with the job to adapt the French Gothic–style mansion on Fifth Avenue designed in 1908 by C. P. H. Gilbert for Felix and Frieda Schiff Warburg into a permanent home for the Jewish Museum. Mrs. Warburg's lawyer and fellow Jewish Theological Seminary trustee, Alan

Nassau Community Temple, West Hempstead, 1948. Presentation drawing. Goodman transformed two connected Quonset huts into a modern sanctuary, community center, and school for young suburban pioneers on a minuscule budget.

Stroock, a friend of Goodman's through literary circles, arranged the introduction.[13] It resulted in work that, though architecturally minor, linked him to a high-profile Jewish cultural institution, and it became the springboard that launched him into synagogue design.

In 1947, Goodman published his first article on synagogue design in the magazine *Commentary*. He also spoke on the topic at a Union of American Hebrew Congregations national conference, where he met leaders of congregations who were looking for architects. By 1948, he had landed his first commissions, including synagogues in Baltimore, Providence, and Lima (Ohio), as well as the Nassau Community Temple in West Hempstead. "From then on," Goodman said, "I became a synagogue architect."[14]

Along with such important modern architects as Louis Kahn, Erich Mendelsohn, and Frank Lloyd Wright, Goodman led a transformation of religious architecture in the postwar era.[15] American-Jewish identity was undergoing a major transformation of its own during this period, affected not only by the Holocaust but also by the founding of the state of Israel in 1948, the general economic upturn in the United States, and the accompanying migration of the middle classes from cities to suburbs. As new Jewish communities took shape in suburbs, synagogue construction boomed. Modernism became the style of choice, replacing the historical-revival styles popular since the nineteenth century. Goodman made the argument, which appealed strongly to his clients, that the emergence of a new Jewish identity necessitated a new architectural vocabulary. "To employ the best modern architects working in their best functional and constructivist style," Goodman wrote in 1949, was the best way to fulfill the practical needs and express the values of contemporary congregations.[16]

The Long Island communities that employed Goodman consisted of young, middle-class individuals and families who identified predominantly with Reform Judaism and its tendency toward the modernization of traditional practices and symbiosis with the larger culture. Their congregations often originated as small groups, concerned as much with forming social ties in their new communities as with practicing religion. Janet Loewy, a founding member of the Nassau Community Temple in West Hempstead, recalls that her congregation began with eleven couples who had little money but a powerful sense of freedom and possibility.[17] Shoestring budgets and makeshift meeting quarters—vacant storefronts, American Legion Halls, even tents—were not uncommon as these groups of Jewish pioneers first staked their claims on the suburban frontier.[18]

For Goodman, the challenge was to design buildings that would express the progressive spirit and accommodate the needs and budgets of these young congregations. Humble, undisguised building materials were an important part of his designs—and the ethos of the congregations—as was abandonment of historic styles for a modern vocabulary and spirit. He designed the Nassau Community Temple on a minuscule budget of $62,000, transforming a pair of Quonset huts that the congregation had bought cheaply from the military into a stylish essay in modern form. The sanctuary of the Temple Beth Sholom in Roslyn Heights features soaring wood beams and walls of rough brick. The hallways of the Union Reform Temple in Freeport are inlaid with ornamental wheat-colored concrete blocks. All of the sanctuaries include heavy, angular wooden pews, lecterns, and chairs, which demonstrate Goodman's talent for furniture design, a skill he developed in his early career as a designer for department stores.

Often his interiors were embellished with abstract art, which Goodman viewed as an important component of a distinctly modern, Jewish architecture. His Congregation B'nai Israel in Millburn, New Jersey, became famous for featuring sculpture and tapestries by young abstract expressionists Robert Motherwell, Herbert Ferber, and Adolph Gottlieb. Most of the Long Island synagogues, however, were designed later, when such artists, according to Goodman's design partner Chiu-Hwa Wang, had "become too famous for our owners to afford."[19] Art remained important nevertheless. The Roslyn temple featured an abstract expressionist sculpture by Irwin Touster mounted above the ark. The eternal flame and menorah in the Great Neck sanctuary was the work of artist Ira Lubin, a member of the congregation. Often, when budgets were tight, members happily contributed to the making of art quilts and tapestries. The women's committees of the Merrick Reform Congregation and the Nassau Community Temple in West Hemsptead sewed ark curtains and chuppahs (wedding canopies), as if they were in quilting bees.[20]

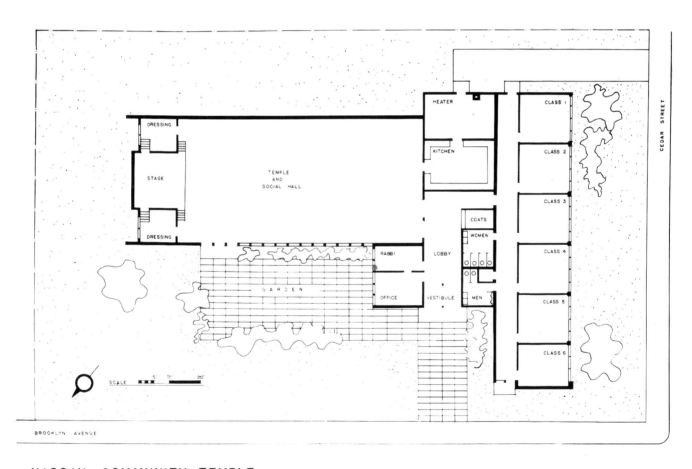

NASSAU COMMUNITY TEMPLE
WEST HEMPSTEAD NEW YORK

PERCIVAL GOODMAN ARCHITECT

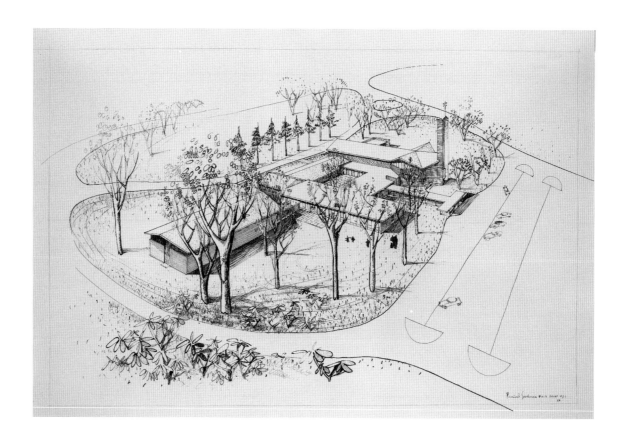

Temple Beth Sholom, Roslyn Heights, 1954 and 1960. Final presentation drawing, 1958. In the foreground is the social hall addition, built in 1960.

Temple Beth Sholom schoolroom, Roslyn Heights, 1954 and 1960. Presentation drawing. Goodman's drawing style had distinct charm.

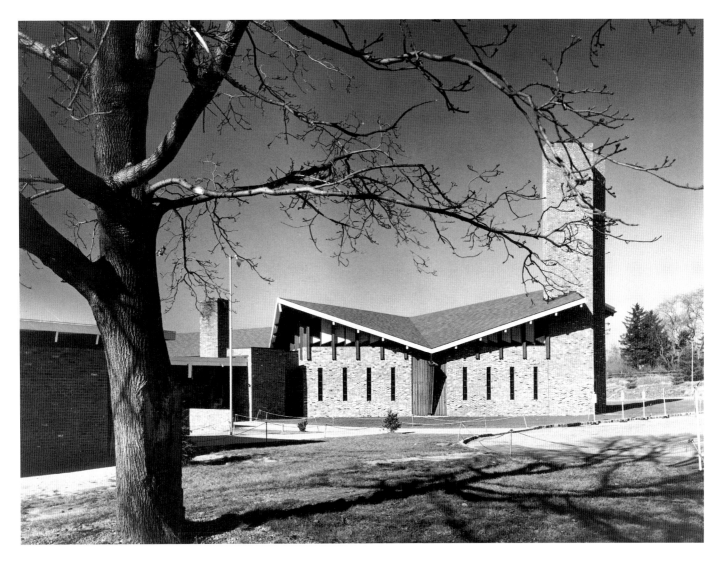

Temple Beth Sholom, Roslyn Heights, 1954 and 1960. The sanctuary building. Its expressionist shape is enhanced by irregular-sized, multitoned red bricks, carefully offset from one another in the manner of Alvar Aalto.

Temple Beth Sholom, Roslyn Heights, 1954 and 1960. Sanctuary interior. Intricate wood joinery in the structural elements and simple, clean-lined furnishings are hallmarks of Goodman's synagogue design, as is the incorporation of natural light, for a "spiritual" atmosphere, through clerestory windows.

Great Neck Synagogue, Great Neck, 1962. Final presentation drawing. The drum-like sanctuary is clad in red brick; all the expressively designed support structures are precast concrete.

Critical to Goodman's notion of "functionalist" design was the way spaces conformed to the unique requirements of modern Judaism, as he understood them. He felt that not only worship but also social gathering and education were essential functions, and his plans included a distinct space for each. Classrooms were typically situated in a separate wing with a more utilitarian appearance. Social halls were always connected directly to the sanctuary, separated by an accordion partition that could be opened to expand seating for the High Holidays. The sanctuary was the grandest space; it was always double height and often had a distinctive form that marked it as a sacred place. Sometimes it was covered by a gently pitched roof, an allusion to the tent of the meeting in the wilderness from which the synagogue originated.[21] For congregations with larger budgets he designed more dramatic spaces. The most striking are the drum-like sanctuary of the Great Neck Synagogue, with a soaring vertical window at the altar and a semicircular series of elevated benches, and the angular geometries of the Roslyn sanctuary, inspired by Frank Lloyd Wright's famous Beth Sholom Congregation in Elkins Park, Pennsylvania.

Attention to the Jewish liturgy was essential to Goodman. Although not religious, he was deeply fascinated by how architecture could be used to enhance spiritual experience and symbolically convey sacred meaning. He described himself as a "sort of fundamentalist" who said, "Let's just stick to the Bible" to find the most authentic forms of worship.[22] He believed that the Jewish religious ceremony should be communal and participatory, in contrast to what he saw as the passive receipt of instruction in Christian services. "The rabbi is in no sense a priest or minister . . . the only religious actor is the congregation," he wrote.[23] In the Great Neck Synagogue, he positioned the *bimah*, or platform from which the Torah is read, in the center of the sanctuary, rather than on a stage at the head of the space. At Roslyn Heights, he positioned the cantor facing away from the congregation and toward the ark, to stress the communal act of addressing the Torah. Ario S. Hyams, a founding rabbi of the Roslyn temple, wrote that this arrangement not only made the service more deeply spiritual but also resulted in an architecture with true "Jewish individuality."[24]

Light was a final important component. Goodman argued that stained glass was "contrary to the spirit of the Jewish service," which was fundamentally rational and centered around reading.[25] He favored large, clear-glass windows (though congregations often added stained glass later). In Freeport, Long Beach, and elsewhere, he employed clerestory windows to bring in extra light from above. He always choreographed light to dramatic effect. Those who attended services in Goodman's buildings used words like "spiritual" and "ethereal" to describe the effect of light, especially at the liturgically significant moment of sundown, when light would strike the congregation through west-facing windows.[26]

Built for communities in transition, Goodman's Long Island synagogues remain subject to the inevitably shifting tide of demographics. In some cases, the original congregations have prospered and grown, and additions have been made to Goodman's buildings, as in Roslyn Heights and Great Neck. In other communities, the original congregations have dispersed, leaving the synagogues underused or threatened by dwindling membership, as

Union Reform Temple, Freeport, 1957. Presentation drawing, final version. Though not seen in the drawing, the finished building featured intricate brickwork on the exterior façades and sanctuary walls.

in Long Beach. The Freeport and West Hempstead congregations have closed and sold their buildings. As communities and institutions are buffeted by changes, the continued existence of many of Goodman's synagogue buildings is very much in question. If the buildings do not continue as synagogues, their best new use is as churches, such as the Union Reform Temple, Freeport, which now houses a thriving church with a congregation of first-generation immigrants from Latin America, who enjoy it fully, in keeping with Goodman's original design intent and his almost magical treatment of light.

Like other New York artists, Goodman and his wife, Naomi, bought land in Springs, the area of East Hampton where the old fishing families lived. According to his son Joel, Goodman was too busy with his practice, teaching, and intellectual preoccupations to design a weekend house. Instead, Naomi Goodman purchased a small, prefabricated house she had seen displayed on the roof of the Abercrombie & Fitch sporting goods store in Manhattan.[27] They installed it in an area of fields and woods not far from Jackson Pollock and Lee Krasner's farmhouse and studio. Over the years, her husband made only a few modest additions, including studio space for himself, where he painted and made large assemblages, a beloved avocation. If not for architecture, Joel Goodman recalled, art making would have been Percival Goodman's career.[28] Toward the end of his life, Goodman executed a few nearby residential projects for friends, including a new house and renovations of two existing houses for the Braude family in Amagansett, as well as projects for B. Tina Stronach-Buschel and the Karlin family. Ultimately, however, it is the very insignificance of this residential work in Goodman's career that is most telling. His concern with community, rather than private life, compelled him to remain dedicated to middle-class housing and synagogues. This work, along with his diligent enthusiasm for his teaching career at Columbia, was what the idealistic Goodman deemed to have the greatest social value.

15

RICHARD NEUTRA 1892–1970

John Nicholas and Anne Brown ("Windshield") House, Fishers Island, Suffolk County, 1938;
Lorin and Alice Price House, Bayport, 1951;
Proposal for Levittown (unbuilt), 1951;
Swirbul Library, Adelphi University, 1957–67

The editors of *Time* magazine put a portrait of Viennese-born Richard Neutra's intense, craggy, gentlemanly face on the cover of its August 15, 1949, issue. The accompanying story promoted new modern architecture and touted Neutra as its most imaginative and practical champion, an architect who could design houses for the middle class within budget. The writer proclaimed, "The resale value of Neutra houses has been demonstrated time and again. Real-estate agents never fail to insert the words 'Neutra House' when they advertise one for sale."[1]

The *Time* article brought Neutra popular fame and three very different Long Island–based clients. When William Levitt was calling for proposals for his Levittown housing development, he hired Neutra and his associate Thaddeus Longstreth during the formative phase of the ambitious endeavor. Neutra produced a beautiful set of color drawings of easy-to-reproduce flat-roofed houses in a well-organized landscape. Probably out of fear that modern-looking design would not sell after all, the Levitts dismissed Neutra and Longstreth's proposal and opted instead for traditional New England house types, set in a vast, meandering cul-de-sac road plan. Next to contact Neutra was Broadway producer Lorin Price and his wife, who commissioned a classic version of Neutra's rectangular house designs for their main residence, on land near the ocean in Bayport and within commuting distance of Manhattan. The most elaborate job came from the board of Adelphi University, which

John Nicholas and Anne Brown Windshield House, Fishers Island, 1938. The main living room, called the music room in the plans, overlooks West Harbor.

held a competition for the design of a master plan and a new library for the university's Garden City campus. Neutra and his partner Robert Alexander won the competition hands down.

By the 1950s, Neutra was a senior statesman of modern architecture, very well known among his colleagues. The *Time* article missed this point, as well as how influential his technologically innovative buildings of the late 1920s and 1930s in Los Angeles had been on the development of American Modernism. These radical, sophisticated buildings for the Los Angeles movie crowd epitomized the International Style's machine aesthetic at the dawn of American Modernism, which had its nexus in Southern California. Throughout his long, productive career, Neutra retained the basic language of those early days, adapting it to the latest materials and technologies. His European training in engineering as well as architecture prepared him to understand how to design for the rapidly changing, automobile-dependent way of life in America, which he witnessed unfold in Los Angeles, after he and his wife, Dione, emigrated there permanently in 1925.

As a young architect in Vienna, Neutra had imagined America as a world of endless possibilities for architects, free of the heavy load of history and the class structures of Old Europe. He arrived in the United States in 1923 and first found work as a draftsman in Manhattan, before moving on to employment at Holabird & Roche, one of Chicago's most prominent firms, known for its skyscrapers.

Frank Lloyd Wright was Neutra's hero, as he was to virtually all of Europe's avant-garde architects. After a visit to Taliesin, Wright's school and workshop near Spring Green, Wisconsin, Neutra gave notice to the firm in Chicago and fulfilled an aspiration to work as an apprentice for the master. The Neutras stayed at Taliesin for several months, and although Wright tried to persuade them to stay longer, Neutra was anxious to reach his final destination, Southern California, where he hoped to set up a practice. Ultimately, the young architect became disappointed in Wright's use of heavy masonry and ornament, although certainly not in the spirited genius of the man, with whom he remained in touch.[2]

Neutra's Los Angeles practice became enviably prolific. Even during times when it slowed, his theoretical, humanistic, often rambling writings maintained his reputation at home and abroad. His books and articles revealed an eccentric theorist. The basis of his philosophy was that a building's spatial layout and detailing had to provide psychological comfort and satisfy man's primal yearning for a connection to Nature. In his book *Survival Through Design*, he called this philosophy biorealism—the inherent and inseparable relationship between man and nature: "bio" from the Greek bios, meaning "life," and "realism," which to him connoted human beings' sensory apprehension of their environments. As Barbara Lambrecht, the most recent biographer of Neutra, has written, Neutra believed "quite simply, that good architecture—that which reconciles humanity with nature in an 'exultant dance of interconnectedness'—heals and that bad architecture—that which alienates the human from nature and from his or her essential naturalness—harms."[3]

WINDSHIELD

From 1936 to 1938 Neutra labored on a grand, exquisitely detailed thirty-four-room International Style house with distinct American accents and a nautical bent for a site on Fishers Island. Although closer to the Connecticut shore than to Long Island, Fishers Island is politically part of the town of Southold in Suffolk County.

Neutra's clients were the supremely wealthy, architecturally sophisticated John Nicholas Brown and his wife, Anne. As a child, Brown inherited the bulk of his family's shipping and textile-manufacturing fortune. The family had founded Brown University in Providence, Rhode Island, among many other institutions of learning, social service, and culture. Soon after marrying, the John Nicholas Browns restored his family's colonial-era house in Providence. For a summer house, however, they wanted to put their keen interest in modern architecture into full effect. They were well aware that a newly built modern house on Fishers Island would attract a great deal of attention and demonstrate their support for progressive ideas in architecture and design. As Brown wrote to Neutra, "I hope it will be a distinguished monument in the history of architecture."[4]

Avid readers of architecture journals, the couple had followed Neutra's West Coast avant-garde projects. But what convinced them to contact him was their visit to the 1932 International Style exhibition at the then fledgling Museum of Modern Art. The show, which had a great impact on American architecture, was based on a field survey of progressive architecture in Europe, carried out by Philip Johnson and Henry-Russell Hitchcock, under the guidance of the museum's first director, Alfred Barr, who coined the term International Style. The only American residence included in the exhibition, besides Kocher and Frey's experimental Aluminaire House (see page 38), was the technologically pioneering house that Neutra had designed for Dr. Philip Lovell, a naturopath and celebrity health and fitness columnist for the Los Angeles Times.

The construction of the Lovell House, also known as the Lovell Health House, was based on skyscraper technology, the very building method that had brought Neutra across the Atlantic in the first place. Its rectangular volumes literally hung out over a canyon in the Hollywood Hills. What made this effect possible was a light steel frame that Neutra made sure was erected in forty-eight hours and his daring use of cantilevered rooms—essentially steel cages covered with concrete panels and bands of steel window sashing.

Besides the stark, unadorned modernism of the Lovell House, the Browns were no doubt impressed by the fact that it was not just a family dwelling but also a private sanatorium, with exercise rooms, sleeping porches, and a wonderful interconnectedness with the outdoors, including an outdoor lap pool tucked beneath the main living quarters.

In the early stages of their collaboration with Neutra, the Browns wanted their new house to duplicate the Lovell House, with white stucco for the façade, steel windows, and steel framing. But in the end, they decided to deviate from the standard hard white look of the International Style's concrete houses and make theirs completely, gleamingly, metallic looking. To achieve the appearance of steel without the cost, Neutra specified wooden framing and shiplap siding covered with silver gray aluminum paint. The local contractor knew very well how to install shiplap siding, a time-tested material for New England boat and house building. It was the only vernacular accent incorporated into the house design.

Absolutely modern, however, was the pioneering use of aluminum window frames, Solex window glass, and wide corner aluminum angles to hold the wooden façades in place. Equally pioneering was the Browns' purchase of two of Buckminster Fuller's prefabricated copper and sheet-metal bathrooms, designed for the prototype of his aluminum Dymaxion House, exhibited in 1929. The Browns met with "Bucky" at the Phelps Dodge plant on Long Island, where nine of these ultimate cabinets de toilette had been manufactured. The Browns were Fuller's only clients for the fully equipped chambers, which he had hoped to mass-produce and ship all over the country.

Neutra and his clients enjoyed an intense collaboration, fully documented in frequent correspondence and questionnaires crafted by John Nicholas Brown. Notable in this documentation are Brown's fascination with American ingenuity in the creation of new products and gadgetry and Anne Brown's enjoyment in furnishing the interiors with modern furniture, including some Alvar Aalto pieces shipped over from Finland, her delight in bringing bright, saturated colors into the decorating scheme, and her choice of nubby, textured fabrics that contrasted strongly with the shiny linoleum and rubber floors.

From afar, the house, perched on a hilltop overlooking the island's deepest harbor, looked like a steel ocean liner on land. With its numerous gadgets and careful space planning, it functioned quite like one, a true "machine for living." And like a ship at sea, it was equipped with its own telegraph. The Browns' son Carter proclaimed as a small boy, "It doesn't look like a house, it's a twain!"[5] Growing up in the Neutra-designed house gave him a deep appreciation of modern architecture, and when he oversaw the creation of a new wing at the National Gallery as assistant director of the museum, he selected I. M. Pei to design the magnificent, spatially extravagant modern addition.

In the summer, the Browns used the house as a base for sailing their yacht, which they could see anchored in the main harbor from their windows. On the flat rooftops they could deploy meteorological instruments and a mechanically hoisted system of flags to signal their yacht crew or other boats out on the water. There were telescopes at some of the windows, all of which had sweeping views out to sea.

John Nicholas Brown's love of mechanical efficiency and ingenuity was incorporated into all aspects of life in the house. He and his wife played music with their children in a large music

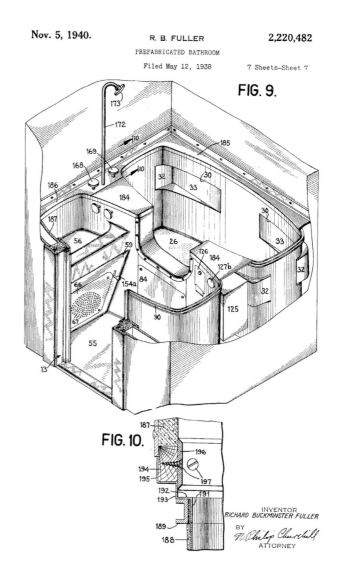

John Nicholas and Anne Brown Windshield House, Fishers Island, 1938. Buckminster Fuller, Prefabricated Bathroom for the Dymaxion House, patent application drawing. Two bathrooms of this type were installed side by side in the master bedroom suite.

room, which was the hub of the house and as state-of-the-art as any radio sound studio. Stowaway built-in drawers and closets were built to size for specific musical instruments, as well as for the family's sailing and sports gear. Neutra designed laundry shoots, dumbwaiters, and other conveyances. Garage doors were controlled electronically. One memorandum to Neutra mentioned that Anne smoked in bed and would like an ashtray installed in her bedside table that would send ash down a chute to the servant's level.

The couple named their house Windshield. With its horizontal composition of rectangular wings and wide, rhythmic bands of windows and sliding glass doors, it was as sleek and modern as the tempered-glass car windshields that were widely introduced in the late 1920s, replacing the need for anyone to wear goggles at the wheel of a high-speed vehicle. With their choice of name, the Browns proclaimed their allegiance to modernity and all the arts that were catching up with the speed of the automobile, ocean liner, train, and airplane during the so-called Machine Age of the interwar years.

Apparently solidly built and impermeable, as well as the most expensive modern house erected in America at that time, Windshield suffered serious damage during the great hurricane of 1938, soon after the family moved in. Upset but undeterred, the Browns rebuilt. After the house was sold to a new owner in the late 1970s, it caught fire one muddy, foggy evening, and the fire department could not reach it in time to save it. Few people are left on Fishers Island who can remember the great flat-roofed house, changing color in different weather and literally glowing when sunlight reflected off its metallic-colored façades. Yet the house lives on in myth, a testament to the bravado of the Browns' utterly modern statement in an enclave where few break away from conventional behavior, let alone traditional building styles.

PRICE HOUSE

Lorin Price came into an inheritance in 1951 that enabled him and his bride to buy six acres with waterfront in Bayport, on the Great South Bay.

Lorin and Alice Price House, Bayport, 1951. Presentation sketch, final version, 1950. The rugged post-and-beam redwood structure supports window walls that offer constant engagement with the outdoors.

Lorin and Alice Price House, Bayport, 1951. Bayside view of the house on an early spring day.

They commissioned Neutra to create drawings for a substantial year-round family house and paid all the travel expenses for Neutra and themselves to meet either at the Long Island site or at his Los Angeles office.

An up-and-coming theatrical producer, Lorin Price enjoyed Manhattan's fast pace, whereas Alice, his Swedish-born wife, wanted to bring up their two children in the great outdoors. The couple divorced in 1956, and she raised the children in the Bayport house, while he launched a successful bicoastal career, producing a number of hit Broadway shows and Hollywood films.

Neutra sought both camaraderie and adulation from all his clients, and the Prices gave him both in spades. Alice Price had only kind words for him, "He was wonderful! We became friendly and it all worked out very well."[6] As was his custom, Neutra made a concerted effort to get to know the Prices' every need through lengthy questionnaires and face-to-face meetings.

In the 1940s, Neutra's style changed from his pronounced machine aesthetic to a lighter, more seemingly Japanese-derived appreciation of simple post-and-beam architecture, as well as a greater blurring of the boundaries between indoors and outdoors. Gone were the flat, solid planes and rhythmic windows of the International Style years and so much a part of Windshield's aesthetic. His mid-career buildings featured rectangular sliding window walls for the main rooms, which always opened out onto patios that were created as

Lorin and Alice Price House, Bayport, 1951. East bedroom façade and a spider-leg roof support—a Neutra signature device by the early 1950s. These supports served both to anchor his buildings and frame the views.

open-air rooms. By 1950, reflecting pools, sometimes indoors, and extensions of the framing into the landscape—his signature spider-leg outriggings—were constants.

Yet, compared to Neutra's rather suggestively tentlike house designs of the same period, the Price House was atypically solid looking. The eastern climate necessitated a more classically derived and contained modern house than those he was designing out west. The Price House was a Romantic statement, its thick, rough-hewn granite walls textural foils to the large glass window walls. Irregular granite flagstones covered the floors in the living spaces and extended outdoors to the rectangular patios. Spider legs appeared to anchor the entire house to its flat, windswept site and also served to frame the views.

In some respects, the house recalled the Usonian houses Frank Lloyd Wright built for cold climates: its L-shaped plan, horizontal shape, rooflines extending into the landscape, strong post-and-beam redwood structure, and rugged stone fireplace. Yet unlike the Usonians, the Price House was not a low-cost, cozy container centered around the fireplace wall. It was a sharp-edged structure, wide open to the outdoors, with walls entirely of glass framing the views. The core idea of Neutra's architecture, its psychological focus, was embodied in the window wall. The Prices could see the ocean on the low horizon and the vast sky from almost every vantage point. Even when they warmed themselves near the huge double fireplace, which separated the main living space from a small den, the built-in seating faced the outdoors, not the fire.

Neutra was putting the final touches on *Survival Through Design* when the Price House was being finished, and his theories about how architecture must serve people's sensory needs were given practical application in its design. The house was elegantly appointed with custom cabinetry from expensive woods and carefully crafted stonework, but this material richness was a sideshow. Like the great Romantic artists who depicted lonely human subjects contemplating the magnificence of their surroundings, what Neutra most wanted the family to experience was a sense of awe toward the ever-changing seascape. Thus, he sited the house close to the water to optimize the view, smell, and feel of sea and sky.

After Alice Price moved out of the house, it had a number of owners, including Sean Hannity, the conservative television host, and its design remained relatively intact. In 2003, however, it was altered beyond recognition.

SWIRBUL LIBRARY

In 1937, Dr. Paul Dawson Eddy, a Methodist minister, took over the presidency of Adelphi College, then a small women's liberal arts college in Garden City and one of the few institutions of higher learning on Long Island. A progressive thinker, he was determined to turn Adelphi into an important educational hub for the rapidly growing suburbs of Nassau and Suffolk counties and improve its

Lorin and Alice Price House, Bayport, 1951. The living room has a woodsy, Scandinavian feel; there is even some furniture by the Finnish designer Alvar Aalto. To encourage interaction with nature, Neutra positioned his built-in seating facing outward, rather than toward the fireplace.

Adelphi University, Garden City, 1957–67. Presentation perspective drawing, south entrance to the "Living Library and Center for Communication Arts."

national profile to attract students from across the country and abroad. An active board of governors drawn from the worlds of business, technology, finance, media, and advertising oversaw the organization of departments tailored to prepare students for careers in Long Island's burgeoning aerospace and defense industries, as well as healthcare and social service agencies.

Soon after World War II ended, the college went coeducational, and returning male veterans made up a large part of the increased enrollment. Because many of them held day jobs, the college introduced night classes and part-time schedules. The veterans paid for their education through the Servicemen's Readjustment Act of 1944, or GI Bill, which also provided the low-cost housing loans that triggered new housing developments all over Long Island, including Levittown, a short car drive away from the campus. By the mid-1950s, with enrollment up to nearly six thousand students, there was urgent need for a new master plan to redefine the college's program.

The original plan for the sixty-eight-acre campus was designed by McKim, Mead & White. It consisted of six buildings in a setting conceived with landscape architect Helen Swift Jones, who arranged the planting of rows of elm trees, some of which still stand. The architects left plenty of site options in their master plan for additional buildings. No doubt they envisioned it filling out to become Long Island's version of their massive, cohesive design for Columbia University in upper Manhattan. But the reality turned out quite differently; in a rush to accommodate the boom in student enrollment after the war, the college trucked in a number of prefabricated buildings from the Army's Camp Upton in Yaphank, and a large, corrugated-metal Quonset hut, which was used as the college theater.

In 1956, a board-appointed selection committee ran a competition for the design of a Communications Center, to include a much-needed state-of-the-art library, radio and television facilities, and studios for recording and listening to tapes and records. An important member of the selection committee was Tex McCrary, the legendary public relations man and political strategist who had already done an impressive job marketing Roosevelt Field for William Zeckendorf and Levittown for William Levitt. McCrary and others knew that a conceptually dramatic design from a star architect would help boost the college's name recognition and fund-raising efforts. They also knew that a technologically innovative building would signal Adelphi's readiness to educate a generation intent on winning the Cold War, which was in full swing by the mid-1950s. One committee memorandum stated that the new campus master plan should allow Adelphi "to make a contribution to the emergency needs of the United States today for experts."[7]

The committee decided to seek an architectural firm that would lend prestige to the campus while breaking away from McKim, Mead & White's grand Beaux-Arts style. James A. Linen, president of Time Inc., was on the Adelphi board at the time, and soon to become its president. He introduced the committee to his staff at *Architectural Forum*, a Time Inc. publication, and they put together a list of sixteen recommended architects.[8]

The list read like a who's who of the American architectural vanguard: Marcel Breuer and Associates; Chapman, Evans & Delehanty; Harrison & Abramovitz; Ludwig Mies van der Rohe; I. M. Pei for Webb and Knapp; Richard Neutra; Pereira & Luckman; O'Connor & Kilham; Moore & Hutchins; Shepley Bulfinch Richardson & Abbott; Skidmore, Owings & Merrill; Eero Saarinen and Associates; Urbahn, Brayton & Burrows; Minoru Yamasaki; and Frank Lloyd Wright. The college invited all of these firms, as well as Kelly & Gruzen, Welton Becket and Associates, Edward Durell Stone, and Watterson and Watson to meet with the committee. Among this constellation of architectural stars, the

Adelphi University, Garden City, 1957–67. Presentation perspective drawing. Connectivity to the world at large is the theme for a library and communications center, with a "Time Space" gate in the form of an enormous, illuminated, translucent globe in the building's atrium.

173

Entrance to Swirbul Library soon after its opening in 1963—a pared-down version of the elaborate prior proposals.

winners were Neutra and his partner Robert Alexander for their overall conception and schematic drawings, and Urbahn, Brayton & Burrows, who were chosen as the local firm to execute the project from their Manhattan office. The runners-up in the competition were Edward Durell Stone's firm and Kelly & Gruzen.[9]

Neutra and Alexander's presentation tremendously impressed the committee "with its imagination and comprehension of design,"[10] to use the committee's words. A practiced showman, Neutra knew how to engage the committee members and persuade them to embrace his wildly ambitious proposal. With a set of vivid color crayon drawings, some beautifully rendered by him, and elaborately written and diagrammed preliminary study pamphlets, he presented a master plan consisting of fifteen new buildings, many more than the competition for a Communications Center called for, several of them clustered into five interrelated institutes.

The Institute of Communication Arts was the key complex among them, the others being the Institute of Business and Commerce, the Institute

of Health, Education and Welfare, the Institute of Man, and the Institute of Science and Industry. As Neutra wrote in one of his illustrated brochures, "Communication between human beings full and unwarped, whether these beings are close or distant around the globe and beyond the far ranges of the past—communication in the broadest sense is at the core of education."[11] The Institute of Communication Arts consisted of two buildings, the first a rectangular three-story "Living Library" with an entrance atrium and the second an adjacent tear-drop-shaped "World in Focus Auditorium"[12] with three hundred seats and equipped with movie projectors and "closed circuit T-V" for televised interviews from "The Adelphi Room" at the Waldorf=Astoria Hotel in Manhattan. The Institute would function, Neutra wrote, "as a Service Center for all the Institutes of the College, as well as the surrounding community and industries."[13]

In this initial design proposal, Neutra enticed students to become active participants in the Pax Americana, as they approached the "Living Library" along an adjacent elevated walkway and entered the glass-walled atrium. Indoors, the walk

Adelphi University, Garden City, 1957–67. Swirbul Library, "Ascent to Wisdom" stairway. The gray-blue propeller balustrades and bed of greenery were signature devices of Neutra's California buildings. The mirrored wall creates the illusion of a sweeping, baroque double stair, a successful bow to budgetary restrictions.

continued on a bridge through the "Time Space" gate, an enormous, translucent, illuminated globe, with the topography of the world in full relief on the inside. This globe promised an intense spatial and sensory experience upon entry and, visible from across campus, was meant to be a beacon promoting internationalism and Adelphi's connectivity to the world at large. Electrification allowed for a sound system and lighting to show the world's hot spots, air travel routes, and a clock that ringed the space and showed the time in different time zones. Once out of this cartographic-cum-architectural space, initiates next encountered Associated Press ticker-tape machines and carrels, where selected stories were projected on screens. Also in the plan were long-distance telephone booths, so students could conduct interviews with sources overseas. Neutra envisioned students going on foreign study tours, so he included a travel agency, at a time when air travel was prohibitively expensive and the so-called junior year abroad was a rare opportunity bestowed on only a few exceptional students.

Neutra's futuristic vision for the center wowed the administration. For the next three years, Neutra and Alexander engaged in amiable, prolific correspondence with the administration and mailed blueprints from the firm's Glendale, California, office. They also visited the campus on a number of occasions. Their trips east had a dual purpose, as the firm was also designing the Gettysburg Cyclorama Center in Pennsylvania for the National Park Service. When visiting the campus, the Neutras stayed at the grand Garden City Hotel, sometimes for a week or two, and got to know the college well. Their son, architect Dion Neutra, worked as the project architect for the Communications Center, from the California office.

Neutra's method of conferring was to get committees in a room for an entire day to brainstorm, while he took voluminous notes. As Dean William Condon remembered, "He wanted our full attention, so at his insistence we met in a locked room, with lunch already there on the table. He was a talented humanist who liked to gather a warehouse of ideas by leading discussion in many directions. His ultimate desire was to make sure his buildings reflected the ideas of the institution, as much as his own, although for him the students' educational experience was paramount."[14] President Eddy and his wife took advantage of the Neutras' presence by hosting soirees to introduce the celebrated couple to prospective donors. At these events, Richard was the center of attention, until Dion gave them the pleasure of near virtuoso cello performances.

Fundraising for Neutra's Communications Center did not match its ambitious reach, not for lack of enthusiasm from the college; until 1960 the college administration seemed to want to go ahead with the entire proposal. In 1961, however, the decision was made to break ground for the library building only, the Swirbul Communications Center and Living Library, named for Jake Swirbul, the recently deceased cofounder of the Grumman Aircraft Engineering Corporation and an Adelphi board member. His sudden death prompted such an influx of donations, mostly from Grumman employees, that there were finally enough funds to start construction. He was much liked by his employees, and important, as corroborated by Admiral George Anderson, Chief of Naval Operations for the United States, who was the main speaker at the library's dedication ceremony.

The finished library building, which opened in 1963 after seven years of planning, is a most decent version of the many elegant modular schools, office buildings, and clinics Neutra and Alexander had designed in California. Based on a grid consisting of a series of open 22½-foot-square concrete frame modules placed side by side to form a rectangle, the two-story concrete, brick, and glass building was designed to be a flexible space inside and easy to add onto on its solid concrete west façade. The building envelope is a combination of opposites, with each façade different from the others. The windows on the south façade are protected from temperature changes and sunlight by a system of automatically controlled, anodized aluminum louvers, which Neutra first used in 1946 for the famous Kaufmann Desert House in Palm Springs, California. The louvers give the south façade a distinct rhythm and modern appeal, in dynamic contrast to the static materiality of the entrance façade, which is faced with a protruding slab of white textured concrete and a wall of red soldier bricks to echo the brick McKim, Mead & White buildings on campus. The north façade is a sheer curtain wall of glass, with the spandrels between the windows arranged in rectangular panels of milky brown, mocha, and beige, Neutra's signature colors.

As Neutra wrote, "An architect cannot forget about the future, which does not stand still. Swirbul Library can double with Adelphi; it can double in all idealism unimpeded."[15] The architect anticipated that any additions to the library would be built by his own firm, but an addition was added to the west end in 1986 by Long Island–based architect Ted Bindrim. Incidentally, Bindrim ran his practice out of the small barn that Mies van der Rohe adapted beautifully in 1954 for the artist Mary Callery (see page 223). As he recalled, "The President wanted an anonymous addition, meant to be a giant book file."[16]

In 1977, Gropius's firm TAC, The Architects Collaborative, designed an elaborate addition to Swirbul that involved demolishing Neutra and Alexander's entry vestibule, which pushes out from the building box. This addition was never built, fortunately, so the original Neutra entrance, with its glass front wall and glass curtain wall opposite, as well as the surrounding landscaping remain intact, including a rectangular reading courtyard, with its original plantings, and two pools and a waterfall that can be seen upon entering the building and from the south windows of the library. Neutra asked for a gently sloping berm to the south and at the entrance, a kind of earthworks on what had been flat Long Island prairie. Visitors have to ascend to enter the building and then cross a bridge over a narrow moat that is connected with the pool system. Neutra's attention to the outdoors and his penchant for a constant interaction with Nature are

Adelphi University, Garden City, 1957–67. South side of Swirbul Library, soon after its opening in 1963, and before plantings created a shaded reading courtyard.

present in the building, as in all of his architecture, with views from window walls of the plantings on patios on either side of the building and of the greenery-laden built-in planters in the interior courtyards.

Once Neutra knew that the Time Space gate was no longer in play, his rhetoric changed from the theme of internationalism and modern communication to nature and the quest for knowledge in an atmosphere of calm reflection. As he said in a lecture at Adelphi, "Quiet and lasting shapes, not novelty of fashion, must be the background of world literature and should tune the interior of a library to the needs of our sensitiveness, making it a soul-anchorage place. This makes it a living library, even if it doesn't have a news ticker and a stock exchange ticker to draw people in to it."[17]

To the left of the lobby Neutra installed a massive freestanding staircase, with the same gray-blue airplane-propeller balustrades that he had used in some of his California buildings. He originally wanted a double staircase, but when the cost proved prohibitive, he created the illusion of one with a mirrored wall, from which he hung a headlight lamp, not unlike the two Model A headlights he installed in 1929 at the Lovell Health House, to signify modernity.

The gentle ascent to reach the entrance was the beginning of an ascent to knowledge, but a walk up the staircase was, in his words, an ascent to "wisdom": "Ascent to wisdom is not so much straight as spiraled. That is how I tried to design that stairway. The entering reader sees this stairway doubled by illusion—seemingly a bridge under whose arch green plants grow, bloom in color, and accompany his passage to the offerings of the main reading room. This quiet, lastingly shaped space opens through a transparent glass front into a play of seasonal changes in a garden court. When, as readers, we ever so often raise our head from the book, we must refresh our eyes by distant accommodation, resting them on trees, and those colorful perennials of nature."[18]

The library in its first incarnation was a place of quiet contemplation, with simple, low-key interior decor. Individual study carrels lined the window walls and students sat in straw-backed chairs by Marcel Breuer either at the carrels or at long tables with chrome legs rather than wooden ones, which Neutra believed would not provide a sense of lightness. The senior library staff occupied glass-walled offices adjacent to the garden courts. The stacks stood in long, rectangular rows in the middle of the building, both upstairs and down. In line with his biorealistic principles, the palette of materials was warm and intended to harmonize with the outdoor greenery: white Formica for table- and desktops, blond woods for chairs and the veneer at the end walls of the stacks. The floors were beige linoleum or a terra-cotta wall-to-wall Berber wool carpeting. An array of colors for the interior walls, mostly blues, yellows, and beiges with names such as bayberry, foxglove, and raffia tan, were all carefully worked out with Emily Malino Associates. Malino chose the fabrics, as well as furniture from Knoll, which she and Neutra recommended to the library's staff and faculty committee.

The calm, contemplative atmosphere of the interior of the building lasted until computer stations became necessary, after which the college administration decided to convert much of the second-story space into an Information Commons, with computer stations and comfortable sofas for student study groups. The downstairs space was turned into a lounge and a much larger reference desk was installed. Neutra and Alexander's carefully thought-out interior plan has been changed; even the A. Conger Goodyear Special Collections Room was dismantled upstairs for more open space. Neutra must have been disappointed when his original futuristic schemes for the Communications Center were pared down but glad to see Swirbul Library built as an elegant, functional modern addition to the campus. With the benefit of hindsight, his early schemes can now be understood as architectural analogues to the interactivity of the Web and a testament to Neutra as a great visionary thinker.

The building housing the School of Business, completed in 1968, was also designed by Neutra and Alexander's firm and built by the New York City firm of John Shober Burrows Jr., on the very spot specified in Neutra and Alexander's masterplan drawings from the late 1950s. Their association with this building became almost undetectable, however, after it was drastically altered in the late 1980s; when Dion Neutra visited the campus, he merely stood silent in front of it.[19] The Swirbul Library has been changed also, but it remains very much a Neutra building, a wonderful showplace for many of his signature devices.

Adelphi University, Garden City, 1957–67. Swirbul Library. Each of the building's façades is different. As seen here, the east façade is clad in concrete and red vertical bricks; the north façade is a sheer glass curtain wall with horizontal panels of milky brown, mocha, and beige. The walls of the projecting reading court are brick.

16

WILLIAM LESCAZE 1896–1969

Calderone Theatre, Hempstead, 1945–49;
Spinney Hill Houses, Manhasset, 1947–52;
Harbor Homes, Port Washington, 1950–52;
Pond View Homes, Manhasset, 1956;
Laurel Homes, Roslyn, 1956;
Dune Deck Hotel, Westhampton Beach, 1952

n 1945, Dr. Frank Calderone, whose family owned cinemas and stage theaters across Nassau County, hatched plans for a flagship venue in Hempstead. To design a visually striking, luxuriously appointed building complex that would become a destination for area audiences and would represent the Calderone brand, he called on William Lescaze, the Swiss-born, New York–based architect known as one of the pioneers of modernism in the United States. Calderone wanted a theater that would rival any in the Northeast and his choice of Lescaze reflected his desire for a work of architecture that would convey a level of sophistication not commonly found in popular entertainment.

Lescaze had a well-established practice by the 1940s, producing office buildings, theaters, public-housing projects, and houses for affluent clients in and around New York City and Philadelphia. On Long Island, Lescaze executed six projects, including a beachfront hotel and four low-income housing complexes in addition to the Calderone Theatre. His Long Island projects were of a smaller scale and are much less known today than his Philadelphia Savings Fund Society (PSFS) bank and office tower in Philadelphia, which rocketed him to fame, the Williamsburg Houses in Brooklyn, or the CBS Columbia Square studios in Los Angeles. But they reflect the same commitment to European modernism that made him one of the most renowned American architects of the 1930s and 1940s.

After completing his architectural training in Zurich and emigrating to the United States

in 1920, Lescaze quickly worked his way from unknown draftsman to internationally renowned architect. His first major commission was the 1929 PSFS tower, which he designed in partnership with George Howe. Described by Philip Johnson and Henry-Russell Hitchcock in their 1932 exhibition on architectural modernism at the Museum of Modern Art as the first ever International Style skyscraper, the building immediately established Lescaze's reputation as a leading American architect and a technical innovator. The steel-framed, severely rectilinear tower, with a shiny granite base, aluminum and stainless-steel windows, and gorgeous, colorful marble surfaces in its main banking hall and hallways, was topped with an iconic, red neon "PSFS" sign. Everyone knew that PSFS was primarily designed by Lescaze and that he had been brought into the partnership to provide a modern syntax. The building amounted to the most ambitious appropriation of European modernist principles in American architecture to date and helped initiate a dramatic shift in national taste. According to architectural historian William Jordy, "American acceptance of the International Style" began with the PSFS building.[1]

During the Depression, Lescaze remained productive. Among his projects of this period were several pavilions at the 1939 New York World's Fair and the New Deal–funded Williamsburg Houses in Brooklyn, one of the first public-housing projects in the United States. He also managed to find private clients interested in cutting-edge design. His own

Calderone Theatre, Hempstead, 1945–49. Presentation drawing, Calderone Theatre and mixed-use retail/office complex, Hempstead, 1945. Lescaze designed an all-white, International Style concrete building complex in the manner of the studio complex he built for CBS in Los Angeles, 1936.

181

1933 townhouse and office, a sleek white structure with enormous glass-block windows, described in the *New Yorker* as the first modernist residence in the city, led to a number of commissions for townhouses and suburban villas. Another major facet of his activity in the 1930s was his work for the entertainment industry, especially theater design.

Lescaze's interest in theaters dated back to his student days at the ETH Zurich, where he chose to design a theater within a multi-use commercial complex as his diploma project. In 1931, he designed newsreel movie theaters for the Trans-Lux chain in New York and Philadelphia. When the film industry was trying to woo its dwindling audience back from television in the early 1950s, the Cinerama company hired Lescaze to renovate a series of theater interiors in New York, Los Angeles, Detroit, Chicago, and Philadelphia.

In 1934, Lescaze became the house architect for CBS, designing the rapidly growing company's radio broadcast theaters in cities across the country. These theaters consisted of sound stages and seating for live audiences, who helped make the "theater of the air" seem more tangible to listeners at home. Lescaze's radio production interiors were highly functional; the materials, the angles of walls and ceilings, the positioning and design of seating, and even the light fixtures were all designed with acoustical considerations in mind. His approach was influenced by broadcasting studios designed in the early 1930s for the BBC in England by Wells Coates, Serge Chermayeff, Erich Mendelsohn, and Raymond McGrath.[2] After renovating the CBS headquarters in Manhattan, Lescaze was commissioned to design a four-building facility in Hollywood, which included a five-story office building with a projecting, curvilinear sign advertising station KNX, street-level stores, and a restaurant with a curved glass window. Audience members entering the 1,500-seat theater for live on-air performances could see into the station's master control booth, which had thick plate-glass walls curving out into the complex's colorful main entrance hall.

CALDERONE THEATRE

After World War II, Lescaze's business slowed somewhat, so the Calderone Theatre commission must have been especially welcome. The project also provided him with an opportunity to return to theater design.

The Calderone family had been in the theater business since Dr. Calderone's father, Salvatore, a Sicilian immigrant, began operating vaudeville theaters for working-class audiences on Manhattan's Lower East Side in the first decade of the twentieth century. In 1911, Salvatore Calderone made his first foray onto Long Island, buying and renovating the Strand Theatre in Hempstead, which attracted soldiers from nearby Mitchel Field. Over the next twenty years, he built up a chain of Long Island venues, including the Rivoli in Hempstead and theaters in Glen Cove, Lynbrook, Valley Stream, and Mineola. The Calderone theaters were located along trolley lines to attract customers without cars. Each had a full stage, an orchestra pit, an organ, and a comfortable lounge area, and the program was usually a mix of film and vaudeville or musical productions. Salvatore often situated his theaters within multi-use complexes that incorporated apartments and stores to generate additional fixed income. Frequently, he provided an apartment for the theater's manager and his family.

Toward the end of his life, Salvatore Calderone is said to have told his son Frank, "I know you want to be a doctor, but you've got to keep these theaters going. You owe it to the audiences."[3] In 1924, after finishing his training as a physician, Frank Calderone took a four-year leave from medicine to manage the family business. He eventually went on to become an authority on public health and served as an early leader of the World Health Organization. He attributed his abilities as an administrator to what he had learned organizing staff and talent at his family's theaters.

As a theater manager, Frank Calderone most likely knew of Lescaze's work for Trans-Lux and CBS. It is also likely that the men met socially. Calderone's wife, Mary, herself a physician and pioneer in the field of reproductive rights and birth control, was the daughter of photographer Edward Steichen. Steichen had worked closely with photographer, writer, and social activist Dorothy Norman, who often held gatherings at her Lescaze-designed townhouse on East 74th Street in Manhattan. Calderone may well have been introduced to the architect at one of Norman's parties.

When he hired Lescaze, Calderone had grand ambitions to establish a major regional attraction on Hempstead's busiest shopping street. Because

Long Island's ever-expanding network of expressways was creating a more mobile customer base, he believed that a distinctive venue would attract customers from a wide radius of towns. Wanting his theater to rival Radio City Music Hall or even the CBS facility in Hollywood in size and allure, he envisioned a stylish multi-use complex, incorporating a stage, a cinema, shops, and offices.

The original scheme had to be altered somewhat when an underground stream was discovered during excavation, making it impossible to build the foundation necessary to support a proscenium stage for theatrical productions. Lescaze had to reconfigure the auditorium to serve primarily as a movie theater. But the essential multi-use concept remained. The two-part complex consisted of a tall auditorium structure rising above a long, low façade with shops at ground level and offices on the second floor. The theater, which seated 2,500, was the largest cinema built in the New York area since the war. It was unmatched from the standpoint of comfort and technology, with air conditioning, spacious, lavishly appointed ladies' and gentlemen's lounges, and the first-ever escalator installed in a theater in the United States.

For the exterior, Lescaze employed an International Style vocabulary of rectangular volumes and horizontal strips of windows. Engineered by Fred Severud, later the structural engineer for Eero Saarinen's Gateway Arch in St. Louis, the complex was supported by a steel frame and faced with red brick and hollow tile. Especially important to the complex's formal character was its illumination. Like the German modernist Erich Mendelsohn, whose department-store designs of the 1920s Lescaze admired, he gave the exterior a striking effect at night, when illuminated windows turned the façade into bands of light and dark. Above the ground-floor shop windows, the second story seemed to float, and the window that stretched its length appeared as an unbroken ribbon of light.

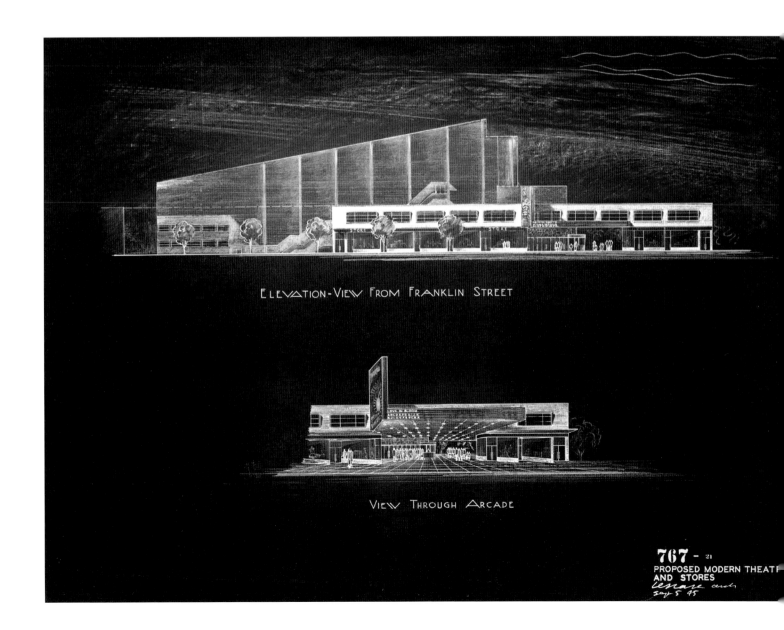

Calderone Theatre, Hempstead, 1945–49. Presentation drawing. Elevation and perspective view through an arcade, 1945. The façade fronting the sidewalk features a modern, rectilinear design in white concrete.

Calderone Theatre, Hempstead, 1945–49. Drawing, Calderone Theatre complex, as built, 1945. The all-brick façades were no doubt Lescaze's concession to a traditional-minded planning board and community.

In a 1950 article on lighting and theater design, Lescaze stated his belief that "artificial lighting, form and color should be combined into a single entity."[4] Throughout the interior of the Calderone Theatre, light and color played an essential role in giving the space visual drama. When customers passed under the marquee, past the aluminum-framed glass ticket booth, and into the vestibule, they entered a space flanked on one side by a wall of cobalt blue Belgium marble and on the other by a wall of Madre Cream Alabama marble. The lighter, cerulean blue ceiling was dotted with a matrix of recessed downlights, "spaced further and further apart as the inner portion of the lobby is approached, reducing the intensity of the lighting gradually, to effect a transition from outdoors to the inside. All of these spot lights recessed in the blue ceiling resemble, in a way, stars in the sky."[5] Ticket holders proceeded from the vestibule down a sloping floor, through two sets of aluminum-framed glass doors and into the grand, double-height lobby. Walls of solid golden yellow and blue, red cylindrical structural columns, and gray ceilings, all painted in high gloss, gave the space the abstract look and clearly defined colors of the Dutch de Stijl movement, a key proponent of which was Piet Mondrian. The space was lit by giant, concave, disclike fixtures in the ceiling.

One of the most distinctive features of Lescaze's interior was the escalator that rose from the lobby up to the balcony level. Although tickets for balcony seating were more expensive, the novelty of riding the escalator, along with the fact that smoking was permitted only in the upper-level lounge, made the balcony the most popular choice. As customers ascended the escalator, flanked by a black marble wall on one side and a wide staircase with slender aluminum railings on the other, a mirrored wall straight ahead reflected the sixty-foot-wide mosaic mural above the entrance doors, which could also be seen as a reflection when ticket holders entered the building. The mural was created by Max Spivak, a student of Arshile Gorky. Spivak began his career decorating schools and post offices for the Works Progress Administration (WPA). The enormous mural featured abstract, loopy shapes, including one that resembled a giant hotdog, in bright colors that complemented Lescaze's chromatic scheme and the aubergine walls of the

Calderone Theatre, Hempstead, 1945–49. Grand lobby, with sixty-foot-wide mosaic mural by Max Spivak. With its gray ceilings, yellow and blue walls, red columns, and even cobalt blue on the elevator casing, the double-height space made reference to an anti-cubic giant, three-dimensional De Stijl structure.

OPPOSITE
Calderone Theatre, Hempstead, 1945–49. Smoking lounge. Top-tier tickets were the most expensive but popular, because they afforded moviegoers the opportunity to ride the first ever escalator in an American movie theater and to smoke, both in the lounge and in the theater.

Calderone Theatre, Hempstead, 1945–49. Opening night. From left, poet Carl Sandburg, an unidentified woman, architect William Lescaze, and photographer Edward Steichen, father-in-law of the theater's owner, Frank Calderone.

upstairs smoking lounge. The mural was fabricated by a team of craftsmen from the DePaoli Mosaic Company in Long Island City, who were trained in the ancient Byzantine technique of tesserae mosaics.

Lescaze's striking use of light and color continued inside the auditorium. The walls were covered with huge red, green, yellow, and blue panels. Fluorescent bulbs concealed behind the panels created a subtle glow. Beneath the panels was wainscoting veneered in Hawaiian koa wood. The movie screen was mounted in a red lacquered frame, with strips of red and yellow incandescent lighting around it. Lescaze draped the screen with bright yellow fiberglass curtains and spotlighted them before the show. From the projection room, which had thirty-five dimmer switches and three projectors, operators not only changed the film reels but also manipulated the auditorium lighting, to create the desired atmosphere. Lighting hues were warmed up or cooled down, depending on the genre of movie being shown and the season. Reds were used in winter, cool colors in summer, and leaf colors in fall. Remote controls regulated other flourishes, including the opening and closing of two additional curtains besides the yellow one.

Floors in both the lobby and the auditorium were covered in a red carpet with a swirling plant-tendril pattern in gray. Lescaze, who was a prolific furniture designer and created unique pieces to complement many of his larger architectural commissions, was not given the budget to design seating for the Calderone Theatre. Instead, he chose stock chairs and side tables from the Herman Miller company to furnish the lobby areas. For the auditorium, he installed Bodiform spring-back chairs upholstered in a cocoa-colored fabric.

On opening night in June 1949, a brochure proudly announced the Calderone Theatre as "the largest and most beautiful post-war theatre in America . . . Modern as tomorrow."[6] The large crowd attending the opening night celebration included such prominent figures as Frank Calderone's father-in-law, Edward Steichen, and the celebrated American poet Carl Sandburg, who was married to Steichen's sister Lilian. Afterward, people continued to come from all over western Long Island to attend the movies but also to ride the escalator and enjoy the lavish atmosphere. Dr. Calderone, who believed that theater going should offer "a little pleasure in life at its best,"[7] staffed his theater with a manager, who greeted customers on Friday and Saturday nights in a tuxedo, and a cadre of smartly dressed ushers to complement the elegance of Lescaze's design.[8]

The theater prospered for about fifteen years, but staggeringly high fixed operating costs, including taxes, heating, and air conditioning, eventually made it impossible to sustain. Nationwide, cinema attendance began to plummet, dropping 22 percent between 1948 and 1949,[9] and the grand movie palaces that had flourished since the silent-film era began to die out. Also, after Roosevelt Field and other shopping malls opened, people flocked to theaters there. In the late 1960s, Dr. Calderone sold the family's theaters to the Associated Independent Theatres chain,[10] which soon thereafter went bankrupt. The end of the Calderone Theatre as a feature-film venue came in 1972. Ironically, its last screening was of the Oscar-winning blockbuster *The Godfather*, which packed the house. Used as a rock-concert venue for a while, then converted to a multiplex, and finally taken over in 1998 by a church, the complex lost many of its original features and its once grand atmosphere. Nevertheless, much of Lescaze's original design remains intact in the interior behind partitions and dropped ceilings or otherwise in plain view.

PUBLIC-HOUSING PROJECTS

In addition to theater design, another field that occupied Lescaze throughout his career was public housing. Influenced by the social concerns of European modernism, he began designing subsidized public housing in the 1930s, when New Deal financing supported the first such developments in the United States. He first achieved recognition in the field in 1932, when he, George Howe, and Albert Frey were asked by Philip Johnson and Henry-Russell Hitchcock to exhibit a model of their Chrystie-Forsyth Street Housing Development in the Museum of Modern Art's 1932 International Style exhibition. Lescaze solidified his standing as a public-housing designer after the completion in 1938 of the 1,622-unit Williamsburg Houses in Brooklyn, the country's first large-scale public-housing project, for which he served as chief designer. An astute politician, from 1949 to 1959 Lescaze sat on the New York State Building Code Commission, which did not preclude him from employment by state-funded agencies, such as the North Hempstead Housing Authority.

The five-person authority was set up in 1946 to address appallingly unsanitary and dilapidated housing clusters within the township, which had jurisdiction over some of the most affluent commuter suburbs in the country. To get five new low-rent housing projects under way in unincorporated areas in Manhasset, Port Washington and Roslyn, the authority needed to do a convincing job of justifying them to the townspeople and to state and federal grant committees. A group of local volunteers, under the supervision of a New York State Division of Housing economist, produced a town-wide survey of substandard housing. They documented a ramshackle village in deplorable condition on Spinney Hill in Manhasset, which was only a quarter of a mile away from the gatehouse to Greentree, then Jock Whitney's 500-acre horse farm. Similar

Spinney Hill Houses, Manhasset, 1947–52. Officials from the Town of North Hempstead. April 17, 1954. A rendering of the recently built Spinney Hill Houses hangs on the wall behind them.

Spinney Hill Houses, Manhasset, 1947–52. As-built drawing of Spinney Hill Houses, April 1950.

OPPOSITE
Spinney Hill Houses, Manhasset, 1947–52. The redwood siding, ample windows, and overhanging roof lend visual interest to the simple architecture. The new plantings are by landscape architect Leo A. Novick, 1952.

slum conditions were found in an area of Harbor Hill, outside Port Washington and across the road from the large cast-iron gates of Solomon Guggenheim's 250-acre estate, originally known as Villa Carola. The extensive report documented, among other things, the absence of indoor plumbing and modern heating in many buildings, some of which were originally chicken coops and stables.

The housing authority's pitch to state and federal grant committees proved effective. In 1946, funding was secured to build 66 housing units on Harbor Hill in North Port Washington and 102 units on Spinney Hill. Lescaze was hired to design both developments. A few years later the housing authority commissioned Lescaze to design Pond View Homes in Manhasset and Laurel Homes in Roslyn as well. The housing authority also apparently succeeded in convincing local residents of the need for the low-rent housing. Commentary in local newspapers revealed no objections to it. Editorials and letters were enthusiastic and conveyed a sense of civic pride in the endeavor.

When Lescaze took on the North Hempstead housing projects, he designated one of his most trusted partners, Henry Alfred Dumper Jr., as project architect, as he had been for the Calderone Theatre. Dumper lived in Syosset, knew Nassau County inside and out, and his family was well connected in the area. His grandfather ran a large farm and pickle-processing business in Farmingdale and his architect father had designed civic buildings in Nassau, as well as warehouses along the Brooklyn waterfront in the last two decades of the nineteenth century. Dumper attended the meetings in the housing authority's Manhasset office and proved to be an effective liaison between the firm and public officials.[11]

Both Spinney Hill Houses and Harbor Homes are complexes of long, two-story, flat-roofed buildings set back from the street in large, parklike green spaces. Spinney Hill's steep slope allowed the architects to place the buildings on flat, graded areas, parallel to each other, but at a 15-degree angle to the street. Six uphill buildings are oriented southeast to northwest; the other four are oriented southwest to northeast. They are faced with red brick on the first story and horizontal redwood siding on the second. Costs were kept to a minimum, but as Lescaze wrote in a press release about Spinney Hill Houses, "We tried to make the buildings

Spinney Hill Houses, Manhasset, 1947–52. Cooking lesson at the community house demonstration kitchen, June 1952.

BELOW LEFT
Spinney Hill Houses, Manhasset, 1947–52. A typical kitchen, June 1952. Note the curtain-covered cupboards.

BELOW RIGHT
Spinney Hill Houses, Manhasset, 1947–52. A typical living room, June 1952.

look like homes, rather than institutions."[12] The architecture is decidedly plain, yet compared to the design of most of the public housing built at that time, these buildings have a level of detailing that keeps them from being monotonous. The redwood siding, as well as ample windows, overhanging roofs, and doors painted in bright primary colors all contributed visual interest. The interior design was also bare boned. Cupboards and closets had curtains instead of doors to keep costs down. But the units benefited from ample natural light and modern kitchens and bathrooms.

In the spirit of the Garden City movement, the landscape design was an integral part of the scheme for all of the housing communities that Lescaze designed, with shared spaces and walkways contributing to the enjoyment of the outdoors and sociability. Landscape architect Leo Novick designed the central green spaces and outdoor walkways for the developments. He had worked for the New York City Housing Authority before the war, and later for I. M. Pei & Associates' Kips Bay Plaza, among other important projects. A knowledgeable plants man, he used a wide variety of deciduous trees and evergreens. Parking lots were kept on the periphery of the developments, reserving interior areas for communal green space. The Spinney Houses site was particularly parklike, with buildings covering a mere 16 percent of its seven acres. The complex included two playgrounds and an outdoor patio area next to the community house. Pathways were well lit with fixtures that Lescaze designed with Claude R. Engle and Morris Shapiro, who went on to found the most widely used engineering firm for speculative suburban developments in the Washington, D.C., area. In addition to the communal outdoor spaces, each apartment had a designated plot for gardening. The New York State Division of Housing, which partially funded all of the projects, promoted the activity by distributing a booklet called "Hints on Tenant Gardening."

DUNE DECK HOTEL

The smallest of Lescaze's Long Island projects was a 1952 renovation and expansion of a hotel in Westhampton Beach. The original Dune Deck Hotel was a collection of somewhat dilapidated wood-framed structures located on the barrier island between the Atlantic and Moriches Bay. It was built in the early 1920s out of decommissioned World War I barracks, which had probably been purchased at auction from the Camp Upton military installation in Yaphank. In the late 1940s, the area was populated mostly in the summer, and the Dune Deck was one of few hotels. It drew a clientele from Long Island and New York City, as well as personnel from Suffolk County Air Force Base, which had opened inland in 1943 on nearby Riverhead Plain. At the time, Lescaze's firm was engaged with much larger projects, including an office tower on Third Avenue in Manhattan. How he came to take on this diminutive project is unknown. Perhaps Hyland Chester, the hotel's owner, had a personal connection to the architect. In any case, Lescaze seems to have been happy with the commission, as he allowed the results to be published in *Architectural Record*.[13]

The commission involved replacing one of the original barracks with a new guest-room building, expanding the hotel's dining room, and creating decks for lounging. Lescaze's new guest-room structure was a long, two-story white box in a minimal modernist style. The rooms were small, but each featured a private veranda and large plate-glass windows with views of the beach and the ocean. For the dining room in the main building, Lescaze added a space that juts out over the beach, supported by stilts. He also designed upper-level decks for lounging and sunbathing, with elegantly curving walls of vertical cedar siding.

In addition to these new structures, Lescaze refurbished the entire hotel with simple modernist interventions. He installed large windows to open up the façades, designed staircases with white metal banisters and wooden railings painted a vivid red, and outfitted the verandas with nautical ropes and sailcloth awnings. His changes to the interior included cork floors, plywood wall paneling, and modern Swedish furniture.

Following Lescaze's renovations, the hotel became a more fashionable destination and attracted prominent guests. Among the regulars was the cartoonist Charles Addams. In 1950, Addams bought a Victorian house not far from the

Dune Deck. He converted a double-height children's playhouse into a studio and let a thick hedge of poison ivy grow around it to ward off unwanted visitors. At the end of the day, he would often emerge from this eccentric workspace and relax at the Dune Deck bar.

While Lescaze was renovating the hotel, Hyland Chester asked Addams to create an artwork to adorn the hotel. The result was an ink-wash mural depicting his humorously ghoulish Addams Family picnicking and fishing at the beach. The mural, which hung in the bar, was an odd decorative complement to Lescaze's spare, white architecture, but apparently Chester liked the combination. In June 1952, he threw a party to celebrate the renovation of the bar with the unveiling of the mural. For the event, the owner had the barroom decorated with Addams-like Gothic touches and dubbed it the "Haunting Room." A crowd of cultural luminaries, including illustrator Ludwig Bemelmans, fashion designer Oleg Cassini, furniture designer George Nelson, and novelist John O'Hara attended the party, which featured hors d'oeuvres shaped like bats, octopi, and skulls.

Today the Dune Deck has lost some of the stylishness that characterized it in the period following Lescaze's renovations. The Addams mural was removed from the bar in 1990 by the hotel's owner, Walter Goldstein, who donated it to his alma mater, Pennsylvania State University. Yet the Dune Deck remains a comfortably unpretentious resort and Westhampton's favorite "watering hole."

OPPOSITE
Dune Deck Hotel, Westhampton Beach, 1952. Staircase to the hotel sundeck, above the dining room addition.

ABOVE
Dune Deck Hotel, Westhampton Beach, 1952. The hotel bar. Above the banquette, cartoonist Charles Addams's ink-wash mural *Addams Family Holiday*. Addams's house and studio were across the street from the Dune Deck, and he frequented the bar and restaurant almost every evening.

17
GORDON CHADWICK 1915–1980
WITH GEORGE NELSON 1908–1986

Holiday House, Quogue, 1950;
Julius and Anne Abeles House, Roslyn, 1954;
Otto and Eloise Spaeth House, East Hampton, 1956;
Rudolph and Ethel Johnson House, Montauk, 1962

George Nelson—editor, writer, and founder of the design firm George Nelson & Associates—was a preeminent representative of American modernism from the early 1940s until the end of the 1970s. Nelson wrote lively commentary on the pages of *Architectural Forum*, *Interiors*, *McCall's*, and many other periodicals. He also wrote several books about product and industrial design. He and his staff designers created practical yet witty and inventive furniture, office systems, household products, textiles, lighting, and graphics. Many of his products were sold through the Herman Miller showrooms around the country.

Nelson also maintained an architectural practice, though building design was perhaps the least significant of his professional pursuits. He left much of the responsibility for architectural projects to his partner, Gordon Chadwick. The lesser-known Chadwick joined Nelson in 1950. In 1953, the partners launched a new architecture division, which they named George Nelson and Gordon Chadwick Architects. It proved to be a productive partnership. Chadwick's reserve, practicality, and thoughtful, determined approach to the design process served as a counterpart to Nelson's exuberant creativity and energetic self-promotion. The projects they took on included a visitor's center at Colonial Williamsburg, exhibitions for the State Department, notably the American National Exhibition in Moscow, site of the infamous Nixon-

Khrushchev "kitchen debate" of 1959, and the Chelsea Passage section of Barneys New York's first store in lower Manhattan.

On Long Island, they were responsible for four houses, including a model weekend house commissioned by the travel magazine *Holiday*; the Abeles House, which was based on the Holiday House; and the larger Spaeth and Johnson beachfront houses. All four have at times been attributed to George Nelson alone. In every case, however, Chadwick played a primary role; indeed, he was the sole architect of the Spaeth and Johnson houses. Tellingly, these two houses are quite distinct from most of Nelson's own work, incorporating vernacular forms and rustic materials. In certain ways, Chadwick's architecture points away from Nelson's modernism toward elements of the postmodern architecture that began to emerge in the 1960s.

Nelson's engagement with modernism began in 1932, when he arrived at the American Academy in Rome with a grant for independent architectural study. Earlier that same year, the International Style exhibition at the Museum of Modern Art had drawn attention to European modernism. Nelson decided to use his time in Europe to visit some of the buildings featured in the exhibition and to seek out and interview their architects, including Mies van der Rohe, Le Corbusier, and Walter Gropius. Returning to New York in 1934, he was able to get the

Holiday House, Quogue, 1950. The Holiday House allowed the public to experience the new gadgetry and building materials of modern American living. The boxcar-shaped house is to the left. The arcade leading to the "Garden Room" is accessed from the path on the right.

legendary architecture and graphic design journal *Pencil Points* to publish his interviews, to which he added lively, incisive introductions. From there, he landed an entry-level writing job at the widely read professional journal *Architectural Forum*. Nelson quickly caught the attention of Henry Luce, owner of the journal's parent company, Time Inc. By 1935 Nelson was associate editor at "The Forum," and in 1943 he became co-managing editor.

In addition to his burgeoning journalistic career, by the mid-1930s Nelson had formed an architectural partnership with William Hamby in New York. In 1940, he and Hamby designed an innovative house in Manhattan for inventor and entrepreneur Sherman Fairchild that featured window walls overlooking a central courtyard. The project brought the partners substantial recognition, but Nelson parted ways with Hamby the following year to branch out into other areas of design. In 1945, D. J. DePree, the founder of Herman Miller, persuaded Nelson to become director of design for the company, the start of a long and productive relationship. The following year, Nelson founded his own design firm in Manhattan.

Gordon Chadwick, known as Chad, began his architectural career as an apprentice to Frank Lloyd Wright from 1938 to 1942. He apparently impressed Wright, who in 1939 made him project architect for the Pope-Leighey House, a modestly scaled Usonian dwelling in Falls Church, Virginia. Chadwick left Wright's office to enlist in the army. After the war, he served as head of the Monuments, Fine Arts, and Archives section of the United States Army in Germany. In 1948, at the conclusion of his army service, he began working for Nelson and quickly became an essential part of the firm. Chadwick was the only person to get attribution for his design contributions to the Nelson brand, and when the company moved in 1956 to larger quarters on 50th Street and Madison Avenue, only Chadwick and Nelson had private offices.

With their distinctly different personalities and working styles, Nelson and Chadwick assumed complementary roles in the design process. Nelson, although trained as an architect at Yale University, admitted to disliking the minutiae of architectural design and the endless communication required to manage a building project. His strength lay in attracting and working with clients and in the conceptual aspects of a project. Appearing frequently on the lecture circuit, Nelson wowed audiences with his charismatic speaking style and visually dynamic presentations. After securing commissions, he took charge of the initial contact with clients, who expected and liked to meet with him. Then Chadwick, who was less personally engaging but more adept at developing a project from an initial idea into a finished building, would take over the commission.[1]

HOLIDAY HOUSE

In 1950, a slow time for architectural commissions, Nelson and Chadwick were working on design concepts for prefabricated housing, but they were unable to find a manufacturer. Seeking new opportunities, the tireless Nelson approached the editors of *Holiday* magazine and convinced them to commission a prototypical vacation house that would put into practice design ideas that he had developed in his best-selling book *Tomorrow's House*, written with architect Henry Wright in 1945. Nelson was perhaps inspired by the exhibitions at the Museum of Modern Art of model houses by Marcel Breuer in 1949 and Gregory Ain in 1950. Like the museum showhouses, Nelson's model dwelling was meant to promote a new concept of modern domestic architecture and lifestyle that was affordable and suited to middle-class American families. And like the museum commissions, the Holiday house was conceived as a mutually beneficial arrangement among architect, host institution, and commercial manufacturers. Nelson would get a public forum for his architecture and furniture designs, and the magazine would receive an exclusive cover story on a major architectural event. Manufacturers would supply free building materials and home products in exchange for publicity, and would also become new advertisers in the magazine.

The result of this symbiotic collaboration was the Holiday House in Quogue, the closest to Manhattan of the East End's summer colonies, where Nelson owned a nineteenth-century inn that he and his family used as a country house. The Holiday House was located in the middle of a one-acre site, set a hundred feet back from Beach Drive, across from the Quogue Field Club. The house itself was "a kind of deluxe boxcar," a long, boxy, 20- x 100-foot volume constructed of concrete blocks insulated with Celotex sheeting and clad in stained-cedar siding. Inside, a central living room

Holiday House, Quogue, 1950. Dining area of the living room. All the furniture was designed by George Nelson & Associates.

was flanked by the kitchen and service spaces on one side and by bedrooms on the other. The bedrooms were reached by a narrow corridor lined with built-in cabinets below a high ribbon window, a configuration reminiscent of the Pope-Leighey House and other Usonian designs. The house's flat roof was pierced by several Plexiglas bubble skylights, a novel type of glazing that came out of the War Department's testing and use of Plexiglas for airplanes and easily assembled housing.

The design was meant to suit the kind of indoor-outdoor living and efficiency that was emerging in postwar America as a domestic ideal. Along the rear façade, off the master bedroom, large sliding glass doors opened onto an intimate garden space flanked on one side by an enclosed patio. Across the square front lawn, seen from the plate-glass windows of the main living rooms, was a semi-open pavilion, reached by an enclosed walkway, in the manner of Japanese house design. The pavilion was used for outdoor entertaining and for enjoying views of the lawn—essentially a large garden court—where the architects had left a grove of ailanthus trees. This lightweight pavilion structure, appointed with lounging and dining furniture, a kitchenette, and a built-in radio and television set, epitomized an informal modern lifestyle enhanced by both nature and technology.

When *Holiday* magazine opened the house to the public in June 1951, visitors came in droves and were fascinated by the house's many novel features. Perhaps most appealing were the technical gadgets, some seen for the first time as affordable products for the mass market, such as dimmers for indoor and outdoor lighting, an intercom, and motor-operated large-pane windows, draperies,

Holiday House,
Quogue, 1950.
The hallway to the
bedrooms is lined with
built-in storage cabinets.

ABOVE RIGHT
Holiday House,
Quogue, 1950.
Master bathroom
and dressing area.

RIGHT
Holiday House,
Quogue, 1950.
Dressing area closet.

OPPOSITE
Holiday House,
Quogue, 1950.
The master bedroom,
viewed from a patio.
The commodious closet
is on the far side of
the wall separating
the bedroom from
a dressing area.

Holiday House, Quogue, 1950. The modern kitchen. Walls of gray Marlite and red-brown mahogany paneling contrast with dusty blue metal cabinets and a dove-gray linoleum floor.

OPPOSITE TOP LEFT
Holiday House, Quogue, 1950. Space-saving cabinetry.

OPPOSITE BOTTOM LEFT
Holiday House, Quogue, 1950. A retractable typewriter for the busy housewife.

OPPOSITE TOP RIGHT
Holiday House, Quogue, 1950. A drawer-type refrigerator, ideal for a compact kitchen.

OPPOSITE BOTTOM RIGHT
Holiday House, Quogue, 1950. A serving trolley, an emblematically modern furniture staple of informal living.

Holiday House, Quogue, 1950. The "Garden Room," on the far side of the lawn, which is shaded by a grove of ailanthus trees.

and blinds. The house was for the family without a maid, explained the editors of *Holiday*. It was a house designed for a "button-pushing squire." In the kitchen, the refrigerator, stove, and dishwasher were all built into the counters, an arrangement that we take for granted today as a "fitted kitchen," but that at the time was a wholly new concept. Even the time-saving countertop appliances—toaster, electric mixer, small typewriter—which could be neatly tucked away behind sliding panels were exciting to the public. Although most Americans had replaced their iceboxes with electric refrigerators by the early 1950s, many families still did not have dishwashers, washing machines, or dryers. Kitchens were often poorly organized spaces in transition from the days when they had coal- or wood-fired stoves. Visitors were also struck by new design features such as sliding bamboo screens and

"Thru-Vu" nylon blinds, which could be adjusted for greater privacy or openness. Unexpected shots of bright yellow and blue, complementing warm, reddish mahogany paneling, accentuated the kitchen and living room cabinets and the bedroom walls. Formica and other synthetic materials were mixed with natural wood throughout the house. The furniture included pieces designed by Nelson and Ray and Charles Eames, whom Nelson had recruited to design for the Herman Miller company in the late 1940s.

ABELES HOUSE

As Nelson had hoped, the feature in *Holiday* generated plenty of publicity and brought numerous visitors to the house. Among them were Anne Abeles, an industrial design student at Cooper Union, and her husband, Julius, who had recently started a meat freezer storage business in Queens. The newly married couple, eager to move out of their apartment in Hempstead, wanted to build a modern house that could accommodate later additions to the family. Having studied with furniture and industrial designer Gilbert Rohde at New York University's College of Architecture and Arts, Anne Abeles was attracted to the Holiday House for its versatile, clever, stowaway storage elements and its openness to the outdoors. Moreover, George Nelson was one of her design heroes.

As she later recalled, Anne Abeles was intimidated by the prospect of meeting Nelson, and she and her husband hesitated for a year or so before contacting his firm.[2] Eventually they arranged to meet with the designer at his office on East 22nd Street in Manhattan. At their first meeting, Nelson suggested that they build a steel-frame house with panels made out of cemesto wallboard, which had first been used in experimental prefabricated building systems developed by Robert Davison and his team at the John B. Pierce Foundation in the 1930s. Nelson and Chadwick had been working on concepts for a low-cost modular house and

Holiday House, Quogue, 1950. Inside the "Garden Room." Orlon acrylic fiber drops serve as flexible walls.

Julius and Anne Abeles House, Roslyn, 1954. The exterior of the rectilinear house, here seen from the driveway, belies the light-filled, cleverly planned spaces within. The screened corridor on the second level, above the front entrance and garage, permits light, breezes, and views into the bedrooms.

they hoped that the Abeles commission would afford them the opportunity to build a prototype. Nelson had his eye on land in Pennsylvania, where he wanted to build an entire community.

When preliminary drawings arrived, the design, a rectangle like the Holiday House, was very much to the Abeleses' liking. They had a fixed budget of $20,000, however, and when the plans were put to bid, local contractors wanted $100,000 or more, mainly because of the custom-designed metal framing. The couple mulled over what to do for two years. Anne Abeles thought about contacting Frank Lloyd Wright after seeing his model Usonian house at the exhibition Sixty Years of Living Architecture, a retrospective of Wright's work, which opened in October 1953 on the plot of land the Guggenheim family had purchased for its eventual museum building. All the while, Julius Abeles had been talking to contractors about building the Nelson and Chadwick design with more affordable wood framing. When he found someone willing to do the job within their budget, he contacted Nelson to ask if he would give up the original steel-frame and cemesto concept.

The project was turned over to Chadwick, who took a keen interest in giving the Abeleses what they wanted, doing it efficiently, and adhering to their budget. "Even though I knew how to read drawings, we were not privy to the design process," Anne Abeles remembered during an interview. "Probably our limited budget made Chadwick want to expedite things. Things moved fast. He was quick and efficient by nature, although he paid close attention, visited numerous times, and was involved with every detail. George Nelson popped in for a five minute walk-through after the house had been completed in July of 1954, to give his final approval."[3] Nelson's one suggestion was that the Abeleses build a fence to create an outdoor room and to block the view of a more traditional house going up next door. Shortly thereafter, their general contractor received a drawing of an eight-foot louvered fence, just like one at the Holiday House, from Chadwick.

The house was built on a steeply sloping,

heavily wooded half-acre lot found by the Abeleses in Roslyn Estates, not far from the North Shore village of Roslyn in North Hempstead. The housing development, which sat on the highest point on Long Island, began in 1906 with traditional houses on large lots along winding roads. Working with a hillside site must have been a familiar challenge for Chadwick, as he had been apprenticing with Frank Lloyd Wright while Fallingwater was being built into a rocky embankment over a stream in Bear Run, Pennsylvania. Like many of Wright's designs, the Abeles House is positioned so that it projects out over the hillside. A 30- x 60-foot flat-roofed rectangular box clad in gray wood siding, it is approached from below.

The visitor first encounters a two-story façade, the lower story of which is painted a vivid turquoise. On the second level, a narrow screened walkway adjacent to the bedrooms projects out over the garage and the front door. Its underside, painted a bright red, shelters the entrance. The otherwise unassuming entry leads to service spaces and a wooden stairway straight up to the main living and sleeping rooms. As in the Holiday House, living spaces are compact but open to the outdoors. Large windows and Plexiglas bubble skylights bring in daylight. Doors in the rear façade open onto patios and lawn. Other design features shared with the Holiday House are mahogany paneling, bright-colored walls and furnishings, accordion screens, built-in storage, and recessed lighting. The kitchen cabinetry and counters were originally faced with white Formica and dark mahogany, and one of its walls was back-to-back with the mahogany-clad wall of the living room. Sliding shoji screens separated the kitchen from the dining area on one side and from the hallway on the other. Nelson and Chadwick proposed designing the kitchen as an open "workspace," meant to put the housewife at the center of domestic activities. But when Anne Abeles resisted the idea, the sliding screens, made of laminated fabric stretched across mahogany frames, were offered as a compromise.

The shoji screens, along with other Japanese-inspired elements, appeared elsewhere as well, becoming a kind of leitmotif of the design. In the living room, the same sliding screens were installed parallel to the wide-pane glass windows,

Julius and Anne Abeles House, Roslyn, 1954. Dining area, with kitchen to the left. Shoji-type sliding screens can close off the kitchen and provide privacy at the windows. The cabinetry and "saucer" bubble lamp are by George Nelson & Associates.

to filter light during the day and replace the need for curtains or blinds. The hard, polished concrete floors in the entry hall were covered with woven straw mats, a westernized version of the tatami mats used for the flooring of traditional Japanese houses. In June 1954, just about the time the Abeleses occupied their new house, the Japanese Exhibition House opened in the sculpture garden at the Museum of Modern Art, initiating a craze of sorts, promoted by house magazines, for incorporating Japanese elements into American homes. Nelson and Chadwick's design was thus ahead of its time. Nelson had visited Japan in 1951 for the first time, and was enormously impressed by traditional Japanese architecture. Most likely, the Japanese features in the Abeles House were his idea.

Anne Abeles recalled that the Village of Roslyn Heights's planning board tried to prohibit the construction of her modern house but found no legal recourse. Soon after she and her husband moved in, local gossip reached her by way of a boy scout who had stopped to admire the latest addition to the neighborhood. "Everybody talks about your house because it looks like a shoe box," she remembered him saying. Coming inside, the young man expressed his amazement at how light and bright it was, with the skylights and touches of bright yellow. "But I think it's wonderful in here!"[4]

SPAETH HOUSE

In 1955, Otto and Eloise Spaeth asked the Nelson-Chadwick partnership to design a house overlooking East Hampton's Two Mile Hollow Beach, not far from the Maidstone Club. The Spaeths had bought land on what everyone used to call the "eastern plains" of the village from a family who had farmed potatoes there for generations. After getting permission to develop the property, the Spaeths put in a new road, Spaeth Lane, and sold off parcels to friends, keeping the spot with the most spectacular ocean views for themselves.

Otto Spaeth had built his fortune with the Meta-Mold Aluminum Company, among other ventures, from his base in Dayton, Ohio. In 1950, when their children were grown, he and Eloise moved to Manhattan. One reason for their move was their devotion to the visual arts. The Spaeths collected works by Alexander Calder, Mary Callery, Lyonel Feininger, and Edward Hopper, among others, out of connoisseurship and a desire to bring public recognition to these artists. They even organized their collection into a traveling exhibition that toured the country in the mid-1950s in a converted school bus, "The Spaethmobile."

After moving to New York, the Spaeths spent their summers in East Hampton. During their first summer there, Eloise Spaeth curated an exhibition at Guild Hall, A Historic Survey of American Art,

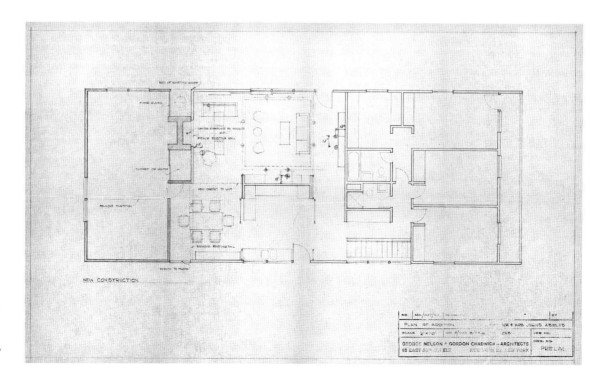

Julius and Anne Abeles House, Roslyn, 1954. The 1954 floor plan with "New Construction" addition, built in 1961.

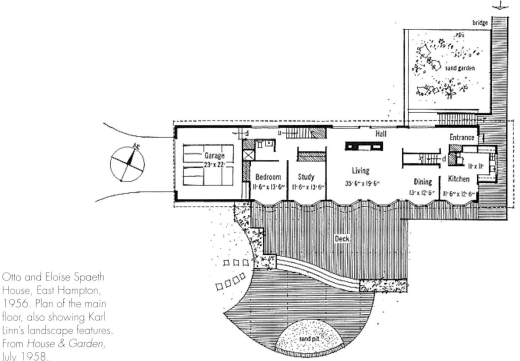

Otto and Eloise Spaeth House, East Hampton, 1956. Plan of the main floor, also showing Karl Linn's landscape features. From *House & Garden*, July 1958.

Otto and Eloise Spaeth House, East Hampton, 1956. The entrance façade. Chadwick may have explicitly quoted the shape of McKim, Mead & White's 1887 Shingle Style Low House, but he made it distinctively his own by incorporating features from vernacular farm buildings, such as the grouping of square, white-framed windows on the second-story gable, and by adding modernist touches, such as the band of white brick punctuated with large rectangular windows on the ground floor.

in which eighteenth- and nineteenth-century works such as Quaker artist Edward Hicks's *Peaceable Kingdom* were shown in the same room as paintings by Jackson Pollock, Willem de Kooning, and other then not-so-well-known artists, many of whom had studios in East Hampton. In 1954 she mounted Contemporary Religious Art, featuring stellar examples of stained glass, statuary, and models of houses of worship by modern architects, including Marcel Breuer and Percival Goodman. In 1955, she stood firm against a widely circulated petition decrying the showing of abstract art at Guild Hall. In Manhattan, she joined the boards of the Whitney Museum and the Smithsonian's Archives of American Art.

Chadwick conceived and built the Spaeth House on his own, as Nelson later confirmed, stating that it was "100 percent Chad's."[5] But there was another contributor to the design process—Otto Spaeth, Jr., known as Tony, who accompanied his parents to meet with both Nelson and Chadwick at their offices. Tony had studied architecture at Princeton University, where he had designed a beach house for his master's thesis. He recalled that it was he who came up with the idea of building the structure on the edge of the dunes, not a common practice then for a winterized "summer cottage," as the denizens of East Hampton's summer colony called their commodious houses. The younger Spaeth was also responsible for the design of the gently S-curved driveway, which brought visitors from the main road to the house through four acres of meadowland.[6]

In the context of both the Nelson office and American modernism in general, the Spaeth House embodied a significant stylistic shift. On the East End, local architects and the press saw the Spaeth House as a bolt from the blue. International Style designs, with big window walls and flat roofs, were popular in the area, as were low-budget wood A-frames, such as those Andrew Geller produced as a sideline to his day job at the Raymond Loewy firm. But with rebellious conviction, Chadwick chose instead the peculiarly American Shingle Style, characterized by wood framing, pitched roofs, and rustic shake siding, which first Henry Hobson Richardson and later Stanford White and others made popular in the 1880s.

Chadwick was familiar with the Shingle Style because, as a boy, he spent summers with his family in an old Victorian house near the Montauk Association colony, a group of seven Shingle Style houses built by White.[7] And he most likely would have seen East Hampton's distinctive shingled houses from the early days of English settlement, the saltboxes with their long roofs sloping all the way to the ground in the back. In his design for the Spaeths, Chadwick alluded to McKim, Mead & White's 1887 Low House in Bristol, Rhode Island, demolished in 1962. The house, which is vastly different from the monumental Beaux-Arts edifices for which the McKim, Mead & White firm is best known, had recently been featured in architectural historian Vincent Scully's widely read 1955 book, *The Shingle Style*. Chadwick was no doubt familiar with the book and influenced by Scully's

Otto and Eloise Spaeth House, East Hampton, 1956. The ocean-side façade is animated by Chadwick's witty "eyebrow" bulges, which alleviated the need for canvas awnings.

Otto and Eloise Spaeth House, East Hampton, 1956. View of the house from the beach.

description of the Low House as an archetypically American house[8] with poetic, democratic associations. He based the shape of the Spaeth House quite explicitly on McKim, Mead & White's design; like the Low House, its main façade is formed of a single, broad gable pierced by rows of bay windows.

Chadwick did not simply reiterate Stanford White's Shingle Style design, however, but added his own distinctive modern twists and historicist allusions, which seem to refer to those Precisionist paintings and photographs from the 1930s depicting the simple geometries of old wooden American farm buildings. On the approach side of the Spaeth House, he articulated the enormous second-story gable with a cluster of square, small, white-framed windows. The windows draw on another aspect of the local vernacular, the English-style barns and sheds that were once ubiquitous on the largely agricultural East End. On the lower story, a band of white brick punctuated by large rectangular windows has a more modernist character and contrasts with the shingled gable above. (A later owner added a living room that protrudes out from this wall, compromising Chadwick's taut façade.) Another departure from traditional Shingle Style houses is the lack of an embellished central front door. Chadwick located the main entrance on a side porch under deep eaves, a reference perhaps to the hidden front doors of Frank Lloyd Wright, and he designed an approach that requires visitors to cross a wooden bridge over a Japanese sand garden in order to reach the door.

The beach side of the house is even more distinctive, and quite witty. A large deck with subtle curves and an oval sand pit for children was designed by Karl Linn, a landscape architect who was responsible for the exterior and interior landscape features of Mies van der Rohe's Seagram Building before dedicating his career in the 1960s to building community gardens in low-income urban neighborhoods. The house's beach-side façade is particularly distinguished by the "eyebrow" bulges that shade each of the bay windows. The effect is a gentle rippling of the

surface—evoking waves—that breaks the austere flatness and imposing mass of the enormous gable and adds a playful touch to the design.

The interior of the Spaeth House, though not visually dramatic, is spacious and cleverly organized within the restrictions of the house's triangular shape. The rectangular living and dining room, anchored by a central fireplace, is the largest space. Floor-to-ceiling bay windows and doors connect the room to the deck and the beach beyond. This sense of openness to the outdoors pervades the front of the house as well; the hallway

Otto and Eloise Spaeth House, East Hampton, 1956. The ocean-side deck, including a sand pit, designed by landscape architect Karl Linn.

that runs along it, leading to a modern version of the New England boxed-in stairway, is bathed in light from the first-floor windows. Every room has southern exposure and windows with breathtaking views of the dunes and ocean, and no other houses in sight.

One of the Spaeths' requirements for the interior was to provide space in which to exhibit their extensive art collection. The long entry hallway wall served as a gallery. An Edward Hopper and other large paintings hung in the living area. Chadwick tailored his design to accommodate the

OPPOSTIE
Otto and Eloise Spaeth House, East Hampton, 1956. A gallery hallway leads from the main entrance, which is tucked under the east eave, to the main living space.

ABOVE
Otto and Eloise Spaeth House, East Hampton, 1956. Dining area, with a view of the kitchen beyond. Edward Hopper's painting *South Carolina Morning*, 1955, hangs above a wall cabinet designed by George Nelson & Associates.

art. The eyebrows above the bay windows limited direct sunlight. Doors were kept to a minimum to provide maximum wall space for hanging. Built-in furniture and storage compartments kept the house uncluttered. According to Tony Spaeth, his parents enjoyed their collection without all of the state-of-the-art temperature and humidity controls that collectors of precious possessions feel compelled to live with today.

Another distinctive feature of the interior was Chadwick's use of Nelson's Omni storage system. The Omni was one of Nelson's pioneering adaptable storage designs, in which storage containers, shelving, colored panels, and desktops were hung in flexible arrangements between brass-colored aluminum uprights. At the time when Chadwick was working on the Spaeth House, Nelson had just contracted with Aluminum Extrusions Inc. to begin manufacturing the Omni system.[9] Chadwick installed the Omni poles, fitted with walnut shelves, in the upstairs hallway, surrounding the square windows. He also used Omni poles to support the main staircase. This may well have been the first time that the new Omni design was employed.

JOHNSON HOUSE

Chadwick again turned to the Shingle Style for his design of the Johnson House, built in 1961–62. This commission originated when architecture aficionado Richard Johnson heard from his parents that they were looking into buying a factory-made A-frame house for land they owned along the cliffs east of Montauk. Insisting that they let him search for a "proper" architect, he took leave from his job managing Chrysler's sales in Latin America and started an architectural tour of modern houses in the Northeast. "I studied art and architectural history at Williams College during the great art professor Lane Faison's years, so I had learned how to know what to like, or not like, and how to understand modern architecture."[10] After viewing many variations on the International Style, including Philip Johnson's Glass House and houses by Marcel Breuer, Johnson realized that he wanted something different, without strictly rectangular geometries and large horizontal windows. The search for an architect was settled after Olga Raymond, the previous owner of his parents' land, took the family to visit her friend Eloise Spaeth. Johnson said, "As soon as I walked through the Spaeth House, I could see here was an architect who knew how to design spatial flow, use light, and integrate the building with nature, in the manner of Frank Lloyd Wright."[11]

In his design for the Johnson House, Chadwick turned to his old master Wright's Arnold Friedman Lodge. Chadwick had been responsible for executing the working drawings for the Friedman Lodge, built in 1945 in Pecos, New Mexico. Wright's design featured an unusual plan of parallelograms and hexagons, and Chadwick incorporated these geometries into his design for the Johnson House. And like Wright, he paid close attention to integrating the house and its setting, a hillside that slopes gently toward the ocean. He designed the house as a long, narrow volume and positioned it perpendicular to the slope, so that it projects outward from the hillside and toward the ocean below. Chadwick even experimented with the shingled pyramidal roofs that Wright had designed for the Friedman Lodge. These distinctive features appeared in his original drawings for the Johnson House but were not built because the cost was prohibitive. Instead, he settled on a flat-roof design, which made the house look something like a Shingle Style crenellated fortress, with the façade angling in and out, large expanses of blank, windowless, cedar-shingle sheathing, and a tall, hexagonal tower looming over the downhill end of the house.

Among the most distinctive features of the exterior design is a ramp that ascends from the driveway, wraps around the side of the house, and leads to a second-story entrance. Its purpose was partly functional, to allow groceries to be pushed on a cart up to the kitchen, rather than carried up the internal stairs. But it also added a dynamic line that stretches outward from the house's main volume. According to Richard Johnson, a blown-up photograph of the ramp was displayed across from the elevator at the George Nelson & Associates office for several years, suggesting that Nelson was was particularly fond of this piece of Chadwick's design.[12]

The interior of the house consisted of a series of interlocking hexagonal spaces with the kind of distinctive "spatial flow" that Johnson had sought when he commissioned Chadwick. On the lower floor, a studio apartment, built for Richard

Rudolph and Ethel Johnson House, Montauk, 1962. The house under construction.

Johnson, was separated by a breezeway from the entrance hall, a bedroom, and service spaces. On the second floor, bedrooms were at the rear, the dining room and kitchen were in the middle, and a large living area occupied the tower at the front. The interior spaces were distinguished not only by their angular geometries and openness to the surrounding landscape but also by the treatment of their materials. Chadwick played with contrasts, juxtaposing the natural and the synthetic, rough and smooth surfaces, earth tones and bold colors. Walls were clad in the weathered shingles of the exterior, ceilings were covered with polished wood, and some rooms had rough flagstone floors like those of the patios. The massive living room fireplace was built of large, ocean-polished stones collected from below the cliffs at Montauk Point.

Against this background of organic materiality, which Chadwick derived from the Shingle Style and from Wright, he incorporated design features characteristic of the Nelson office and a few quirky screens, probably influenced by a recent journey to the Far East. Seating, spiced with brightly colored cotton cushions, was arranged around the periphery of the rooms to open the spaces. Built-in furniture, cabinetry, and paneling were designed with precision. Color, which was of particular interest to Nelson, who asked his staff to use the Munsell color system when choosing colors for their designs, appears throughout the house. Doors and cabinetry were faced with sheets of white and colored Formica, and bright-colored, matte-lacquered panels were used on the specially designed rectangular chests of drawers in the bedrooms.

The distinctively shaped Johnson House attracted a great deal of attention and became a modern landmark along Old Montauk Highway. During the 1960s and 1970s, the house was used frequently for fundraisers and meetings of Concerned Citizens of Montauk, the group responsible for conserving the area's open space and beaches as parkland. Every New Year's Day, Richard Johnson, a board member and leading activist, hosted a bonfire party below the house, with plenty of whisky and boisterous tales of battles with developers. In the late 1960s, Johnson and his group successfully fought against Robert Moses's scheme to build a four-lane highway through Napeague State Park all the way to the Montauk Point Lighthouse.

Despite the importance of the house to the community and the local landscape, Johnson sold it in 1989. The new owners remodeled it into an utterly traditional house with a pitched roof. Quickly regretting the loss, Johnson set to work replicating Chadwick's design on a lot next to Montauk Point State Park. Chadwick died in 1980, and at his funeral Johnson met George Nelson for the first time.[13] Using the original contractor and Chadwick's drawings, as well as all the modern furniture designed by George Nelson's studio that Chadwick had selected, Johnson directed the project himself. The new house differs in certain respects from the original. It lacks the breezeway and is 20 percent larger. Perhaps most significantly, the site is not the same; hence, the superb engagement with the landscape that characterized the original house has been lost.

TOP
Rudolph and Ethel Johnson House, Montauk, 1962. The completed house from the driveway.

ABOVE LEFT
Rudolph and Ethel Johnson House, Montauk, 1962. The hexagonal living room.

ABOVE RIGHT
Rudolph and Ethel Johnson House, Montauk, 1962. The living room and view of the hallway, which leads past the kitchen to the dining room.

18

LUDWIG MIES VAN DER ROHE
1886–1969

Mary Callery Barn Renovation, Huntington, 1950

Few who are familiar with the work of German architect Ludwig Mies van der Rohe, who immigrated to the United States in 1938, are aware of a small red barn in Huntington that he remodeled in 1950 as a weekend house for the artist Mary Callery. The barn, originally built in the 1720s for the Thomas Whitson family, descendants of early Quaker settlers,[1] was one of several agricultural buildings on acreage purchased in the 1950s by Wallace and Ellen Harrison, adjacent to their property on Round Swamp Road (see pages 26–35). The barn renovation was most unusual for Mies, an innovative architect of perfectly polished, modern buildings of steel, plate glass, and marble or fine brickwork. Yet Mies's involvement is evident. The austerity of the smooth white walls, the structural clarity of the exposed wooden beams, the openness of the living space to a terrace on the brow of a hill, and the integration of house and landscape recall some of his most famous designs, such as the Tugendhat and Farnsworth houses, and clearly reflect the central principles of his domestic architecture.

MARY CALLERY, 1903–1977

Today, Mary Callery's prominence as an artist in the mid-century New York art world has largely been forgotten, but in the 1940s and 1950s, she was recognized as a leading American sculptor

Mary Callery Barn Renovation, Huntington, 1950. Mary Callery sculpture on the south façade of the "living barn."

whose work was included in major exhibitions and collected by museums. In 1923, after marrying Frederic Coudert Jr., later a congressman, she began attending the Arts Students League in Manhattan. The Couderts owned a family compound in Cove Neck, Long Island, where she turned an old stable into her first art studio. When Coudert was transferred to the Paris office of his family's law firm, she continued her art studies there. The young couple divorced in 1930, and she remained in Paris. Her second brief marriage, a love match this time, unlike her socially acceptable marriage to Coudert, was to Carlo Frua de Angeli, a well-to-do Italian, who introduced her to an art world beyond classrooms, the milieu of avant-garde practicing artists. His family opposed the marriage, as she was not Italian or Catholic, and they insisted on an annulment through their connections at the Vatican.

The daughter of a moneyed Pittsburgh family, Callery had an independent spirit and was endowed with intellect, a forceful personality, and Junoesque beauty, all qualities that, along with artistic talent, made her a personage in the Crazy Years, when Paris was the center of the art world. In 1927, when the newly wed Wallace and Ellen Harrison visited Paris, Callery introduced them to Henry Matisse, Alexander Calder, Aristide Maillol, and Fernand Léger. Picasso was Callery's friend and a mentor, Léger a lover.[2] Picasso's 1938

Mary Callery Barn Renovation, Huntington, 1950. Mary Callery stoking the fire. View is from the sleeping loft, above a small kitchen and bathroom, at the south end of the "living barn."

portrait of her elegant head and neck was the cover of the catalogue of a 1945 exhibition of her collection of his drawings at the Curt Valentin Gallery in Manhattan.[3]

In 1938, in advance of the invading German army, she returned to the United States, her luggage packed with rolls of drawings and paintings, some owned by her and others on consignment from her artist friends. Settling in New York, she showed this collection to Alfred Barr, the first director of the Museum of Modern Art, who over time purchased from her important works by Picasso, Léger, Matisse, and others, now at the core of the museum's collection of European art.

Callery's own work quickly found recognition in New York as well. In a converted carriage house on 63rd Street, she produced sculptures mostly of steel, brass, and aluminum, many of which depicted attenuated figures of animals, acrobats, dancers, and characters from fairy tales. In 1943, she and Léger exhibited two painted plaster works, which they collaborated on and co-signed, at the Tate Gallery in London. Her first solo show was hung in 1944 at the Curt Valentin Gallery in New York, where she exhibited frequently, before moving to the Knoedler Gallery. In the 1940s, she taught at Black Mountain College's summer art program. Her work was featured in the Museum of Modern Art's 1953 Sculpture of the Twentieth Century exhibition and was subsequently purchased by the Modern and the Metropolitan Museum of Art. Among her most impressive works are several massive architectural sculptures, including *Three Birds in Flight* (1953), which hangs in the lobby below a dropped ceiling of cloud-shaped cutouts in the Alcoa Building, designed by Max Abramovitz and Wallace Harrison, in her hometown of Pittsburgh, and a colossal escutcheon, known by operagoers as "the giant chastity belt,"[4] of curving bronze forms mounted above the stage at the Metropolitan Opera House at Lincoln Center in New York. Callery made the piece as an homage to Léger, as its forms recall his works of the early 1940s, in which he included twisted raw metal shapes to evoke nature and images of the American city. Her large works were always tours de force of metalwork, unusual for a woman artist at the time. For the American Pavilion designed by Edward Durell Stone at the 1958 Brussels World's Fair she created *Fountains*, a ten-foot-high wheel of smooth bronze that whirled in a pool of water.

Ellen Harrison had known Callery since they were classmates at Manhattan's Spence School. Callery had a major influence on the Harrisons' social acquaintance with artists and on Wallace Harrison's penchant to incorporate large artworks into his public buildings. As a visiting professor at Yale in the late 1930s, Wallace Harrison helped transform the architecture school, infusing its Beaux-Arts tradition with a breath of modernism. He invited artists he had met through Callery, including Léger, Amédée Ozenfant, and Calder to be critics in the drafting room.[5] Harrison made sure that Nelson Rockefeller, who gave Harrison several architectural commissions, had first pick from his artist friends' studios, either for Rockefeller's own collection or for the Museum of Modern Art. Both Léger and Matisse did murals for Rockefeller's New York apartment, at the insistence of Callery and Harrison.

The Harrisons made a practice of inviting artists to live on the grounds of their large property in Huntington, sometimes in exchange for artwork. Callery had been a regular visitor at the Harrisons' house since her return from war-torn Europe. Around 1947, the couple offered her two eighteenth-century barns for use as a retreat. The larger of the barns became a studio, while the smaller served as living quarters. She most likely paid for the barns by giving the Harrisons artworks.[6]

CALLERY AND MIES

Callery asked Mies to give her specific ideas and plans for the remodeling of the smaller barn, which she called "the living barn." She had known the German architect since the early 1940s through Philip Johnson. A former director of the Bauhaus and a leader of the Modern movement in Europe, Mies had first been championed in the United States by Johnson, who featured his buildings in the exhibition Modern Architecture: International Exhibition at the Museum of Modern Art in 1932. Mies emigrated in 1938, having closed the Bauhaus in 1933 and failing to find support for his work from the Third Reich government. He first came briefly to New York on the encouragement of Barr, who hoped to have him design the Museum of Modern Art's new building. But he settled instead in Chicago, where he assumed the directorship of the school of architecture at what is now the Illinois Institute of Technology.

In 1947, Mies visited New York frequently to consult with Johnson on the Mies van der Rohe exhibition that Johnson was organizing at the Modern. Mies was in the midst of a temporary falling out with his lifelong companion, the artist Lora Marx.[7] According to his biographer, Franz Schulze, that year Mies and Callery began "the kind of light, desultory romantic affair to which he was long accustomed in the old country."[8] Only a few architectural historians have noted the relationship, including architect and critic Peter Blake,

who mentioned it in his memoir *No Place Like Utopia*. In reference to Mies, Blake wrote, "He had re-modeled a townhouse in the East Sixties for his charming friend the sculptress Mary Callery, and on Long Island, where he had re-modeled an old barn for Mary into a studio next to Wally Harrison's country house."[9] By all accounts, Callery and Mies kept up their friendship,[10] even after she moved back to Paris in 1958. Callery owned some of Mies's architectural drawings, which she donated to the Museum of Modern Art.

Mies's role in the Callery barn renovation is apparent from photographs, from anecdotal evidence, and from observing the barn itself. But in the various archives that hold the architect's

Mary Callery Barn Renovation, Huntington, 1950. View of the dining and fireplace zones from the east patio, early 1960s. The "living barn" was sold to Armand and Celeste Bartos in 1958.

papers, no drawings or records of the project are to be found. Perhaps he considered the renovation too minor to be recorded. Perhaps, after the public turmoil of his relationship with Edith Farnsworth, who commissioned the now famous Farnsworth House on the Fox River outside Chicago, he wanted the project to remain anonymous to prevent Lora Marx from finding out about his affair with Callery. Whatever the case may be, the project has been all but forgotten by historians.

Callery probably first took Mies to see the barns in the summer of 1947. They must have come to an agreement for him to transform the smaller barn into a permanent living space by 1950. Mies's renovation consisted of several components. First, the original barn structure was dismantled, moved to a new location, and rebuilt on a new foundation. Second, the exterior siding, interior walls, and interior floor were replaced, new windows were added, and a kitchen, bathroom, and fireplace were installed. Finally, Mies designed the landscape around the house, including box hedges, a lawn, and a stone patio.

THE ARCHITECTURE

The original Yankee- or English-style barn was a simple, rectangular post-and-beam structure clad in vertical board-and-batten siding, three bays long, with haylofts at either end and broad doors in the middle of the long sides. The idea of working with a humble, rough-hewn vernacular structure must have had a certain appeal to Mies, despite his penchant for industrial materials and machine-tooled precision, and his famously rarefied approach to design. As a boy in Aachen, Germany, Mies had learned traditional building techniques while apprenticing with his father, a master stonemason and bricklayer. Later in life, Mies voiced his admiration for traditional wooden buildings and their honest use of materials. Museum curator and art historian James Johnson Sweeney, a close friend, recalled the architect saying, "'Where can we find greater structural clarity than in the wooden buildings of old? . . . They seem to be the echo of old songs.'"[11] The expression of structure and materials was among the essential qualities of his mature architecture. The Farnsworth House in Illinois and the Seagram Building in New York, for example, feature naked, skeletal frameworks of steel I-beams, which Mies referred to as "skin and bone construction."

On the interior of the Callery barn, the structural members were completely exposed. Mies embraced the visibility of the frame as a primary aesthetic feature, taking great care to preserve and accentuate its character. He substantially altered the physical nature of the supports, anchoring the posts in a concrete foundation and inserting steel rods and plates into the mortise and tenon joints, but he carefully concealed these twentieth-century additions to retain the appearance of the original structure.[12]

Mies balanced the rusticity of the irregular, hand-cut beams with the clean, flawless look of new materials. He replaced the original threshing floor with uniform, run-of-the-mill oak boards, and reclad the exterior in standard pine siding from a local lumberyard. He covered the interior walls between the framing elements with beaverboard, a low-cost, wood-fiber wallboard used frequently in the 1950s. Its stucco-like surface was painted white to contrast with the dark wood. The resultant effect resembled medieval half-timbering, with a lattice of beams crisscrossing white walls at irregular intervals. But the white walls also had a minimal, modernist quality that served as an ideal background for Callery's art collection.

In the Farnsworth House, Mies experimented with the idea of a country retreat consisting of a single big room that accommodated different living functions and facilitated constant interaction with nature. Its continuous space, resting on a raised plinth, was broken only by a central rectangular module that contained a gallery kitchen, bathroom, and fireplace. The Callery barn was a variation on this theme of spatial simplicity and openness. The interior was essentially a single room for living, dining, and sleeping. In its northern bay was a seating area arranged around a fireplace, the dining area occupied the middle, and the southern bay contained a birch-clad module—similar in its simplicity to the Farnsworth House's utility core—that concealed a small kitchen, bathroom, closet space, and a stair leading down to the basement and up to a sleeping area in what had once been the hayloft.

Besides the enclosed kitchen-bathroom unit, the only interference with the barn's open interior came in the form of white linen curtains installed on curved rods high up on the barn's wooden

Mary Callery Barn Renovation, Huntington, 1950. View from the sleeping loft of the dining area and patio, early 1960s. The outdoor tables were assembled by Mies for Callery.

trusses. They were quite similar to the curtains he and interior designer Lilly Reich had fashioned for a café at an exhibition in Berlin in 1927. Throughout his long career, Mies experimented with ways of making interiors more open and flexible, and he often included retractable hanging fabric—literally curtain walls—that could be used to divide a room when needed. In the Callery barn, Mies installed one curtain arrangement to enclose the fireplace zone and another to separate the dining table from the seating area during meals. Mies turned the two barn doors into large plate-glass windows, creating some of the sense of permeability and connection to the outdoors that had defined the all-glass Farnsworth House. However, he chose not to open the space further, save for a few small windows punched into the east wall for light, and he left the solid walls around the fireplace fully intact. This decision was surely in part to allow space for Callery to hang her art collection, but it also gave the interior a greater sense of enclosure and intimacy than was typical in his houses.

THE LANDSCAPE

Mies did much to enhance the connection between the barn and its surroundings. From the very outset of his career, he had devoted a great deal of attention to siting his houses, framing views of the landscape, and using plantings, walls, and outdoor furniture to create constructed garden spaces. This aspect of his work was long obscured by a stereotype of him as an uncompromising rationalist whose designs were based primarily on pure geometries, industrial materials, and the overt expression of structure. Philip Johnson had promulgated the idea of Mies as a rationalist, going so far as to erase wavy lines representing plantings on his plans, when in fact they had been devices integral to the architecture.[13] More recently, however, historians have reemphasized the role of landscape in his work and have recognized how closely his ideas about gardens and vistas were in fact related to the classical tradition and to a nineteenth-century Romantic conception of nature.

To take full advantage of the scenic potential of the gently rolling terrain, Mies had the barn moved across a field to the edge of a slope that fell away toward an expanse of open fields. Mies had favored hillside sites for a number of his earlier houses, most famously the Tugendhat House in the city of Brno in what is now the Czech Republic. Because of the way that house is situated on the crest of a steep slope, the view is not revealed to anyone entering on the hilltop side. Only when one descends a staircase to the main level does the landscape below open up dramatically through large windows. For the Callery barn, Mies had subtler topography to work with, but he was nonetheless able to enhance the spectacle of the landscape by controlling the visitor's encounter with the view. He positioned the barn's entrance on the sheltered west side to keep the view hidden. When the visitor steps inside and looks straight ahead, the sightline leads directly to the opposite picture window, which frames a panorama of the fields below.

Mary Callery Barn Renovation, Huntington, 1950. View from the "living barn" to the entrance court, with its yew hedge marking the perimeter and rectangular topiary "bench," early 1960s.

Mies surrounded the barn with simple yet carefully constructed garden spaces that further mediated between the interior and the landscape. Using perfectly clipped, flat-top yew hedges, he created a perimeter boundary around three sides of the structure. The hedges' rectilinear, architectonic form conveyed their function as a kind of low wall demarcating outdoor "rooms." About three feet tall, they provided a sense of privacy, while maintaining a connection between the house and its surroundings. On the west side, a small opening in the hedge led visitors from the road into a grassy space—an outdoor room— at the barn's entrance. In front of the entrance, a freestanding topiary about two feet tall and shaped like a rectangular bench referenced one of his signature devices, the rectangular bench in the court garden. Its very benchlike appearance drew attention to the architectural quality of the plantings. On the opposite, embankment side of the barn, he had the earth built up so that he could create a patio paved with flagstone. Directly outside of the east window he installed a table made of two thick tree stumps and a raw granite slab—a permanent piece of outdoor furniture that turned the patio into an extension of the indoor dining area. The patio was also a platform from which to take in the view. In this regard, the yew hedge not only served as a physical boundary for the space but also framed and enhanced the view by blocking the immediate foreground, and thus drew the eye into the distance, heightening the sense of expansiveness.

Beyond the flagstone patio, Callery installed a round swimming pool. Similar to the round pool at Wallace Harrison's house, it was probably built with the guidance of Harrison rather than Mies. The pool is also similar to the one at Philip Johnson's Glass House. As Callery and Johnson were friends, it is possible that his was inspired by hers.

THE BARN AFTER CALLERY

In 1958, Callery moved back to Paris and sold the barn to the architect Armand Bartos and his wife Celeste. Bartos was in partnership with the Austrian-American architect Frederick Kiesler, with whom he had designed the Shrine of the Book in Jerusalem, opened in 1965 to house the Dead Sea Scrolls. Callery would have known Armand and Celeste Bartos from her involvement with the Modern. After purchasing the barn, Bartos moved another small barn onto the property, which he converted into sleeping quarters for his family. In the Callery barn, the Bartoses did not alter Mies's design, although they installed their own furniture and art, including a large rope and wood assemblage by Kiesler that is now in the collection of the Museum of Modern Art. The art dealers Harold and Hester Diamond purchased the two barns in 1967, before moving into the Harrison house in 1981.[14] Long Island architect Theodore Bindrim was the last owner to fully appreciate Mies's work. He turned Callery's residence into his office and drafting studio and built a family house nearby that recalled Mies's interventions on Callery's living barn. Callery's studio barn was demolished in 1999, and even though the residential barn that Mies remodeled still stands, it has been substantially altered, as has its once bucolic setting.

Mary Callery Barn Renovation, Huntington, 1950. Mary Callery entertaining, 1952. *Photograph by Hans Namuth.*

19

PHILIP JOHNSON 1906–2005

Eugene and Margaret Farney House, Sagaponack, 1945–46;
Robert and Mary Leonhardt House, Lloyd Neck, 1954–56;
New York State Pavilion, Queens, 1962–64

Three buildings designed by Philip Johnson on Long Island provide an excellent means of tracking the course of his early architectural career, which he began at the age of thirty-seven. Two are relatively unknown water's-edge houses: a small wooden beach house at Sagaponack, one of the first commissions that he received after opening his practice, and a steel, brick, and glass year-round residence overlooking Huntington Harbor on the North Shore, a larger, more mature work of a decade later. Both of these houses adhere to the radically simplified formal vocabulary of Mies van der Rohe, whose influence on Johnson during the initial part of his career was enormous. The third, which he designed with Richard Foster Architects, is one of his most well-remembered works—and one of his most original: the New York State Pavilion for the 1964 World's Fair in Queens. With its curves, bright colors, and exuberant spirit, the design signaled a dramatic departure from the Miesian "less is more" approach. Linked to Pop art, the pavilion stands at the beginning of a larger shift in American architecture, away from the influence of the International Style and toward an architecture of wit, contrast, and historical references.

Johnson was as mercurial, eclectic, and prolific as anyone on the architectural scene of the twentieth century. In his later years he became a kind of senior dean who nevertheless remained restless and quizzical until his death

at age ninety-eight. Both in his early activities as a curator and critic, which were marked by his advocacy of the modernist architecture and design emanating from Europe, particularly his curating of the seminal Modern Architecture: International Exhibition at the Museum of Modern Art in 1932, and in his practice as an architect, he possessed a unique ability to reinvent himself. Not a radical innovator, he was instead a consummate tastemaker who was quick to recognize others' innovations, incorporate them into his own architecture, and in so doing, simultaneously confirm their importance and take his own work in new directions. Johnson has often been criticized as an imitator, yet it cannot be denied that he contributed enormously to shaping modern architecture over the span of his long career.

Johnson received his architectural training at Harvard in 1940–43, when Walter Gropius was dean of the Graduate School of Design. In 1945, Johnson returned to the Museum of Modern Art to reclaim the position of director of the Department of Architecture, which he had originated in the early 1930s. At the same time, he opened his own architecture practice with Landis Gores, a Harvard classmate, who oversaw the design, drafting and job-site responsibilities while Johnson was busy at the museum. Over the next two decades, Johnson executed some of his best designs, including his own Glass House in New Canaan, Connecticut

Eugene and Margaret Farney House, Sagaponack, 1945–46. North façade. A long ramp leads to the front entrance, which opens into the glass-walled living and dining room.

(1947–49), which he surrounded with other buildings, including follies and a museum for the art collection he acquired with his domestic partner, David Whitney.

FARNEY HOUSE

For Eugene and Margaret Farney's beach house in Sagaponack, Johnson balanced Mies's austere minimalism with an element of rusticity, achieved through the use of traditional construction methods, simple materials, and unfinished surfaces. A nod in part to the simple weekend cottages on Cape Cod designed by his Harvard teacher Marcel Breuer, this rusticity suited the house's isolated oceanfront site. It was also likely a response to the taste of his clients, who were enthusiasts of the Arts and Crafts movement.

The Farneys had the wealth to build any type and size house they wanted. Eugene Farney inherited a fortune from his mother, the daughter of Rudolf Wurlitzer, who turned his family's musical instrument-and-jukebox manufacturing company into a booming enterprise. Entirely on his own, Eugene Farney created another fortune as founder of the Telecoin Corporation, a pioneer in the coin-operated laundry business. As a 1947 article in *Time* magazine on Telecoin, run by "handsome Harvard-man Eugene Farny [sic]," quipped. "Nobody has made such a good thing out of washing dirty linen in public."[1]

Years before capitalizing on modern technology, Eugene Farney developed an interest in modern architecture, most likely sparked by growing up at Craftsman Farms in Morris County, New Jersey, which his father purchased from Gustav Stickley in 1917. Stickley, a furniture designer, architect, publisher of *The Craftsman* magazine, and leading American advocate for the English Arts and Crafts movement, filed for bankruptcy following the collapse of his manufacturing and publishing empire. Craftsman Farms, today owned by a foundation and open to the public, was then a six-hundred-acre property with a working farm, part of Stickley's romantic vision of life close to the land, and a rustic bungalow of rough-hewn chestnut logs, fieldstone, and shingles, similar to the house designs that he popularized on the pages of *The Craftsman*. Stickley filled his house with exquisitely constructed oak furniture, fireplaces with hammered-copper hoods, and hand-woven rugs. Architecture, landscape, and furnishings all came together in a harmonious ensemble of Arts and Crafts form, at once archaic and strikingly modern.

In the early 1940s, Eugene and Margaret Farney began thinking about building a retreat for themselves. To that end, they purchased a four-acre plot on the dunes, reached through acres of flat potato fields, not far from Sagaponack, a sparsely populated village with few summer residents at the time. They were introduced to Johnson by his sister Theodate, who may have known Margaret Farney as a fellow Wellesley College alumna.[2] When they engaged Johnson as their architect, the Farneys were most likely envisioning a house that, like Stickley's rough-hewn bungalow, would both complement its idyllic rural setting and express a quality of modernity. Johnson was not the most obvious designer to fulfill this vision of a rustic modernism, as his architectural proclivity had been defined by the pure volumes, shiny smooth surfaces, and industrial materials of the European avant-garde and the work of Mies van der Rohe.

Yet the recently trained Johnson proved capable of accommodating his clients' wishes. In creating the Farney House, Johnson looked to Mies, but he chose from the German architect's oeuvre a unique and particularly well-suited unbuilt design from 1938, the Stanley and Helen Resor House project for their ranch in Jackson Hole, Wyoming. Helen Resor was on the board of the Museum of Modern Art and, at Philip Johnson's insistence, she and her husband sponsored Mies's emigration to America and engaged him to prepare drawings for the house. Mies's design played subtly with the frontier landscape. Instead of the noble materials like marble, travertine, and chrome that had given his earlier projects their characteristic abstraction and play with sheen, Mies chose cypress siding and fieldstone to connect the structure to its rocky, wooded surroundings and magnificent views of the Grand Teton Mountains. He oriented the house's long, rectangular façade with its expanse of floor-to-ceiling glass toward the mountains. The great living room at the center afforded an open view, carefully framed by the positioning of internal elements, including a massive fieldstone fireplace and slender structural columns.

Johnson's Farney House is a smaller, more simplified version of the Resor House project. The exterior of the long, rectangular volume is clad in vertical boards at each end and has floor-to-ceiling windows and sliding doors in the middle, opening onto a deck. This central living area, with its sweeping views of the Atlantic and fluid connection between indoor space and outdoor terraces, contrasts with the small, relatively enclosed bedrooms and service areas situated to either side.

Johnson produced two schemes for the Farney House. In the first, from 1945, the exterior included a massive battered-concrete base, giving the structure a sense of weight and solidity that diverged markedly from the gracefully floating Resor prototype. After the Farneys' contractor rejected the first scheme as too costly, Johnson eliminated the battered-concrete base and lifted the building onto wooden pilings. This solution was not only cheaper but allowed the structure to hover instead of hulk above the dunes. According to Landis Gores, Johnson intended the slender, cylindrical piers as a direct reference to Le Corbusier's pilotis. Johnson reinforced this connection by adding a long entrance ramp, another signature feature of Le Corbusier's 1920s houses, to the north façade of the house.[3]

Designed as a simple beachside cottage, the proportions of the Farney House were compact, with eight-foot ceilings and rooms just big enough to accommodate their functions. The house was constructed with a cypress wood frame and clad in tongue-and-groove cedar on the exterior. Johnson employed a low-tech method of insulating the house, pouring sand from the dunes between the exterior and interior wall panels. Inside, he faced the walls with the same bare, tongue-and-groove vertical cedar boards, laminated the interior columns with cypress, and covered the floor with cork tile. To complement the architecture, Johnson designed simple furniture, including a dining table, coffee table, and cabinets. Constructed of unpainted cypress planks and embellished only with quarer-inch plate-glass tops, these pieces presented the same minimal, boxy profile as the house. It was one of the few times in his career that Johnson designed furniture. Perhaps the Farneys requested it in order to lend the house the kind of architectural and decorative harmony typical of the Arts and Crafts movement.

In adding a rustic dimension to his design, Johnson looked to the work of architects who pursued forms of modernism concerned with regional identity and traditional building techniques. Gores recalled that while working on the Farney commission, he and Johnson studied Marcel Breuer's "small, jewel-like Chamberlain House"[4] in Wayland, Massachusetts (1940–41), a diminutive cottage in the woods clad in vertical pine siding and resting on a fieldstone base. According to Gores, he and Johnson were also interested in the work of two lesser-known American architects whose work had appeared in the Museum of Modern Art's 1944 exhibition Built in U.S.A.: 1932–44. One was John Yeon's 1937 Watzek House, located on a wooded hillside in Portland, Oregon, which featured fir siding from regional forests and gently pitched gables that echoed the profile of the Cascade Mountains in the distance, as well as the rooflines of Arts and Crafts bungalows, so common in the area. Another was Pietro Belluschi's Kerr House, built on the Oregon coast in 1941, which was similarly defined by its use of local spruce and its low gables, a hallmark of the Pacific Coast regionalist movement with which he and Yeon were associated.[5]

Eugene and Margaret Farney sold their house in the late 1970s, and it has changed hands several times since then. Although still standing, the structure has been substantially altered. A coat of gray paint was applied to the bare cypress siding to give the exterior a more finished quality. A local architect filled in the open area between the ground and the base of the house and lengthened the entire structure, increasing the interior space to about 5,000 square feet, but negating the sense of lightness and the careful balance of proportions that gave Johnson's design its appeal. The once modest and charming house surrounded by farm fields has been transformed into a large and luxurious Hamptons house, complete with a putting green and a swimming pool.

LEONHARDT HOUSE

The Leonhardt House presented Johnson with a different set of challenges. Commissioned by an urbane, jet-setting couple, the house called for a refined, sophisticated design to accommodate the family and their art collection. Its location on Lloyd Neck, a peninsula of hilly land on the North Shore, was in many ways antithetical to the farm fields and dunes of Sagaponack. The Neck, so called by its denizens, has a rich history dating back to colonial times, when it was a manor; in the early twentieth century it became a desirable location for wealthy industrialists and professionals in search of a baronial way of life close to sandy beaches.

One such baron was Wilton Lloyd-Smith, a prosperous corporate lawyer, who purchased eighty-six acres of hilly land in 1924 and commissioned Bertram Goodhue, the architect of the Nebraska State Capitol and St. Bartholomew's Episcopal Church in Manhattan, among other important projects nationwide, to design a house for the property. The result was a forty-six-room brick structure with the half-timbering, steep gables, and tall chimneys of an English Tudor country house.[6] In 1954, Prentice Brower, a New York lawyer, and his wife, Mary, bought the Lloyd-Smith estate, tore down parts of the Goodhue-designed house, and subdivided the land into twelve plots. They sold one of the best—four acres with a clear view of the bay—to Robert Leonhardt, an investor and owner of McGrath Securities, and his wife, Mary Gay Leonhardt.

Bringing with them modern tastes of the postwar era, the Leonhardts wanted a very different kind of house from Goodhue's Tudor mansion up the hill. The couple traveled widely, often jetting off to Europe to attend events like the Venice Biennale exhibition of contemporary art or balls with an international set from both sides of the Atlantic. They had little interest in being tied to a property that required a well-trained staff. Their itinerant lifestyle was best served by a much smaller dwelling, with just enough space for their young family and the occasional glamorous European guest, such as their friend Sophia Loren, whose visits caused a stir in the neighborhood. The historically inspired architectural styles typical of the great estates were equally ill suited to the Leonhardts. Rather than reprise the grandiosity of the area's older mansions, they turned to Philip Johnson to design a house in a style that would not only satisfy their taste for modernism but suggest a more modern set of cultural values than those of the previous generation.

Natives of New Orleans, the Leonhardts moved to New York City in 1950. Acquaintances remember them as a strikingly attractive, energetic, even flamboyant couple. After they moved into the Lloyd Neck house, Robert Leonhardt often commuted to his Manhattan office in his seaplane. At the time, small aircraft were allowed to fly low and underneath the East River bridges, making for a

Robert and Mary Leonhardt House, Lloyd Neck, 1954–56. The volume on the left contains the living and dining spaces. The volume on the right houses the master bedroom suite on the lower level and a separately accessed children's wing above. Flanking the path to the entrance are a sculpture by Mary Callery, left, and a Rodin torso.

dramatic approach along Long Island Sound and down the East River to Lower Manhattan.[7]

Mary Leonhardt's great passion was art. An amateur furniture designer and avid collector of painting and sculpture, she was actively involved with the Museum of Modern Art. Soon after arriving in New York, she gained entrée into the exclusive circle of well-connected, cultured supporters of the Modern. Her initiation into the museum's International Council was no doubt facilitated by her cousin Ellen Milton Harrison, whose husband, Wallace, was a board member. Mary Leonhardt also most likely benefited from her friendship with the sculptor Mary Callery, another museum insider. The Leonhardts collected Callery's sculpture and she was godmother to their daughter.

The Leonhardts' interest in modern architecture began when they moved into an unusual weekend house on the Harrisons' Huntington property soon after they arrived in New York. Harrison, always experimenting with new materials and building techniques in the fields near his house, built several on-site mass-produced concrete houses, prototypes for a housing project in Lomas, Puerto Rico, which was built in 1953 as part of Nelson Rockefeller's International Basic Economy Corporation (IBEC) housing initiative.[8] The Leonhardts were so intrigued by these bunkerlike structures that they decided to buy a pair and combine them into one house. Mary Callery's charming barn, renovated by Mies van der Rohe (see pages 216–23), was directly across Round Swamp Road from the Leonhardts' concrete house. Callery, or perhaps the Harrisons, most likely provided them with an introduction to Philip Johnson.

The Johnson-Leonhardt match was a success, enduring as a friendship beyond the construction of the house. In 1964, the Leonhardts purchased a second Johnson design, a small townhouse originally built for Blanchette and John D. Rockefeller III in 1950. In 1958 the Rockefellers sold the house to the Museum of Modern Art, which used it as guest quarters for important visitors before selling it to the Leonhardts for $100,000. After Robert Leonhardt died in 1971, Mary Leonhardt rented the house to Johnson, who lived there for several years in the 1970s.

The Leonhardts' son, Clifton ("Cliff"), remembers Johnson telling him, "Your father was an easy client,"[9] suggesting that his parents accorded the architect a healthy measure of creative latitude.

Robert and Mary Leonhardt House, Lloyd Neck, 1954–56. The glass and exposed-steel living space projects dramatically over Huntington Harbor. A Mary Callery sculpture, right, reclines on the outdoor path between the two volumes.

The house that Johnson designed for them met their needs on both artistic and practical levels, combining modernist elegance and visual drama with convenience and comfort. Like the older Lloyd-Smith estate house, the Leonhardt House was meant to attract attention as a work of architecture. Its polished materials and dynamic forms showed off the owners' bold modern taste and ability to afford it. But at the same time, the relatively compact layout suited more down-to-earth ends. Johnson tailored the house's interior to fulfill the day-to-day needs of the couple, who wanted a quiet, restful place for themselves and their two young children, who lived there year round. The parents had a pied-à-terre in Manhattan, where they typically spent three nights a week, in between their frequent travels.

Like his own Glass House, Johnson positioned the Leonhardt House at the edge of an embankment that dropped about seventy feet to a rocky beach. Site and especially approach were longstanding concerns of Johnson, who often described his architecture as "processionalism." Looking to the example of the eighteenth-century English landscape garden, he composed spaces and views in such a way that they would be experienced as an unfolding sequence. For the Leonhardt House, he orchestrated the sequence to heighten the inherent drama of the site by progressively revealing and reframing the expansive view. The road to the house ran down the hill from the old estate house to a parking area, where the view of the water was obscured by the house and trees. From there, a straight path led to a raised entrance platform between the house's two volumes, where the full expanse of the water and sky came into view. An inconspicuous door to the left led into a windowless entrance hall, at the end of which large wooden doors opened to reveal the glass-walled living room dramatically floating over the embankment and the bay.

To match the impact of the approach, Johnson gave the house a striking profile. From the initial rear view, the house presented only light-colored brick walls. Like Frank Lloyd Wright's Fallingwater, the exterior could only be fully appreciated from below. If one walked around the house and down the slope, the slender projecting volume of the raised living room loomed into view. Even more striking was the view of the house from the bay. Sailing past, members of the Seawanhaka Corinthian Yacht Club across the harbor were treated to the sight of the cantilevered prism shooting out from the trees and the light brick façades of the rest of the house. According to Cliff Leonhardt, the original plan called for the house to extend even farther from the hillside, but Hurricane Carol eroded the bluff in 1954 and compelled Johnson to situate the structure at a more cautious remove from the edge.

The focal point of the house, the cantilevered living room, was an idea Johnson borrowed directly from a 1934 freehand sketch by Mies for a "house on a hillside."[10] Johnson most likely came across a photograph of the sketch in 1947 while preparing his retrospective exhibition on Mies's career at the Museum of Modern Art. He may also have seen renderings of a preliminary design by Charles Eames and Eero Saarinen for the Case Study House No. 8. Sometimes referred to as the Bridge House, the Eames-Saarinen design featured a rectangular volume extending from a hillside with diagonal braces. It, too, may have been derived from Mies's concept.

Johnson unabashedly copied the outward appearance of Mies's "house on a hillside" design, down to the distinctive diagonal braces that bisected the glass panels. But he also elaborated on the original concept. Mies's plan featured a single rectangle that contained a glass-walled living space at the projecting end and solid-walled sleeping and service rooms at the hillside end. Johnson transformed this utterly simple arrangement into something more complex. His version featured two parallel volumes extending in opposite directions from a perpendicular core. Of identical dimensions, the twin volumes played off each other. One was rooted in the hillside, the other hovered in the air. One featured solid, mostly windowless brick walls, the other an open steel frame and glass walls. Bedrooms were relegated to the closed wing, public living space to the open volume.

The visual impact of the Leonhardt House's glass living room, like that of its famous forebears Glass House and Mies's Farnsworth House, was defined not only by the panoramic view of the natural surroundings but also by its precise details and expensive materials The slender, black steel supports framed the view with crisp vertical and diagonal lines. The floor was a mosaic of tesserae. The large doors at the entrance end, set flush to the wall, were covered in an elegant wood veneer, as was the cabinet in the middle of the room. At the far end of the room, a fireplace contained in an austere black steel drum punctuated the space.

In early black-and-white photos by Ezra Stoller, the interior is furnished with Mies's Barcelona chairs and other modernist pieces, but this sparse phase did not last long. According to Cliff Leonhardt, his mother inherited her parents' traditional furniture, which she placed in the house.[11] An eclectic art collection was a critical component of the house as well. The Stoller photos show several pieces of outdoor sculpture, including a Rodin torso and a few works by Mary Callery. A reclining human figure by Callery was positioned on the entrance platform in such a way that it seemed to gaze out and gesture toward the water, mediating between the visitor and the view. Indoor pieces included a mobile by Alexander Calder, Picasso drawings, a Renoir painting, a Tang Dynasty horse, a Giacometti sculpture, and a Willem de Kooning painting.

The Leonhardt House was in many ways quite formal, yet Johnson also gave substantial consideration to how the house could best serve the needs of the family. Marcel Breuer had devoted a great deal of attention to the dynamics of middle-class domestic life, and Johnson no doubt looked to his former professor when contemplating the organization of interior spaces. Breuer designed many of his houses according to his binuclear plan, which split the spaces into two zones with different uses, both public vs. private and adult vs. children's (see pages 70–73).

Johnson adhered to the binuclear plan in the Leonhardt House. The cantilevered volume contained the open-plan living and dining room, as well as the kitchen, while all of the private and service functions were housed in the other volume. Within the private zone, the space was further separated by generation. On the lower floor were the master bedroom and a large adjoining dressing room. The upper floor was entirely devoted to children: a den and a kitchen at the front and two bedrooms toward the rear. To reach the sleeping area from the living area, one could either walk across the terrace that connected the two wings or down a flight of stairs and through a tunnel-like corridor lined with shelves full of books and art objects that ran beneath the terrace. This lower route allowed the parents to reach their bedroom from the living area without entering the children's space.

Johnson's quirky system of circulation contributed to an environment that balanced the grownup elegance of the house's modernist forms with a measure of youthful freedom. According to Cliff Leonhardt and his neighbors Ann and Peter Brower, who remember playing there as children, the privacy and informality of the house had great appeal. "I feel tremendously fortunate," Cliff Leonhardt has said about growing up there. "The living room was an amazing place to be in a snowstorm."[12] The rambling grounds around the house, which included outbuildings from the old estate and bunkers from World War II, contributed to the sense of adventure for the children.

Although much loved by the Leonhardt family, the house failed to gain acceptance from neighbors, many of whom were shocked by the departure from the historical styles of the older estate houses. Peter Brower remembers that someone tried to impede construction by filing a complaint with the zoning board that the design was actually two houses. His sister, Ann, recalls that some neighbors referred to it as a "glass factory."[13] When the Leonhardts put the house on the market in 1971, Andy Warhol, who worked with Johnson at the 1964 World's Fair, tried to buy it. But again the conservative culture of the area stood in the way and the neighborhood association vetoed Warhol's application. Subsequent owners had little taste for Johnson's Miesian minimalism. In the 1990s, the house was refaced and reroofed to give it a more conventional appearance, leaving little trace of the original design.

NEW YORK STATE PAVILION

A one-hundred-foot-tall, multicolored, concrete and plastic "Tent of Tomorrow," a circular "Theaterama" decorated with brash works of Pop art, and a trio of flying saucer–like observation towers—these were the unorthodox structures that made up the New York State Pavilion at the 1964 World's Fair, which Johnson designed with Richard Foster. Although perfectly suited to the carnival atmosphere of the fair, the buildings confounded many of the expectations that Johnson had established for his own buildings. *New York Times* critic Ada Louise Huxtable wrote that his architecture could exhibit a "painstaking refinement" and that "his houses are extravagant pleasure-palaces of carefully unostentatious richness for a Who's Who of art patrons and wealthy collectors."[14] Yet his oeuvre did not remain monolithic, if it ever really was completely so, and by the late 1950s, a change of aesthetic direction from his earlier hard-edged modernism had become apparent. Circles, arches, and domes began to show up in his buildings, especially when he collaborated with Foster, whose circular Revolving House of 1968, built for his family in Wilton, Connecticut, turned 360 degrees on ball bearings around a stair core. With the 1964 World's Fair pavilion, Johnson's approach to architecture took an even more dramatic turn, not only exhibiting a different vocabulary of forms, but also expressing a new populist spirit. Lively and accessible, these structures were in a sense a rebuke to the cool tastefulness of his previous work.

Johnson's pavilion also spoke to a broader development in American culture, a new attitude and a more experimental spirit that was just beginning to emerge in the mid-1960s. In architecture, modernism's confident claims of universality were being ever more forcefully challenged by critics and designers. Johnson's whimsical, exuberant pavilion seemed to offer an alternative to both the seeming aloofness of modernism and the buttoned-up conformity of postwar American society.

Johnson's connection to New York governor Nelson Rockefeller, who was president of the Museum of Modern Art from 1939 to 1958, put him in an excellent position to receive the commission for the pavilion. Rockefeller, along with the fair's director, Robert Moses, had long favored modernist architects for major public commissions such as Lincoln Center, where Johnson designed the New York State Theater, and the new State University of New York campuses. Rockefeller participated in the groundbreaking ceremony for the pavilion in October of 1962. According to a newspaper account of the event, the pavilion was to include industrial, government, artistic, and agricultural exhibits, as well as fashion shows and orchestral performances. Dubbed the "County Fair of the Future," its projected cost was $5,000,000.[15]

The pavilion differed substantially from his earlier work, as its most striking feature is the predominance of curves over right angles. In his earlier Miesian houses, Johnson occasionally introduced a single circular form, such as the stout brick cylinder containing the fireplace and bathroom in the Glass House or the smaller steel-drum fireplace in the Leonhardt House living room, to relieve the otherwise relentless rectilinearity. By the early 1960s, some of his projects featured plans made up entirely of circular spaces. If Mies had inspired his boxlike designs of the 1950s, it was likely Frank Lloyd Wright who sparked his subsequent experimentation with new geometries. Wright's Guggenheim Museum, which was under construction in the early 1960s, offered the most prominent example of a circular plan.

The layout of the New York State Pavilion was an essay in circles and ovals. The tent structure consisted of an enormous ellipse with a smaller circle nested inside it. It was ringed by sixteen circular, hollow concrete piers of the same diameter as the shafts supporting the observation towers. Fronting the tent were the circular theater and the three overlapping circles of the towers.

These carefully calculated geometries were part of a highly ordered, symmetrical, harmonious plan that suggested classical influences. A concourse between the theater and the observation towers led directly to the grand entrance of the tent's elliptical plaza, which was encircled by an elevated promenade, reached via escalator or stairs. The promenade served as a path for strolling, an exhibit space, and a vantage point from which to take in the views of the fair and Manhattan in the distance.

A precedent for the elliptical structure is Bernini's colonnaded piazza fronting St. Peter's Basilica in Rome, which Johnson praised a few years later in an interview as one of his favorite urban spaces. His fascination with neoclassical urban spaces also influenced his contemporaneous design for the plaza at Lincoln Center, with its pattern of concentric circles and radiating axes paved in travertine. The idea of Johnson as an architect of neoclassical grandeur was expressed by *New York Times* critic Ada Louise Huxtable, who praised the historical aspect of the New York State Pavilion and hailed Johnson as a throwback to turn-of-the-century giants of Beaux-Arts-style architecture such as McKim, Mead, and White.[16]

If the pavilion's sense of space and geometric order were inspired by classical sources, other elements were thoroughly modern and derived their appeal more from a sense of whimsy than classical gravitas. Fair exhibits, on subjects ranging from the state legislature to the Hudson River School, were installed in a modular scaffolding of interlocking, diamond-shaped metal frames that resembled an oversized toy construction set pieced together in random configurations.

New York State Pavilion, World's Fair, Flushing, Queens, 1962–64. The "Tent of Tomorrow," the "Theaterama" (foreground), and one of the two "Observation Towers."

The roof of the main structure looked very much like a circus big top. Lev Zetlin was the engineer responsible for what was described at the time as the world's largest suspension roof. Consisting of forty eight cables stretched between the elliptical perimeter ring and circular center ring, and fifteen hundred colored, translucent plastic panels, the roof was assembled on the ground and then housed into place. Enormous, toothlike metal forms, to which the cables are attached, give the appearance of festive pennants hanging from the perimeter.[17]

In addition to his use of plastic, which several contemporary accounts noted as a widely celebrated material at the fair, Johnson turned to concrete, which had grown rapidly in popularity in the 1950s. Instead of the delicate polished steel and glass of Miesian construction that Johnson had previously favored, he now looked to Le Corbusier, who pioneered the use of exposed concrete to achieve heavy, visceral, monumental effects. He might also have been inspired by Paul Rudolph's concrete architecture such as the nearby Endo Laboratories (see pages 278–83).

The pavilion also diverged sharply from Mies's aesthetic in the use of color. For the Leonhardt House Johnson had relied on a subtle palette of black steel beams, white brick walls, and transparent glass. Here he flooded the space with bright color. The plastic roof panels were red, orange, pink, and sky blue, and many structural elements were painted bright yellow, including the perimeter ring supporting the roof and the edges of the

New York State Pavilion, World's Fair, Flushing, Queens, 1962–64. The "Tent of Tomorrow" had a brilliantly colored fiberglass-tile roof. The circular balcony promenade afforded views of both the pavilion and the fair.

observation tower platforms. The "sky streak" elevator that took visitors to the top of the towers was also bright yellow, as was the promenade's balustrade, on which were mounted yellow lampposts with blue globes. At ground level, the exterior wall of the tent structure was striped with red and white canvas panels, as was the interior wall.

The festive character was enhanced by prominent graphic elements. The floor of the tent was covered with an oversized map of the state of New York made of terrazzo with plastic inlays. Sponsored by Texaco, this was a 4,000-fold blowup of the company's touring map and was billed as "the largest map in the world." The fabrication, handled by the Port Morris Tile and Marble Shop, was labor intensive. First, tiny sections of the published map were projected onto 4- x 4-foot pieces of paper, and every mark on the map was traced. Then plywood pattern boxes were made of each drawing and terrazzo was poured in, colored with pigments, and polished. Symbols and markers were cut out of plastic and metal and set into the forms. Finally, 576 finished tiles were pieced together on the pavilion floor. A mix of advertising and decoration, the map not only allowed visitors to symbolically traverse the length and breadth of the state inside the exhibit hall but also promoted the Texaco brand by showing the location of every one of the company's gas stations.

The most controversial embellishment of the pavilion architecture was the installation of a series of large-scale paintings and sculptures by New York-based Pop artists on the exterior of the Theaterama. This cylindrical structure housed a 360-degree movie screen on which was projected footage of state tourist destinations. To adorn its plain concrete façade, Johnson commissioned artworks from Roy Lichtenstein, Alexander Liberman, Robert Indiana, James Rosenquist, John Chamberlain, Robert Mallary, Peter Agostini, Robert Rauschenberg, Ellsworth Kelly, and Andy Warhol. One work, Warhol's *New York's Most Wanted*, a grid of blown-up mug shots, mostly of male Mafia leaders, attracted immediate opposition from fair organizers, who feared lawsuits from the pictured figures. Governor Rockefeller, it has been suggested, worried about offending his Italian American constituents. Told the piece was unacceptable, the mischievous Warhol quickly made a new version, replacing the mug shots with a repeated image of Robert Moses flashing a sinister grin. This time it was Johnson who vetoed Warhol's work, not wanting to offend his powerful patron. In the end, the original version remained on the wall, but it was covered with a coat of silver paint that left the faces only faintly visible.

The drama of the Warhol controversy aside, this feature of Johnson's design is a particularly intriguing one. The act of decorating his architecture with Pop art suggests that he felt an affinity with the movement. Just as artists like Warhol began incorporating images from popular culture into their art in the early 1960s as a critique of what they viewed as the aloofness of the abstract art of the 1950s, so Johnson, in combining the democratic openness of a public square with the color and festivity of the big top, offered an alternative to the architectural modernism—especially his own—that had been dominant for so many years.

The pavilion's fanciful design was widely celebrated at the time. According to Huxtable, it was "immediately hailed as the architectural delight of Flushing Meadow,"[18] even if its "decorative" aspect offended some orthodox modernists. Certainly its patrons were satisfied. At the dedication ceremony for the pavilion in April 1964, Rockefeller and Moses announced that because of its architectural quality, the pavilion would be left as a permanent monument.[19] It still stands today, although as a partly abandoned shell, the colorful plastic panels that covered the tent roof conspicuously absent. Only the theater building is currently in use, having been renovated for stage productions. The entire complex has recently been nominated for landmark status, so there is hope that its serious deterioration will someday be halted.

New York State Pavilion, World's Fair, Flushing, Queens, 1962–64. Texaco Road Map. West view of the 130 x 166 foot terrazzo road map of New York State on State Legislators Day, July 1, 1964.

20

I. M. PEI b.1917

Roosevelt Field Shopping Center, East Garden City, 1956;
Franklin National Bank, East Garden City, 1957

Today Roosevelt Field probably strikes most visitors as just another suburban shopping mall. Yet this expanse of parking lots and low-slung retail buildings along the Meadowbrook Parkway in central Nassau County was once an innovative and architecturally distinguished commercial development, designed by a team of young, progressive architects led by I. M. Pei.

Opened in 1956 as America's largest suburban retail complex,[1] Roosevelt Field was built on hallowed ground. The site, a flat, treeless piece of the vast, grassy Hempstead Plains, was once the world's premier aviation field. Two generations of military pilots had trained at Roosevelt Field, named for President Theodore Roosevelt's youngest son, Quentin, who was killed in aerial combat over France during World War I. In 1927, Charles Lindbergh took off from Roosevelt Field in the Spirit of St. Louis on his famous transatlantic flight. History could not be ignored, and in a canny mix of patriotism and public relations, the developer, William Zeckendorf, staged a dedication ceremony on August 8, 1956, at which he stood alongside a major general of the U.S. Air Force, an Air Force chaplain, and the chairman of Macy's, as well as two hundred aviation cadets representing twenty-two foreign nations.[2] Two weeks later, fifty thousand shoppers jammed into Macy's, the center's flagship retailer—an event that was indeed a poignant illustration of the

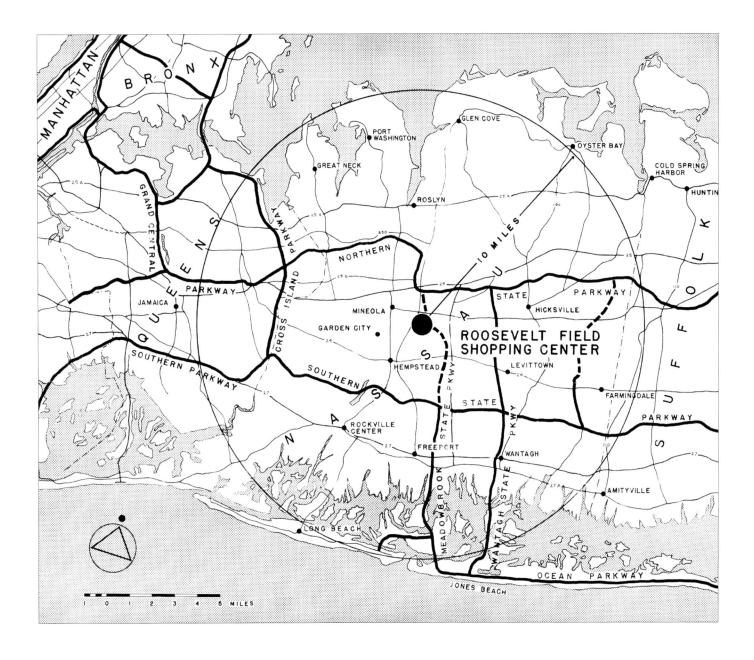

Roosevelt Field Shopping Center, East Garden City, 1956. Map of ten-mile-radius catchment area, showing how easily accessible Roosevelt Field was by car, thanks to the Robert Moses system of parkways.

paradigm shift from wartime sacrifice to postwar prosperity and materialism.

When Zeckendorf acquired the site in 1950, Nassau County was in the midst of rapid demographic and physical changes. Recently dominated by farmland, rural villages, and rail suburbs like nearby Garden City, the county was experiencing a population and building boom. New housing had sprouted with the influx of workers at the Grumman, Sperry, Republic, Liberty, and Fairchild aviation plants during World War II. After the war, returning soldiers continued to fuel population growth, and housing developments such as Levittown sprang up on former agricultural land all over the county.

Development in the region was increasingly governed by the expansion of automobile travel. Robert Moses, the titan of automobile-based planning, was at the time in charge of developing Long Island's parkway system. This was the era of the concrete cloverleaf, "the pretzel approach," or what *New Yorker* architectural critic and urbanist Lewis Mumford derisively dubbed our "National Flower."[3] The proliferation of new roadways allowed for a complete revision of community planning. Instead of the older model of small towns centered around pedestrian-accessible main streets and rail hubs, new housing development could spread with the highways. Retail services could be concentrated in larger,

Roosevelt Field, East Garden City, 1931. In the 1930s, Roosevelt Field was America's busiest airfield, but by the 1950s it had become a near-derelict wasteland.

more distant regional centers reachable primarily by car.

Like other developers and architects of the new shopping centers, Zeckendorf and Pei understood their projects as the modern, automobile-based equivalents of the ancient Greek agora or medieval cathedral square, where people would come to shop, stroll, and work. Indeed, though it was surrounded by parking lots and removed from housing, Roosevelt Field was not entirely different from a traditional urban center in terms of its dense internal layout and the variety of services it offered. Retail outlets, two supermarkets, restaurants, outdoor food stands, European-style kiosks, an ice-skating rink, a movie theater, and community meeting rooms were arrayed along pedestrian malls and around small squares and plazas. Escalators, called "electric stairways" at the time, descended beneath the open-air streets to an underground, air-conditioned concourse where there were twenty-five additional shops, restrooms, administrative offices, a radio broadcasting studio, a four-hundred-seat community meeting room, a home-building-products display center, and the Art Center, which exhibited top-quality paintings and sculpture chosen and purchased by Mrs. Zeckendorf, usually with her favorite art dealer, André Emmerich, or lent by the developer's many art-world acquaintances.

The presence of the art gallery was indicative of a remarkable level of attention to design that pervaded the entire project. Pei's buildings were elegant, light-filled modernist structures of steel and glass. The superb landscape design included gardens, concrete planters and benches, pools, water walls, fountains, and a variety of large trees and flowerbeds. Colorful graphic design, intended to recall the aviation history of Roosevelt Field, contributed a distinctive, unified visual character and an element of whimsy to the entire complex. The commitment to the integrity of Roosevelt Field's design extended even to the management

Roosevelt Field Shopping Center, East Garden City, 1956. Webb and Knapp presentation model, including a cloverleaf ramp running off the Northern Parkway. With Robert Moses's permission, the ramp was extended to allow direct access to the shopping center.

of tenants. The company's leasing office kept close watch on individual retailers, policing their signage and even internal displays to make sure that they adhered to guidelines for colors, materials, and scale. Equally vigilant was the Village of Garden City board, which worked with the Roosevelt Field Corporation for nine months on the planning issues for retail development and the removal of most buildings from the airfield. Mrs. Irwin Smith, appointed official historian of the village in 1959, wrote that "the area was to be limited to three-story professional or business buildings with minimum land coverage and 232 foot set-backs; that brightly-lit signs were to be outlawed; and that the unsightly hangars were to be removed."[4]

INNOVATIVE RETAIL DESIGN

However crass commercial shopping centers may seem today, in the 1950s this new architectural type attracted innovative thinking and high-quality design. The pioneering architect of American shopping malls, Austrian émigré Victor Gruen, brought European modernist taste and progressive social thinking to the type. Like Gruen, Roosevelt Field's developer, Zeckendorf, believed in the higher value of his work. Zeckendorf was a flamboyant self-promoter and an idealist who saw himself as a patron of great architecture. In his autobiography, he wrote that he consulted with his friend Nelson Rockefeller, then president of the Museum of Modern Art, on finding an unknown but promising architect to provide fresh ideas for his projects. Zeckendorf asked him, "Nelson, don't you think it is about time that the modern Medicis began hiring the modern Michelangelos and Da Vincis? I plan to go into a great building program on a national scale, and I'd like to put together an architectural staff to provide new thinking."[5]

In 1948, Zeckendorf recruited Pei, then an assistant professor at Harvard's Graduate School

of Design, to work at his development company, Webb & Knapp. Pei was given the title Director of the Architecture and Planning Division, ample workspace at the company's Manhattan headquarters, and a mandate to expand the firm's in-house design staff. Pei brought together a team of young designers who, like himself, had been trained in the principles of European modernism. He chose the thirty-four-year-old Don Page, an architect with a then rare background in graphic design as well, to head the Graphics Division. According to Page, "Webb & Knapp was the first development company to have in-house graphic design to enhance architecture and everything else."[6] Pei knew Page from Harvard, where they had both studied architecture under German émigré architects Walter Gropius and Marcel Breuer. A young Sol LeWitt was also briefly a member of the Graphics Division staff, from 1955 to 1956, before going on to his own acclaimed career as a sculptor of minimalist

Roosevelt Field Shopping Center, East Garden City, 1956. Steel framework 26- x 32-foot modules create light-filled, expansive spaces in the manner of Mies van der Rohe.

"structures"—modular configurations of open cubes in varied sizes—and wall paintings and drawings executed by others according to his specific instructions. LeWitt's desk was taken over by another young graphic designer, Ken Resen, who had just completed an MFA at Yale under the influential German artist and former Bauhaus teacher Josef Albers. To direct the Landscape Division, Pei hired the twenty-seven-year-old Robert Zion, another Harvard acquaintance and Gropius-Breuer protégé, who had recently attracted attention for a modernist garden that he created for his parents' house in Lawrence, Long Island.

According to those who worked with "Zeck," the developer believed that the design side of his business should operate as a freely collaborative fellowship of artists and intellectuals. He was willing to provide extensive resources and creative leeway in order to foster a dynamic environment in which his carefully chosen staff could come up with their best ideas. Zeckendorf enjoyed cultivating the camaraderie and spirit of his young designers. According to Resen, "Webb & Knapp was an exciting place to work, we became very caught up in giving 'Zeck' the best we could do. We believed we invented super graphics, or rather, integrated applied graphics."[7]

WILLIAM ZECKENDORF THE DEVELOPER

Pei and Zeckendorf's collaboration was amicable and highly productive. The two men worked together in the easy manner that comes from mutual admiration and friendship. They even lived in the same building at 30 Beekman Place, where Pei renovated the developer's penthouse apartment. Pei's output for Zeckendorf was prodigious. A year after designing a small office building in Atlanta in 1951, Pei began working on Roosevelt Field and the nearby Franklin National Bank building. He then moved rapidly through an impressive catalog of office, retail, and residential projects in Denver, Washington, D.C., Philadelphia, Montreal, and New York. Perhaps the most distinctive of his designs for Zeckendorf was a small but striking cylindrical glass turret perched on the roof of the Art Deco building that housed the Webb & Knapp headquarters at Madison Avenue and 46th Street. By 1955 the architect had gained so much autonomy within the company that he began working under the name I. M. Pei Associates at Webb & Knapp. In 1960, Pei left Webb & Knapp to launch an independent firm, today the successful Pei Cobb Freed & Partners.

Ultimately, Zeckendorf's attempt to fashion himself as a "modern Medici" contributed to the collapse of his real estate empire. Henry Cobb, a Pei associate since 1955 and today a principal at Pei Cobb Freed, recalls an inauspicious incident that reflected Zeckendorf's fatal weakness for art, his generosity to others, and his extravagance. At the opening ceremony of the Franklin National Bank, Zeckendorf unveiled a large, abstract sculpture by Jacques Lipschitz, remotely suggesting a male and female figure in coital embrace. It was an

Roosevelt Field Shopping Center, East Garden City, 1956. Clad in off-white brick, the Macy's store was one of several buildings with a closed, solid aesthetic complementing those with exposed I-beam framing.

244 I. M. PEI

Roosevelt Field Shopping Center, East Garden City, 1956. The Flight Mall. The kiosk on the right is one of ten dotted around the center. Like all the signage in the center, posters on the kiosks had to meet with official approval.

important piece from Zeckendorf's own collection and yet, as Cobb remembers, "Everyone blanched as Zeck gleefully presented what he thought was the perfect gift to stand on the lawn in front of the new building at a busy highway intersection."[8] Although the bank's executives delighted in the modern building that Pei had designed for them, Zeckendorf's sculpture was gone by the next day and soon replaced with a statue of Benjamin Franklin that had stood in front of the bank's prior headquarters at nearby Franklin Square.

Whatever his failings as a developer, Zeckendorf was both a visionary architectural patron and a savvy deal maker. While the formerly rural expanse of central Nassau Country was rapidly filling up with small-scale housing and retail developments, Zeckendorf saw the possibility for something much more ambitious. Since the opening of Idlewild and LaGuardia airports closer to New York City, the former Roosevelt Airfield had become a shabby, neglected expanse of open land. By 1950, when Zeckendorf clinched the deal to buy the airfield, its runways were used for little more than auto racing and its hangars housed a handful of warehouses. But the 125-acre parcel, combined with an adjacent 235 acres that Zeckendorf acquired from the Old Westbury Golf & Country Club, provided the developer with an enormous tract in the middle of the quickly developing area.

Zeckendorf understood that turning this space into a hub for shopping and community life would be enormously profitable, but would first require easy driving access for the area's growing population. So he struck an ingenious deal with Robert Moses, then in charge of the Jones Beach State Parkway Authority, donating forty-eight acres bisecting the airfield to the Parkway Authority. This enabled Moses to build the Meadowbrook

Parkway through Zeckendorf's site and provided space for a cloverleaf interchange that brought traffic from both the Meadowbrook and the Hempstead Turnpike directly into the shopping complex. Webb & Knapp made much of this convenience, marketing the project to prospective retailers and entertainment outlets with colorful brochures that publicized the far-reaching accessibility of the site. According to the brochures, 1,300,000 people could reach Roosevelt Field in thirty minutes or less.

THE PLANNING

Pei played several roles in the design of Roosevelt Field: site planner, architect of the core buildings, and overseer of the landscape and graphic design components. This was the first large-scale, multifaceted project that he undertook for Webb & Knapp, but his years at Harvard studying under and teaching alongside Gropius, who understood the design process as a collaborative effort, had prepared him well for this sort of task.

In Pei's recollection, his biggest concern was the layout of the complex. Situated to the west of the Meadowbrook Parkway, the shopping center was a tight cluster of structures nested inside a parking lot. He recalls how it all began: "Zeckendorf came to me and said, 'Make me a plan so I can invite Macy's and Gimbel's as magnets for either end of the shopping plaza and then everything else will make sense.'"[9] The Macy's building, the largest in the complex, sat at the south end. Gimbel's could not be persuaded to buy into the plan, so the north end of the site instead featured a skating rink, movie theater, and supermarket. The remaining structures, which housed small retailers, were aligned along north–south pedestrian malls and around small plazas. Pei designed the overall layout of the buildings to be compact rather than expansive, keeping the pedestrian corridors narrow enough to create a sense of intimacy.

According to Pei, the most crucial and complicated aspect of the plan was parking and traffic flow. How to guide heavy traffic into large parking lots with the greatest efficiency and how to connect parking areas with pedestrian zones were new issues for planners at the time. "I did considerable work on the parking, even though I didn't like having to deal with so many cars," Pei recalls.

"Unique to our plan was the vast amount of space we needed to allocate to cars and how to design things so shoppers would not have to walk very far or worry about finding them."[10] To circulate traffic around and into the 11,000-car lot, Pei designed a ring road. Two interchanges funneled cars from the Meadowbrook Parkway onto the ring, from which drivers could quickly reach the desired side of the complex without increasing internal congestion. On the lots, bold signage suspended from light poles identified parking zones. On the western side of the complex, a visually arresting, pergola-like bus-stop structure marked the main entrance into the complex. This glass-topped lattice of steel I-beams provided disembarking shoppers with shelter, as well as with a sense of arrival from the functional parking area to the more refined space of the shopping center itself.

THE ARCHITECTURE

Pei was responsible for the design of most of the buildings. Exceptions included Macy's, for which the department store hired the firm Skidmore, Owings and Merrill, in collaboration with Webb & Knapp architect A. Preston Moore; and the Century Circuit Cinema, which was designed by John J. McNamara, the venerable theater architect, who had his own firm, which converted or restored several Broadway theaters and designed a number of movie theaters in the Northeast.

Pei's buildings borrowed their architectural vocabulary from Mies van der Rohe. As Kellogg Wong, a former I. M. Pei Associates partner and brother of Pershing Wong, who was project architect for Roosevelt Field, explained, "We had three ways to go then—Mies, Frank Lloyd Wright, or Corbusier. We chose Mies, as he was the master of steel builders and we really liked the simplicity of his work."[11] Following the example of Mies's recently completed Illinois Institute of Technology campus in Chicago, Pei created two types of buildings: one that was extremely light and open in appearance, with slender I-beams of dark brown steel framing broad expanses of glass and supporting delicately cantilevered roofs, and another that was closed and solid, with unbroken walls of off-white brick. The design had both practical advantages and visual appeal. The modular architecture of bare steel beams was an efficient means of erecting large structures, and the thinness and strength of the frame enabled the creation of expansive, light-filled, and inviting spaces. The contrast of light and dark materials and the play of volumes gave the buildings a visual rhythm. And the European modernist vocabulary made the complex seem fashionable, even somewhat elegant.

DESIGN AND CORPORATE IDENTITY

The success of the complex as an attractive and cohesive work of architecture was due not only to Pei's graceful modernist architecture but also to Don Page's graphic design, which included extensive signage, brochures and company reports, and even the shopping bags and wrapping paper used by retailers. The idea of integrating architecture and graphics to create a distinctive visual identity was at the time becoming increasingly popular among American corporations. As companies expanded rapidly in the postwar economic boom, savvy businessmen embraced design as a means of making a lasting impression. In 1956, just as Zeckendorf's team was completing Roosevelt Field, IBM initiated its famous design program, led by Eliot Noyes, another Gropius disciple from Harvard. The scale and ambition of Noyes's work at the multinational IBM Corporation, which included designs for typewriters, advertising graphics, and office buildings, vastly exceeded what was happening at Roosevelt Field. Yet both IBM and Zeckendorf held a similar belief, born from the principles of Bauhaus graphics and wedded to an American concern with brand identity and marketing, in the value of comprehensive design to business and industry.

Page saw his graphic design as complementing the refined modernism of Pei's overall conception:

Roosevelt Field Shopping Center, East Garden City, 1956. Important artworks were sold by the Roosevelt Field Art Center, Inc., which exhibited in this outdoor sculpture court, as well as in an adjacent indoor gallery.

"Pei's minimal buildings were perfect for our applied graphics."[12] This look was no stretch for the young designer, as he, too, had connections to German modernism. After earning his undergraduate degree at Harvard, Page taught at Black Mountain College from 1938 to 1942, alongside German painter Josef Albers, another former Bauhaus instructor. Albers was best known for his series of paintings begun in 1950 titled *Homage to the Square*, starkly minimalist compositions of superimposed squares, which he intended as experiments in the optical effects of color juxtapositions. Page's graphics for Roosevelt Field consist of bright colors applied in simple, geometric patterns. The back of one of Page's promotional brochures, for example, is adorned in Albers-like fashion with four rectangles in contrasting shades of orange, yellow, and green.

But Page also brought a touch of whimsy to Roosevelt Field. He created a stylized hot-air balloon motif as the center's primary logo. Its buoyant form appeared, typically in bright green or orange, as a bold, colorful icon emblazoned on walls, awnings, shopping bags, and brochures, and in a repeating pattern on the wrapping paper. It also appeared on a string of illuminated, white plastic globes, forty inches in circumference, perched atop aluminum poles, a jaunty advertisement along the roadway that looked like a row of colossal lollipops or floating Ping-Pong balls. Similarly light touches were found in the round, brightly colored parking-lot signs and the outsized white telephone receivers stenciled on red brick walls to mark banks of public phones. Ultimately, Page seems to have understood his work as striking a careful balance between warm and cool. "We wanted to create an atmosphere of festivity, but quietly, elegantly, rather than with the blare of commercial promotion, which is the tendency today," he later noted.[13]

THE LANDSCAPING

In addition to his graphics, Page designed outdoor architectural features, including benches, seating enclosures, drinking fountains, and kiosks, all in distinctively sculptural, curving forms made of white concrete. On these features, Page worked closely with landscape architect Robert Zion, whose fountains, planters, paving, and foliage added a final element to Roosevelt Field's comprehensive design.

Along the Fountain Mall, one of the main pedestrian corridors, Zion placed large water features that emitted 2,200 gallons a minute, 25 percent of which passed through filters for recirculation in welded-steel tanks clad in stone. At night, the jets were illuminated by amber, blue, and green underwater lights controlled by rheostat. In the winter, the water temperature was regulated by special heating units. Zion punctuated Roosevelt Field's other corridors and squares with smaller fountains and raised planters, which also functioned as seating. The rectilinear forms of these concrete structures effectively harmonized with Pei's architecture. Complementing the planters were square beds of flowers, typically of a single variety and color, and low shrubs. An expert arboriculturist, Zion was skilled at selecting plants and trees for their sculptural effects. Great expense went to trucking in mature trees from long distances and building elaborate below-ground planting boxes

Roosevelt Field Shopping Center, East Garden City, 1956. The supermarket pick-up area, another example of Don Page's festive signage.

Roosevelt Field Shopping Center, East Garden City, 1956. Brick-walled telephone banks were instantly identifiable thanks to the whimsically oversized telephone receivers graphic designer Don Page stenciled on the side.

with deep wells, so that the trees appeared to grow directly out of the pavement. The roof over the underground shopping concourse supported large granite boxes planted with specimen trees that weighed as much as twelve tons.

Zion took particular interest in the paving of the squares and malls. In a 1962 article on paving in *Architectural Forum* titled "Who's Minding the Floor?" he lamented that "pavement design has been abandoned to the concrete mixer. Texture, color, and pattern are shunned as needless luxuries—a strange phenomenon." Noting that there had been much recent talk among architects about the revival of the "piazza," he argued, "As surely as the Renaissance exterior used the restrained elegance of the plaza floor as a foil, so the chaste contemporary building can gain by contrast with a richly patterned pavement."[14] At Roosevelt Field, Zion urged Zeckendorf not to use inexpensive concrete, which he felt was not only visually bland but produced excessive glare and noise. He convinced the developer to spend the money on more varied and interesting materials. For most of the paving, he chose relatively inexpensive hexagonal asphalt blocks, but he interspersed these with what he called "carpets" of granite cobblestones, which were laid down by masons trained in Italy. The materials and patterns changed as pedestrians moved from the main malls to the smaller connecting alleyways and courtyards, but the layout and

Franklin National Bank, East Garden City, 1957. The building was referred to affectionately as the "birdcage" because of its gridlike façade and the gold-anodized aluminum that coated the louvered screens and mullions of its windows, giving them a warm metallic sheen.

patterning were always based on the scale of the building bays.

Zion left Webb & Knapp soon after his superlative landscape scheme for Roosevelt Field was completed. He formed Zion and Breen with Harold Breen and later Donald Richardson. The firm executed a wide range of projects, including realizing Philip Johnson's design concepts for additions to the sculpture garden at the Museum of Modern Art (1961–2004), the landscaping for the Endo Laboratory designed by Paul Rudolph in nearby Garden City (1964; see pages 278–83), and some of the grounds of Long Island's State University of New York at Stony Brook (1968; see page 265). Among his masterworks are the diminutive Paley Park (1967), a beautiful vest-pocket park with a water wall off of a busy street in midtown Manhattan, and the grounds at the base of the Statue of Liberty (1986).

FRANKLIN NATIONAL BANK

Zeckendorf envisioned not only a shopping center at Roosevelt Field but an office complex as well. Pei's original master plan included a group of five office buildings on fifty-five acres on the western part of the site. However, only one was ultimately constructed: the five-story Franklin National Bank, designed by Pei, which opened in 1957. Previously housed in a grand Neo-Georgian edifice built in 1926 by the institution's founders in the nearby hamlet of Franklin Square, the bank came to Zeckendorf seeking a new look to represent the new culture of postwar America.

Just as he had done for the shopping center, for Franklin National Bank Pei created an elegantly minimal, modernist structure that derived its visual appeal from the simplicity of its overall volume, the subtle articulation of its façade geometry, and the quality of its materials. The bank was built of concrete, but its windows' louvered screens and mullions were faced with gold-anodized aluminum, which gave the structure a distinctive bronze sheen, while deflecting heat and sunlight. With its light, metallic, gridlike façade, the building became affectionately known as "the birdcage." Here again Pei followed the example of Mies van der Rohe. The German architect's Seagram Building was at that very moment under construction on Park Avenue, just a few blocks from the Webb & Knapp offices. Pei borrowed a number of Mies's elements, including the metal sheathing of the structure; the recessed, glass-clad ground floor, which creates a pedestrian arcade and adds to the sense of structural lightness; and the surrounding plaza, punctuated with shallow, rectangular pools. The plaza, which also included rectangular flowerbeds and lawns set between concrete-and-stone-aggregate walkways, was the work of Zion. In the lobby, Pei used travertine—a favorite material of Mies—for the walls and flooring. On axis with the main entrance, the building's service core included two elevators to the office floors and to the Sky Room, a penthouse cocktail lounge and restaurant. In the basement were two enormous vaults, along with—another characteristic sign of postwar culture—a large fallout shelter.

The Franklin National Bank had been successful primarily as a major lender for Long Island's housing and commercial development, but it also distinguished itself with forward-thinking approaches to retail customer service. Recognizing the importance of convenience and the automobile in the new suburban culture, the bank's president, Arthur Ross, invested in drive-through facilities, which were still a novelty across the country but beginning to attract customers. Pei gave the task of designing drive-through kiosks to Don Page. The elongated oval forms of Page's brick pavilions gave clever visual expression to the idea of seamless movement that the bank hoped its customers would associate with the drive-through experience.

Today Polimeni Enterprises, a real estate development company, owns the building, which they purchased from European American Bank, the institution that took over use of the banking hall and building in 1974, when the Franklin went bust in the then largest bank failure in American history. Vincent Polimeni has his corporate headquarters in the building, and he has said, "We are proud to own a timeless, magnificent office building in the best and busiest location on Long Island."[15]

The structure of the Franklin National Bank Building is still intact, but because of alterations, it has lost much of its original character. The aluminum cladding has been painted beige, the arcade has been glassed in to create new retail space, and the lobby, though some of its travertine walls remain, now has a burgundy marble floor.

The Roosevelt Field Shopping Center has been changed far more drastically. Though many of the trees and some of Zion's original paving have survived, Pei's architecture has been altered beyond recognition, starting in 1964, when the mall's interior streets were converted into glass-roofed gallerias.

In fact, Roosevelt Field was already suffering from the rapid turnover of retail culture by the 1960s. In its initial years, when the novelty of its stylish modern design captivated Long Islanders, the place seemed excitingly modern to consumers seeking the new, the convenient, and the different, especially in contrast to crowded downtown areas, with limited parking and the deprivations of the immediate postwar years. Beginning in the early 1960s, however, increasing traffic congestion along the expressways, which had become what people called "stressways," and the proliferation of new shopping centers in central Nassau County began to draw away visitors. Zeckendorf had to sell the entire property in 1963, in what amounted to a prelude to his company's bankruptcy two years later.

Roosevelt Field may have quickly fallen victim to the inexorable forces of development and changing taste, but it remains a shining memory for many Long Islanders and a significant historical site. The complex was the East's earliest example of large-scale suburban commercial architecture and a direct precursor of the enclosed shopping mall. It represented a pioneering use of European modernism in American retail design. And it was the first large-scale project in the prolific career of I. M. Pei.

Franklin National Bank, East Garden City, 1957. Don Page's drive-through banking kiosks were novel at the time.

21

DAMAZ, POKORNY & WEIGEL, GRUZEN & PARTNERS, ET AL.

State University of New York at Stony Brook, begun 1964: Student Union, Administrative Building, Library, Fine Arts and Humanities Center, Auditorium Building, 1964–75;
Earth and Space Sciences Building, 1969;
Stage XI Gruzen and Kelly Dormitory Complex, 1969;
Stage XII Complex (Roosevelt Quad), 1971;
Math and Physics (Graduate Physics-Mathematics) Building, 1973;
Health Sciences Complex 1976–80

Located on the North Shore, approximately equidistant from Manhattan and Montauk Point, Stony Brook is one of the largest and most architecturally rich of the many campuses erected in the late 1960s and early 1970s by the State University Construction Fund (SUCF). Launched by Governor Nelson Rockefeller in 1962, this powerful fund oversaw the design and building of more than twenty new branches of the State University of New York (SUNY) system, spending over four and a half billion dollars in the process. The fund commissioned firms like Edward Larrabee Barnes, Marcel Breuer and Associates, I. M. Pei & Partners, Skidmore, Owings and Merrill, and Benjamin Thompson & Associates to design campuses from the ground up, resulting in a network of institutions notable for the high quality of their buildings, planning, and landscaping.

Nelson Rockefeller had long believed in the social and cultural importance of public building on a grand scale. Indeed, by his own admission he had an "edifice complex."[1] He was involved in the development of Rockefeller Center in the 1930s and the United Nations complex in the 1940s, but the most ambitious of his endeavors was the creation of the SUCF, which he regarded as his single greatest accomplishment as governor.[2] Like his contemporary Robert Moses, Rockefeller favored publicly funded projects of a scope almost unthinkable today and was famous for using his

State University of New York at Stony Brook, 1964–80. Northward aerial view of the campus, mid-1980s.

executive powers to tap state funds to get buildings off the drawing boards and ready for occupancy in record-breaking time.

The SUNY system was in its infancy when Rockefeller took office in 1959 and grew to maturity during his tenure. New York had chartered its public universities only in 1948—the last state to do so—in response to the dramatic increase in demand by returning servicemen wanting to take advantage of the GI Bill for free higher education. At first the system consisted primarily of small colleges and technical schools, but in 1960, a private commission led by Ford Foundation president Henry T. Heald issued a report urging SUNY to substantially increase its budget, the number and size of its campuses, and its research ambitions. Taking advantage of Cold War–instigated federal funding for scientific research and an American public worried that the Soviet Union would outperform the U.S. in educating its citizens, Rockefeller initiated a complete overhaul to create bigger and better universities.

Under the auspices of the SUCF, architecture became a primary focus. Rockefeller chose George

Dudley as one of the fund's trustees. An architect, planner, and founding dean of the UCLA School of Architecture and Urban Planning, Dudley had worked under Wallace Harrison on the U.N. complex and been president of the Rockefeller-initiated International Basic Economy Corporation (IBEC). Working closely with Dudley to promote high-quality design was Anthony Adinolfi, the SUCF's manager of planning at its inception and its chief executive from 1968 until his premature death in 1971. Adinolfi had previously worked as deputy superintendent of the Detroit public schools, where he oversaw a major expansion. In New York, he drew praise not only for his managerial efficiency but also for his ability to collaborate with architects. Following his death, the Museum of Modern Art inaugurated a lecture series on architecture in his name. *Architectural Record* proclaimed him "one of the most knowledgeable and strongest advocates of good architecture ever to have the fiscal and administrative power to accomplish it."[3]

Adinolfi commissioned firms both large and small and approved a wide variety of architectural and planning solutions, from Edward Durell Stone's orientalist-inspired campus for Albany with its arcades of slender white arches gracing the façades of all of the buildings to I. M. Pei partner Henry Cobb's monolithic, poured-in-place concrete buildings at Fredonia. On Long Island, the SUCF constructed two new campuses: one for the small, locally oriented liberal arts college of Old Westbury (see pages 268–75) and another for Stony Brook, which was designated in 1965 as one of the state's four principal research institutions, or "university centers," along with Albany, Buffalo, and Binghamton. The "Berkeley of the East" became Stony Brook's unofficial slogan.[4]

In each case the designers were faced with a basic challenge: how to lend a distinctive personality to a fledgling institution. In the postwar era, as modernism evolved from an avant-garde experiment to the lingua franca of corporations and public institutions, architects were compelled to move beyond questions of utility and efficiency and address the more traditional concern of representation. A new discourse on "monumentality" arose as architects sought a new language that could apply collective values, cultural and political authority, and modernism to continuity with the past.

At Stony Brook, the architects sought to evoke a more traditional conception of the academy to suit the role of flagship institution. In contrast, the more radical architecture of Old Westbury reflects the experimental educational philosophy on which that school was founded. Two firms were largely responsible for giving shape to the new campus at Stony Brook. Damaz, Pokorny & Weigel produced the first master plan, the Library, and several other central buildings; Gruzen & Partners designed the science buildings and dorms, as well as the revised master plan, which they took over after Damaz, Pokorny & Weigel departed. The buildings and plazas that these two firms created were thoroughly contemporary in form and materials, avoiding any trace of nostalgia for traditional collegiate styles, but at the same time capturing something of the pomp and ceremony found at the nation's established older university campuses.

The new campus was located on 478 acres of heavily wooded land donated by Ward Melville, founder of the Thom McAn shoe store chain, the largest retailer of American shoes at the time. Founded as a teachers college in 1957, Stony Brook was located in nearby Oyster Bay before moving to the land donated by Melville in 1962. For the next several years, it was housed in a temporary collection of boxy, red brick buildings designed by the New York City firm of Voorhees, Walker, Smith, Smith & Haines. In 1965, after receiving its designation as a university center, Stony Brook hired a new president, John Toll, formerly chair of the Department of Physics and Astronomy at the University of Maryland. Toll was brought in to transform the university into a world-class institution of scientific research and to lead the campus expansion. It was during Toll's tenure, which lasted until 1978, that much of the present-day campus was planned and constructed.

The architectural firm hired to execute a master plan was a newly formed enterprise made up of three architects with little experience as principal designers. Jan Pokorny, a Czech émigré born in 1914, trained and practiced briefly as an architect in Prague before fleeing the Nazis in 1939. Settling in New York, he enrolled at Columbia University's architecture school to gain American credentials and then spent several years at the firm of Skidmore, Owings and Merrill. In 1946, he opened his own practice. Several smaller commissions for academic buildings led him to the Stony Brook project, after which he enjoyed a long, productive career specializing in the

State University of New York at Stony Brook, 1964–80. Pedestrian Circulation Plan from SUNY Stony Brook's "Design Vocabulary," dated March 16, 1967.

rehabilitation of historic structures. He was also a highly respected professor at Columbia University and an outspoken member of the New York City Landmarks Preservation Commission, on which he served from 1997 to 2007.

Pokorny first heard about the proposed Stony Brook project from George Dudley, with whom he was acquainted. Interested in being considered for the job of designing the Student Union, he asked the SUCF trustee to propose his name to Adinolfi, who engaged Pokorny first as architect of the Student Union and eventually as chief architect of the campus master plan. Having only a small practice, however, Pokorny needed collaborators to fulfill this larger role. Dudley suggested Paul Damaz and H. Bourke Weigel, two architects with whom he had worked under Wallace Harrison on the United Nations (U.N.). Damaz, born to French and Portuguese parents in 1917, studied architecture in Lyon before coming to New York with Le Corbusier in 1947. After Le Corbusier failed to win the U.N. commission, Damaz joined Harrison's firm. The slightly older Weigel, a New York City native born in 1912, was the U.N. project coordinator under Harrison. In the early 1960s, shortly before Dudley asked them to join with Pokorny, Damaz and Weigel struck out together to form their own firm.

The resulting partnership was, according to several involved parties, more a marriage of convenience than a natural merging of personalities. Pokorny later characterized Damaz somewhat dismissively as "a flashy kind of designer."[5] Ervin Galantay, then an associate professor at Columbia, whom Pokorny hired as the associate in charge of design, expressed a similar opinion.[6] Galantay and Damaz, both active critics used to arguing their views, clashed over aesthetic questions. As the two primary designers in the firm, each perhaps saw the other as infringing on his creative autonomy. Whatever the precise nature of these personal conflicts and animosities, by the time Galantay left the project to take a teaching position in Switzerland in 1970, he and Damaz had had a complete falling out. When the firm completed its work at Stony Brook the following year, Pokorny parted ways with Damaz and Weigel, who resumed their previous partnership.

Between 1964 and 1970, however, Damaz, Pokorny & Weigel's contributions to Stony Brook were substantial. In addition to the initial master plan, they designed the Library, Auditorium Building, Fine Arts and Humanities Center and Administration Building. They also laid out the plaza around which these structures were grouped and designed a long pedestrian bridge to connect the Student Union to the Library (known as the "bridge to nowhere" because it sat unfinished for ten years). Pokorny assumed primary responsibility for the master plan, Student Union, Library and Administration Building, although he delegated most of the actual design and drafting work to younger employees, including Galantay. Damaz was responsible for the design of the Auditorium Building and the Fine Arts and Humanities Center, and acted as coordinator among the project's many architects, engineers, and contractors. Weigel, whom Pokorny described as "a perfect administrator" and "famous for specifications,"[7] apparently acted exclusively as an overseer.

The initial phase in 1964 involved the design of the Student Union, which was handled primarily by Pokorny. He began before Galantay arrived and before the partnership with Damaz and Weigel was formed, though official credit for the final scheme was given to the whole firm. Pokorny hired a pair of younger architects, Rolf Ohlhausen and David Glasser, to draft the design under his supervision.

The building that Ohlhausen and Glasser produced, on a site across a service road from the central campus, is a rectangular, two-story, solid-looking brutalist structure with an exposed frame of rugged concrete and infill of dark, glazed brick. The exterior, though softened by carefully placed plantings, has a closed, almost fortress-like appearance, broken only by narrow slits in the heavy walls. Entrances are few and not immediately discernible. The primary mode of access was the pedestrian bridge, which extended over

State University of New York at Stony Brook, 1964–80. The "bridge to nowhere," leading into the Student Union. This elevated-access plan was later abandoned, and the bridge was demolished.

State University of New York at Stony Brook, 1964–80. The "bridge to nowhere" spanned the service road that separated the Student Union from the rest of the campus. Across the service road from the Student Union are two exedras, signature landscape designs by M. Paul Friedberg.

State University of New York at Stony Brook, 1964–80. The lounge in the Student Union, designed by Jan Pokorny.

State University of New York at Stony Brook, 1964–80. The cafeteria in the Student Union was skylit by day; hanging globe fixtures illuminated the space at night.

State University of New York at Stony Brook, 1964–80. The Library, designed by Ervin Galantay, looms over the Academic Forum. Originally designed for academic parades, concerts, and rallies, the vast plaza has since been covered over with grass.

OPPOSITE
State University of New York at Stony Brook, 1964–80. Library. This arcade is an addition to the original library's entrance façade.

the service road to the central campus. This broad, elevated promenade punched through the Student Union's façade and connected to a turret-like stair tower that led directly down to the heart of the building.

The building's interior spaces are remarkably varied in scale, with expansive, double-height public areas flanked by intimate, recessed spaces. The largest public room is the ballroom; large glass dome fixtures hang from its superb honeycombed concrete ceiling. A dark-glazed, brick-paved concourse runs through the center of the building like an interior street and provides access to the theater and bookstore, as well as to a sheltered courtyard filled with plantings and overlooked by balconies. Reflecting the moment in which it was built, the courtyard featured a built-in brick podium that one reviewer described as useful for "impromptu speeches or student rallies."[8]

The design of the Student Union convinced the SUCF of the firm's abilities and won them the larger assignments of creating a master plan for the whole campus and designing several of the larger buildings. The architectural vocabulary and materials used by Ohlhausen and Glasser in their design for the student union set the precedent for subsequent structures, as did a dearth of affordable steel at the time of the Vietnam War and building of the World Trade Center.[9] Indeed, the SUCF compiled a book of standards in which the materials that could be used were prescribed. Thus, exposed-concrete bearing structures and red brick walls for infill predominate in Pokorny's Administration Building, Galantay's Library, Damaz's Fine Arts and Humanities Center (to which Galantay contributed) and the Auditorium Building. Another feature common to all the buildings is the dark-glazed, brick-paved interior corridor, the most prominent example of which is found in the skylit, atriumlike space that stretches along the front of the Library. It is lined with benches, potted shrubs, and large globe lamps built into the wall.

Galantay's Library, on the western edge of the central plaza, is the largest and most formally

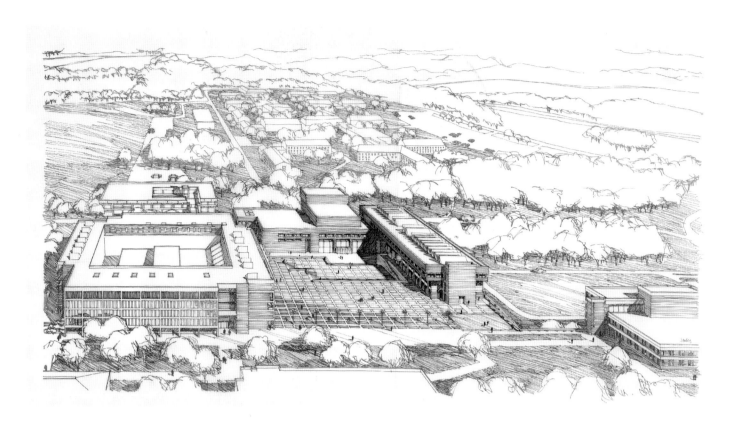

OPPOSITE TOP
State University of New York at Stony Brook, 1964–80. Fine Arts Building and Central Campus. Damaz, Pokorny, & Weigel's as-built massing study, November 5, 1970.

OPPOSITE BOTTOM
State University of New York at Stony Brook, 1964–80. Fine Arts Center, designed by Paul Damaz.

State University of New York at Stony Brook, 1964–80. Aerial view of the Academic Forum, surrounded by the Library (in the center of the photo) and the Fine Arts Center and Auditorium (foreground).

imposing of the firm's buildings. Designed as an addition to the original library, it wraps around the older brick box, which remains partly intact in the center. The exterior of the new building is a five-story grid of concrete piers that conveys a thoroughly classical sense of order and weight. Galantay, born in Budapest in 1930, studied architecture in Zurich, where his favorite teacher was the architectural historian Sigfried Giedion. A leading voice in the discourse on monumentality, Giedion was a strong proponent of Le Corbusier and the Bauhaus masters, though he also insisted that his students approach their studio design work with a solid knowledge of time-honored, iconic architecture. Galantay found himself critical of the work of the modern masters, heretically so in the presence of Giedion, and more drawn for inspiration to the massive architecture of the world's military training fortresses, the solid monumentality of Roman stone architecture, and the New Classicism practiced by architects in the Nordic countries.[10] After coming to the United States, Galantay entered a design in the Boston City Hall competition. The winning design, by Kallmann McKinnell & Knowles, a looming mass of gigantic concrete slabs, pushed monumentality to its outer limit. Galantay's Stony Brook library might be seen as his response to that building.[11]

The colonnaded first level and otherwise gridded façade of the Library certainly resembles that of Boston City Hall, but in subdued form. The result is an imposing building with a well-organized cadence to its façade. It was a near perfect example of poured-in-place concrete construction, in which the impressions of the wooden formwork are left raw on the untreated building surface. Near perfect, until the university painted over the light brown concrete surface. Well-designed, primarily concrete buildings always exhibit a dramatic interplay between mass, shadow, and void, but a paint job mutes the drama.

Damaz, Pokorny & Weigel sought to capture a sense of monumental grandeur not only in their buildings but also in the layout of the plaza around which the Library and Fine Arts and Humanities Center were situated. Known as the Academic Forum, this space was a central element of the overall campus design and underwent several revisions during the planning phase of 1964–67. Led by Galantay, the architects' aim was to create a space that could accommodate all-university events and project an aura of ceremony. An early version included a round, amphitheater-like area to be used as an outdoor stage for gatherings and performances. In the realized design this evolved into a series of terraces that step down from the library toward the Fine Arts and Humanities Center. Galantay's intention was to capture something of the spirit of older urban plazas like Venice's St. Mark's Square. Seeing the library as analogous to the Doge's Palace, he designed third-floor balconies from which university officials dressed in academic regalia could oversee proceedings below, like modern-day Venetian *nobili*. Part of this vision was the planned, but never built, humanities tower, a tall, slender structure that would have punctuated the south end of the plaza like a campanile.[12]

In addition to designing the Library and Academic Forum, Galantay contributed to the master plan. He was the only one of the firm's architects with large-scale planning experience. In 1956, he won a fellowship to work on the Philadelphia City Planning Commission under the visionary architect and planner Edmund Bacon and with architect Willo von Moltke. Then I. M. Pei and William Zeckendorf hired him to work on the Society Hill neighborhood development project in Philadelphia. While teaching at Harvard and MIT in the early 1960s, he participated in the design of a new industrial town in Venezuela, and in 1975 he published a book on the history of new towns. In his work on the Stony Brook plan, Galantay was aided by Ohlhausen and Glasser, who had started their own firm but stayed on as "planning consultants." Together, they produced several versions of the master plan in late 1965 and early 1966. On February 1, 1967, Pokorny, Glasser, Ohlhausen, and Damaz traveled to Albany, where they received approval for the plan from Adinolfi and other officials.

Damaz, Pokorny & Weigel's master plan confirmed the symbolic importance of the Academic Forum by positioning it as the hub to which all other areas were linked by radiating spokes. This arrangement, referred to as the "five fingers plan," created secondary spatial nodes for the liberal arts, engineering, physical sciences, and health sciences, as well as non-academic activities like athletics. Pedestrian paths connected these nodes to the center. The plan kept automobile traffic on the perimeter of the campus, though cars were by no means banished. Given the campus's rural location, the firm recognized that convenient and plentiful parking was an essential element of the campus infrastructure. To allow automobile access to the center of campus while maintaining a pedestrian-oriented environment, the planners proposed building an enormous parking garage beneath the Academic Forum.

The underground garage was never built, but its inclusion in the original plan indicates the importance the architects accorded to pedestrian traffic. In their view, a pedestrian-filled campus was essential to creating the atmosphere and character of an "urban space." The issue of density came to the fore in discussions between representatives of Damaz, Pokorny & Weigel and SUCF and SUNY officials in Albany. To promote density, the architects proposed building several high-rise towers with separate floors for faculty offices and classrooms near the Academic Forum. President Toll countered this proposal, arguing for a single humanities tower with faculty and student facilities sharing the floors.

In the end, all of the planned high-rise buildings remained on the drawing board because of budget cuts, and the Academic Forum was left without its crowning structure on the south side, resulting in a much lower concentration of users. In 2002, the concrete and brick plaza was torn out and replaced with grass, and the pedestrian bridge between the Library and Student Union was torn down—modifications that appeal to current taste but undermine the vibrancy and interconnection of the Student Union with the plaza and all of the outdoor spaces as originally envisioned by the designers.

By 1971, when the Library and Student Union had opened, the work of Damaz, Pokorny & Weigel at Stony Brook was largely complete. The brick-clad Fine Arts and Humanities Center did not open until 1975, and by then the partnership had disbanded. Responsibility for the master plan had been passed to Gruzen & Partners, the other firm originally hired by the SUCF to design a major segment of the campus. Known until 1967 as Kelly & Gruzen, the firm had been established by B. Sumner Gruzen, who passed leadership to his son, Jordan, and to his younger partners, in the late 1960s. By that time, it had established itself as a leading firm for large institutional commissions. Its most

State University of New York at Stony Brook, 1964–80. Graduate Physics-Mathematics Building, designed by Gruzen & Partners, 1973.

acclaimed projects of those years were Chatham Towers near City Hall in Manhattan and the nearby New York City Police Headquarters. Chatham Towers were the first poured-in-place concrete high-rise buildings in America and a distinguished model for affordable housing.

At Stony Brook, Gruzen & Partners was responsible for several science buildings. Because President Toll aimed to make scientific research Stony Brook's primary calling, these buildings dominated the central campus. The first to be completed, in 1969, was the Earth and Space Sciences Building. Situated at the terminus of the main pedestrian path leading west from the Administration Building and past the paths to the Academic Forum, it featured a large archway, under which students could pass to reach the path to a dormitory quadrant. Designed in poured-in-place concrete, with the wooden formwork crafted to express crisp decorative detailing of vertical and horizontal lines, the L-shaped building wrapped around a landscaped sunken courtyard garden, accessed via several broad series of steps, which served as the central plaza for the science area.

A provocative assignment for the young architects from Gruzen & Partners was to design an underground counting chamber for the university's prized collection of moon rocks, brought back from the first lunar mission in 1969. These were donated by the federal government to help President Toll establish the new university's high profile in the sciences. Over the next five years, Gruzen & Partners completed the brick-faced Graduate Physics-Mathematics Building, reminiscent of Louis Kahn's Richards Medical Research Laboratories in Philadelphia, as well as buildings for life sciences, engineering, computer sciences, and social sciences.

In addition, the firm was responsible for two complexes of undergraduate dormitories, the Stage XI complex (originally known as Gruzen and Kelly, but today known as the Kelly complex), and the Stage XII complex (today the Roosevelt Quad). Jordan Gruzen was the primary designer for the XI buildings, intended to accommodate a thousand students. Rather than house them all in one large, vertical building, he came up with the concept of what he called a "daisy chain" of strung-together Y-shaped buildings, each housing sixty or so students. Built with exposed-concrete frames and brick infill walls, the dormitories were situated around landscaped plazas. In layout, if not in design, the complex emulated the intimacy and social cohesion found in student housing at old, venerable universities.

The courtyards of the Stage XI quad and the Earth and Space Sciences Building, as well as the plaza in front of the Physics-Mathematics Building, which could be viewed from the so-called "bridge to nowhere," were designed by M. Paul Friedberg, well known by the end of the 1960s for his creation of urban outdoor spaces. Several of his award-winning projects were funded by the Astor Foundation, notably the grounds of the Jacob Riis Houses in Lower Manhattan. The aim of Friedberg's designs was social more than formal; he specialized in the creation of gathering spaces to foster human interaction. At Stony Brook, in addition to the science and residential quad courtyards, Friedberg created built-in outdoor seating with attached concrete lighting columns near the Student Union and below the bridge. The seating consisted of large exedras, like miniature amphitheaters of poured concrete, which were meant to inspire casual conversation, as well as to add visual punctuation marks to open spaces. These exedras are still there and are often used for outdoor classes in sunny weather, as mature, well-chosen shade trees now

OPPOSITE TOP
State University of New York at Stony Brook, 1964–80. Presentation drawing, Earth and Space Sciences Building, designed by Gruzen & Partners, 1969. M. Paul Friedberg designed the steps and the sunken garden of the building's main courtyard.

OPPOSITE BOTTOM
State University of New York at Stony Brook, 1964–80. Earth and Space Sciences Building, 1969. Note the observatory on the roof.

BELOW
State University of New York at Stony Brook, 1964–80. Aerial view of the Stage XI (Gruzen and Kelly) dormitory complex in the foreground and the Stage XII complex (Roosevelt Quad) in the background, 1969 and 1971.

State University of New York at Stony Brook, 1964–80. Gruzen and Kelly dormitory complex, exterior view, 1969.

provide a further sense of enclosure. As Friedberg has said of his approach to his design for Stony Brook, "On a campus, students interact as much outside of buildings as they do inside. I deal with shared space, so it has to facilitate the opportunity for people to interact informally as well as in scheduled activities."[13]

Still other architects contributed to the campus in the early stages. Richard Roth Jr., of Emery Roth & Sons in Manhattan, executed a dormitory complex (known today as the Roth Quad). William Kessler, a Detroit-based architect, designed a windowless, multipyramidal structure as a main lecture hall named for New York State's Senator Jacob Javits. Its exterior walls are of battered, textured concrete, and it was originally offset by landscape design by the firm of Zion and Breen. The Health Sciences complex, at the southeast edge of the campus, was the work of the futuristic Chicago architect Bertrand Goldberg, best known today for his Marina City complex, the so-called Corn Cob apartments, completed in 1964, in Chicago. Construction of Goldberg's cubic raw concrete Clinical Sciences Tower and Basic Sciences Tower, and two hexagon-shaped Hospital towers, sheathed in shiny dark brown glass squares, took place between 1976 and 1980. Raised on stilts above a seven-story base building built into a hill, the towers can be seen from miles away and serve as distinctive signage. They are reminiscent of the fantasy architecture of the Japanese Metabolists and are among the university's most arresting buildings.

Although today less unified than some of the campuses built by the SUCF, Stony Brook contains a rich collection of structures and outdoor spaces of remarkably high-quality design and construction. The campus remains a testament to the achievements of the SUCF. The construction of New York State's vast public university system in the late 1960s and early 1970s, carried out in a short span of time, on a controlled budget, and with commendable architectural results, amounts to one of the great public building campaigns of the late twentieth century.

State University of New York at Stony Brook, 1964–80. Gruzen and Kelly dormitory, interior view, 1969.

BELOW
State University of New York at Stony Brook, 1964–80. Health Sciences Complex, designed by Bertrand Goldberg, 1976–80. Built on stilts above a seven-story base building, the complex could be seen for miles around.

22

JOHN JOHANSEN b.1916, ALEXANDER KOUZMANOFF 1915–2004, AND VICTOR CHRIST-JANER 1915–2008

SUNY Old Westbury, 1966–82: master plan until 1972;
Academic Village A, 1972;
Campus Center, 1982

The College at Old Westbury differed sharply from its much larger Long Island sibling, Stony Brook University (see pages 252–67). Rather than a flagship research institution cut from an essentially traditional mold, Old Westbury was a small liberal arts college that posed a vigorous challenge to standard academic practices. Its founders created the school in response to the era's changing social norms and widespread student discontent as a model for the reform of higher education. The design of the campus, situated on 570 acres of open space surrounded by woodlands, adjacent to the Long Island Expressway, reflected this antitraditional ethos. John Johansen, Alexander Kouzmanoff, and Victor Christ-Janer, the architects in charge of designing the new campus, created adventurous buildings that they hoped would reflect and enable Old Westbury's radical educational and social ideals.

The notion of adding an ultra-experimental college to the State University system, known as SUNY, was initiated by its progressive chancellor, Samuel B. Gould. A close associate and friend of Nelson Rockefeller's, he fused fifty-eight campuses into today's SUNY system. As Gould's obituary in the *New York Times* observed, he "sought to mesh the parts while keeping SUNY from deteriorating into a chain of clones."[1] To lead the new Old Westbury institution, Gould chose Harris L. Wofford, a former civil rights lawyer and associate director of the fledgling Peace Corps. Wofford, who was

among the protestors arrested at the 1968 Democratic National Convention in Chicago, was openly supportive of a radical agenda and embraced the mandate given to him by Gould to make Old Westbury "the most ambitious laboratory in the world for innovation in higher education."[2]

Before opening SUNY Old Westbury in 1968, Wofford convened a group of students and faculty to define the college's mission. The result was a program that emphasized student empowerment, racial equality, and social activism. Students were granted "full partnership" with the administration and faculty and "the right to determine, in large measure, their own areas of study and research."[3] There were to be no traditional exams, no failing grades, and no prescribed pace of study. The usual academic departments were replaced by an interdisciplinary curriculum that emphasized contemporary urban social problems. Fieldwork conducted among disadvantaged urban populations formed a large a portion of the course of study. The college also sought to include in its student body a high percentage of individuals from groups with traditionally limited access to college. Over half were African-American and Latino, and the average age of the students was twenty-nine.[4]

The architecture and planning of the Old Westbury campus was designed to be similarly progressive, with indoor and outdoor spaces intended to encourage socializing and group learning.

SUNY Old Westbury, Academic Village A, 1972. Aerial view of the Academic Village. Built on the highest hill of a former "great estate," the architects designed a picturesque hill town of archaic forms from amber-colored cast stone. The campus plan originally called for a federation of academic villages, each with distinct clusters of buildings for learning and residential use.

Classrooms and hallways featured large-pane windows open to spacious courtyards. Like Stony Brook, the college occupied a former great estate, symbolically displacing the grandeur and rarefied living of the Gold Coast's Great Estate era with a new egalitarianism. The property, formerly known as Broad Hollow, had been one of several country properties, including a 5,000-acre horse farm in Cooperstown, New York, and a bona fide Georgian country mansion in Leicestershire, England, owned by Ambrose Clark, an heir to the Singer Sewing Machine Company fortune. He and his first wife were noted Anglophiles, and he was the quintessential amateur equestrian sportsman of his generation.

In 1965, a year after Clark's death, the state of New York worked out an arrangement with his executors for the state to assume ownership of Broad Hollow, including its extensive parks and fields and its forty-two-room brick-and-stone Georgian Revival mansion, designed in 1912 by Harry St. Clair Zogbaum. Today, students wander along the riding trails, and the polo fields are used for football, baseball, and other sports. The mansion was converted into a temporary campus center with administrative offices and classrooms, but was destroyed in a fire just months before the college was set to open in 1968. Arrangements were quickly made for the college to set up a library and classrooms at another former great estate, Planting Fields, in nearby Oyster Bay, where geodesic domes, an architectural form with strong countercultural associations, were hastily erected to house the first class of students. Nevertheless, some classes did open at Broad Hollow, in an enormous ballroom, a 1922 addition to the mansion that was saved from the fire, and in buildings that once housed scores of horse trainers and servants.

Meanwhile, Johansen, Kouzmanoff, and Christ-Janer had completed the master plan for the permanent campus at Old Westbury. Like the Stony Brook partnership of Damaz, Pokorny, and Weigel, this was a temporary alliance of architects formed at the bequest of the State University Construction Fund. Each of the three architects came to the project through connections to the SUCF leadership. Johansen and Kouzmanoff knew architect George Dudley, who as an SUCF trustee was in charge of selecting architectural firms. Christ-Janer was acquainted with Nelson Rockefeller, who employed him as chief graphic designer at the Office of the Coordinator of Inter-American Affairs

SUNY Old Westbury. Geodesic domes at Planting Fields, another former great estate in nearby Oyster Bay, provided temporary classrooms and a library in 1968.

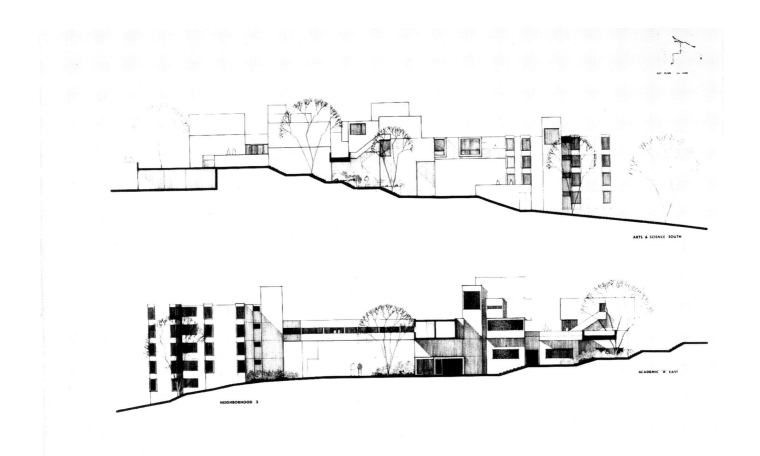

SUNY Old Westbury, Academic Village A, 1972. Elevation drawings of the Arts and Science Building and other classroom facilities in the complex.

in 1941–42. There were further connections among the three architects: Johansen and Kouzmanoff had both worked with Wallace Harrison on the United Nations in the early 1950s. Kouzmanoff and Christ-Janer knew each other from Columbia University, where they taught in the architecture school; and Christ-Janer and Johansen were both part of the coterie of young modernist architects who had set up offices and designed numerous houses in New Canaan, Connecticut, in the late 1940s.

The master plan for Old Westbury reflected the organization and ideals of the school. Old Westbury was to be structured as a federation of independent colleges, each with its own disciplinary emphasis, students, and faculty. Accordingly, the master plan consisted of distinct clusters of buildings for four separate colleges, each with its own classrooms, faculty offices, and dormitories. The colleges were situated like satellites around a central group of administrative, library, and arts facilities. On the whole, the plan was much more diffuse and less grand than that of Stony Brook or other, more traditional campuses. There were no quadrangles, axes, focused vistas, or spatial hierarchies. Instead, buildings were scattered irregularly around the parklike estate in a way that suggested the individualism and informality of the new institution itself.

Construction began in 1968 on the first of the colleges, which was soon after named the Academic Village. The design was primarily the work of Alexander Kouzmanoff, a superb architect with a Beaux-Arts education who turned to modernism at the start of his career, when he was designing for the Navy, and John Johansen, an iconoclast whose architectural ideas were well suited to Old Westbury.[5] Johansen attended the Harvard Graduate School of Design (GSD) from 1939 to 1942, studying with Walter Gropius, Marcel Breuer, and others from the German Bauhaus. By the late 1960s, the GSD came to be associated with an oppressively conformist brand of architectural modernism, derisively referred to by postmodernists as the architecture of the "Harvard Box." Johansen, however, took a restlessly innovative and highly personal approach to design and in the late 1950s he turned away from the austere boxes of his Harvard training toward more varied forms. He embraced the sculptural quality of buildings like Le Corbusier's chapel of Notre Dame du Haut at Ronchamp, France, as seen in his 1955 designs for a series of unbuilt houses in swelling, shell-like, sprayed-concrete

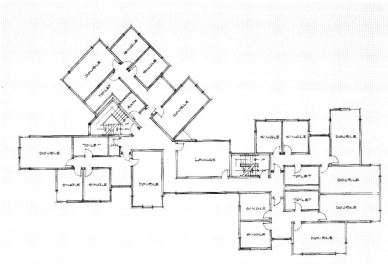

SUNY Old Westbury, Academic Village A, 1972. Floor plan of student housing, designed to encourage community, with four separate suites and a central lounge and large pane windows with views of outdoor courts.

forms. He also experimented briefly with neoclassical symmetry, notably in his cylindrical American Embassy in Dublin (1964).

In the late 1960s, Johansen shifted toward an approach that he described as "ad hoc" or "organic" design, in which form developed in an apparently natural way out of how the building was to be used. He wanted his designs to convey a sense of unplanned growth and change. "In biological terms, one might describe the assemblage as an accretion of shells (enclosures) or as barnacles attaching themselves to a rock of their own free will," he wrote of one of his earlier projects.[6] This sense of radical self-determination, with its strong social undertones, was most strikingly reflected in Johansen's Mummers Theater in Oklahoma City (1965–70; now called Stage Center). Drawing inspiration from the British group Archigram and its countercultural fantasies for modular, "plug-in" cities, Johansen designed a network of brightly colored, sheet-metal-covered tubes, wooden ramps, and massive concrete drums. The theater was commissioned by an avant-garde stage director and was meant to reflect the experimental quality of the productions within.

At Old Westbury, begun soon after Mummers Theater, Kouzmanoff and Johansen followed a similar ad hoc approach, but used a vocabulary of heavier, more archaic forms in masonry. Johansen recalled that he "really wanted to have colored

OPPOSITE TOP
SUNY Old Westbury, Academic Village A, 1972. View of rooftop faculty office buildings.

RIGHT
SUNY Old Westbury, Academic Village A, 1972. Classroom buildings on either side of stairs leading to an upper plaza.

BELOW RIGHT
SUNY Old Westbury, Academic Village A, 1972. View towards an area of classroom buildings. Note the ramps and bridges to connect buildings of blocky irregularity.

sheet-metal panels added to the complex, like we were able to do with Mummers,"[7] but was forced by external considerations at Old Westbury to use only concrete, something he later greatly regretted after seeing how well the combination of materials worked in the completed theater. In contrast to the colorful tubes and panels of Mummers, which Johansen meant to echo the look of electronic circuit boards, the rough, poured-in-place concrete of Old Westbury emulates brutalist buildings like Kallmann McKinnell & Knowles's Boston City Hall (1963–68).

Above all, Kouzmanoff and Johansen's design for Old Westbury reflects their interest in the layout and formation of medieval cities. Like Louis Kahn, another contemporary to whom their work was indebted, both architects had spent time in Italy sketching and painting views of quaint winding streets, jutting towers, and massive fortifications. Their taste for medieval townscapes was likely reinforced by reading the work of Camillo Sitte. The Viennese architect's influential book *City Planning According to Artistic Principles*, first published in 1889, argued for a return to the picturesque and intimate qualities of winding medieval streets as an alternative to the imposing boulevards and open plazas of nineteenth-century urbanism. It appeared in a new English translation in 1965 and was widely read by younger architects and their professors, such as Christ-Janer, Johansen, and Kouzmanoff, who viewed modernist planning as excessively monumental and uniform.

Johansen described the Academic Village at Old Westbury college as a picturesque hill town and as an organic cluster of forms that "had grown together casually over time."[8] In profile, the concrete buildings are characterized by their blocky irregularity, with towers projecting here and there

LEFT
SUNY Old Westbury, Academic Village A, 1972. A second-level view from within the academic buildings complex.

BELOW LEFT
SUNY Old Westbury, Academic Village A, 1972. Dormitory buildings connected by a bridge at an edge of the village.

like turrets. In plan, the complex has the meandering quality of an ancient village positioned on a gently sloping hillside. According to Johansen, "The idea was to have the hill determine the organization and character and life of the project," a planning strategy that he described as "a great success."[9] The complex is anchored at the top of the rise by a core of academic buildings, including a lecture hall, classrooms, a small library, and faculty offices. These feed into the rooftop plaza of a two-story building, from which bridges lead to peripheral dormitory buildings. The bridges, along with ramps, twisting stairways, small courtyards, sheltered corners, and small gardens, contribute to a highly varied and rich composition of spaces and circulation routes. As at Stony Brook, the architecture follows the spirit of the institution's original mission. But whereas SUNY Stony Brook's classically ordered façades and quadrangles conjured academic tradition, the organic design of SUNY Old Westbury's Academic Village suggests student autonomy, academic freedom, and community.

After the completion of the Academic Village in 1972, the SUCF leadership decided to break up the joint venture, as they liked to call it, between Christ-Janer, Johansen, and Kouzmanoff and give each architect individual commissions.[10] Christ-Janer was assigned Academic Village B, which was never realized. Kouzmanoff and Johansen were assigned pieces of the Campus Center. Kouzmanoff designed the administration offices, a cafeteria, and an art gallery referred to as Core West, while Johansen designed the library and a theater, or Core East. Johansen and Christ-Janer had apparently left the SUCF's employ before completion of the Campus Center, thus leaving Kouzmanoff as the architect in charge of the design process. The Campus Center buildings share some of the compositional freedom of the Academic Village, and except for Johansens's Library, they incorporate

SUNY Old Westbury, Academic Village A, 1972. A stair landing and terrace on the way up to rooftop community spaces. The view ahead is to a dormitory building. Today, the wooden railings have been replaced with metal fencing.

the metal panels that Kouzmanoff and Johansen had hoped to include in the Academic Village's design. The Campus Center has an impressive, glass-ceilinged rectangular atrium, crisscrossed at the second level by ramps. Otherwise, the building volumes are clad in thin, white panels of sheet metal and feature plenty of horizontal windows, giving this second grouping a much lighter, brighter appearance.

After this second building phase was completed in 1982, the original master plan for multiple colleges was abandoned. Today, the Old Westbury campus suffers somewhat from the aborted progress of its original concept. Johansen's rock-solid and intricately designed Academic Village lacks connection to the rest of campus. Both Johansen's and Kouzmanoff's buildings have fallen into partial disuse and are threatened by increasing obsolescence in the overall scheme of the campus. Small alterations—the removal of exterior lamps, the addition of new railings and new paving on the central terrace—have subtly compromised the architectural integrity of Johansen's design for the Academic Village. Nevertheless, the genius of the place and the spirit of experimentation in the architecture remain tangible. The brutalist architecture has stood the test of time, not only because of its fortresslike concrete construction but also because of its exceptional formal beauty, which has even been enhanced by the growth of vines and other lush vegetation in and around the complex. Recently, there have been requests from college planners to demolish the Academic Village as part of an overhaul of the Old Westbury campus. The complex is significant within the context of John Johansen's internationally recognized career; in addition, adapting it for the use of future generations of students would allow it to stand as an exceptional example of the architecture of its time and the pride of a college originally established to represent high ideals of democracy and community.

23

PAUL RUDOLPH 1918–97

Endo Laboratories, Garden City, 1964;
Maurice and Barbara Deane House, Kings Point, 1970;
Daniel Siegel Beach House, Westhampton Beach, 1978

Over the course of two decades, Paul Rudolph executed three projects on Long Island, each a distinct iteration of his bold, varied, and innovative architecture. None of these buildings is well known nationally, but the three works, one a pharmaceutical factory and the other two oceanfront residences, reflect the range of his output, which spanned from enormous commercial projects to the smallest private houses. He deployed forms both massive and delicate, rough and refined; he made use of rustic materials and craft techniques, as well as steel, glass, and concrete; and he drew on influences as diverse as American vernacular styles and the modernism that he learned to appreciate during his training at Harvard's Graduate School of Design. Furthermore, certainly in the late phases of his career, he relished incorporating modern materials, such as plastic, Mylar, and anything that glimmered, into his multifaceted, always spatially complex architectural language.

Rudolph grew up in Kentucky, the son of an itinerant Methodist minister who took his family with him on his travels throughout the South. Rudolph received his first architectural training at the Alabama Polytechnic Institute, but came to the Northeast in 1940 to train with Gropius and Breuer at the GSD. During World War II, he left Harvard to serve in the Navy, working as a shipbuilding supervisor at the Brooklyn Navy Yard, where he had the opportunity to hone his drafting style and

Endo Laboratories, Garden City, 1964. Final perspective drawing of entire pharmaceutical plant, including office, manufacturing, and laboratory facilities. Drawing by Bryant Conant, project architect for Paul Rudolph.

to learn about large-scale construction and interlocking vertical and horizontal space. After the war, he returned to Harvard to complete his studies with the European émigré masters. He then headed South again and set up a practice in Sarasota, Florida, where, from the late 1940s through the late 1950s, he designed a number of small but elegant beach houses, using low-cost materials and devoting careful attention to site and climate. On the basis of his Florida work, Rudolph was named dean of the Yale Architecture School when he was just thirty-seven years old.

During the 1960s, Rudolph executed a number of larger institutional commissions, from the Yale Art and Architecture Building (1958–64) to the Government Service Center in Boston (1962–71). His buildings exerted worldwide influence and received critical acclaim for their originality. Among the many influences apparent in his work were the teachings of Breuer and Gropius; the organic qualities and spatial arrangements of Frank Lloyd Wright; Le Corbusier's sculptural forms and use of concrete; and even the southern vernacular buildings he had first seen as a boy. But his architectural language was also highly personal and unquestionably his own. Rudolph combined influences in new, surprising ways and typically disregarded prevailing architectural fashions. Peter Blake, the architect and editor of *Architectural Forum*, praised this originality when

Endo Laboratories, Garden City, 1964. One side of the sweeping double stair that leads to the building's main entrance.

OPPOSITE
Endo Laboratories, Garden City, 1964. A "chipper" perched on a window sill on the turreted west façade.

he wrote of Rudolph's "absolutely staggering and incorruptible talent."[1]

By the 1970s, however, Rudolph's architecture was losing favor in the United States. During the Vietnam era, his sometimes fortresslike buildings came to be associated with unpopular establishment forces. With the waning of his reputation at home, Rudolph accepted a number of large-scale corporate and government commissions in Southeast Asia. In these later works Rudolph stuck to his modernist principles, never adopting the historical forms of postmodernism. He paid a price, becoming known as the embodiment of everything that was perceived to be wrong with modernism. His highly individualistic, sometimes wildly flamboyant interiors were panned by journalists as Space Age chic, even kitschy. In their widely read 1972 book, *A Significance for A&P Parking Lots, or Learning from Las Vegas*, architects Denise Scott Brown and Robert Venturi called his architecture overly abstract, passé, and even hostile. Since his death in 1997, however, architects, critics, and scholars have begun to reevaluate his work and to recognize its rigor and inventiveness. The three Long Island buildings offer compelling examples.

ENDO LABORATORIES

In 1960, the owners of Endo Pharmaceuticals, based in Richmond Hill, Queens, approached Rudolph to design a new headquarters and state-of-the-art research and drug-manufacturing facility on the former site of the Nassau County Polo Fields in Garden City. David Ushkow founded Endo in 1918 as a supplier of intravenous solutions. In the 1950s, the company became hugely profitable through sales of Coumadin, a blood thinner and anticoagulant, and several painkillers. Joseph Ushkow, the founder's nephew, and his partner, David Klein, handed management of their successful enterprise to their sons-in-law Howard Barnet, Maurice Deane, and Jerome Serchuck. The younger generation hoped to build a new headquarters that would represent Endo as a thriving, stable, and innovative company at the forefront of pharmacology. They sought an architect who could produce such a building, as well as handle a complex program that included not only corporate offices but also research laboratories and manufacturing facilities.

Endo first received a proposal from Edward Durell Stone, who favorably impressed the senior management. According to Saretta Barnet, it was her husband, Howard Barnet, a serious art collector and admirer of modern architecture, who pushed for Rudolph instead.[2] Barnet was enthusiastic about Rudolph's Yale Art and Architecture Building, under construction at the time. Although Rudolph had no experience with the type of office and manufacturing facility that the Endo project represented, Barnet convinced the others to hire the architect, apparently based solely on the promise of the Yale building.

Endo's managers were delighted with the design process and the results. As Maurice Deane recalled, "Paul was a pleasure to work with."[3] Rudolph asked for complete artistic freedom. According to Deane, "We had to allow him to use his creativity to full force with the architecture and interior design."[4] Indeed, the result shows an exceptional degree of formal inventiveness and attention to materials and finishes. Remarkably, though Rudolph used labor-intensive fabrication methods and custom-designed much of the furniture, at $23 per square foot and a total cost of $4 million, not including the landscaping by Zion and Breen Associates, the building was a paragon of cost-effectiveness. Most important, it fulfilled the desire of the Endo managers for both a striking corporate emblem and a facility that would accommodate the company's functional needs and allow it to grow.

The building's exterior sets a tone of imposing solidity. The long, three-story structure is characterized by broad expanses of rough concrete broken only by narrow bands of windows along the top level. The massive forms nevertheless possess a decided energy and elegance. Projecting volumes offset the overall sense of weight and create a visually dynamic interplay of forms. Prevalent curves, including round turrets that house stairways and air-intake and exhaust systems for the manufacturing facilities, lend a sculptural quality. Rudolph had designed these sorts of utilitarian features during his years in the Navy, and there is indeed a nautical quality to his shapes. He was inspired as well by Le Corbusier's sculpturally expressive concrete buildings of the 1950s, such as Notre Dame du Haut chapel, with its weightiness and undulating, organic forms.

Curves predominate at the entrance as well; a sweeping, referentially Baroque double stair ascends to the building's main doors. This grand staircase of four-inch risers and wide treads creates a long, slow procession that led visitors, during the days of Endo's authority over the building, past a large, bronze Endo plaque and into the reception area, which is housed in an assertively prowlike, rounded volume surrounded by glass. Inside, another sweeping stair rises from the lobby to a recessed landing and then to the executive floor. Hanging over the stair is a large Plexiglas sculpture that complements the Baroque aspect of Rudolph's design. A tour de force of the medium in scale, voluptuousness, and pearlescent surface, this work was created by sculptor Erwin Hauer, a colleague of Rudolph's at Yale. Rather like a giant elongated conch shell, it was created both to resonate with the design and to contrast with the fluted, hammered-concrete walls.

Curving forms and flowing spaces continue throughout the building. The round turrets form skylit interior alcoves in which Rudolph placed kidney-shaped wooden platform desks. The ceilings in the executive areas are gently vaulted. Conference rooms are oval shaped. The landscape architecture firm Zion and Breen, which had designed the outdoor spaces for I. M. Pei's Roosevelt Field Shopping Center nearby (see pages 248–50), used a similar sinuous language for the landscaping. On the rooftop, Zion and Breen created an outdoor space with circular flowerbeds set into undulating fields of anthracite, which strongly recall the wavy forms of Brazilian landscape architect Roberto Burle Marx's mid-century garden designs in Brazil.

Endo Laboratories, Garden City, 1964. A "chipper" at work on Rudolph's signature hammered-concrete surface.

In addition to its sculptural curves, the Endo building is distinctive for its hammered-concrete surface. The expressive use of rough concrete was pioneered by Le Corbusier in the late 1940s. Referred to as "brutalism" after Le Corbusier's term *béton brut*, or raw concrete, this type of architecture, a leading strain of modernism in the 1950s and 1960s, often features massive, imposing forms. In his Yale Art and Architecture Building, Rudolph developed a unique treatment of concrete by chiseling the walls to create a highly textured surface of corduroy-like vertical ribs. For the Endo building, he mixed cement with quartz, which was mined in nearby Port Jefferson, Long Island. Not only was it a local material, but it was also the best choice to add shimmer to the walls. The mix was poured from above into fluted wooden forms. Concrete finishers—workmen known as chippers—used bush hammers to expose the light-catching quartz and create the vertical striations. The exceptional degree of care taken in treating the wall surfaces was recognized by the Concrete Industry Board, which named Endo Laboratories its Concrete Building of the Year in 1964. Artist Louise Nevelson was engaged to design a Lucite award.

On the interior, Rudolph's treatment of materials was equally striking. Throughout, the brutalist concrete set the tone. Many of the interior wall surfaces were chiseled with the same ribbed pattern as the exterior walls. In some spaces, such as the stair towers, Rudolph followed Le Corbusier's technique

Endo Laboratories, Garden City, 1964. Undulating fields of anthracite surround flowerbeds in the upper roof garden, designed by Zion and Breen. The cafeteria is to the left.

Endo Laboratories, Garden City, 1964. Erwin Hauer's shell-like sculpture hangs above the stairway leading from the reception area to the executive offices.

of leaving the slat patterns of the formworks on the concrete walls, creating a coarse surface, but one that was certainly smoother than the hammered concrete. Rough textures were found in many other finishes as well, such as the furry-looking vaulted ceilings in the executive suites, which were covered with a pulp of asbestos fibers shot out of a spray gun. Sadly, Rudolph's frequent exposure to asbestos, which was not known to be carcinogenic at the time, eventually caused the illness that ended his life.

Rudolph always favored textural contrast. He juxtaposed polished finishes and furniture to the coarse, irregular wall surfaces. In the areas for management and senior scientists, he used walnut paneling, desks with walnut sides and white plastic laminate tops, and chrome and leather chairs, all of which offset the ruggedness of the architecture. The floors in the executive and reception areas were covered either in cleaved slate or in flame orange carpet. Rudolph designed and oversaw the fabrication of the cabinetwork and much of the furniture, including pieces for the executives' offices, the switchboard room, and the conference rooms. Stand-alone desks for the executives and their secretaries were kidney shaped, as were the built-in desktops in the turret spaces. He also incorporated a few pieces of furniture from other designers, including Ward Bennett's black tufted-leather chairs with chrome legs in the executive conference rooms.

Light was critical to bringing out the textures of his wall surfaces. As Rudolph said of his work, "What is architecture but concrete, glass, light and shadow blended to create imaginary spaces."[5] Some of the spaces, such as the conference rooms, were fully enclosed by solid wood-paneled walls and illuminated by carefully orchestrated artificial light. Elsewhere, natural light was admitted through Plexiglas skylights in the turrets and ceilings. Some of the large public spaces, such as the cafeteria and the lobby, were flooded with light from floor-to-ceiling windows.

In addition to the poetic forms and textures that distinguished the building visually, the planning of the spaces and the incorporation of the building's technical functions were critical to its success. According to Deane, Rudolph allowed Endo management to "choose the engineering firm and work out the manufacturing machinery design with them."[6] Henry Pfisterer was the engineer and the firm of Walter Kidde Constructors was in charge of mechanical engineering. Collaborating with these groups, Rudolph addressed a complex set of functional and spatial requirements, which he was well qualified to do, given his wartime experience retrofitting large ships. For example, some drugs necessitated a five-story, gravity-driven assembly line in which chemicals were poured into giant hoppers at the top and then funneled down from story to story as they passed through various stages of production. Other drugs such as morphine derivatives had to be made in highly controlled environments involving special ventilation systems, autoclaves, and secure areas. At ground level, he laid out a huge warehouse facility with forklift access and a 10,000-square-foot narcotics vault accessed through a sally port with a government-mandated checkout center. On the research level, there were operating rooms for animal testing, as well as an elliptical balcony that served as a dog exercise run. Bryant Conant, the project architect, said in hindsight that the challenges of accommodating all of the functions were staggering. "It was spatially like designing a tower for NASA, it was that complicated."[7]

The Endo building stood out dramatically from the neighboring factories and office buildings. It was widely admired, although apparently not by Robert Moses, who, as president of the Long Island State Park Commission, ordered the planting of a row of hemlock trees along the Meadowbrook Parkway to block passing motorists' view of the building. Sadly, the brutalist behemoth was allowed only a brief existence in its original state. Only eight years after the completion of their new headquarters and manufacturing facility, the families of the original founders sold Endo Pharmaceuticals to DuPont de Nemours and Company, who in turn sold it to Bristol-Myers Squibb. When its was first sold to DuPont, the building was stripped of much of Rudolph's woodwork, doors, paneling, lighting, and built-in furniture. Over the years, the building was refurnished and badly cared for. The raw concrete surfaces were painted over, and Zion and Breen's landscaping was neglected. A hodgepodge of corrugated metal additions was added to the back façades. Until 2003, the building continued to be used as a pharmaceutical plant. Then, after sitting empty for three years, it was converted by Metropolitan Realty Associates into rental space for commercial use. Today the primary tenant is Lifetime Brands, whose president, Jeff Siegel, has collaborated with Metropolitan Realty on restoring it to its original condition. According to Siegel, "The building is built like a fortress, so it is basically all here."[8]

DEANE HOUSE

In 1969, around the time the Endo company was sold, Maurice and Barbara Deane commissioned Rudolph to design a family house for them in Kings Point. Rudolph remembered Maurice Deane asking during the heroic effort to complete Endo, "If we ever build a house, will you be the architect?"[9] The Deanes invited Rudolph to accompany them on a boat trip to see a number of waterfront sites. Eventually they secured an acre site at the bottom of a hill overlooking Manhasset Bay. Soon a site along the water's edge became available, as well as one above the house, and the Deanes purchased these as well.

Endo Laboratories, Garden City, 1964. Concrete interior staircase.

Burroughs Wellcome Company Corporate Headquarters, Research Triangle, NC, 1969. Presentation drawing by Paul Rudolph. In his design for the Deane House, Rudolph used hexagonal geometry similar to the stacked hexagonal pods he designed for the Burroughs Wellcome Company building.

RIGHT
Maurice and Barbara Deane House, Kings Point, 1970. Final presentation drawing. Elevations of the wood skeleton and hexagonal frames, waterside vantage. Note the slanted walls for a swimming pool at ground level.

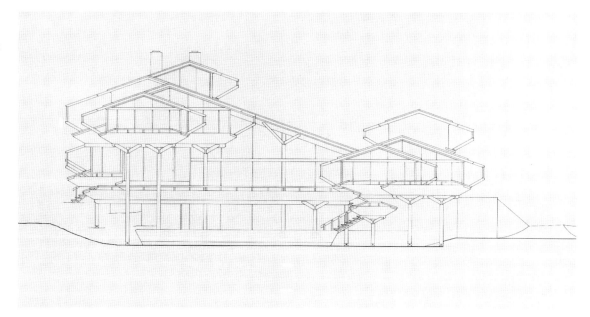

Maurice and Barbara Deane House, Kings Point, 1970. Wood framing under construction. Note the interlocking latticework.

Maurice and Barbara Deane House, Kings Point, 1970. View of completed waterside façades, with the swimming pool in the foreground.

Donald Luckenbill, the project architect on the house, remembers how quickly Rudolph produced the design. "He was like Frank Lloyd Wright was with Fallingwater. After seeing the site on a Friday, Rudolph drew a sketch in an hour or so, which convinced the Deanes to want to go ahead."[10] By Monday morning, his staff had made a model of the house, which he could take apart and share with his clients. But the Deanes did not want to rush the project. Having complete trust in Rudolph's methods and talent, they told him that they wanted a masterpiece. They gave the architect ample freedom and resources to create a house that was not only large but structurally daring, decoratively rich, and highly orchestrated in all of its facets, from landscaping to interior finishes.

In many ways the Deane House is the architectural antithesis of Endo Laboratories. Built of wood reinforced with steel, it is open and light. Its exterior is defined by an exposed skeletal structure that seems to lift upward, in contrast to Endo's solid, grounded masses. The visible frame, pitched roofs, and deep eaves distance this work from Rudolph's earlier concern with the abstract volumes of Le Corbusier and suggest instead an affinity with Arts and Crafts architecture and traditional Japanese buildings. Above all, even to this day the house has a powerful presence as ultramodern architecture out of the future.

In the late 1960s, Rudolph began to experiment with a new kind of architecture based on repeating geometric modules attached to an exposed structural frame. When he received the Deane House commission, he had just started working on the Burroughs Wellcome Company Corporate Headquarters in North Carolina, a villagelike cluster of hexagonal pods stacked one on top of another and raised up on slender steel stilts. He used a similar hexagonal geometry for the Deane House. But in contrast to the enclosed pods of the Burroughs Wellcome building, the Deane House's hexagonal forms are part of the frame itself. Rudolph designed the entire house as a complex, open lattice of interlocking beams, giving it a sense of structural lightness and integrity as well as visual dynamism.

With much of the house raised on slender piers, the structural system was an impressive feat of engineering. Earl Anderson, the contractor, recalls its complexity, "The house was a complicated piece of construction and very few other contractors wanted to bid on it. It was really like a big Tinkertoy set, with us building all the parts on site and with separate drawings for every single bolt connection. Mr. Rudolph said to me, 'Does this design scare you?' To which I said, 'If you can design it, I can build it.'"[11] Originally, Rudolph had planned to use a steel frame but opted instead for redwood beams with steel plates sandwiched between them, thus creating a structure that harks back to older building traditions but also provides the strength of modern materials. The reinforced-redwood Y columns are bolted at ground level to steel tubes embedded in underground concrete anchors. The Y-shaped braces help resist lateral wind stress and at the same time recall the rustic joinery of Arts and Crafts architecture. The solid chimney at the center of the house further buttresses the frame. The façades were made of plywood carefully made to look like stone through a most primitive process. Workmen simply went around the building day after day with buckets of stones that they threw onto a cementitious binder. Rudolph specified a transparent whitewash for the warm beige-colored pebble surface to increase its delicate appearance. "Mr. Rudolph wanted the Deane house to look structurally elegant, even soft and light, as a piece of architecture as sculpture," Luckenbill recalled.[12]

Viewed from the eastern side of the slope on which it is situated, the house rises dramatically above a large, rectangular swimming pool set into a concrete plinth, the walls of which are angled 45 degrees and run parallel to the lines of the house framing. From this perspective, the architecture asserts itself over the landscape. Seen from the west, however, the house appears nestled into the hillside, partly hidden by trees that provide a feathery contrast to the seemingly stone-clad forms of the house. The integration of the house into the site is enhanced by the landscaping, which was created by Robert Zion, Rudolph's landscape design colleague from the Endo project. For the approach to the house, Zion designed a meandering driveway, and his workmen used a bulldozer to form grass berms along the drive. The berms serve to dramatize the approach to the house, which is at first hidden and then gradually revealed as one gets closer. Zion also planted a bank of evergreens along the north side of the drive and a number of oak trees around the site to further conceal the house.

The entrance façade is largely opaque, providing a sense of privacy. Just inside the front door, however, the house opens up spectacularly, its expansive living spaces overlooking panoramic views of the slope and the bay. The interior is organized around a central core. As in Frank Lloyd Wright's Prairie Style houses, spaces pinwheel out from a massive fireplace surrounded by built-in seating that anchors the house in both a symbolic and a physical sense. The living spaces at the center of the house form a kind of village square surrounded by a parapet, beyond which are arrayed the more enclosed, private areas, including the bedrooms. Another distinctive feature of the interior is the constantly changing level of the floor, creating a highly kinetic spatial experience as one moves between raised and sunken areas. As Philip Johnson said of Rudolph's architecture, "His space flowed like water through his buildings."[13] Indeed, the subtle breaks in elevation serve to divide the living areas into smaller, more intimate spaces without interrupting the overall sense of openness.

Taking another cue from Frank Lloyd Wright, Rudolph carefully integrated the interior and exterior of the house. Terraces extend interior spaces outdoors, and planters built into interior walls bring the outside in. In the main living area, a planter runs along one wall just beneath the ceiling, its lush greenery cascading down like a

Maurice and Barbara Deane House, Kings Point, 1970. Mrs. Deane's mirrored bathroom and dressing room. On the wall to the left, copper mesh is studded with glass.

curtain. Observing Wright's notion of an "organic architecture" in which all elements are designed in harmony, Rudolph used the same materials and the same hexagonal geometries for the interior detailing and furniture as he did for the exterior of the house.

Two generations earlier at Laurelton Hall in nearby Oyster Bay, Louis Comfort Tiffany broke sharply with nineteenth-century historicism by adorning the house with exotic, colorful, and highly unconventional elements. Rudolph's sensuous, eccentric decoration of the Deane House amounted to a similarly iconoclastic gesture, in his case a refutation of the functionalist orthodoxy of modernism. He experimented with unusual materials, colors, and ornamental forms. His search for materials took him to hardware stores and party-supply shops on the Bowery in New York, dental catalogues, manufacturers of airplane parts, and theatrical-supply houses.

Rudolph created clever, playful combinations out of these materials and textures, some chosen for their startling, incongruous artificiality. Against the predominantly beige surfaces of the house, shiny, colorful touches with glass, mirrors, Mylar, and polished metal caught the eye. In Barbara Deane's dressing room, the countertops and cabinetry were faced with mirrors. The walls were covered in copper mesh studded with small rectangles of glass laboriously set in place with double-sided

Daniel Siegel Beach House, Westhampton Beach, 1978. View from the beach.

OPPOSITE
Daniel Siegel Beach House, Westhampton Beach, 1978. The stairway curves around a tree to access the drum-shaped entrance volume.

tape by a group of Rudolph's students from the Pratt Institute in New York. The adjacent bathroom featured a luminous wall of Plexiglas painted red on the reverse side. The house's front door was a lattice of clear green plastic strips. Alternating bands of wood and mirror on the ceiling above the entryway created a broken, shimmering reflection of the curtain of plants on the opposite wall. Blinds were made of strips of copper sheeting from a roofing-supply company and Ultrasuede, a synthetic microfiber fabric that had just been invented by Dr. Miyoshi Okamoto and that Halston made all the rage for women's clothing in his Fall 1972 collection. The ceiling of the ground-floor recreation room was clad in silver Mylar, which reflected the Y beams supporting it, the pool, the grassy knolls, and the bay beyond.

SIEGEL BEACH HOUSE

In contrast to the grand, structurally dramatic Deane House, with its honeycomb phalanx of fauxstone façades and elaborate, whimsical interior, the beach house that Rudolph created for Daniel Siegel in Westhampton Beach conjures up archetypal associations with primitivism and comprises a compendium of devices used throughout his career. In 1978, when he was approached about the project, Rudolph was working on several skyscraper projects in Southeast Asia, as well as his own New York City house, but he accepted the commission gladly. He had not designed a beach house since the 1950s in Sarasota, Florida.

Siegel, a graphic-display artist, is a bon vivant and consummate party giver. He wanted a casual house, where he could invite friends to enjoy the sun, sea air, and ocean views. A collector of art and folk objects, he also wanted to be able to display paintings and sculpture. Rudolph created a complicated two-story structure with smooth white walls, an open, loftlike informal living area below, bedrooms above, and a rear deck that leads onto the beach. Though he could have simply dipped into his repertoire and chosen one of the early beach-house designs that had made him famous, Rudolph concocted an entirely novel creation.

Like the Deane House, the Siegel Beach House is primarily a wooden structure. But unlike the visually intricate framing system of the earlier project, the approach here is more elemental, with vernacular and rustic elements playing a prominent role. The materials include rough-hewn tree trunks, traditional New England gray cedar shingles for the roof, and vertical cedar plank siding. Vernacular influences are especially pronounced on the beach side of the house. The two-story gallery, steeply overhanging pitched roof, and tree-trunk columns

Daniel Siegel Beach House, Westhampton, 1978. Chaim Gross's *The Juggler* presides over the dining area of the living space.

strongly suggest the Southern plantation houses and Creole cottages that Rudolph saw as a boy when he traveled through the deep South with his preacher father.

The Siegel Beach House incorporates these historical references, as well as a white-walled modernist purity that recalls Le Corbusier's houses of the 1920s, without any of the punning and pastiche characteristics of the Postmodern movement, which was in full force at the time. Indeed, Rudolph reviled postmodernism and never gave into it. The façade on the driveway side is defined by a series of drum-shaped volumes, reminiscent of the turrets at Endo, and second-story rectangular bay windows that project boldly from the façade, creating a striking play of masses. A gently angled stairway crosses the front of the house and makes its way around a tree to the side, where it meets a drum-shaped entrance volume.

The front door leads into an enclosed hall, to the right of which is another drum-shaped volume, an elliptical washroom. Beyond the hall, the soaring living area opens up. Daylight pours into this large rectangular space from a skylight along the roof ridge and from the large, glass sliding doors that lead to the beach. The sculptural volumes of the exterior are echoed inside as well, and wide, round columns—both tree trunks and concrete-clad steel columns—support the complex floor arrangements of the second level. At one end of the space is a massive fireplace surrounded by a raised seating area, formed from sinuously curving white concrete. At the opposite end, another wood-clad drum provides storage for the kitchen beyond.

The stylistic precedent for the interior was the Mediterranean peasant village, where ledges, tables, and seating were customarily part and parcel of the masonry. According to Luckenbill, who served as project architect, as he had for the Deane House, these forms were inspired by conversations he had with Rudolph about the vernacular architecture on Ibiza, where Luckenbill had once spent several months.[14]

Luckenbill recalled Rudolph's penchant for editing and reworking the design of a project as it was being built, and how ad hoc his approach to designing the interior was. The undulating shapes that form the sculptural fireplace in the lounge area also curl around vertical piping containing the fireplace flue and ductwork for the central heating and air conditioning. The seating is actually made out of wood and plaster to resemble masonry or carved rock, as it would have been in primitive villages. Siegel balked at the length of time it was going to take for custom-made upholstery pieces to be designed and fabricated. To hasten Siegel's inhabitation of the house, Rudolph and Luckenbill asked the Matranis, Quogue's well-known plaster craftsmen, who were doing the extensive plasterwork on the walls and columns, to create the village seating arrangement and fireplace as they went along. These forms are echoed in the curving concrete staircase, with its clear Plexiglas tubular railing, which leads from the rear of the living area up to a second-floor gallery and the bedrooms and bathrooms with their expansive views of the ocean on one side and the bay on the other. Upstairs, rooms open onto cantilevered balconies and window seats jut out into space for maximum enjoyment of the views.

The Siegel Beach House reaffirmed Rudolph's dedication to the language of modernism and his inventiveness and individuality. As Luckenbill stated, "It is a house of great artifice. Extremely intricate drawings were part of the process, along with the trial-and-error approach, as with all of Rudolph's architecture."[15]

From the brutalist concrete surfaces of Endo Laboratories to the futurist-looking Deane House to the blending of the modernist and the rustic in the Siegel Beach House, Paul Rudolph's three Long Island buildings show the remarkable variety that makes him among the most intriguing of American architects. As architect Der Scutt, who in 1962 managed Rudolph's office in Manhattan, recalled, "Paul Rudolph understood how to conceptualize space and scale better than any other architect, and he had the same kind of creative spirit as Frank Lloyd Wright. He could draw immediately and beautifully, with pen and ink, generating images from a single point, as if he was unfurling space."[16] As the Paul Rudolph Foundation staff can attest, his works are more appreciated in the history books than in real life. Several important Rudolph buildings, including a school in Florida and a house in Connecticut, have been demolished in recent years. The Long Island buildings are due for National Register of Historic Places designations and the protection of local landmark ordinances, as they have stood the test of time and never lost the sense of being from the future.

Daniel Siegel Beach House, Westhampton Beach, 1978. The sculptural volumes of the exterior are echoed inside. The raised, built-in seating area in front of the fireplace was inspired by Mediterranean peasant village interiors, where furnishings were an integral part of the masonry.

24

JOHN W. STEDMAN JR. 1908–1977

John Stedman House, Laurel Hollow, 1952;
Peter and Margaret Luce House, Cooper's Bluff, Cove Neck, 1953;
Robert and Mary Lindsay House, Cold Spring Harbor, 1957;
John and Frances Fennebresque House, Cove Neck, 1960

In the 1950s and 1960s, architect John Stedman enjoyed a busy practice designing modern and traditional houses for a North Shore–based clientele consisting primarily of fellow sailors from the Seawanhaka Corinthian Yacht Club on Centre Island. Word had it that his modern architecture was admirable—even if one disapproved of modern architecture. Though able to subtly adapt his style to suit his clients' preferences, he was always a modernist by inclination, as evidenced by his design for his own house in Laurel Hollow in 1952, a flat-roofed, cedar-clad split-level, with a stone fireplace wall extending out to terraced gardens and views of Oyster Bay.

Besides having the right social credentials for acceptance by the well-to-do inhabitants of the North Shore (he had ancestors who signed the Declaration of Independence), Stedman's education and early career prepared him well to manage an eclectic practice based out of his office in the Town of Oyster Bay. Stedman graduated from Harvard in 1930 and went on to study architecture. As he wrote two decades later in Harvard's alumni journal, "I put in four years of interesting, but extremely grueling, work at Columbia Architectural School, learning, as I thought at the time, all there was to know about architecture."[1] He won most of the prizes at the Columbia graduation, making him eligible for a prestigious fellowship to study at the École de Beaux-Arts in Paris—de rigueur for ambitious young American architects. Yet Stedman chose

Peter and Margaret Luce House, Cooper's Bluff, Cove Neck, 1953. Presentation plan, final version, drawn by John Stedman.

to stay close to his family's summer compound in South Dartmouth, Massachusetts, so he could continue a winning streak racing sailboats. His first job, held only for a year, was with Coolidge Shepley Bulfinch and Abbot in Boston, a nationally prominent firm and successor to Henry Hobson Richardson's practice.

During World War II, Stedman distinguished himself as commander of a destroyer escort for four Pacific island invasions. His full immersion into modern architecture came only after the war, in 1946, when he joined the office of Harrison & Abramovitz to work on the design of the United Nations complex in New York. As he later wrote of his postwar readjustment to architecture, "I could hardly remember the size of a bathtub."[2]

To reinforce his knowledge of the architectural process, in 1952 Stedman made the creation of his Laurel Hollow house a do-it-yourself project. As he said, "By doing most of the work myself, I discovered many things that could not be learned in an office, but commuting on the famous Long Island R.R., mixing mortar when I got home, and getting up at four a.m. in the mornings to do my private architectural work made it a very busy schedule."[3]

PETER AND MARGARET LUCE HOUSE

Stedman's first break, designing a big-budget modern house for Peter and Margaret Luce on sixteen acres on Cove Neck peninsula, meant he could set up shop nearby in Oyster Bay with hopes of making a living, and at the same time enjoy his house, garden, and sailboat. The Luces' outcropping of land was up the road from Sagamore Hill, President Theodore Roosevelt's summer house. The Luces bought it from Billy Weekes, then the preeminent land and real estate broker along the North Shore. Stedman relied on Weekes, a Harvard College classmate, to bring him clients. The Weekes family had farmed along various Oyster Bay–area coves and inlets since colonial times; besides having his own land to sell, Weekes had a steady business managing the subdivision and sale of acreage for families no longer able or willing to sustain their great estates.

As the second son of Time Inc. founder Henry Luce and his first wife, Lila Hotz, Peter Luce had the means to build whatever type of house he wanted on his new property. He had grown up in a French-style château in Chester, New Jersey, and in a South Carolina retreat, Mepkin Plantation, designed by Edward Durell Stone. Margaret Luce, on the other hand, had been raised far from the rarefied world of modern architecture, in a Nova Scotia farmhouse. Their new Long Island site had the best vantage point in the area, with views of Oyster Bay Harbor, Lloyd Neck, and Long Island Sound, as well as a wide expanse of beach accessed along an old Matinecock Indian trail. "There was no question of anything other than a modern house for us at that time and with scenery like that," Margaret (Luce) Howe recalled.[4] The couple approached Walter Gropius about designing their house, as they had seen and liked his house in Lincoln, Massachusetts, where they lived when Peter Luce was a graduate student at MIT. They also contacted Frank Lloyd Wright. But Stedman won the Luces' trust and the job, because he was talented, likable, and local.

Stedman sited the large, rambling composition of varied geometric shapes and overhanging rooflines at the very edge of the bluff, on a narrow strip of land adjacent to a kettle hole, an Ice Age crater, from which there was a steep 160-foot drop to the sandy beach below. In the kettle hole he installed a sunken Japanese garden and he put a ramp—a ship's gangway of sorts—along and across it to access the split-level house, which was partially set on top of concrete slabs supported by wide concrete pilings sunk deep into the kettle hole. The house has water views from every room and a 180-degree bird's-eye view of Long Island Sound from the living room, with its three-sided terrace looming out over the bluff. The flow of space takes a zigzag path between the three zones of the house: the kitchen and staff wing; the living room, dining room, and study wing; and the five-bedroom sleeping wing.

Peter and Margaret Luce House, Cooper's Bluff, Cove Neck, 1953. The triangular terrace projecting out from the dining room, seen from the bottom of the Ice Age kettle hole.

Peter and Margaret Luce House, Cooper's Bluff, Cove Neck, 1953. In this aerial view, the house's varied geometric shapes and overhanging roofs are clearly visible.

There are no right angles anywhere—the rooms and their respective built-ins are hexagonal, pentagonal, and triangular. Maurice Remie was the master carpenter for the house, and, thanks to his training as a boat builder in his native Norway, he had no difficulty constructing the geometric modules.

Henry Luce, whose magazines promulgated fear of and readiness for a Soviet nuclear attack on American cities, insisted that his son and daughter-in-law incorporate a large, comfortable fallout shelter in the basement. Underneath the thick concrete floor slabs of the house, Stedman built an enormous basement that included the fallout shelter—an apartment with bedrooms and a storage space big enough to stock sufficient supplies for the Luces and their young children to wait out the direst effects of a nuclear attack on New York. All summer long the Luce's sixty-five-foot schooner, also well stocked for an escapade (or an escape), was moored in the deep water offshore, in sight of a five-room bathhouse near the beach.

The Luce house was the talk of the neighborhood, not only for its sublime sea views but also because it had a number of unusual features that would not become common in modern architecture until the mid-1960s. The basic design of the house is a version of the International Cottage Style, a term coined by the Museum of Modern Art's Alfred Barr to describe the wood houses built in the San Francisco Bay area during the late 1930s, 1940s, and 1950s that were softened, cozier versions of the white, concrete, and rather severe International Style houses of the 1920s and 1930s. Like the Bay Area houses, the Luce House is designed for casual living, with balconies providing access to the outdoors, and wood everywhere, including plenty of built-ins, window frames, and walls clad in various wood veneers.

The vaulted living room, surmounted by a rectangular Lucite skylight, had a high brick chimney wall. In front of the fireplace, Stedman designed a large, sunken seating area, a precursor to the funky "conversation pits" that became so popular in the decade to come. The bedrooms and kitchen also had Lucite dome skylights, another feature that gained popularity in the 1960s. The children's bedrooms had a whimsical shiplike quality, complete with bunk beds and stowaway spaces angled into the corners. The large playroom accommodated a six-sided, glassed-in atrium porch with an open roof to accommodate a tree. The house was sparsely furnished with antique pieces from the Luce family houses and modern furniture designed or found by Paul Letz, a neighbor and decorator who worked with textile designer Jack Lenor Larsen.

ROBERT AND MARY LINDSAY HOUSE

Stedman designed a modestly budgeted, but no less remarkable house for Robert Lindsay, brother of New York mayor John V. Lindsay (1966–73), and

Robert and Mary Lindsay House, Cold Spring Harbor, 1957. This low-budget ranch house with astounding views of Oyster Bay is sited on land that was once part of Laurelton Hall, the Louis Comfort Tiffany estate.

OPPOSITE TOP
Robert and Mary Lindsay House, Cold Spring Harbor, 1957. The U-shaped entry courtyard.

OPPOSITE BOTTOM
Robert and Mary Lindsay House, Cold Spring Harbor, 1957. The window wall in the high-ceilinged living room affords spectacular views of the water.

his wife, Mary, who chose the architect because they were impressed by the siting of the Luces' house, and by "how he commanded the whole Sound for them," Mary Lindsay recalls.[5] The Lindsay House sits on a four-acre rise above Oyster Bay, a site that was once the easternmost part of Laurelton Hall, the Louis Comfort Tiffany estate. The Tiffany property was sold and the land subdivided in 1949, and the Lindsays bought their parcel from its previous owners, the Dudley Millers. Tiffany's visionary house design had been an orientalist oddity, one of the most eccentric and storied houses in America. Mary Lindsay saw the great house burn to the ground in 1957 from across the bay, where she and her husband were renting an eighteenth-century cottage while Stedman was building their new house. When the three Lindsay children were growing up, they would find and bring home bits of metal and other items from the former Tiffany estate stables and farm buildings at the edge of their property. They also collected pearlescent tile fragments from around the nearby minaret, which had survived the fire along with an icehouse and a few terraces.[6]

The family had moved to Long Island from an apartment in Peter Cooper Village in Manhattan. Instead of buying new furniture, they asked Stedman to design plenty of ship-cabin-like, double-aspect built-ins to complement a few hardy neo-Georgian pieces, a dining room table and chairs, and a tall bookcase and English china inherited from Mrs. Lindsay's family. Stedman's mandate was to give them what looked like a decidedly modern house with multisided views of the water and a strong sense of being surrounded by nature. Yet the Lindsays also wanted the house plan to retain some old-fashioned formality, and here again Stedman accommodated them, creating a separate dining room and living room and a children's wing far from the master suite.

As a sailor, Stedman knew how to design the house to take full advantage of the prevailing winds. One day he showed up for a client meeting on the site with a set of cardboard models, and Mary Lindsay remembers him putting them on the ground and deciding then and there how the house would be positioned. The house has never had air conditioning and still does not need it, according to Mary Lindsay, except on rare hot summer days when wind blows in from the west. Until oil prices went up in the early 1970s, the Lindsays kept Stedman's system of louvers throughout the house. But the louvers leaked cold air in the winter months, so they were eventually replaced with drywall.

When one arrives at the Lindsay House, its U-shaped entry courtyard and front façade promise a rather formal, neoclassical plan on a single level inside. Yet the entrance belies the freer, more modern distribution of the interior spaces. The house consists of three distinct volumes that step down the slope. The children's wing is a split-level unit with a large romper room on the first floor and bedrooms above. Perpendicular to it is a large, long unit containing the kitchen and the dining room. From there, three steps lead down to the high-ceilinged living room, which boasts a large window wall. The master suite, comprising a cozy study, small bedroom, and bathroom, leads off the living room and has windows overlooking the bay and the entry courtyard.

Whereas the old Tiffany estate was associated with Arabian Nights mystery and no-holds-barred expense, the Lindsay House is a charming modern villa, an understatement in Arcadia with a uniquely American air of Protestant asceticism. It is important as a rare, unadulterated example of the American ranch-house style prevalent in the late 1950s, and it demonstrates how a well-trained architect could use simple elements and spatial arrangement to create a sense of elegant grandeur and good taste within a limited budget. An important precedent in this regard was a showhouse in nearby Upper Brookville, designed as a special feature for *House & Garden* magazine in 1951 by architect John Callender that Stedman most likely would have seen. Intended to demonstrate exactly the kind of efficiency, economy through the use of basic building materials, and reserve that Stedman brought to the Lindsay residence, Callender's "House of Ideas" was part of an ongoing project by tastemakers in the design community to popularize modern architecture; its slim silhouette, spread-out plan, and glass window walls all appear to have had an influence on Stedman's design of the Lindsay House.

John and Frances Fennebresque House, Cove Neck, 1960. View of the house from the driveway.

JOHN AND FRANCES FENNEBRESQUE HOUSE

Stedman's other big-budget modern Long Island project was also located on Cove Neck, not far from the Luces' house. Completed in 1960, Stedman's design for client John Fennebresque and his family was very different from the precociously ultramodern residence he had created for the Luces.

A petrochemical engineer by training, John Fennebresque became president of Mobil Chemical Company in the early 1960s. He and his wife, Frances (Fritzie), had been living on the North Shore since World War II, with a brief hiatus in Los Gatos, California. The couple's stay in the Bay Area village apparently convinced John Fennebresque of the superiority of what became known as the California lifestyle. After returning east, he went in search of a waterfront property for his young family—and an architect who would build an East Coast version of a one-story, close-to-the-ground California ranch house, with plenty of patios.

The triangular plot that Fennebresque selected was purchased from the Nichols family, which had been farming in the area since before the Revolutionary War. As with the Luce house and other Stedman projects, developer Billy Weekes acted as matchmaker between client and architect, selling the land to the Fennebresques and recommending his designer friend for the project. Also like Stedman's other Long Island projects, the site boasted magnificent views, with vistas stretching as far as Centre Island and Cold Spring Harbor. The Fennebresques employed the same contractors (including the Norwegian master carpenter) for their cedar-shingled house as the Luces, and they too kept a sailboat moored nearby.

Ironically, considering that they commissioned the same architect and contractors as the Luces, Mrs. Fennebresque recalls that she did not particularly care for the Luce House. "I thought their kitchen was too small. . . . I did not like how their living room seating turned away from the view, and . . . it was very much my husband's idea to want a contemporary house."[7] But Stedman, adaptable in his design approach and eager to please, created a plan calibrated to his clients' preferences. The basic envelope of the house follows the outline of the classic California ranch house, with a V-shaped plan splayed wide open to encompass more outdoor space and an orientation away from the long, steep uphill driveway; all of the main living spaces, including the kitchen, face the water view. The house also featured a three-car garage, five bedrooms, a bluestone floor in the front hallway and all of the main living spaces, and ample stowaway cabinetry that appealed to sailor and ex-Navy-man Fennebresque. Fully air-conditioned, it was an expensive house to build, with a fieldstone fireplace and wall in the living room, high ceilings, a paneled library near the front door, and a master bedroom with an adjoining terrace overlooking the water. The Fennebresques' interior decorator, Thorndike Williams, appointed the house with elegant modern and traditional furniture from his shop in Cold Spring Harbor.

In true California ranch style, the house combined a modern sensibility with vernacular building materials and methods. The rustic post-and-beam construction was deliberately made visible in some areas, contrasting with the decidedly industrial-looking basement-level steel pilotis supporting the terraces and the large expanses of glass on the outside. But in retrospect, two other, somewhat tangential factors make the house worthy of note.

The first is the landscape design, a system of fieldstone-walled terraces above and beyond a basement-level pool, which is set in a kind of sunken courtyard. Meandering paths wend their way from the pool and around the house to low sitting walls within distinct garden rooms or under trees. To design the landscape, Mrs. Fennebresque secured the services of American landscape architect Thomas Church (1902–1978), then at the height of his fame, thanks to constant endorsement of his work in American house magazines. Author of the popular *Gardens Are for People*, Church understood that most people had no desire to handle a great deal of garden maintenance; furthermore, they were more interested in living in their gardens than in merely looking at them. Church came to the Fennebresque project by way of Abby Rockefeller Milton O'Neill, whose house and Church-designed garden was in nearby Oyster Bay Cove. Mrs. Fennebresque had seen O'Neill's

John and Frances Fennebresque House, Cove Neck, 1960. California ranch house living on a terrace above the pool area. All of the landscape features were designed by Thomas Church.

garden and Church's book, and, impressed by both, engaged him to make sense of their triangular site, especially in its widest part, where the house was located. Heretofore unknown to landscape architecture enthusiasts, the project is an intriguing example of Church's work. According to his client, he provided the plans after visiting the site twice—arriving on site in his customary khaki uniform and with a briefcase full of grass samples—and then stepped aside to let John Stedman and local contractors oversee the masonry work and nurserymen fill in the specified plants.

The second notable fact about the Fennebresque House is even more tangential to its design. In 1977, several years after its original owners had decamped for Virginia, the house was sold to musician and singer Billy Joel. It was featured on the cover of his multiplatinum 1980 album *Glass Houses*, with Joel—a Long Islander himself, raised in Hicksville—rearing up to strike one of its glass-fronted façades with a stone.

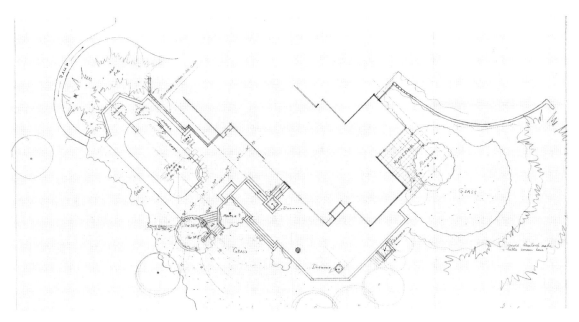

John and Frances Fennebresque House, Cove Neck, 1960. Thomas Church's final drawing, the "Pool Study," showing the waterside pool and landscape features.

25

RICHARD MEIER b.1934

Saul Lambert House, Fire Island, 1962;
David and Anita Hoffman House, East Hampton, 1967;
Renny and Ellin Saltzman House, East Hampton, 1969;
Alvin and Joan Weinstein House, Old Westbury, 1971;
Richard Maidman House, Kings Point, 1971–76;
Alfonse M. D'Amato United States Courthouse and Federal Building, Central Islip, 1993–2000.

Richard Meier, a son of the suburbs, has always preferred to design buildings outside the confines of dense urban environments. Often a neutral backdrop of open land suits him best, allowing him to shape his buildings as autonomous sculptural objects. He works equally well with dramatic natural settings, which he treats as a decorative feature, framing views through enormous windows or creating elevated terraces to take in the surrounding panorama. At the outset of his career, in the 1960s and early 1970s, Meier received commissions for both kinds of sites on Long Island. By that time, much of the island's farmland and beachfront, which had once provided an open frontier for the construction of weekend houses, had been transformed by development. Yet Meier's clients still managed to find room to build, sometimes on flat expanses of former potato fields, other times on picturesque sites overlooking the ocean or the Sound.

Given the number of commissions that Meier has executed on Long Island, it is fair to call it a laboratory in which his career took shape. In the late 1960s, Meier worked alongside like-minded young architects, such as Charles Gwathmey and Julian and Barbara Neski, who also began their careers on Long Island and who shared his fascination with the International Style modernism of the 1920s. Quoting directly from modernist pioneers, especially Le Corbusier, Meier developed

David and Anita Hoffman House, East Hampton, 1967. The exterior of the low-budget house resembles a Constructivist sculpture. The entrance is behind the bicycle.

his readily identifiable style of white walls and abstract geometries.[1] He designed these early buildings making extensive use of models, a practice that allowed him to give play to his fascination with the manipulation of forms in space, as he continues to do to this day.[2]

Yet certain unexpected qualities show up in Meier's Long Island work as well. These houses are quite modest compared to the enormous institutional commissions like the Getty Center in Los Angeles that catapulted him to "starchitect" status. Most were commissioned by young couples with children who wanted secluded and casual family retreats, rather than conspicuous status symbols. They reflect the constraints of budget and program under which the architect worked. Despite the sleekness of their forms, the Long Island houses are constructed primarily of wood. Most are relatively compact in plan and exhibit an easy informality with features like sleeping lofts or study areas on landings open to living rooms below. They allot as much space for children's playrooms as for formal dining rooms. Perhaps most surprisingly, they are not as abstract and homogeneous as they appear in Ezra Stoller's black-and-white photographs, the images through which they are predominantly known. Nor are they as uncompromisingly conceptual as the "Whites"—the group, including Gwathmey, Peter Eisenman, Michael Graves, and John Hejduk, with which Meier became associated around this time—espoused.[3] Rather, Meier incorporated touches of saturated color and elements of whimsy into his early architecture that suited his young clients and reflected the cultural ferment of the 1960s.

Today Meier is among the most international of architects, with projects from Prague to Kuala Lumpur to Rome. But early in his career, he operated on a local stage, cultivating his clients and contacts within the orbit of New York City.[4] After completing his architecture degree at Cornell in 1957, he took jobs with a series of New York firms: Davis, Brody and Wisniewski (1958–59), Skidmore, Owings and Merrill (1959–60), and Marcel Breuer (1960–63). He also was active as a painter and formed connections in the New York art world, sharing a studio with Frank Stella and collaborating with Barnett Newman on a design for a synagogue. Indeed, his first architectural commission came from the art world.

LAMBERT HOUSE

In 1962, the painter and book illustrator Saul Lambert hired Meier to design a beach house on Fire Island. Given a minuscule budget of $11,000, Meier turned for inspiration to the work of his boss, Breuer, particularly the small weekend cottages on Cape Cod that combined modest materials and a rustic sensibility with dynamic structural and spatial features. He took as his prototype the elevated, rectangular box with an asymmetrical façade that Breuer, Philip Johnson, and others had developed in the 1940s and 1950s from the model of Mies van der Rohe's Resor House project. In Meier's version, the box rests on a pair of I-beams raised above the dunes on wooden piers. In plan, the house consists of nothing more than a closed service core flanked by a bedroom on one side and an open living space on the other. The two long façades are almost completely open to breeze and views. To meet the budget, Meier contracted a Michigan log house manufacturer to prefabricate the whole structure using an easy-to-assemble system of tongue-and-groove boards rather than traditional framing. Meier and a team of workmen assembled the house in just a few days while camping out on the beach.[5] Like Breuer's and Johnson's houses, Meier's unpainted wooden structure was at once a minimalist machine and a rugged frontier cabin. Its later owners, the film and stage royals Mel Brooks and Anne Bancroft, apparently grew tired of the house's simplicity and altered it so completely that it became largely unrecognizable.

With one independent commission under his belt, Meier left the Breuer office to set up his own practice in his apartment, a two-room walkup on East 92nd Street in Manhattan. For the next several years, he executed a variety of small projects. He curated an exhibition at the Jewish Museum, which was then dedicated to showing contemporary American art, on recent synagogue architecture, in which he featured the work of Percival Goodman (see pages 152–63) and others.[6] He also began what became a long teaching career at the Cooper Union. In his architectural practice he took on small residential and commercial projects that have mostly been forgotten today, including a house for his parents in New Jersey and the interior of Sona, a shop on East 55th Street that sold arts and crafts imported from India.

For the interiors of these early projects, Meier collaborated with Elaine Lustig Cohen,[7] who in the 1950s had worked as a graphic designer with Philip Johnson on the Seagram Building and Eero Saarinen on the TWA Terminal, and had designed exhibition catalogues for the Museum of Modern Art in the 1960s. Together, Meier and Lustig Cohen created spaces characterized less by the aesthetic purity for which the architect later become known than by bold contrasts. Against the background of Meier's clean, white walls, Lustig Cohen added colorful decorative embellishments, using the latest art, patterned textiles, and folk crafts. Their mix of cool and vibrant, modern and primitive, captured the spirit of the moment, when the rigid prescriptions of postwar culture were giving way to freer, more experimental attitudes in manners and lifestyles, and artists were shifting from Minimalism to Pop and Op Art in rebellion against the Abstract Expressionists.

Design writer Barbara Plumb recognized the work of Meier and Lustig Cohen as fitting into the 1960s' zeitgeist. In several pieces on home design for the *New York Times Magazine*, she featured Meier–Lustig Cohen interiors, pointing out the play of different colors, textures, and cultures. In her article "The Home: One World of Design" she highlighted the living room from Meier and Lustig Cohen's Renfield House expansion in New Jersey (1965), which included African masks, cushions covered in Indian fabrics, a rainbow-striped Stella painting, and ceiling beams painted in Day-Glo colors, all offset by glossy, white, Formica-covered furniture designed by Meier.[8] Although he did not work with Lustig Cohen on his Long Island commissions, the color and eclecticism that she brought to their collaboration continued to play a role in his design.

HOFFMAN HOUSE

Plumb's interest turned out to be important to the advance of Meier's early career. Her *New York Times* articles introduced several future clients to his work. One was Anita Hoffman, who with her husband, David, had bought a flat piece of land on the edge of East Hampton's historic village and wanted to build a small weekend house for her family. The Hoffmans were in their twenties and had three young children. Mrs. Hoffmann recalled that she turned to Meier after first consulting a more traditional architect. "David hired someone he worked with to do a design and we got a pretentious French château. I was leafing through the Sunday magazine one day and I said, 'This is what I want.'"[9] She showed Plumb's article to her husband, who realized that it was the same Richard Meier who had been a grade-school friend in Maplewood, New Jersey.

The couple approached the architect in 1966 with a budget of $40,000 and a request to design something that would suit their family.[10] The result, which was hastily completed in time for the following summer season, was modest but ambitious. In essence, it was a two-bedroom cottage with an open living room and a loft above that served as a play area for the children. The interior was cozy and informal rather than grand, recalling the intimate quality of Marcel Breuer's houses and fulfilling the clients' desire for a relaxed, private retreat instead of an ostentatious space for entertaining.[11] Also like Breuer, Meier resorted to built-in seating, bunk beds, and cabinets to address constraints of space and budget.[12] He designed much of the furniture himself, including round tables of butcher block covered with white Formica mounted on round steel bases and a U-shaped sofa of white-lacquered wood with ovoid edges that surrounded the living room fireplace, forming a kind of room within the room. Stemming from his experience with the Lambert House, he used inexpensive four-by-eight sheets of plywood with caulked joints for the exterior walls, although he later replaced the plywood with clapboard siding.[13]

Money-saving measures shaped the project, yet compared to the Lambert House or many of Breuer's designs, the architecture was much more aesthetically experimental. As the site did not afford an ocean view, the house itself became the focus, standing like a piece of constructivist sculpture on the flat land. To achieve a bold, formal effect, Meier turned from the minimalist Miesian box, which had been the model for the Lambert House, to a more dynamic set of forms. The Hoffman House originally consisted of two rectangular volumes, one of which was rotated forty-five degrees off-axis to create a starlike configuration and a complex play of interpenetrating planes. The exterior is completely white, striking a bold contrast with the green lawn and blue sky. Since the site abuts busy Georgica Road, Meier gave the house an almost blank street façade and opened the opposite side to the landscape with a gridlike wall of wood-framed windows. Inside, the

David and Anita Hoffman House, East Hampton, 1967. View from the guest sleeping loft of the lower-level living space and the hallway to the bedrooms. Several doors and ceilings throughout the house were painted Day-Glo Kodak yellow and red.

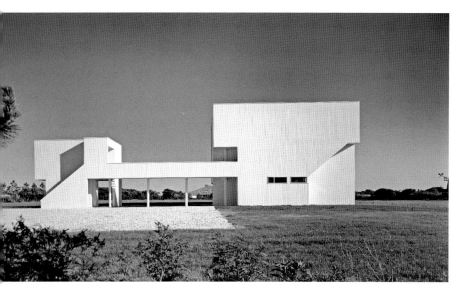

TOP
Renny and Ellin Salzman House, East Hampton, 1971. Southward view of the bridge connecting the main and guest houses.

ABOVE
Renny and Ellin Salzman House, East Hampton, 1971. The west façade.

stark whiteness of the double-height living room is enlivened by views of trees and sky through this grid of windows. Recalling Lustig Cohen's decorative work, Meier added a few splashes of bright color, which one critic described as contributing a "constant surprising delight" as one moves through the house.[14] A strip of red wall at the base of the staircase was a prelude to another red wall and at the top of the stairs a brilliant "Kodak yellow" ceiling, as Anita Hoffman described it. Although she liked the calm quality of white walls, Mrs. Hoffman recalled that she was open to Meier's addition of Day-Glo colors. "I was in my twenties and was a little wilder . . . so I went along with it."[15]

At some point in the 1970s, Mrs. Hoffman removed the original red and yellow colors and now enjoys living in an interior in which all appliances, furniture, and bedding are white. As she says, "White is a sort of a canvas and you can put whatever you want with it. It is a backdrop for wearing your clothes and your personality. It brings the outdoors in. You feel peaceful and part of the outdoors."[16] And she has enlarged the house to accommodate her grandchildren. Designed by Peter Stamberg and Paul Aferiat, who worked for Meier in the past, the additions blend seamlessly with the original structure while greatly expanding it. The only nonwhite element is the modern, blocky birch furniture that the architects designed for the much enlarged kitchen.

SALTZMAN HOUSE

Renny and Ellin Saltzman also read Plumb's pieces and contacted the architect around the same time as their friends the Hoffmans. Like the Hoffmans, the Saltzmans had recently become parents and wanted a weekend and summer place for their family. They approached Meier with high aesthetic ambitions. Both were professionally active in the design world—Renny was a successful interior designer with a roster of wealthy clients and Ellin had recently become the top fashion editor at *Glamour* magazine—and they wanted their house to make a bold statement about their own progressive taste and enjoyment of the outdoors. The result was a grander, more complex piece of architecture than the Hoffman House, designed to accommodate live-in help, as well as large dinner parties. An enormous south-facing window without any mullions runs the three-story height of the house and opens the interior to the outdoors to such an extent that, as Renny Saltzman once remarked, "On nights when the moon is full, one can dine without electric or candlelight."[17]

The Saltzmans' property was close to the shore and though not directly on the beach—Gordon Chadwick and George Nelson's Spaeth House stood in the way (see pages 206–13)—it had great scenic potential. "You can't see the ocean until you get onto the third floor,"[18] noted Meier. There, above the double-height living area and the small master bedroom on the second floor, he designed a loft with a sun deck so the Saltzmans could enjoy the ocean views. The kitchen and dining room are on the ground floor, as is a rectangular wing containing a den and dormlike rooms with bunk beds for the

Renny and Ellin Salzman House, East Hampton, 1971. The south façades.

children and the nanny. The main house was connected to a guesthouse—a box in the sky held up on pilotis—by a bridge, also on pilotis, accessed from the living room. Like the main house from the second story up, it provides guests with the sensation of being on an ocean liner, "without the seasickness," as Renny Saltzman described it.[19] The house sits on a flat lawn; Meier added a small cluster of trees to frame the approach along a gravel drive. He also designed a swimming pool with a low white wall and a small changing cabin, situated far enough away so that the sounds of playing children—the family hosted swimming lessons there every summer for a summer camp attended by their son—couldn't be heard from the house.

Like the Hoffman House, the Saltzman House is white and austerely abstract, but it is more monumental; its indoor *promenade architecturale*—to use the language of Le Corbusier—offers a circuitous route up through the structure to the ultimate destination, the ocean views. Like the guesthouse, the main house is partially raised above the ground on slender pilotis, clearly suggesting Meier's fascination with Le Corbusier. Curved corners south and east, versus sharply angled corners elsewhere, and the interplay of solid walls and recessed terraces pushed deeply inward through the taut outer skin give the house a sculptural, Cubist quality, as if the architect were creating a collage of architectural layers and shapes. Instead of inexpensive plywood, the house is clad in a more refined vertical wood siding, lending the otherwise rigorously modern structure a subtle connection to traditional American wood-frame construction.[20] Inside, the

Renny and Ellin Salzman House, East Hampton, 1971. Second-story living room.

living spaces are more formal and expansive than the almost cabinlike interior of the Hoffman House.

Meier relinquished the decorating to Renny Saltzman, who chose fabrics, furniture, and art pieces.[21] Like Elaine Lustig Cohen, Saltzman treated the white surfaces as a backdrop for pattern, color, and the exotic. He upholstered the living room banquette in a leopard print and displayed African statuary and masks, along with bright contemporary prints. A zebra skin adorned a bathroom floor and bright red Formica counters accented the kitchen. Ellin Saltzman recalls having left the decorating entirely to her husband, but she seems to have shared Renny's aesthetic sensibility. A photo in *House & Garden* magazine in 1969 shows her standing outside the house wearing a skirt made from a traditional American quilt.[22] This juxtaposition of architecture and fashion perfectly illustrates the play between whiteness and color and between ultramodern design and rustic folk-inspired patterns that seems to have contributed greatly to the appeal of Meier's houses in the late 1960s.

WEINSTEIN HOUSE

By the time the Saltzman House was completed in 1969, Meier had won major professional awards and his work was becoming increasingly known through national and international publications. That year he received his largest commission to date, a house in Old Westbury for a family with six children, a grandmother, and a live-in staff. The clients were Alvin Weinstein, who owned Concord Fabrics, a manufacturer of textiles for residential decorating, and his wife, Joan, who later became the company's fashion director. Concord had recently gone public, giving the Weinsteins the wherewithal to commission a grand house.[23] Meier designed a twelve-bedroom, three-story structure that stretched across its five-acre site. In sheer size, it recalls Windshield, the huge modern house that Richard Neutra designed in 1938 for the John Nicholas Browns on Fishers Island (see pages 166–71). The setting, a clearing in a wooded suburban area, was similar to that of the Hoffman and Saltzman houses in that it contributed no visual drama of its own but presented a plain backdrop for Meier's sculptural architecture. In this case, however, the clients' deep pockets enabled Meier to devote more attention to landscaping; the berms and the small pond that he added to the expansive lawn framed views of the house and lent a sense of ceremony to the approach.

The Saltzman and Weinstein houses were Meier's most direct homages to Le Corbusier: white, shiplike, with ribbon windows, pilotis, and a few massive, drumlike forms providing counterpoint to the overall rectilinearity. The main entrance of the Weinstein House is an oversized door on a central pivot like the entrance to Le Corbusier's chapel at Ronchamp. The central feature of the interior was a long ramp—another favorite Le Corbusier motif—that served to integrate the space not only vertically, from the first to the third level, but also

Alvin Weinstein House, Old Westbury, 1971. Entrance façade. The pilotis are an homage to Le Corbusier.

Alvin and Joan Weinstein House, Old Westbury, 1971. Walkway to the playroom pavilion.

Alvin and Joan Weinstein House, Old Westbury, 1971. The house, a modernist mansion, in its parklike setting.

TOP
Alvin and Joan Weinstein House, Old Westbury, 1971. Richard Meier designed the seating in the living room.

ABOVE
Alvin and Joan Weinstein House, Old Westbury, 1971. View of the dining space and the kitchen beyond. To the left is the ramp that Meier designed in lieu of stairs.

horizontally, from the public spaces at one end to the sleeping areas at the other. Meier recalled that he conceived of the ramp in social as well as formal terms. It was to serve as the communal heart of the house, a place "where everyone can kind of get together as they're moving around from one level to another."[24] One reviewer described the ramp as serving "to express an open and informal style of living," in which individuals can drift leisurely back and forth across the large interior.[25] Another significant feature of the spaces is the built-in furniture. As for the Hoffman and Saltzman houses, Meier designed a white-lacquered wooden couch that created an intimate seating enclosure within the otherwise open living space. The room-within-a-room seating unit harked back to the "conversation pit" concept that Eero Saarinen, Paul Rudolph, and other architects embraced. Meier also placed a banquette beneath a large-pane window beyond the couch.

Another important consideration in the spatial planning was how to accommodate the Weinsteins' six children. With so many, the house became "an indoor playground," in which "the ramps are alive with running, shouting youngsters."[26] Meier gave the children their own area on the top level of the house, at a remove from the master bedroom on the second floor and the living spaces on the first. He created a large playroom in an outlying pavilion, which, like the Saltzman guesthouse, is connected to the main body of the house by an elevated walkway. And a separate staircase at the west end of the house gave the children direct access to the entrance hall and breakfast room on the first floor from their third-floor bedrooms.

Perhaps also in response to the presence of the children, the interior of the Weinstein House was Meier's most colorful to date. Each of the children's bedrooms was painted a different combination of purple, blue, green, red, and orange. Adult spaces received some of the same treatment: the entrance door was coral red, the second-floor sitting area was flanked by walls of blue and green, and the kitchen was brightened with blocks of red, blue, and yellow. Folk-patterned textiles—perhaps from the clients' fabric business—accentuated the otherwise pure white living room and master bedroom. One reviewer, commenting on the architect's use of color, wrote that the house "brims with a multitude of surprises and moods. It is friendly and warm, more colorful inside than its sculptural, white-painted redwood exterior suggests."[27] The house's current owner, Long Island–based architect Michael Harris Spector, who was the co-architect with Meier on the United States Courthouse in Islip, has made all of the walls white. However, Spector has added color by embellishing the house with works from his extensive collection of first-rate contemporary painting and sculpture.

Richard Maidman House, Kings Point, 1971–76. South façade. The rooflines of the preexisting building are visible through the cutout windows.

Richard Maidman House, Kings Point, 1971–76. Entrance façade. The walkway on the right leads to Long Island Sound.

MAIDMAN HOUSE

The last, and by far the most colorful, of Meier's Long Island houses was commissioned in 1971 by Richard Maidman, a Manhattan lawyer and real estate developer. It is arguably the most unusual of all Meier's houses, as the architect himself has acknowledged, saying it allowed him a great deal of experimentation.[28] Its distinctiveness arose from the contingencies of the commission. Maidman had purchased a piece of land that featured a striking view of Long Island Sound but was already occupied by an old, abandoned house. Renovating the decaying structure, which had been constructed in 1869, was out of the question, but Maidman disliked the idea of simply demolishing it. So he stipulated that Meier incorporate the foundation, exterior supporting walls, chimney, main staircase, and gambrel roof of the original house into a new design.

Maidman, who relished the process of working with the architect, hoped that the challenge of reusing an existing structure might add an extra

Richard Maidman House, Kings Point, 1971–76. Visible out of a window in the second-level sitting room is the metal spiral slide that served as a fire escape from the top-floor children's rooms.

spark to the architect's creativity.[29] Indeed, the commission generated several unique features. First is the curved profile and flying beam of the upper story, clever visual details that played off the old gambrel roof. Another is a spiral slide—a tube of unpainted metal—that provides a memorable Arte Povera accent to the otherwise white, planar exterior. This highly sculptural flourish was Meier's solution to the clients' request for a fire escape for the third-story children's rooms. It is yet another example of how creatively Meier designed for children. One of Richard Maidman's daughters, Dagny, remembers the house as "big and fun" with an "element of fantasy."[30] This quality came not only from the slide that the children could use to shoot from their upstairs rooms to the big lawn below, but also from the myriad colors that Meier used to decorate the interior, more than in any of his past or later designs. Almost every room contains color. Often, adjacent walls feature contrasting hues: the angular rear staircase has panels of aquamarine, pink, and coral; in the living room the emerald green HVAC duct plays against the orange-red velvet cushions of the sofa. In total, the house contains perhaps thirty different shades, from the Day-Glo hues of Frank Stella's paintings in the living areas and bedrooms to the softer tones of the kitchen walls, which mimic Le Corbusier's Purist paintings. Meier has said that he likes to use color to enliven spaces that get less natural light. Because the Maidman house incorporated preexisting brick supporting walls, it would have been difficult for Meier to cut large openings in the façade. Without the enormous windows and intensity of natural light that characterized his other houses, he employed color as an alternative means to create visual energy. Interestingly, photographs of the Maidman House are almost never published in color, perhaps because these interiors contradict too dramatically the impression of whiteness that is so strongly associated with Meier's architecture.

UNITED STATES COURTHOUSE AND FEDERAL BUILDING

Meier's career as an architect of houses peaked around 1970, when he began to shift his practice toward civic commissions, beginning with public institutions in the New York area such as the

Bronx Developmental Center (1970–77), now, shamefully, largely demolished, and moving on to museums and corporate offices around the world. He would eventually return to Long Island to execute commissions for the Swissair North American Headquarters in Melville (1991–95) and the United States Courthouse and Federal Building in Islip (1993–2000). Both of these buildings defy the stereotype of so-called exit-architecture—the building as mere billboard, designed for function and to attract the distracted gazes of motorists passing at high speeds. The latter building, which was the result of a federal program during the Clinton years to increase the architectural quality and public recognition of government buildings, is one of Meier's most critically acclaimed works.

The Islip courthouse is also greatly admired by its users. Leonard Wexler, the senior judge of the United States District Court for the Eastern District, and his wife, Barbara, are great admirers of Meier. They championed Meier during the architectural competition, in which the architect was chosen from among a group of other high-profile candidates. Judge Wexler, who spends his days in a top-floor office and courtroom, has nothing but praise for the building, both as a smoothly functioning courthouse and inspiring work of architecture.[31] The citizenry, who use the building as members of juries or applicants for United States citizenship, can likewise enjoy the building's grand ceremonial spaces and views overlooking Fire Island and the Great South Bay. The building's complexity is a confident homage to Meier's hero, Le Corbusier, and the huge courthouse complex that the Swiss architect designed for Chandigarh, India. The Islip courthouse, like much of Meier's mature work, seems to spring from the concepts he developed in his houses, and it stands as a fitting bookend to the architect's long and productive association with Long Island.

Alfonse M. D'Amato United States Courthouse and Federal Building, Central Islip, 2000. The imposing civic building is impossible to miss from the Southern State Parkway.

NOTES

1 WALLACE HARRISON
1. Max Abramovitz became an associate of Harrison & Fouilhoux in 1935. In 1940 he was made a partner and the firm was renamed Harrison, Fouilhoux & Abramovitz. After Fouilhoux's death in 1945 and until 1976, the firm was known as Harrison & Abramovitz.
2. Thaddeus Crapster, interview with author, August 2004.
3. Ibid.
4. Abby Rockefeller Milton O'Neill, interview with author, February 16, 2005.
5. Hester Diamond, interview with author, July 2004; Thaddeus Crapster, interview with author, August 2004.
6. Abby Rockefeller Milton O'Neill, interview with author, February 16, 2005.
7. Ibid.
8. Thaddeus Crapster, interview with author, August 2004.

2 A. LAWRENCE KOCHER AND THE FORT SALONGA COLONY
1. Walter Gropius, letter to A. Lawrence Kocher, July 7, 1934. Courtesy Kocher Collection, Colonial Williamsburg Foundation.
2. Ibid.
3. "House-to-House Canvas." *The Texaco Star*, vol. 22, no. 4. (1936), p. 10.
4. Ibid.
5. Gloag, John. "A Week-End House in New York." *Architectural Review*, May 1935, p. 187.
6. McAndrew, John, ed. *Guide to Modern Architecture: Northeast States* (New York: Museum of Modern Art, 1940), p. 54.
7. A. Lawrence Kocher, letter to Mary Mix Foley, July 11, 1968. Courtesy Kocher Collection, Colonial Williamsburg Foundation.
8. Sandra Kocher, interview with author, March 26, 2010.
9. Ibid.
10. Robert L. Davison. "The Autobiography of Robert Leavitt Davison" (unpublished, ca. 1960), p. 25.
11. John Hancock Callender. "Aluminum Foil for Insulation: An Impartial Research Report." *Architectural Forum*, January 1934, pp. 67–71.
12. Robert L. Davison, John H. Callender, and C. O. Mackey, eds. *The Engineered Dwelling: Research Study 8* (New York: The John B. Pierce Foundation, 1944).
13. "Portfolio of Small Houses and Apartment Buildings." *Architectural Record*, October 1936, p. 278.
14. Robert L. Davison. "Horizontal Prefabricated Type: Plywood House." *The Timberman*, February 1937.
15. Anita Davison Engelman and Pat Davison Savadove, interview with author, October 10, 2010.
16. John Hancock Callender. "The Scientific Approach to Design." In Davison, Callender, and Mackey, eds. *The Engineered Dwelling*, p. 9.
17. Davison. "The Autobiography of Robert Leavitt Davison," pp. 31–32.
18. John Hancock Callender, letter to John McAndrew, Curator, Department of Architecture, Museum of Modern Art, June 6, 1941.
19. *Styling Your Home: Forty Exteriors in the Redwood Mode* (San Francisco: California Redwood Association, ca. 1938), p. 16.
20. Beth Bogie, interview with author, August 2006.
21. Alfred Bruce and Harold Sandbank. *A History of Prefabrication* (New York: The John B. Pierce Foundation, 1945), p. 12.
22. John Hancock Callender, letter to William P. Bogie, July 3, 1946. Quoted in "Steel Houses." *Architectural Forum*, April 1933, p. 331.

3 FRANK LLOYD WRIGHT
1. Ben Rebhuhn, letter to Frank Lloyd Wright, Thanksgiving 1937. Frank Lloyd Wright Foundation.
2. Ben Rebhuhn, telegram to Frank Lloyd Wright, December 7, 1937. Frank Lloyd Wright Foundation.
3. Anne Rebhuhn, letter to Frank Lloyd Wright, January 3, 1938. Frank Lloyd Wright Foundation.
4. Edgar Tafel, A Quick Rememberance of the Background of the Anne and Ben Rebhuhn House, Great Neck, NY, October 20, 1992. Courtesy of the Frank Lloyd Wright Foundation.
5. Edgar Tafel, interview with author, August 2004.
6. Anne Rebhuhn, in reply to an owner questionnaire from the Frank Lloyd Wright Foundation, Taliesin West, Scottsdale, Arizona.

4 ANTONIN RAYMOND
1. David Leavitt, interview with author, July 28, 2004.
2. Alice Krakauer, Larry Krakauer, and Phyllis Krakauer Jeswald (all of whom grew up in the Krakauer house in Great Neck), interviews with author, July 20, 2002.
3. Mrs. Shirley Rosen, interview with author, August 28, 2005.
4. Patricia Rosen Burgman, interview with author, August 28, 2005.
5. David Leavitt, interview with author, July 28, 2004.

5 DAVID L. LEAVITT
1. Ernest Silva and Arlene Silva, telephone interview with author, July 2010.
2. David Leavitt, interview with author, July 2003.
3. Ernest Silva and Arlene Silva, telephone interview with author, July 2010.
4. Judith Nasatir. "Arranging Nature." *House & Garden*, August 2006, p. 62.
5. David Leavitt, interview with author, July 28, 2003.

6 MARCEL BREUER
1. Joe Geller, interview with author, March 3, 2005.
2. Michael Geller, interview with author, February 22, 2005.
3. Stanley Geller, interview with author, December 14, 2004.
4. Michael Geller, interview with author, February 22, 2005.
5. Bea Hanson, interview with author, August 2004.
6. Ibid.

7 JANE YU
1. Jane Yu, interview with author, October 17, 2005.
2. The tapestry was donated to Dartmouth College in 1981 by the Geller family. The donation was accompanied by a certificate from Modern Masters, Inc. The Charles E. Slatkin Collection of Contemporary Tapestries, New York.
3. Jane Yu, interview with author, October 17, 2005.

8 WILLIAM LANDSBERG
1. William Landsberg, interview with author, November 4, 2005.
2. "Houses: 8. Dr. Rudolph Joseph House, Freeport, N.Y." *Architectural Record*, May 1955, p. 155.
3. Randall McIntyre, interview with author, November 24, 2005.
4. Ibid.
5. William Landsberg, interview with author, November 4, 2005.
6. Ibid.
7. Ibid.

9 HAMILTON P. SMITH
1. Hamilton Smith, interview with author, April 19, 2004.
2. Debra Miller Gates, interview with author, October 31, 2011.

3 Ibid.
4 Matthys Levy, interview with author, October 31, 2011.
5 Ibid.

10 JOSEP LLUÍS SERT

1 Miani Johnson, interview with the author, October 19, 2011.
2 "Remodelled Dairy Building Becomes a Colorful Suburban House." *Architectural Forum*, July 1950, p. 96.
3 Josep Lluís Sert, quoted in Peter Blake. "Sert's Piazza." *Harper's Bazaar*, March 1952, p. 232.
4 Sigfried Giedion, as quoted in Knut Bastlund. *Jose Luis Sert: Architecture, City Planning, Urban Design* (New York: Frederick Praeger, 1967), p. 7.
5 Saul Steinberg, quoted in Blake. "Sert's Piazza," p. 232.
6 Ibid.

11 HERMANN HERREY

1 *Locust Valley Leader*, January 14, 1971, p. 9.
2 "Victorian Stable Becomes Modern House." *Architectural Record*, April 1952, pp. 168–73.
3 Ibid.

12 BENJAMIN THOMPSON WITH THE ARCHITECTS OLLABORATIVE (TAC) AND SHOGO MYAIDA

1 Terry Rankine, interview with author, March 28, 2011. Rankine worked at TAC from 1958 to 1962. He is a founder of Cambridge Seven Associates, an architecture and design firm.
2 Mary Burke. "Twisted Pine Branches: Recollections of a Collector." *Apollo*, February 1985, p. 77.
3 Ibid.
4 Ibid.
5 Ibid.
6 Mary Griggs Burke. *Personal Selections from The Mary and Jackson Burke Collection* (Delray Beach, Florida: The Morikami Museum and Japanese Gardens, 1993), p.18.
7 "Informal Landscaping Keynotes a New House." *Architectural Record*, August 1956.
8 Charles B. Fahs, Director, Division of Humanities, The Rockefeller Foundation, to Walter Gropius, The Architects Collaborative, July 5, 1955. RG 1.2 Series 60R Box 45, Folder 493.
9 Connie Legakis Robinson, interview with author, April 10, 2011. Her father was a gardening assistant to Shogo Myaida, who was her neighbor when she was growing up.
10 C. W. Post Campus, B. Davis Schwartz Memorial Library, Special Collections and Archives, Archives of Shogo Myaida. Uncatalogued landscape design drawings for Mr. and Mrs. Jackson Burke house from 1956, 1960, and 1971.
11 Ibid. Information from Myaida's résumé of November 1, 1988.
12 Shogo Myaida papers, 97.77.1, Japanese American National Museum, Los Angeles, CA.

13 EDWARD DURELL STONE

1 A. Conger Goodyear. *The Museum of Modern Art: The First Ten Years* (New York: The Museum of Modern Art, 1948), p. 70.
2 Ibid.
3 Edward Durell Stone. *The Evolution of an Architect* (New York: Horizon Press, 1962), p. 37.
4 Ibid.
5 Ibid.
6 Ibid., p. 38.
7 Ibid., p. 89.
8 Ibid.
9 "The Scent of Money." *Vanity Fair*, January 1990, pp. 90–92.
10 Amei Wallach. "From Austerity to Opulence." *Newsday*, August 8, 1979, p. 4A.

14 PERCIVAL GOODMAN

1 Percival Goodman. "A Note on the Modern House." *Architectural Progress*, November 1931, p. 6.
2 Ibid.
3 Ibid.
4 Ibid., p. 23.
5 Percival Goodman. "Week-End House: Architect, Percival Goodman." *Architectural Record*, July 1934, p. 52.
6 "Builders Active on Long Island. Many New Homes Being Erected to Meet the Increased Spring Demand." *New York Times*, May 17, 1931.
7 "Modernity's First Subdivision." *Architectural Forum*, January 1935, p. 112.
8 Joel Goodman, interview with author, February 7, 2010.
9 Taylor Stoehr. "The Goodman Brothers and *Communitas*." In *Percival Goodman: Architect, Planner, Teacher, Painter*, ed. Kimberly J. Elman and Angela Giral (New York: Miriam and Ira D. Wallach Art Gallery, 2001), pp. 24–26.
10 Percival Goodman. "Notes on Community Planning." *Architectural Progress*, February 1932, p. 4; quoted in Stoehr, "The Goodman Brothers and *Communitas*," p. 25.
11 "Modernity's First Subdivision," p. 28.
12 Percival Goodman, unpublished transcript of an interview with Suzanne O'Keefe, 1979, Columbia University Oral History, p. 429.
13 Ibid., p. 334.
14 Ibid., p. 431.
15 See Kimberly J. Elman, "The Quest for Community: Percival Goodman and the Design of the Modern American Synagogue." In *Percival Goodman*, pp. 53–61.
16 Percival Goodman and Paul Goodman. "Modern Artist as Synagogue Builder: Satisfying the Needs of Today's Congregations." *Commentary*, January 1949, pp. 51–55; reprinted in *Percival Goodman*, p. 69.
17 Janet Loewy, interview with author, February 24, 2010. See also Nassau Community Temple, "25th Anniversary Journal: 1945–1970" (pamphlet in the author's collection).
18 Peter Sobel, interview with author, February 23, 2010.
19 Chiu-Hwa Wang, e-mail to author, February 19, 2010.
20 Gladys Kruh, interview with author, February 2010; Janet Loewy, interview with author, February 24, 2010.
21 See Elman, "The Quest for Community," p. 56.
22 Percival Goodman, unpublished transcript of an interview with Suzanne O'Keefe, p. 434.
23 Goodman and Goodman. "Modern Artist as Synagogue Builder," pp. 51–55; reprinted in *Percival Goodman*, p. 69.
24 Ario S. Hyams. "Sacred Ark: Focus of Worship." *United Synagogue Review*, 1962, p. 11.
25 Percival Goodman, unpublished transcript of an interview with Suzanne O'Keefe, p. 576.
26 Gerald Weinstein, interview with author, March 15, 2010.
27 Naomi Goodman. "A Memoir." In *Percival Goodman*, p. 178
28 Joel Goodman, interview with author, February 7, 2010.

15 RICHARD NEUTRA

1 *Time*, August 15, 1949.
2 Barbara Lamprecht. *Neutra* (Cologne, Germany: Taschen, 2006), p. 13.
3 Ibid., p. 7.
4 John Nicholas Brown, letter to Richard Neutra, October 9, 1936. Collection John Nicholas Brown Center for the Study of American Civilization at Brown University.
5 Anne Brown to Thomas S. Hines, April 11, 1979. In

Thomas S. Hines. *Richard Neutra and the Search for Modern Architecture* (New York: Rizzoli, 2005), p. 171.
6 Alice Price, interview with author, July 7, 2004.
7 Suggested Outline for a Description of Adelphi College to be included in Foundation Proposals, October 10, 1955. Adelphi University Archives.
8 Architects and Designers: List of Architects recommended by the *Architectural Forum*, Architect and Design, and the Library Committee at Adelphi. University Archives and Special Collections, Swirbul Library, Adelphi University, n.d.
9 Report of the Committee on Buildings and Grounds: Ratings of Architects. From the Minutes of the Semi-Annual Meeting of the Board of Trustees of Adelphi College, January 22, 1957. Courtesy University Archives and Special Collections, Swirbul Library, Adelphi University.
10 Ibid.
11 Richard Neutra. "Communicating Arts." *The Delphian*, May 21, 1959, p. 9.
12 Ibid.
13 Richard J. Neutra & Robert Alexander, Architects, Planning Consultants. "Preliminary Studies for a Masterplan and the Institute of Communicating & Performing Arts of Adelphi College," May 24, 1957–June 6, 1957, p. 12.
14 William Condon, interview with author, November 2008.
15 Richard Neutra. "Centerpiece of a Library." *Library Journal*, December 1, 1964, p. 4696.
16 Ted Bindrim, interview with author, May 2009.
17 Richard Neutra, from a speech at a meeting of the College and University Libraries Section of the New York Library Association at Adelphi University, October, 1964. Collection of University Archives and Special Collections, Swirbul Library, Adelphi University.
18 Ibid.
19 Eugene Neely, interview with author, June 2004.

16 WILLIAM LESCAZE

1 William H. Jordy. *American Buildings and Their Architects*, vol. 5: *The Impact of European Modernism in the Mid-Twentieth Century* (New York: Oxford University Press, 1986), pp. 87–88.
2 "England, Birmingham Broadcasting House: Erich Mendelsohn and Serge Chermayeff Architects." *Architectural Forum*, June 1936, p. 486.
3 Terry Townsend, past president of Long Island Theatre, which she started with Dr. Frank Calderone in 1967, interview with author, January 20, 2008.
4 William Lescaze. "Light, Color and Form in New Theatre." Lighting & Lamps, January 1950, p. 25
5 Ibid.
6 "Announcing Grand Opening Calderone Theatre, Hempsted Long Island." William Lescaze Papers, Syracuse University Library.
7 Miriam Tulin, Professor Emerita of Drama, Hofstra University, and author of *Calderone Theatres on Long Island: An Introductory Essay and Description of the Calderone Theatre Collection at Hofstra University*, (Hempstead, NY: Long Island Studies Institute, Hofstra University, 1991), interview with author, January 20, 2008.
8 Ibid.
9 Maggie Valentine. *The Show Starts on the Sidewalk: An Architectural History of the Movie Theatre, Starring S. Charles Lee* (New Haven: Yale University Press, 1996), p. 171.
10 Andrew Marglin, Kelmar Systems, interview with author, March 28, 2008.
11 Laura Seitz, Henry Alfred Dumper, Jr.'s daughter, interview with author, March 2, 2008. On Dumper's work for Lescaze, see Lorraine Welling Lanmon. *William Lescaze Architect* (Philadephia: The Art Alliance Press, 1987), p. 125.
12 William Lescaze, quoted in a press release issued for North Hempstead Housing Project, n.d. Syracuse University, William E. Lescaze Archives, George Arents Research Library for Special Collections.
13 *Architectural Record*, January 1953, p. 128.

17 GORDON CHADWICK WITH GEORGE NELSON

1 Jack Masey, interview with author, July 16, 2006; Philip George, interview with author, July 18, 2006; Irving Harper, interview with author, August 12, 2006.
2 Julius and Anne Abeles, interview with author, July 2006.
3 Ibid.
4 Ibid.
5 Stanley Abercrombie. *George Nelson: The Design of Modern Design* (Cambridge, MA: MIT Press, 2000), p. 34.
6 Tony Spaeth, interview with author, June 6, 2006.
7 Mrs. Russell Chadwick, Gordon Chadwick's sister-in-law, interview with author, July 2006.
8 Vincent Scully. *The Shingle Style: Architectural Theory and Design from Richardson to the Origins of Wright* (New Haven: Yale University Press, 1955), pp. 152–53.
9 "Examples of Work by George Nelson." *Architectural Record*, December 1957, p. 132.
10 Richard Johnson, interview with author, August 30, 2006.
11 Ibid.
12 Ibid.
13 Ibid.

18 LUDWIG MIES VAN DER ROHE

1 Building Structure Inventory Form, Division for Historic Preservation New York State Parks and Recreation, Town of Huntington, Summer 1979.
2 Fritz Coudert, interview with author, February 23, 2005. George Mittendorf, Mary Callery's great-nephew, interview with author, May 22, 2006; Marcella Korff, Mary Callery's niece and sole heir, interview with author, May 5, 2006.
3 *Exhibition of Paintings and Drawings by Pablo Picasso from a Private Collection*, February 27–March 17, 1945.
4 Patrice Munsel, opera singer, interview with author, June 2008.
5 Caroll L. V. Meeks. "Yale and the Ivy League Tradition." *Journal of the Society of Architectural Historians*, vol. 24, no. 1, March 1965, pp. 65–66.
6 George Mittendorf, interview with author, May 22, 2006; Marcella Korff, interview with author, May 5, 2006.
7 Franz Schulze. *Mies van der Rohe: A Critical Biography* (Chicago: University of Chicago Press, 1985), pp. 235–36.
8 Ibid., p. 239.
9 Peter Blake. *No Place Like Utopia: Modern Architecture and the Company We Kept* (New York: W. W. Norton, 1996), p. 192.
10 George Mittendorf, interview with author, May 22, 2006; letter from Callery to Mies, April 5, 1957. Mies van der Rohe General Office File, Callery, Mary, 1957, Library of Congress.
11 Schulze, *Mies van der Rohe*, p. 321.
12 Theodore Bindrim, interview, with author, August 4, 2008.
13 Barry Bergdoll. "The Nature of Mies' Space." In Terence Riley and Barry Bergdoll, eds. *Mies in Berlin* (New York: The Museum of Modern Art, 2001), p. 67.
14 Hester Diamond, interview with author, June 2004.

19 PHILIP JOHNSON

1 "Corporations: Wash It Yourself." *Time*, December 29, 1947.
2 Stover Jenkins, e-mail to author, June 2009.

3. Landis Gores. Unpublished memoirs of Landis Gores. Courtesy collection Pamela Gores.
4. Ibid.
5. Ibid.
6. Robert MacKay, Anthony K. Baker, and Carol A. Traynor. *Long Island Country Houses and Their Architects* (New York: W. W. Norton, 1997), pp. 196–97.
7. Clifton Leonhardt, interview with author, June 2009.
8. Victoria Newhouse. *Wallace K. Harrison, Architect* (New York: Rizzoli, 1989), p. 78.
9. Clifton Leonhardt, interview with author, June 2009.
10. Franz Schulze. *Philip Johnson: Life and Work* (Chicago: University of Chicago Press, 1996), p. 214.
11. Clifton Leonhardt, interview with author, June 2009.
12. Ibid.
13. Ann Brower, interview with author, March 2008.
14. Ada Louise Huxtable. "He Adds Elegance to Modern Architecture." *New York Times*, May 24, 1964, p. SM18
15. "Rockefeller Drives First Pile at State's Fair Complex." *New York Times*, October 10, 1962, p. 49.
16. Huxtable. "He Adds Elegance to Modern Architecture."
17. Ibid.
18. Ibid.
19. Walter Carlson. "State Wins Praise For Fair Pavilion." *New York Times*, April 24, 1964, p. 1.

20 I. M. PEI
1. James S. Hornbeck. "It's Fun to Visit America's Largest Shopping Center." *Architectural Record*, September 1957, p. 207.
2. Sid Schectman. "Roosevelt Field, L. I.: On Hallowed Ground." Tex McCrary Inc. press release, August 8, 1956. Collection New York World–Telegram and Sun, Library of Congress.
3. George DeWan. "The Master Builder." In *Long Island: Our Story*. (Melville, Long Island: Newsday, 1998), p. 286.
4. M. H. Smith. *History of Garden City* (Manhasset, NY: Channel Press, 1963), p. 131.
5. William Zeckendorf, with Edward McCreary. *Zeckendorf: The Autobiography of William Zeckendorf* (New York: Holt, Rinehart and Winston, 1970), p. 97.
6. Donald Page, interview with author, December 19, 2006.
7. Ken Resen, interview with author, December 2006.
8. Henry Cobb, interview with author, May 10, 2008.
9. I. M. Pei, interview with author, December 14, 2005.
10. Ibid.
11. Kellogg Wong, interview with author, January 1, 2007.
12. Donald Page, interview with author, December 19, 2006.
13. Ibid.
14. Robert Zion. "Who's Minding the Floor?" *Architectural Forum*, December 1962, p. 118.
15. Vincent Polimeni, interview with author, December 18, 2006.

21 DAMAZ, POKORNY & WEIGEL, GRUZEN & PARTNERS, ET AL.
1. "Promising Jobs, Governor Admits 'Edifice Complex.'" *New York Times*, September 24, 1970, p. 51.
2. Joseph E. Persico. *The Imperial Rockefeller: A Biography of Nelson A. Rockefeller* (New York: Simon and Schuster, 1982), p. 201.
3. "An Analysis of Excellence." *Architectural Record*, January 1971, p. 105.
4. Joel T. Rosenthal. *From the Ground Up: A History of the State University of New York at Stony Brook* (Port Jefferson, NY: 116 Press, 2004), p. 90.
5. Jan Pokorny, interview with author, May 3, 2005.
6. Ervin Galantay, letter to author, August 10, 2009.
7. Jan Pokorny, interview with author, May 3, 2005.
8. "Made for Walking: The Student Union at Stony Brook's State Campus Is Also a Pedestrian Mall." *Architectural Forum* July–August, 1971, p. 60.
9. Ervin Galantay, letter to author, June 20, 2005.
10. Ibid.
11. Ervin Galantay, interview with author, May 25, 2005.
12. Ibid.
13. Paul Friedberg, interview with author, August 2009.

22 JOHN JOHANSEN, ALEXANDER KOUZMANOFF, AND VICTOR CHRIST-JANER
1. Wolfgang Saxon. "Samuel B. Gould, 86, Unifier of SUNY, Dies." *New York Times*, July 16, 1997.
2. Ralph Keyes, Harris Wofford, Jacqueline Grennan, Roger Landrum, and Larry Resnick. "The College That Students Helped Plan." *Change in Higher Education* 1 (March/April), 1969, pp. 12–23.
3. M. A. Farber. "Life and Death of a Far-Out College." *New York Times*, April 26, 1971.
4. Ibid.
5. Jan Kouzmanoff, interview with author, October 31, 2011.
6. John M. Johansen. *A Life in the Continuum of Modern Architecture* (Milan: L'Arca Edizioni, 1995), p. 75.
7. John Johansen, interview with author, May 2006.
8. Johansen. *A Life in the Continuum of Modern Architecture*, p. 87.
9. John Johansen, interview with author, May 2006.
10. Roger Bartels, interview with author, November 24, 2011.

23 PAUL RUDOLPH
1. Peter Blake. *No Place Like Utopia: Modern Architecture and the Company We Keep* (New York: W. W. Norton Company, 1993), p. 261.
2. Saretta Barnet, interview with author, May 2005.
3. Maurice and Barbara Deane, interview with author, July 2006.
4. Ibid.
5. *Spaces: The Architecture of Paul Rudolph*. Short documentary produced by Robert Eisenhardt, 1983.
6. Maurice and Barbara Deane, interview with author, July 2006.
7. Bryant Conant, interview with author, November 2007.
8. Jeff Siegel, interview with author, January 22, 2007.
9. Maurice and Barbara Deane, interview with author, July 2006.
10. Donald Luckenbill, interview with author, April 2007.
11. Earl Anderson, interview with author, April 2007.
12. Donald Luckenbill, interview with author, April 2007
13. *Spaces: The Architecture of Paul Rudolph*. Short documentary produced by Robert Eisenhardt, 1983.
14. Donald Luckenbill, interview with author, April 2007.
15. Ibid.
16. Der Scutt, interview with author, July 2006.

24 JOHN W. STEDMAN, JR.
1. Harvard College Class of 1930. *Twenty-Fifth Anniversary Report* (Cambridge, Mass.: Harvard University Printing Office, 1955), p. 1065.
2. Ibid., p. 1066.
3. Ibid.
4. Margaret Hamilton (Luce) Howe, interview with author, April 8, 2004.
5. Mary Lindsay, interview with author, October 18, 2006.
6. Mary Lindsay, interview with author, October 14, 2006.
7. Frances Fennebresque, interview with author, October 17, 2006.

25 RICHARD MEIER
1. On Meier, Gwathmey, and the Neskis, see Alistair Gordon. *Weekend Utopia: Modern Living in the Hamptons* (New York: Princeton Architectural Press, 2001), pp. 127–46.

2 Richard Meier & Partners Model Gallery is open for view, by appointment, at his firm's warehouse in Long Island City, Queens.
3 See Peter Eisenman, ed. *Five Architects: Eisenman, Graves, Gwathmey, Hejduk, Meier* (New York: Oxford University Press, 1975).
4 For a brief autobiographical account of Meier's early career, see Richard Meier. *Building the Getty* (Berkeley: University of California Press, 1999), pp. 5–22.
5 Ibid., pp. 10–11.
6 Richard Meier. *Recent American Synagogue Architecture* (New York: The Jewish Museum, 1963).
7 Elaine Lustig Cohen, interview with author, November 1, 2011.
8 Barbara Plumb. "The Home: One World of Design." *New York Times*, September 29, 1968.
9 Anita Hoffman, interview with author, April 30, 2010.
10 Ibid. See also "Record Houses of 1969." *Architectural Record*, May 1969, pp. 76–79.
11 See the architect's comments on the commission in Richard Meier. *Richard Meier Houses* (New York: Rizzoli, 1996), p. 32.
12 Ibid.
13 Richard Meier, interview with author, May 11, 2010.
14 "Record Houses of 1969," p. 76.
15 Anita Hoffman, interview with author, April 30, 2010.
16 Ibid.
17 Richard Meier, Paul Goldberger, Sir Richard Rogers. *Richard Meier Houses* (New York: Rizzoli, 1996), p. 42.
18 Richard Meier, interview with author, May 11, 2010.
19 Ibid.; Meier, Goldberger, Rodgers, *Richard Meier Houses*, p. 42.
20 See Meier, *Building the Getty*, p. 12.
21 Ellin Saltzman, interview with author, April 17, 2010; Richard Meier, interview with author, May 11, 2010.
22 "A House That Sets Us Free." *House & Garden*, December 1969, pp. 78–87; illustration also appears in Gordon, *Weekend Utopia*, p. 144.
23 Robert Metz. "Marketplace: Concord Fabrics Bid Splits Investors." *New York Times*, March 1, 1975.
24 Richard Meier, interview with author, April 30, 2010.
25 James D. Morgan. "A House That Glows with Crystalline Transparency." *Architectural Record*, April 1972, p. 98.
26 Ibid.
27 "The Light and Color of Nature in a House for a Big Family: A Sculptured Machine for Living." *House & Garden*, March 1972, p. 69.
28 Meier, Goldberger, Rodgers, *Richard Meier Houses*, p. 66.
29 Richard Maidman, interview with author, March 10, 2010.
30 Meier, Goldberger, Rodgers, *Richard Meier Houses*, p. 66.
31 Judge Leonard Wexler, interview with author, March 22, 2010.

INVENTORY OF ARCHITECTS AND THEIR LONG ISLAND PROJECTS

Asterisks denote architects whose work appears in the book.

BARNES, EDWARD LARABEE 1915–2004
Henry Kaufmann Campgrounds, Wyandanch, 1959
Righter Beach House, Fishers Island, 1964
North Shore Unitarian Universalist Church, Manhasset, 1993

BECKHARD, HERBERT 1926–2003
Herbert and Eleanor Beckhard House, Glen Cove, 1964
Arnold and Rochelle Rosenberg House, Fire Island, 1969
Vasiliou House, "Osprey Nest," Fishers Island, 1984

BENDER, RICHARD b. 1930
Beatrice Simpson House, Springs, 1959. Co-architect: Paul Lester Wiener.
Amenity, a community of houses, Amagansett, 1962
Robert and Ethel Scull House, East Hampton, 1962. Co-architect: Paul Lester Wiener.
Elizabeth de Cuevas House, Amagansett, 1964. Co-architect: Paul Lester Wiener.
"Budget Beach House," Amagansett, 1963
Richard and Sue Bender House, Amagansett, 1963
Peter and Carol Moore House, Amagansett, 1963
Earl Johnson House, Southampton, 1966. Co-architect: Paul Lester Wiener.
Ronald Saypol House, East Hampton, 1966. Co-architect: Paul Lester Wiener (unbuilt).
Marvin and Dory Small House, East Hampton, 1966. Co-architect: Co-architect Paul Lester Wiener (no longer extant).
Amenity 11, a community of houses, Springs, 1968
Saul Steinberg Artist's Studio, Springs, 1970

BENNETT, WARD 1917–2003
Ward Bennett House, Springs, 1968
Hale Allen House, Amagansett, 1969
Marvin Sugarman House, Southampton, 1970

BENTEL, FREDERICK R. and MARIA A. BENTEL 1928–2000
Gloria and George Bock House, East Norwich, 1953
O'Neil and Doris Bouknight House, East Norwich, 1953
Maria and Frederick Bentel House, Locust Valley, 1959
Theresa and Louis Azzarone House, Locust Valley, 1959
Alina Corporation Showroom, Offices, and Warehouse Building, Plainview, 1963
Mr. and Mrs. Dale Denning House, Locust Valley, 1965; addition and alteration as John Gambling House, 1974
North Shore Unitarian Church School, Plandome, 1966
Thompson Aircraft Tire Corporation Office and Plant Building, Brentwood, 1966
Long Island University, C.W. Post Campus, Brookville:
  Finance Center, 1966
  Auditorium, 1970
  Hillwood Commons, 1973
  Field House, 1977
Mark and Eleanor Neitlich House, Oyster Bay Cove, 1967
Regal Cadillac Showroom and Repair Facility, Roslyn Harbor, 1967
Sea Cliff United Methodist Church, Sea Cliff, 1968
Board of Education Building, Locust Valley, 1969
Church of the Redeemer, Merrick, 1969
Croasdale Cadillac Showroom and Office Building, Lynbrook, 1970

Shelter Rock Public Library, Albertson, 1970
Amityville Public Library, Amityville, 1971
Hempstead Bank Executive Headquarters, Garden City, 1971
Woodmere Academy Barbara Steinberg Learning Center, Woodmere, 1971
Jericho Public Library, Jericho, 1972
Calendar House Condominiums, Bayville, 1974
Friends Academy Master Plan development, Glen Clove, 1974–80
New York Institute of Technology, Old Westbury:
   Locker Room Facility and Athletic Department Offices, 1975
   Student Activities Center, 1976
   Nelson A. Rockefeller Building, New York College of Osteopathic Medicine, 1978
Glen Cove Boy's Club, Lincoln House, Glen Cove, 1976
Commack Public Library, Commack, 1977
Friends Academy Commons, Library, and Laboratory Buildings, Glen Cove, 1980
Marjorie and Harry Mayrock House, Old Westbury, 1980

BLAKE, PETER 1920–2006
Ideal Museum at Jackson Pollock House (with Jackson Pollock), Springs, 1949 (unbuilt); model is at the Pollock-Krasner House and Study Center, Springs
Blake "Pin Wheel" House, Water Mill, 1954 (no longer extant)
Jack Russell House, Water Mill, 1956. Co-architects: Julian and Barbara Neski.
Blake House II, Bridgehampton, 1960
Yvonne Hagen House and Studio, Sagaponack, 1960. Co-architects: Barbara and Julian Neski.
Fred Tobey Barn adaptation, Amagansett, 1960. Co-architects: Barbara and Julian Neski (no longer extant).
Hans Namuth House addition, Southampton, early 1960s
Armstrong House, Montauk, 1962. Co-architects: Julian and Barbara Neski.
George and Ruth Eckstein House, Great Neck, 1969. Co-architect: Dorothy Alexander.

BLUM, WALTER E. b. 1920
Usonian Cluster, Great Neck:
Walter Blum House, 1952
Joseph Chasin Handicapped Accessible House, 1954
Henry Haberman House, 1954
Marvin Winter House, 1955
Barnett House, Sands Point, 1953
Douglaston Associates, Douglaston, 1966
Great Neck Park District Administration Building, Great Neck, 1967
Village of Lake Success Golf Facility Building, Lake Success, 1968
With co-architect Robert M. Nerzig (Blum & Nerzig):
   Ten Cutter Mill Road offices, Great Neck, 1972
   Lake Success Community Facilities Building, Lake Success, 1973
   Garfinkle House, Lake Success, 1975
   Great Neck Park Community Facilities Building, Great Neck 1975
   Gilchrest House, Great Neck, 1975
   Solar Heated Office Building, Great Neck, 1979

***BREUER, MARCEL** 1902–81
Bert and Phyllis Geller House, Lawrence, 1945
Long Beach Hospital, Nurses' Residence, Long Beach, 1945 (unbuilt)
Walter Maas House, Lattingtown, 1945–47 (unbuilt)
Apartment House, project for Bert Geller, Lawrence, 1945 (unbuilt)
Gilbert Tompkins House, Hewlett Harbor, 1946 (no longer extant)
John and Bea Hanson House, Lloyd Harbor, 1951
Edmond Witalis House, Saddle Rock, Kings Point, 1951
Abraham & Straus Store exterior, Hempstead, 1951–52
Tibby House, Port Washington, 1952–53 (unbuilt)
Brookhaven National Laboratory, Chemistry Building, Upton, 1960 (unbuilt)
State School for Mentally Retarded, Hempstead, 1969–71 (unbuilt)
Bert and Phyllis Geller House II, Lawrence, 1969
Heckscher Museum expansion, Huntington, 1973–77 (unbuilt)

BUNSHAFT, GORDON 1909–90
International Arrivals Building (Terminal 4), Idlewild (John F. Kennedy) Airport, Queens, 1957
Gordon and Nina Bunshaft "Travertine House," East Hampton, 1963 (no longer extant)
Boardwalk Restaurant, Jones Beach, 1966 (no longer extant)

***CALLENDER, JOHN** 1908–95
Robert L. and Constance Davison Prefabricated House, Fort Salonga, 1936. Co-architect: Robert L. Davison.
Subhi M. Sadi House, Fort Salonga, 1936
Colonel William P. and Betty Bogie House addition, Fort Salonga, 1946. Co-architect: Huson Jackson.
William Shanhouse House, Syosset, 1948. Co-architect: Huson Jackson.
Dorothy Havemeyer House, Syosset, 1949. Co-architect: Huson Jackson.

CHAREAU, PIERRE 1883–1950
Robert Motherwell House, Studio and Guest Cottage, East Hampton, 1946 (no longer extant)

***CHADWICK, GORDON** 1915–80
with **GEORGE NELSON** 1908–86
Holiday House, Quogue, 1950
Woodruff House, Quogue, 1950 (status unknown)
Gerard Spencer House, Seacliff, 1953 (status unknown)
Julius and Anne Abeles House, Roslyn, 1954
Otto and Eloise Spaeth House, East Hampton, 1956
Rudolph and Ethel Johnson House, Montauk, 1962 (no longer extant)

***CHRIST-JANER, VICTOR** 1915–2008
Academic Village A and Master Plan, State University of New York College at Old Westbury, 1972. Co-architects: John Johansen and Alexander Kouzmanoff.
Academic Village B, State University of New York College at Old Westbury, 1972 (unbuilt)

DATTNER, RICHARD b.1937
Estee Lauder Laboratories, Melville, 1964–68. Co-architect: Samuel M. Brody.
Dattner Prefabricated House, Amagansett, 1969
Estee Lauder Automated Warehouse, Melville, 1976. Co-architect: Samuel M. Brody.
Harry Striebel House, Wainscott, 1977
Dattner House, Amagansett, 1980
Estee Lauder Research Park, Melville, 1980. Co-architect: Samuel M. Brody.
Parfums Stern Warehouse, Hauppauge, 1981
Walter and Nina Weiner House, East Hampton, 1981
Walter and Priscilla Reichel House, Water Mill, 1983

DE KOONING, WILLEM 1904–97
De Kooning House and Studio, Springs, 1962

DE PACE, ANTHONY J. 1892–1977
New York State Medical Society Building, Levitt Headquarters complex, Lake Success, 1971

EMBURY, AYMAR 1880–1966
East Hampton Guild Hall, East Hampton, 1931
Triborough (Robert F. Kennedy) Bridge, New York City, 1936
Jamaica Bay Bridge, 1937
Hofstra University South Campus Master Plan and buildings, 1937–62
Bronx-Whitestone Bridge, New York City, 1939
1939 World's Fair, New York City Pavilion, Flushing Meadows, Queens, 1939

FRANZEN, ULRICH b. 1921
Bernstein House, Great Neck, 1963
Ulrich Franzen House, Bridgehampton, 1978–79
Krauss House, Old Westbury, 1978
Arne and Mildred Glimcher House, East Hampton, 1985

FERRISS, HUGH 1889–1962
United Nations project, Flushing Meadows, Queens, 1946 (unbuilt)

FOSTER, RICHARD 1919–2002
1964–65 World's Fair, Flushing Meadows, Queens, with co-architect Philip Johnson:
    New York State Pavilion, 1962–64
    Texaco Road Map, New York State Pavilion, 1963
    New York State Theaterama, 1963
Montauk Golf & Racquet Club, Montauk, 1969
Montauk Manor condominium conversion, 1971
Villas at Montauk Golf & Racquet Club, 1973

FROEHLICH, ARTHUR 1909–85
Roosevelt Raceway, Westbury, 1957
Aqueduct Racetrack, Ozone Park, 1959

FREY, ALBERT 1903–98
Aluminaire House, Wallace Harrison property, Huntington, 1931; moved in 1988 to New York Institute of Technology, Central Islip
Kocher Canvas Weekend House, Fort Salonga, 1934 (no longer extant)

FULLER, BUCKMINSTER 1895–1993
Lunn Laminates Fiber Glass Ray Dome exhibit, Flushing Meadows, Queens, 1953 (no longer extant)

GELLER, ABRAHAM W. 1912–95
Long Beach Homes, Long Beach, 1945. Co-architect: George Nemeny.
Long Beach Condominiums, Long Beach, 1946–47. Co-architect: George Nemeny.
Bernard Applebaum House, Cedarhurst, 1948. Co-architect: George Nemeny.
Jack Diamond House, Woodmere, 1951. Co-architect: George Nemeny.
Temple Beth El, North Bellmore, 1957
J. M. Kaplan House, East Hampton, 1960
Deepdale Hospital additions, Little Neck, 1962
Shelter Rock Jewish Center additions, Roslyn, 1969

GELLER, ANDREW MICHAEL 1924–2011
Merein House, Great Neck, 1953
Morse House, Northport, 1953
Gunst House, Bay Shore, 1954
Elizabeth Reese House I, Sagaponack, 1955 (no longer extant)
Leonard and Helen Frisbie House, Amagansett, 1957
Lois and Beverly Langman House, Sagaponack, 1958
Rudy and Judy Frank House, Fire Island, 1958
Irwin and Joyce Hunt House, Fire Island, 1958
Arthur Pearlroth House, Westhampton Beach, 1959
Sy Fried House, Fire Island, 1959
Roman Catholic Church, Leja Beach, Fire Island, 1961
Phil George House, Sagaponack, 1963
Elizabeth Reese House II, Bridgehampton, 1963
Grishman House, North Haven, 1965
Irving Elkin House, Amagansett, 1966
Howard and Andree Dean House, East Hampton, 1967 (no longer extant)
Jack Lippman House, Huntington, 1967
Zaid House, Old Westbury, 1967
Louis and Racelle Strick House, Amagansett, 1968
Arthur and Carol Greene House, Napeague, 1969
Morley House, Lloyd Harbor, 1970
Christensen House, Eaton's Neck, 1972
Twomey House, Shelter Island, 1975
Upton House, Montauk, 1978
Witkoff House, Westhampton Beach, 1979
Gregg and Hope Geller House, Bridgehampton, 1980

GIFFORD, HORACE 1932–92
Wittstein-Miller House, Fire Island, 1963
Fishman House, Fire Island, 1965
Horace Gifford House, Fire Island, 1965
Bonaguidi House I, Fire Island, 1968
David Luck House, Bridgehampton, 1968
Roeder House, Fire Island, 1969
Lipkins House, Fire Island, 1970
Sloan House, Fire Island, 1972
Travis and Wall House, Fire Island, 1972–77
Ross Runnels house, Sag Harbor, 1974
Bonaguidi House II, Fire Island, 1975
Graham house, Eastport, 1978

*GOLDBERG, BERTRAND 1913–97
Stony Brook University Health Sciences Complex, Stony Brook, 1976–1980

*GOODMAN, PERCIVAL 1904–1995
Philip Batchker House, Long Beach, 1931 (unbuilt)
Weekend Aluminum Beach House, Montauk, 1932 (competition project)
Model house for H. Arthur Colen, Hempstead State Park Homes, Hempstead, 1934
Modern House Development for H. Arthur Colen, Hempstead, 1935 (unbuilt)
1939 World's Fair, Labor Pavilion, "Collective Design," Flushing Meadows, Queens, 1937
Riverview Community House Development, Long Island City, 1944–46
Nassau Community Temple, West Hempstead, 1948
East End Synagogue of Long Beach, Congregation Beth Sholom, 1951
Peters House, Fire Island, 1953 (unbuilt)
Temple Beth Sholom, Roslyn Heights, 1954; addition, 1960
Jewish Community Center, West Hempstead, 1955
Union Reform Temple, Freeport, 1957
Jewish Community Center, Franklin Square, 1958
Temple Beth Israel, Port Washington, 1960
Great Neck Synagogue, Great Neck, 1962
East End Synagogue of Long Beach, Congregation Beth Sholom, Long Beach, 1963 (no longer extant)
Reform Jewish Congregation of Merrick, Merrick, 1963
Unitarian Universalist Congregation of Central Nassau Fellowship Hall, Garden City, 1963.
Unitarian Universalist Congregation of Central Nassau, sanctuary, Garden City, 1963 (unbuilt)
Temple Beth Sholom, Kings Point, 1966 (unbuilt)
Dix Hills Jewish Center, 1972 (unbuilt)
Percival and Naomi Goodman House addition, Springs, 1974
Michael and Lillian Braude House, Amagansett, 1976
Springs Lane Housing Development, East Hampton, 1978 (unbuilt)

Arthur Karlin House addition, East Hampton, 1980
East Hampton Housing for the Elderly, 1984 (unbuilt)

GROSSI, OLINDO 1909–2002
Olindo and Martha Grossi House, Manhasset, 1951 (no longer extant)
Beach House for Westhampton Realty Construction Company, 1954
T. G. Klumpp House, Sands Point, 1954
Stuart Machlin House, Centerport, 1955
Alfred Day Hershey House, Cold Spring Harbor, 1963
Roy Olson House, Sands Point, 1963
Melvin and Audrey Troy House, Sands Point, 1963
Aaron and Blanche Scharf House, Sands Point, 1965
Glen Cove Renewal Project, Glen Cove, 1972

*GRUZEN, JORDAN b.1934 with **GRUZEN AND PARTNERS**
State University of New York at Stony Brook, Stony Brook:
    Earth and Space Sciences Building, 1969
    Stage XI Gruzen and Kelly Dormitory Complex, 1969
    Master Plan, 1970
    Stage XII Complex (Roosevelt Quad), 1971
    Graduate Physics-Mathematics Building, 1973
Jordan and Lee Gruzen House, East Hampton, 1985

GWATHMEY, CHARLES 1938–2009
Gerald Miller House, Fire Island, 1964
Robert and Rosalie Gwathmey House and Studio, Amagansett, 1965. Co-architect: Richard Henderson.
Straus House, East Hampton, 1966. Co-architect: Richard Henderson.
Joseph Sedacca House, East Hampton, 1967. Co-architect: Richard Henderson.
John Steel House ("Steel House I"), Bridgehampton, 1968. Co-architects: Richard Henderson and Robert Siegel.
Arthur and Ruth Steel House ("Steel House II"), Bridgehampton, 1968. Co-architects: Richard Henderson and Robert Siegel.
Rick Lawrence House, Kings Point, 1970. Co-architect: Richard Henderson.
Michael Tolan House, Amagansett, 1970. Co-architect: Robert Siegel.
Marshall and Maureen Cogan House, East Hampton, 1971. Co-architect: Robert Siegel (no longer extant).
Maurice and Marilyn Cohn House, Amagansett, 1973. Co-architect: Robert Siegel.
Ken Charof House, Montauk, 1974. Co-architect: Robert Siegel.
Harry and Sydney Gay Kislevitz House, West Hampton, 1974. Co-architect: Robert Siegel.
Melville I. Haupt House, Amagansett, 1976. Co-architect: Robert Siegel.
Weitz House, Quogue, 1976. Co-architect: Robert Siegel
Francois de Menil House "Toad Hall", East Hampton, 1979. Co-architect: Robert Siegel.
Gabriele Viereck House, Amagansett, 1980. Co-architect: Robert Siegel.

HAMBY, VINCENT b. 1902–90, with co-architect **GEORGE NELSON**
Park House, Great Neck, 1939
W. Taylor House, Bayside, 1941
Sidney Johnson House, East Hampton, 1949

HARRISON, BERNARD ("Quackie") 1907–89
Frank Weissman House, Brookville, 1948. Co-architect: Vincent Furno.
Split Rock Ridge Development, East Norwich, 1951. Co-architect: Vincent Furno.
Norwich Woods Development, East Norwich, 1951
Joseph and Carolyn Robinson House, Westhampton, 1957
Westbury Village Hall, 1957
Augusta "Gussie" and Bernard "Quackie" Harrison House, Centre Island, 1961 (no longer extant)
J. W. and Sally Outerbridge House, Centre Island, 1961. Co-architect: Vincent Furno
R. Evans House, Centre Island, 1961; addition for Jack R. and Eleanor Howard, 1977
Hampton Waters summer house "cabanas" development, Three Mile Harbor, 1960s
Cherrywood residential development Master Plan, 1979
Cherrywood houses:
    George F. Baker House, 1980
    A.J. Powers House, 1980
    Carl and Patsy Timson House II, 1981
    Henry and Georgie Lewis House, 1982
Harry Wilmerding, Mill Neck, 1980
George Walker House, Lattingtown, 1981
Martin and Helene Victor House, Locust Valley, 1982
King House, Centre Island, 1982

*HARRISON, WALLACE 1895–1981
Wallace K. and Ellen Harrison House, Huntington, 1931–62
1939 World's Fair, Flushing Meadows, Queens:
    Master Plan, 1939
    Consolidated Edison Pavilion, 1939 (no longer extant)
    Electric Utilities Exhibit, 1939 (no longer extant)
    Electrified Farm, 1939 (no longer extant)
    Trylon and Perisphere, 1939 (no longer extant)
    Masterpieces of Art Building for A. Conger Goodyear, 1939 (no longer extant)
Plan for United Nations Project, Flushing Meadows, Queens, 1944 (unbuilt)
LaGuardia Airport Master Plan, Queens, early 1950s
1964–65 World's Fair, Flushing Meadows, Queens:
    Master Plan, 1963
    Hall of Science, 1964–65
LaGuardia Airport, Queens:
    Main Terminal, 1964
    Control Tower, 1964 (no longer extant)

HEJDUK, JOHN 1929–2000
William and Barbara Demlin House, Locust Valley, 1963

HENDERSON, RICHARD 1928–2009)
Robert and Rosalie Gwathmey House and Studio, Amagansett, 1965. Co-architect: Charles Gwathmey.
Straus House, East Hampton, 1966. Co-architect: Charles Gwathmey.
Joseph Sedacca House, East Hampton, 1967. Co-architect: Charles Gwathmey
John Steel House ("Steel House I"), Bridgehampton, 1968. Co-architects: Charles Gwathmey and Robert Siegel.
Loring and Dorothy Mandel House, Huntington Bay, 1970

*HERREY, HERMANN 1904–68
Alma Morgenthau House, later Richard Lippold Studio and House, Locust Valley, 1950
Robert and Lola Mautner House, Massapequa, 1950–51

JACKSON, HUSON 1906–2006
with co-architect **JOHN CALLENDER** 1908–95
Colonel William P. and Betty Bogie House addition, Fort Salonga, 1946
William Shanhouse House, Syosset, 1948
Dorothy Havemeyer House, Syosset, 194

JAFFE, NORMAN 1932–93
Barry Lee Cohen House, Eaton's Neck, 1962
Sascha Burland East House, Bridgehampton, 1968
Sascha Burland West House, Bridgehampton, 1968
Schulman House, Bridgehampton, 1968

Harold Becker House, Wainscott, 1969
Barry Cohen House, Eaton's Neck, 1970
Goldman House, Bridgehampton, 1970
Steve and Sandy Perlbinder House, Sagaponack, 1970
Norman Jaffe House, Pheasant Walk, Bridgehampton,, 1971
   Residential grouping, Shelter Island:
   Meyer Osofsky House, 1971
   Bernard Jacobs House, 1971
   Isadore Seidler House, 1971
Chico Hamilton House, East Hampton, 1973
Joseph Wohl House, Old Westbury, 1974
Residential grouping, Sam's Creek, Bridgehampton:
   Marvin Schlachter House, 1973
   John Tozzi House, 1974
   Donald and Ellen Kreindler House, 1977
   Norman Jaffe House, 1978
   Allen Golub House, 1980
   Tony Leichter House, 1982
Residential grouping, Pointe Mecox, Bridgehampton:
   Tony Leichter House, 1975
   Morton House, 1976
   Whitaker House, 1977
Noyac Golf Club, Southampton, 1976
Aron House, Kings Point, 1976
Orest and Tish Bliss House, Southampton, 1977
Philip Datlof House, Sands Point, 1977
Howard P. Krieger House, Montauk, 1977
Martin Turetsky House, Old Westbury, 1977
Alan Alda House, Bridgehampton, 1981
Gates of the Grove Synagogue, East Hampton, 1987

*JOHANSEN, JOHN b. 1916
Academic Village A and Master Plan, State University of New York College at Old Westbury, 1972. Co-architects: Victor Christ-Janer and Alexander Kouzmanoff.
Urban Center for the Creative and Performing Arts, Wyandanch, 1979
Campus Center, Core East, State University of New York College at Old Westbury, 1982

*JOHNSON, PHILIP 1906–2005
Eugene and Margaret Farney House, Sagaponack, 1945–46
Henry Ford II and Anne Ford House, Southampton, 1950 (unbuilt)
Robert and Mary Leonhardt House, Lloyd Neck, 1954–56 (no longer extant)
1964–65 World's Fair, Flushing Meadows, Queens. Co-architect: Richard Foster:
   New York State Pavilion "Tent of Tomorrow" 1962–64
   Texaco Road Map, New York State Pavilion, 1963
   New York State Theaterama, 1963

KAGAN, VLADIMIR b. 1927
Sperry Gyroscope Building and temporary United Nations Headquarters, Lake Success, interior adaptation, 1946–50
Melvin and Audrey Troy House, interior, Sands Point, 1966

KESSLER, WILLIAM 1922–2002
Jacob K. Javits Lecture Center, State University of New York at Stony Brook, Stony Brook, 1967

*KOCHER, A. LAWRENCE 1885–1969
A. Lawrence and Margaret Kocher Canvas Weekend House, Fort Salonga, 1934 (no longer extant)
Colonel William P. and Betty Bogie House project, Fort Salonga, 1938
1939 World's Fair, Plywood House, Flushing Meadows, Queens, 1939 (no longer extant)

*KOUZMANOFF, ALEXANDER 1915–2004
Academic Village A and Master Plan, State University of New York College at Old Westbury, 1972. Co-architects: John Johansen and Victor Christ-Janer.
Campus Center, Core West, State University of New York College at Old Westbury, 1982

*LANDSBERG, WILLIAM W. b.1915
William and Muriel Landsberg House, Port Washington, 1951
Rudolph and Mildred Joseph House I, Freeport, 1953
O. E. McIntyre Plant, Westbury, 1954
Rudolph and Mildred Joseph House II, Freeport, 1956
Ethical Humanist Society of Garden City, Garden City, 1957
Randall and Helen McIntyre House, Deer Park, 1957 (no longer extant)
Angus and Bobbie McIntyre House, Deer Park, 1957 (no longer extant)
Rostock House, Queens, 1958 (status unknown)
Keevil House, Old Westbury, 1960 (no longer extant)
Eugene and Doris Leonard House, Sands Point, 1961
Peter J. White Jr. House, Lloyd Harbor, ca. 1962
Roslyn Animal Hospital, Roslyn, 1963

*LEAVITT, DAVID b. 1919
Bill Miller "Box Kite" House, Fire Island, 1956 (no longer extant)
Ernest and Arlene Silva House, Lloyd Neck, 1956

LE CORBUSIER 1887–1996
Constantino and Ruth Nivola House, murals on ground-floor stairwell walls, Springs, 1956

*LESCAZE, WILLIAM 1896–1964
Calderone Theatre, Hempstead, 1945–49
Spinney Hill Houses, Manhasset, 1947–52
Harbor Homes, Port Washington, 1950–52
Dune Deck Hotel additions, Westhampton Beach, 1952
Pond View Homes, Manhasset, 1956
Laurel Homes, Roslyn, 1956

LESKI, TADEUSZ b. 1916
Tadeusz and Iris Leski House, Huntington, 1962

LOEWY, RAYMOND 1893–1986
Lord & Taylor department store, Manhasset, 1941
Long Island Railroad platform shelters, Floral Park, Mineola, 1948

*MEIER, RICHARD b. 1934
Saul Lambert House, Fire Island, 1962
David and Anita Hoffman House, East Hampton, 1967
Renny and Ellin Saltzman House, East Hampton, 1969
Alvin and Joan Weinstein House, Old Westbury, 1971
Richard Maidman House, Kings Point, 1971–76
Swissair North American Headquarters, Melville, 1991–95
Alfonse D'Amato United States Courthouse and Federal Building, Central Islip, 1993–2000. Co-architect: Michael Harris Spector.

*MIES VAN DER ROHE, LUDWIG 1886–1969
Mary Callery Barn renovation, Huntington, 1950

MOORE, CHARLES 1925–93
Whitman Village, Huntington, 1975
Simone Swan House, Southold, 1975. Co-architect: Mark Simon. Addition by Mark Simon, 2000.
Heyward and Sheila Isham House, Sagaponack, 1977. Co-architect: Mark Simon.
Cold Spring Harbor Laboratory. Co-architects: Moore Grover Harper Associates:
   Airslie House renovation, 1974

Master plans, 1975–80
Jones Laboratory renovation, 1975
Water Treatment Plan and Gazebo Court, 1976
Williams House conversion to apartments, 1977
Hershey Building conversion to offices, 1979
Sammis Hall, 1981

MUSCHENHEIM, WILLIAM 1902–90
Frederick August Muschenheim House adaptation, Hampton Bays, 1925–34
Frederick August Muschenheim Bathhouses, Hampton Bays, 1930 (no longer extant)
Walter D. Fletcher House, Hampton Bays, 1932
Paul Scholze House, Melville, 1935–35
Walter D. Fletcher House, Southampton, 1937–39
A. Whitfield and Jane White Hawkes House, later Alistair and Jane White Cooke House, Nassau Point, Southold, 1941–42
William B. F. Drew House, Westhampton, 1945
Channing K. Jacques House, Hampton Bays, 1947
Irving Diamond House, Hampton Bays, 1947–48
William Schmidt House, Hampton Bays, 1947–48
Robert G. Stewart House, East Hampton, 1948
William J. Murphy House additions, Remsenburg, 1948–51
Bay Avenue Development, Hampton Bays, 1950

*NELSON, GEORGE 1908–86
Park House, Great Neck, 1939 (co-architect)
W. Taylor House, Bayside, 1941 (co-architect)
Sidney Johnson House, East Hampton, 1949 (co-architect)
Holiday House, Quogue, 1950. Co-architect: Gordon Chadwick.

NEMENY, GEORGE 1911–98
Long Beach Homes, Long Beach, 1945. Co-architect: Abraham W. Geller.
Bernard Appelbaum House, Cedarhurst, 1948. Co-architect: Abraham W. Geller.
Lee Everett and Mary Blair House, Kings Point, 1950
George and Patricia Nemeny House, Kings Point, 1953
"The Nemeny" Display House, Bar Harbor Houses, Massapequa Park, 1951
Jack Diamond House, Woodmere, 1952. Co architect: Abraham W. Geller.
Wildwood Pool Club, Kings Point, 1956
Lawrence House, Kings Point, 1957
Castello House, Kings Point, 1958
Marshall P. and Gladys Safir House, Kings Point, 1959
Donald and Ruth Sheff House, Kings Point, 1960
Fleetwood Pool Club, King's Point, 1960 (no longer extant)
Bernie Jacobsen House, East Hampton, 1964
Tennis Club of East Hampton, East Hampton, 1964
Mike Costello House, Kings Point, 1966
Charles and Jane Prussack House, Woodmere, 1967
Billy and Betsy Bell House, Sands Point, 1968
John and Carol Johnston House, Locust Valley, 1968
Seymour and Lorraine Weinstein House, Kings Point, 1968
Selig S. and Gladys Burroughs House, Mill Neck, 1972

NESKI, JULIAN 1928–2004, and
BARBARA NESKI b. 1928
Jack Russell House, Water Mill, 1956. Co-architect: Peter Blake.
Fred Tobey Barn adaption, Amagansett, 1960. Co-architect: Peter Blake (no longer extant).
Yvonne Hagen House and Studio, Sagaponack, 1960. Co-architect: Peter Blake.
Armstrong House, Montauk, 1962. Co-architect: Peter Blake.
Ronnie and Seymour Chalif House, East Hampton, 1965; addition, 1991.
Julian and Barbara Neski House, Water Mill, 1965
John and Millie Cates House, Amagansett, 1968
Edward Gorman House, Amagansett, 1968
Leonard and Ann Hamilton House, Stony Brook, 1968
Bruce Kaplan House, Bridgehampton, 1970
Robert and Hannah Sabel House I, Water Mill, 1970
William and Katharine Batten House I, Oyster Bay, 1971
Stephen and Patricia Kaplan House, East Hampton, 1971
Peter and Merle Simon House, Remsenburg, 1972
Robert and Hannah Sabel House II, Sagaponack, 1973
Norman and Barbara Goodman House, Sagaponack, 1978
Savage House, Springs, 1978
Marvin and Loes Schiller House, Fire Island, 1979
William and Katharine Batten House II, Glen Cove, 1982
Richard and Marianna Chiaraviglio House, 1982

*NEUTRA, RICHARD 1892–1970
Nicholas and Anne Brown ("Windshield") House, Fishers Island, 1938
Lorin and Alice Price House, Bayport, 1951
Proposal for Levittown, 1951. Co-architect: Thaddeus Longstreth (unbuilt).
Swirbul Library, Adelphi University, Garden City, 1957–67. Co-architect: Robert Alexander.
Adelphi University Master Plan, Garden City, 1957. Co-architect: Robert Alexander.

NEWMAN, JUDITH YORK b. 1934 and
RICHARD NEWMAN b. 1933
Newman Beach House, Fire Island, 1975

NOYES, ELIOT 1910–77
IBM Building Garden City, 1963

PARKER, ALFRED BROWNING 1916–2011
Arthur and Jane du Rivage House, Lloyd Neck, 1960 (no longer extant)

*PEI, IEOH MING b. 1917
Roosevelt Field Shopping Center, for Webb and Knapp, East Garden City, 1956
Franklin National Bank, for Webb and Knapp, East Garden City, 1957
National Airlines Sundrome, Terminal 6, Idlewild (John F. Kennedy) Airport, Queens, 1970 (no longer extant)

*POKORNY, JAN HIRD 1915–2008 for Damaz, Pokorny & Weigel
State University of New York at Stony Brook, Stony Brook, 1964–70:
  Student Union, 1964
  Master Plan, 1965–66
  Administrative Building, 1966
  Library, 1971
  Auditorium Building, 1975
  Fine Arts and Humanities Center, 1975

*RAYMOND, ANTONIN 1889–1976
Charles Briggs and Raoul Carrerà House, Montauk, 1941–42
Great River Railroad Station, Islip, 1945
Daniel and Rose Krakauer House, Great Neck, 1946. Landscape by James Rose.
Sidney and Shirley Rosen House, Great Neck, 1947. Landscape by James Rose.

REISER, DEBORA b. 1927
Milton and Marilyn Brechner House, Sands Point, 1975
Sheldon and Myrna Borus House, Sands Point, 1978
Donald and Bonnie Mahara House, Sands Point, 1979
Martin and Arlene Wolf House, Sands Point, 1983
Jerry and Lee Starr House, Old Westbury, 1985

ROBERTSON, JAQUELIN T. b. 1933
Isadore and Joyce Seltzer House, Sagaponack, 1967
Lawrence Flinn House, East Hampton, 1980¬

*RUDOLPH, PAUL 1918–97
Endo Laboratories, Garden City, 1964
Mr. and Mrs. Harry Raich House, Quogue, 1969 (unbuilt)
Maurice and Barbara Deane House, Kings Point, 1970
Central Suffolk Office Park, for Wheeler Associates, Hauppauge, 1970
Mr. and Mrs. Erwin P. Staller House, Lloyd Harbor, 1973 (unbuilt)
East Northport Jewish Center Synagogue addition and Master Plan, East Northport, 1973 (unbuilt)
Mr. and Mrs. Robert Fein House addition, Sands Point, 1977
Daniel Siegel Beach House, Westhampton Beach, 1978

SAARINEN, EERO 1910–61
TWA Terminal, John F. Idlewild (John F. Kennedy) Airport, Queens, 1956–62
1964–65 World's Fair, IBM Pavilion, Flushing Meadows, Queens, 1964 (no longer extant)

*SERT, JOSEP LLUIS 1902–83
Josep Lluís and Moncha Sert House, Locust Valley, former Guthrie Estate, 1947
Marian Willard and Dan Johnson House, Locust Valley, former Guthrie Estate, 1947
Henry and Yela Lowenfeld House, Wading River, 1950 (no longer extant)

*SMITH, HAMILTON b.1925
Hamilton and Caroline Smith House, Springs, 1972

SMITH, TONY 1912–80
Theodoros Stamos House, East Marion, 1951
Betty Parsons House, Southold, 1960

*STEDMAN, JOHN W., JR. 1908–77
John Stedman House, Laurel Hollow, 1952
Peter and Margaret Luce House, Cooper's Bluff, 1953
Bradford and "Gussie" Weekes House, Oyster Bay Cove, 1954
Robert and Mary Lindsay House, Cold Spring Harbor, 1957
John and Frances Fennebresque House, Cove Neck, 1960
Chester Luby House, Oyster Bay, 1967
William T. Tooker, Jr., Oyster Bay, 1968
Charles C. Bunker House, Northport, 1972

STERN, ROBERT A. M. b. 1939
Samuel Wiseman House, Montauk, 1967
Beebe House, Guest House and Cabana, Montauk, 1972
Norman and Carol Mercer House, East Hampton, 1974. Co-architect: John S. Hagman.
Lawson House, East Quogue, 1981 (no longer extant)

*STONE, EDWARD DURELL 1902–78
A. Conger Goodyear House, Old Westbury, 1939; bedroom suite addition, 1950
1939 World's Fair, Food Service Building South, Flushing Meadows, Queens, 1939
Animal Hospital, Hempstead, 1940
Dr. G. H. Cox House, Locust Valley, 1941
Eleanore Potter Ayer Harris House, Locust Valley, 1941
Sperry Gyroscope Building and temporary United Nations Headquarters, Lake Success, interior adaptation, 1946 (unbuilt)
Jacques and Therese Makowsky House, Great Neck, 1946
Bernard Tomson House, Kings Point, Great Neck, 1946 (no longer extant)
Joseph S. and Ronnie Wohl House, Lawrence, 1946 (no longer extant)
Walter C., Jr., and Helen James Janney House, Cold Spring Harbor, 1947
Great Neck Community Hospital, Saddle Rock, 1947 (unbuilt)
Unitarian Church, Plandome, 1953 (unbuilt)
Frederick L. and Ethel Maduro House, Great Neck, 1954
Barrett F. and Mary Scott Welch House, Laurel Hollow, Oyster Bay Cove, 1955
Gulf Station, Idlewild Field, 1958
Murray Gordon House, Hewlitt Bay Park, 1963
Gabriele Lagerwall House (Villa Rielle), Lloyd Harbor, 1963
1964–65 World's Fair, Flushing Meadows, Queens, 1964–65 (not extant):
   Christian Science Pavilion, 1963
   Billy Graham Pavilion, 1964
   Modern House for House of Good Taste Exhibit, 1964
   CBS Pavilion, 1964
   Julimar Farms, 1964
Lake Success Quadrangle Master Plan, Garden City, 1965 (unbuilt)
Levitt and Sons Executive Office Building, Lake Success, 1968
Stone Partners Office, adaptation of existing bank building, Oyster Bay, 1974

*TAC (The Architects Collaborative, firm of Walter Gropius)
Mary Griggs and Jackson Burke House, Centre Island, 1953–61
Chase Manhattan Bank, Great Neck Plaza, 1960. Team architect: Ben Thompson.
Adelphi University Swirbul Library addition, Garden City, 1976 (unbuilt)
Long Island Jewish Hospital, Children's Medical Center, Hillside, 1978
Hillside Hospital, Parking Structure, Hillside, 1979
Hillside Hospital, Hospital Food Processing Plant, Hillside, 1979

VENTURI, ROBERT b. 1925
Dudley Miller House, East Hampton, 1961–62. Co-architect: William Short.
Mr. and Mrs. Burton Brown House, Southampton, 1980 (unbuilt)
Donald and Elizabeth Petrie House, Wainscott, 1983; addition, 1997
Gary Kalpakjian House, Glen Cove, 1985. Nathaniel and Judy Lieb Beach House, Barnegat Light, NJ, 1969, transported to Kalpakjian House site, 2009.
Michael and Georgia de Havenon House, East Hampton, 1991

WIENER, PAUL LESTER 1895–1967
Beatrice Simpson House, Springs, 1959. Co-architect: Richard Bender.
Robert and Ethel Scull House, East Hampton, 1962. Co-architect: Richard Bender.
Elizabeth de Cuevas House, Amagansett, 1964. Co-architect: Richard Bender.
Earl Johnson House, Southampton, 1966. Co-architect: Richard Bender.
Ronald Saypol House, East Hampton, 1966. Co-architect: Richard Bender (unbuilt).
Marvin and Dory Small House, East Hampton, 1966. Co-architect: Richard Bender (no longer extant).

*WRIGHT, FRANK LLOYD 1869–1959
Ben and Anne Rebhuhn House, Great Neck, 1938

*YU, JANE b. 1938
Bert and Phyllis Geller House III, Lawrence, 1978

SELECTED BIBLIOGRAPHY

GENERAL

Arnell, Peter, and Ted Bickford, eds. *Robert A.M. Stern, 1965–1980: Toward a Modern Architecture After Modernism.* New York: Rizzoli, 1981.

Ballon, Hilary, and Kenneth T. Jackson, eds. *Robert Moses and the Modern City: The Transformation of New York.* New York: W. W. Norton, 2007.

Bergdoll, Barry, and Leah Dickerman. *Bauhaus 1919–1933: Workshops for Modernity.* New York: Museum of Modern Art, 2009.

Bitterman, Eleanor. *Art in Modern Architecture.* New York: Reinhold Publishing, 1952.

Blake, Peter. *No Place Like Utopia: Modern Architecture and the Company We Kept.* New York: W. W. Norton, 1996.

Davern, Jeanne M. *Architecture, 1970–1980: A Decade of Change.* New York: McGraw-Hill, 1980.

Ford, James, and Katherine Morrow Ford. *The Modern House in America.* New York: Architectural Book Publishing Co., 1940.

———. *Design of Modern Interiors.* New York: Architectural Book Publishing Co., 1945.

Ford, Katherine Morrow, and Thomas H. Creighton. *The American House Today: 85 Notable Examples Selected and Evaluated.* New York: Reinhold Publishing, 1951.

———. *Designs for Living: 175 Examples of Quality Home Interiors.* New York: Reinhold Publishing, 1955.

Frampton, Kenneth. *Modern Architecture: A Critical History.* 4th ed. London: Thames & Hudson, 2007.

Giedion, Sigfried. *Space, Time and Architecture: The Growth of a New Tradition.* 5th ed. Cambridge, MA.: Harvard University Press, 2009.

Gray, Susan, ed. *Architects on Architects.* New York: McGraw-Hill, 2001.

Heyer, Paul. *Architects on Architecture: New Directions in America.* Revised ed. New York: Van Nostrand Reinhold, 1993.

Hitchcock, Henry-Russell, and Philip Johnson. *The International Style.* New York: Museum of Modern Art, 1932. Reprint, New York: W. W. Norton, 1995.

Hunt, William Dudley, Jr., ed. *Encyclopedia of American Architecture.* New York: McGraw-Hill, 1980.

Huxtable, Ada Louise. *Kicked a Building Lately?* New York: Quadrangle/The New York Times Book Company, 1976.

Isenstadt, Sandy. *The Modern American House: Spaciousness and Middle Class Identity.* New York: Cambridge University Press, 2006.

Jones, Cranston. *Architecture: Today and Tomorrow.* New York: McGraw-Hill, 1961.

Jordy, William H. *American Buildings and Their Architects. Vol. 4, The Impact of European Modernism in the Mid-Twentieth Century.* Garden City, NY: Anchor Press, 1976.

Kassler, Elizabeth B. *Modern Gardens and the Landscape.* New York: Museum of Modern Art, 1964.

Lynes, Russell. *Good Old Modern: An Intimate Portrait of the Museum of Modern Art.* New York: Atheneum, 1973.

McAndrew, John, ed. *Guide to Modern Architecture: Northeast States.* New York: Museum of Modern Art, 1940.

McCallum, Ian. *Architecture USA.* New York: Reinhold Publishing, 1959.

McCoy, Esther. *Guide to U.S. Architecture, 1940–1980.* Santa Monica, CA.: Arts and Architecture Press, 1982.

Mock, Elizabeth, ed. *Built in USA: 1932-1944.* New York: Museum of Modern Art, 1944.

Mock, Elizabeth. *If You Want to Build a House.* New York: Museum of Modern Art, 1946.

Mock, Elizabeth, and John McAndrew. *What is Modern Architecture?* Introductory Series to the Modern Arts, 1. New York: Museum of Modern Art, 1942.

Nelson, George, and Henry Wright. *Tomorrow's House: How to Plan Your Post-War Home Now.* New York: Simon & Schuster, 1945.

Noyes, Eliot F. *Organic Design in Home Furnishings.* New York: Museum of Modern Art, 1941.

Oshima, Ken Tadashi, and Toshiko Kinoshita, eds. *Visions of the Real: II: Modern Houses in the 20th Century.* Special issue of *Architecture and Urbanism*, 2000.

Pearson, Clifford A. *Modern American Houses: Fifty Years of Design in Architectural Record.* Revised ed. New York: Harry N. Abrams, 2005.

Peter, John. *The Oral History of Modern Architecture: Interviews with the Greatest Architects of the Twentieth Century.* New York: Harry N. Abrams, 1994.

Roth, Leland M. *A Concise History of American Architecture.* New York: Harper & Row, 1979.

Scully, Vincent. *The Shingle Style: Architectural Theory and Design from Richardson to the Origins of Wright.* New Haven: Yale University Press, 1955.

Stern, Robert. A. M. *Architecture on the Edge of Postmodernism: Collected Essays, 1964-1988.* New Haven: Yale University Press, 2009.

Stern, Robert A. M., Gregory Gilmartin, and Thomas Mellins. *New York 1930: Architecture and Urbanism Between the Two World Wars.* New York: Rizzoli, 1987.

Tyrwhitt, J., J. L. Sert, and E. N. Rogers, eds. *The Heart of the City: Towards the Humanisation of Urban Life.* New York: Pellegrini and Cudahy, 1952.

LONG ISLAND

The American Institute of Architects, Long Island Chapter, and the Society for the Preservation of Long Island Antiquities. *AIA Architectural Guide to Nassau and Suffolk Counties, Long Island.* New York: Dover Publications, 1992.

The Architecture of Suffolk County. Huntington, NY: Heckscher Museum of Art, 1971.

Bertomen, Michele. *Transmission Towers on the Long Island Expressway: A Study of the Language of Form.* New York: Princeton Architectural Press, 1991.

Bookbinder, Bernie. *Long Island: People and Places, Past and Present.* New York: Harry N. Abrams, 1983.

Goldberger, Paul. *The Houses of the Hamptons.* New York: Knopf, 1986.

Gordon, Alastair. *Long Island Modern: The First Generation of Modernist Architecture on Long Island, 1925–1960.* East Hampton, NY: Guild Hall of East Hampton, 1987.

Weekend Utopia: The Modern Beach House on Eastern Long Island. East Hampton, NY: Guild Hall of East Hampton, 1999.

———. *Weekend Utopia: Modern Living in the Hamptons.* New York: Princeton Architectural Press, 2001.

———. *Beach Houses: Andrew Geller.* New York: Princeton Architectural Press, 2003.

———. *Romantic Modernist: The Life and Work of Norman Jaffe, Architect 1932–1993.* Monacelli Press and Parrish Art Museum, 2005.

Hefner, Robert, ed., essays by Clay Lancaster and Robert A. M. Stern. *East Hampton's Heritage: An Illustrated Architectural Record.* New York: W. W. Norton, 1982. Reprint, East Hampton, NY: Ladies Village Improvement Society, 1996.

Herzig, Helene. *Legendary Long Islanders: Interviews with Famous Residents from the Hamptons to New York.* Green Bay, WI: Mixed Media Memoirs, 2008.

Home Town Long Island: The History of Every Community on Long Island in Stories and Photographs. Melville, NY: Newsday, 1999.

Krieg, Joann P., ed. *Robert Moses: Single-Minded Genius.* Long Island Studies. Interlaken, NY: Heart of the Lakes Publishing, 1989.

———. *Long Island Architecture.* Long Island Studies. Interlaken, NY: Heart of the Lakes Publishing, 1991.

Krieg, Joann P., and Natalie A. Naylor, eds. *Nassau County: From Rural Hinterland to Suburban Metropolis*. Long Island Studies. Interlaken, NY: Empire State Books, 2000.

Long Island: Our Story. Melville, NY: Newsday, 1998.

MacKay, Robert B., Anthony K. Baker, and Carol A. Traynor, eds. *Long Island Country Houses and their Architects, 1860–1940*. New York: Society for the Preservation of Long Island Antiquities and W. W. Norton, 1997.

MacKay, Robert B., and Richard F. Welch. *Long Island: An Illustrated History*. Sun Valley, CA: American Historical Press, 2000.

Noted Long Island Homes. Babylon, NY: E. W. Howell, 1933.

Oser, Marilyn, and Mary Lou Kallman. *Discoveries and Uncoveries: A Sourcebook of Long Island's Collections*. Huntington, NY: Attick Press, 1983.

Porco, Joan Powers. *Holding Back the Tide: The Thirty-Five Year Struggle to Save Montauk. A History of the Concerned Citizens of Montauk*. New York: Harbor Electronic Publishing, 2005.

Smith, M. H. *History of Garden City*. Manhasset, NY: Channel Press, 1963.

Spinzia, Raymond E., and Judith A. Spinzia. *Long Island's Prominent North Shore Families: Their Estates and Their Country Homes*. Vol. 2. College Station, TX: Virtualbookworm.com, 2006.

———. *Long Island's Prominent South Shore Families: Their Estates and Their Country Homes in the Towns of Babylon and Islip*. College Station, TX: Virtualbookworm.com, 2007.

Van Liew, Barbara Ferris. *Long Island Domestic Architecture of the Colonial and Federal periods: An Introductory Study*. Setauket, NY: Society for the Preservation of Long Island Antiquities, 1974.

Viemeister, August. *An Architectural Journey through Long Island*. Port Washington, NY: Kennikat Press, 1974.

Watson, Elizabeth L. *Houses for Science: A Pictorial History of Cold Spring Harbor Laboratory*. Cold Spring Harbor, NY: Cold Spring Harbor Laboratory Press, 1991.

———. *Grounds for Knowledge: A Guide to Cold Spring Harbor Laboratory's Landscapes & Buildings*. Cold Spring Harbor, NY: Cold Spring Harbor Laboratory Press, 2008.

Wayne, Kenneth, and Erik Neil, eds. *Long Island Moderns: Art and Architecture on the North Shore and Beyond*. Huntington, NY: Heckscher Museum of Art, 2009.

Whipple, Enez. *Guild Hall of East Hampton: An Adventure in the Arts. The First 60 Years*. East Hampton, NY: Guild Hall of East Hampton, 1993.

BREUER, MARCEL

"The 1946 Progressive Architecture Awards." *Progressive Architecture* 28 (June 1947): 53–60.

"An Architect Speaks His Mind: 'Much More Interesting Than Stiff Salons Are Areas for Mingling Work and Living,' says Marcel Breuer." *House & Garden* 137, no. 2 (February 1970): 12, 16–17.

Blake, Peter. *Marcel Breuer: Architect and Designer*. New York: Museum of Modern Art, 1949.

Breuer, Marcel. *The House in the Museum Garden: Marcel Breuer, Architect*. New York: Museum of Modern Art, 1949.

Driller, Joachim. *Breuer Houses*. London: Phaidon, 2000.

"Five bedrooms Can Be Added: House for John W. Hanson, Huntington, N.Y." *Architectural Record* 114 (September 1953): 164–66.

Gatje, Robert F. *Marcel Breuer: A Memoir*. New York: Monacelli Press, 2000.

"The Geller House, Lawrence, Long Island." *Progressive Architecture* 41 (February 1947): 50–66.

Huxtable, Ada Louise. "Building's Case History; Award of Capital Contract to Breuer Calls to Mind Hunter College Edifice Exposes Some Problems." *New York Times*, August 9, 1963.

Hyman, Isabelle. *Marcel Breuer, Architect: The Career and the Buildings*. New York: Harry N. Abrams, 2001.

Jones, Cranston. *Marcel Breuer: Buildings and Projects, 1921–1961*. New York: Praeger, 1962.

Masello, David. *Architecture Without Rules: The Houses of Marcel Breuer and Herbert Beckhard*. New York: W. W. Norton, 1993.

Papachristou, Tician. *Marcel Breuer: New Buildings and Projects, 1960–1970*. New York: Praeger, 1970.

"Tomorrow's House Today: The Story of a House Whose Plan Was Shaped by the Needs of Three Small Boys." *House & Garden* 91 (January 1947): 60–67.

"The Tompkins House, Hewlett Harbor, Long Island." *Architectural Record* 102 (September 1947): 66–-73.

"Two Houses by Marcel Breuer." *The Architectural Review* 102 (October 1947): 115–18.

Wallach, Amei. "Breuer Designs Indoors, Too." *Newsday*, February 3, 1974.

"Where Was It?" *South Shore Record*, November 25, 1982.

"Why Not Double the Use of Your Site" *House & Garden* 92 (August 1947): 60–65.

Wilk, Christopher. *Marcel Breuer: Furniture and Interiors*. New York: Museum of Modern Art, 1981.

CHADWICK, GORDON, & GEORGE NELSON

Abercrombie, Stanley. *George Nelson: The Design of Modern Design*. Cambridge, MA: The MIT Press, 2000.

"Above All People Want More Space." *House & Home* (May 1954): 125–30.

Beckman, Ronald. "George Nelson: Prophet of the Modern Office." *Innovation* 9, no. 3 (Fall 1990): 4–7.

Biemiller, Carl L. "Holiday House." *Holiday* (May 1951).

"Castellations and Ramps Add Fun to a New Shingle Style: O. R. Johnson Residence." *Architectural Record* 131 (May 1962): 173–74.

"Examples of Work by George Nelson." *Architectural Record* 122 (December 1957): 127–42.

"The Grand Old Shingle: Otto Spaeth House." *Architectural Forum* 107 (October 1957): 148–53.

Gueft, Olga. "The Design Process at Herman Miller: George Nelson." *Design Quarterly* nos. 98–99 (1975): 11–21.

"Holiday House: Quogue, New York." *Architectural Record* 109 (June 1951): 162–67.

Kellogg, Cynthia. "Modern—With Pedigree." *New York Times*, August 11, 1957.

Linn, Karl. "Reclaiming the Sacred Commons." *New Village Journal*, no. 1 (1999), http://newvillage.net/Journal/Issue1/1sacredcommon.html.

Makovsky, Paul. "Vintage Modern." *Metropolis* 20, no. 10 (June 2001): 113–21, 163.

"Nelson-Kirkpatrick House Local Historic District—2104 Sheffield." Kalamazoo Historic District Study Committee Report, www.kalamazoocity.org/docs/NelsonKirkpatrickHouse.pdf.

Stern, Robert A. M. "Foreword." In Nelson, George. *Building a New Europe: Portraits of Modern Architects. Essays by George Nelson, 1935–1936*. New Haven: Yale University Press, 2007, pp. viii–ix.

Veronesi, Giulia. "Una 'Romantica' Villa di George Nelson e Gordon Chadwick a Montauk, Long Island, U.S.A." *Zodiac* 11 (1963): 158–61.

DAMAZ, POKORNY & WEIGEL, GRUZEN & PARTNERS, ET AL.

"An Analysis of Excellence: A Report on the Accomplishments . . . and the Bold Plans for the Future by the New York State University Construction Fund . . ." *Architectural Record* 149 (January 1971): 105–28.

Augarten, Stanley. "New Library: Stony Brook's Greatest Eyesore." *Statesman*, May 14, 1971.

"The Campus Center Is Almost a Reality." *Statesman*, January 11, 1967.

Damaz, Paul, interviewed by Hartzell, Karl D., September 16, 1987. Stony Brook University Special Collections.

Damaz, Pokorny, Weigel Architects. "Design Program: State University Construction Fund; Central Campus Plaza, State University at Stony Brook, L.I., N.Y." New York: Damaz, Pokorny, Weigel Architects, January 16, 1967.

———. "Design Vocabulary: State University of New York at Stony Brook." New York: Damaz, Pokorny, Weigel Architects, 1967.

———. "Design Manual Report: Library-Humanities Building, State University at Stony Brook; State Construction Fund." New York: Damaz, Pokorny, Weigel Architects, February 15, 1969.

Dudley, George A. "1962–1970... Years of Challenge and New York's Answer." Presentation, State University Construction Fund to New York State Association of Architects Annual Convention, Grossinger's Hotel, Liberty, New York, October 20, 1983.

Geizer, Bernard Paul. "The Construction of Academic Facilities for the State University of New York: A Performance Evaluation of the State University Construction Fund." PhD diss., New York University, October 1974.

Gelber, Sidney. *Politics and Public Higher Education in New York State: Stony Brook—A Case History*. New York: P. Lang, 2001.

"Health Sciences Center: State University of New York at Stony Brook, Long Island, New York, 1968–1971." *Architecture and Urbanism* 55 (July 1975): 74–85.

Jan Hird Pokorny: Czech Architect in New York. Prague: Galerie Jaroslava Fragnera, 2005.

"Made for Walking: The Student Union at Stony Brook's State Campus Is Also a Pedestrian Mall." *Architectural Forum* 135, no. 1 (July/August 1971): 58–61.

"New Buildings to Enhance Learning and Leisure." *Statesman*, May 28, 1975.

Nyitray, Kristen J., and Ann M. Becker. *Stony Brook: State University of New York*. Charleston, SC: Arcadia Publishing, 2002.

Persico, Joseph E. *The Imperial Rockefeller: A Biography of Nelson A. Rockefeller*. New York: Simon & Schuster, 1982.

Pokorny, Jan Hird, interviewed by Mary Kay Judy, "Reminiscences of Jan Hird Pokorny," Columbia University, 1998.

Rosenthal, Joel. *From the Ground Up: A History of the State University of New York at Stony Brook*. Port Jefferson, NY: 116 Press, 2004.

"A State Construction Fund: Management for Quality: How Private Architects and Engineers Are Managing $4.5 Billion Worth of Construction in a Decade of Growth for the State University of New York." *Architectural Record* 149 (January 1971): 55–56.

GOODMAN, PERCIVAL

Elman, Kimberly J., and Angela Giral. *Percival Goodman: Architect, Planner, Teacher, Painter*. New York: Miriam and Ira D. Wallach Art Gallery, Columbia University in the City of New York, 2000.

"Fifty Years: Great Neck Synagogue." Great Neck Synagogue, Spring 2001.

Goodman, Percival. "The Essence of Designing a Synagogue." *Faith & Form*, no. 1 (1967): 16–17.

Goodman, Paul, and Percival Goodman. "Modern Artists as Synagogue Builder: Satisfying the Needs of Today's Congregations." Commentary (January 1949): 51–55.

Goodman, Percival. "Notes on Community Planning." *Architectural Progress* 6, no. 2 (February 1932): 4–6, 23.

———. "20th Century Architecture." In Kuhne, James S., Percival Goodman, and Robert Law Reed. *The Florida Tropical Home at a Century of Progress 1933*. New York: Kuhne Galleries, 1933, pp. 5–6.

———. "The Challenge of Church Design." *Royal Architectural Institute of Canada Journal* 28, no. 1 (January 1951): 14.

———. "The New Synagogue: A New York Architect Has Become the Foremost Creator of Uniquely Designed Synagogues." *Brooklyn Jewish Center Review* (October 1953): 10–11.

Goodman, Percival, and Naomi Goodman, interviewed by Jonathan Lee, June 6, 1989, Easthampton, Long Island. Transcript.

"A Guide for Planning the Synagogue Building." *AIA Journal* (May 1962).

"Houses of Worship." *Building Construction* (December 1964).

Meier, Richard, ed. *Recent American Synagogue Architecture*. New York: Jewish Museum, 1963.

"Modernity's First Subdivision: Hempstead State Park Homes, Inc." *Architectural Forum* 62 (January 1935): 112–14.

"The New Building." Temple Beth Am, Merrick, 1967.

"New Union Reform Temple to Be Dedicated Oct. 14." *The Leader*, October 13, 1960.

Schreiber, Flora Rheta. "Paradox of Percival: Percival Goodman, Architect of Avant-Garde Synagogues, Is a Fundamentalist at Heart." *American Judaism* 9, no. 3 (Purim 1960): 8–9, 34.

Spaeth, Otto. "Worship and the Arts." *Architectural Record* (December 1955): 162–71.

HARRISON, WALLACE K.

The American Institute of Architects, memo to Ludwig Mies van der Rohe, January 27, 1967.

Bohdan, Carol Lorraine. "Living with Antiques: The Wallace K. Harrison House on Long Island." *Antiques* 116, no. 3 (September 1979): 578–81.

Contemporary American Industrial Art, 1940: Fifteenth Exhibition. New York: The Metropolitan Museum of Art, 1940.

Duomato, Lamia. *Wallace K. Harrison: A Bibliography*. Monticello, VA: Vance Bibliographies, 1989.

Greenfeld, Josh. "Curtain Going Up For Wallace Harrison: Wallace Harrison." *New York Times Magazine*, August 21.

Huxtable, Ada Louise. "Reexamining Wallace Harrison." *New York Times*, January 6, 1980.

"La Guardia Airport Gets New Terminal." *Progressive Architecture* 45 (June 1964): 83.

"Life Houses." *Architectural Forum* 69 (November 1938): 341–45.

"Life Houses." *Architectural Forum* 73 (July 1940): 91–92.

"Modern Museum for the Space Age." Stained Glass 60 (Spring 1965): 8–12.

"Museum of Science: City of New York." *Empire State Architect* 25 (May–June 1965): 34–35.

Newhouse, Victoria. *Wallace K. Harrison, Architect*. New York: Rizzoli, 1989.

HERREY, HERMANN

"The Fabled Past: The Artists Among Us." *The North Shore Journal* 27, no. 4 (November 28, 1996).

Herrey, Hermann. "At Last We Have a Prefabrication System Which Enables Architects to Design Any Type of Building with 3-Dimensional Modules." *Pencil Points* 24 (April 1943): 36–47.

"An Interview with Richard Lippold." *Architectural Record* (December 1978).

Richard Lippold, 1952–1962: Willard Gallery, February 6– March 3, 1962. New York: Willard Gallery, 1962.

"Victorian Stable Becomes Modern House: Lattingtown, Long Island, N.Y." *Architectural Record* 111 (April 1952): 168–73.

Willard, Marian Johnson, interviewed by Paul Cummings, June 3, 1969. Archives of American Art.

JOHANSEN, JOHN, ALEXANDER KOUZMANOFF, AND VICTOR CHRIST-JANER

Abercrombie, Stanley. "Hill Town on Long Island: A New College Campus in Old Westbury." *Architecture Plus* 1, no. 11 (December 1973): 57–63.?

"Closely-knit Cluster Campus." *Progressive Architecture* (February 1969): 36–37.

"College in Flux: New, Old Plans Rip Old Westbury." *Long Island Press*, December 2, 1973.

Farber, M. A. "Life and Death of a Far-Out College." *New York Times*, April 26, 1971.

Gray, George Trumon. "The Experimental College at Old Westbury 1966–1971: A Case Study." PhD diss., Indiana University, 1973.

Hadad, Herbert. "A New Regime Tries to Revive Old Westbury." *Boston Sunday Globe*, June 6, 1971.

Johansen, John M. *John M. Johansen: A Life in the Continuum of Modern Architecture*. Milan: L'Arca Edizioni, 1995.

"The Mummers Theater: A Fragment, Not a Building." *Architectural Forum* 128, no. 4 (May 1968): 64–69.

Powers, Thomas. "Autopsy on Old Westbury: The Politics of Free-Form Education." *Harper's* (September 1971): 52–61.

Suckle, Abby, ed. *By Their Own Design*. New York: Whitney Library of Design, 1980.

"SUNY-Old Westbury 'Healthier' After Four-Day Self-Evaluation." The Westbury Times, November 11, 1971.

Vecsey, George. "Students at Old Westbury College Concerned Over State Plan to Enroll More Long Island Commuters." *New York Times*, May 27, 1974.

Weiss, Martin E. "On the Wire." *The Westbury Times*, May 31, 1973.

JOHNSON, PHILIP

Blake, Peter. *Philip Johnson*. Basel: Birkhäuser Verlag, 1996.

"Four Centuries of Painting and Sculpture at the Galaxon New York World's Fair April 22, 1964–October 17, 1965." *Art in America* 50, no. 3 (1962): 34–67.

Fox, Stephen, and Hilary Lewis. *The Architecture of Philip Johnson*. Boston: Bulfinch Press, 2002.

Goldberger, Paul, and Philip Johnson. "Philip Johnson." *Architectural Forum* 138, no.1 (January-February 1973).

Hitchcock, Henry-Russell. *Philip Johnson: Architecture 1949–1965*. New York: Holt, Rinehart and Winston, 1966.

Jacobus, John M. *Philip Johnson*. Makers of Contemporary Architecture. New York: George Braziller, 1962.

Jenkins, Stover, and David Mohney. *The Houses of Philip Johnson*. New York: Abbeville Press, 2001.

Johnson, Philip. *Philip Johnson, Architect: The First Forty Years*. New York: Municipal Art Society of New York, 1983.

———. *Philip Johnson: The Architect in His Own Words*. Edited by Hilary Lewis and John O'Connor. New York: Rizzoli, 1994.

Petit, Emmanuel, ed. *Philip Johnson: The Constancy of Change*. New Haven: Yale University Press, 2009.

Schulze, Franz. *Philip Johnson: Life and Work*. New York: Knopf, 1994.

Whitney, David, and Jeffrey Kipnis, eds. *Philip Johnson: The Glass House*. New York: Pantheon Books, 1993.

KOCHER, A. LAWRENCE, AND THE FORT SALONGA COLONY (ALBERT FREY, ROBERT L. DAVISON, JOHN HANCOCK CALLENDER, AND WILLIAM BOGIE)

Bruce, Alfred, and Harold Sandbank. *A History of Prefabrication*. New York: John B. Pierce Foundation, 1945, pp. 11–12, 26–28, 72–74.

California Redwood Association. *Styling Your Home: Forty Exteriors in the Redwood Mode*. San Francisco, 1940, p. 16.

Callender, John Hancock. "Aluminum Foil for Insulation: An Impartial Research Report." *Architectural Forum* (January 1934): 67–71.

Callender, John Hancock. *Family Living as the Basis for Dwelling Design*. Vol. 1, *Introduction to Studies of Family Living*. New York: John B. Pierce Foundation, 1943.

———. "The Scientific Approach to Design." In Davison, R. L., J. H. Callender, and C. O. Mackey, eds. *The Engineered Dwelling: Research Study 8*. New York: The John B. Pierce Foundation, 1944.

"Corner Windows." *Pencil Points* (January 1937): 34.

Davison, Robert L. "Horizontal Prefabricated Type: The Plywood House." *The Timberman* 38 (February 1937): 11–14.

Davison, Robert L. "The Autobiography of Robert Leavitt Davison." Unpublished, ca. 1960.

Frey, Albert. *In Search of a Living Architecture*. New York: Architectural Book Publishing, 1939. Reprint, Los Angeles: Hennessey & Ingalls, 1999.

"House for S.M. Sadi, Northport, Long Island : designed by S.M. Sadi." *Architectural Record* (December 1936): 434–35.

"House of Robert L. Davison, Northport, Long Island." *Architectural Record* (October 1936): 276–78.

"House-to-House Canvas." The Texaco Star 22, no. 4. (1936): 10.

Kocher, A. Lawrence, and Albert Frey. "Windows." *Architectural Record* (February 1931), 127–37.

———. "Real Estate Subdivisions for Low-cost Housing." *Architectural Record* (April 1931), 323–27.

"The Revolutionary Mr. Davison." *Plumbing & Heating Business* (October 1939): 23–24.

Rosa, Joseph. *Albert Frey, Architect*. New York: Princeton Architectural Press, 1999.

"Six Houses a Day." *Business Week*, no. 628 (September 13, 1941): 65–66.

Vader, Harold W. "Aluminum in Architecture." *Architectural Record* (December 1931): 459–62.

LANDSBERG, WILLIAM

"Raised Basement Expands Hillside House: Residence of William Wallace Landsberg, Arch., Port Washington, Long Island, N.Y." *Architectural Record* 113 (June 1953): 162–65.

"Record Houses of 1957." *Architectural Record* 121 (Mid-May 1957): 172–73.

Leavitt, David

"Eight Houses to Help Home Buyers Raise Their Sights." *House and Home* 14 (December 1958): 120–40.

Nasatir, Judith. "Arranging Nature." *House & Garden* (August 2006): 60–63.

Pepis, Betty. "Japanese Serenity in a Manhattan Apartment: Orient Visit Sparks Ideas for Local Architect." *New York Times*, November 28, 1955.

LESCAZE, WILLIAM

"The 2500-Seat Calderone." *Better Theatres* (July 2, 1949): 24–28.

"CBS Builds New Home for KNX." *Electronics* (April 1938): 21–25.

"Cinerama." *Architectural Forum* 97 (November 1952): 128–29.

Clute, Eugene. "Mosaic for Today's Buildings." *Progressive Architecture* 31 (May 1950): 77–79.

"Colorful Movie Theater, Hempstead, L.I." *Architectural Forum* 91 (November 1949): 95–97.

"Columbia Broadcasting Station." *Architectural Forum* 63 (August 1935): 121–22.

"Columbia Broadcasting Studios." *Architectural Forum* 64 (June 1936): 479–83, 487.

English, Merle. "No Room at the Top of Spinney Hill." *Newsday*, October 20, 1984.

Gutheim, Frederick Albert. "The Philadelphia Saving Fund Society Building: A Re-Appraisal." *Architectural Record* 106 (Oct. 1949): 88–95, 180, 182.

Lanmon, Lorraine Welling. *William Lescaze, Architect*. Philadelphia: Art Alliance Press, 1987.

Lescaze, William. "A Community Theatre." In Isaacs, Edith J. R., ed. *Architecture for the New Theatre*. New York: Theatre Arts, 1935, 71–86.

———. "Art in Buildings: Fund Allocation Urged to Create Works of Lasting Value." *New York Times*, February 3, 1952, Letter to the Times.

"N H Housing Authority Sees Need for 191 Building Units in Manhasset." *The Manhasset Mail*, April 24, 1947.

New York State Division of Housing. "Survey of Housing Conditions: Town of North Hempstead," 1946.

"Steel House, Factory-Built in Seven Pieces, Sets New Standard in Industrialized Housing." *Architectural Forum* 91 (December 1949): 84–87.

"Theater: William Lescaze." Pencil Points 25 (August 1944): 49.

Tulin, Miriam. *Calderone Theatres on Long Island: An Introductory Essay and Description of the Calderone Theatre Collection at Hofstra University*. Hempstead, NY: Long Island Studies Institute, 1991.

Wright, Henry Lyman, and William H. Jordy. "PSFS." *Architectural Forum* 120 (May 1964): 124–29, 143.

"Year's Work of Twenty-One Designers." *Interiors* 109 (August 1949).

MEIER, RICHARD

Ain, Stewart. "For Central Islip, A Renaissance." New York Times, September 17, 2000.

"Architects Now on Board: Huge L.I. Federal Court Complex." *New York Times*, January 10, 1993.

"Beach House at Fire Island." *Arts & Architecture* (January 1964).

Chester, Marjorie. "Adding on to a Meier House." *The East Hampton Star*, August 14, 1997.

"Crafting New Forms for Living from Old." *House Beautiful's Building Manual* 76 (Fall/Winter 1978–79).

"Fire Island House Built in Nine Days with Precut Lumber." New York Times, April 21, 1963.

Futagawa, Yukio, ed. "Houses in U.S.A." *Global Interiors* 1 (1971): 152–69.

———. "House in Old Westbury, Long Island, New York, 1971." *Global Architecture* 22 (1973).

———. "House in Sands Point." *Global Architecture Houses* 5 (Winter 1978): 116–23.

———. "United States Courthouse and Federal Building." *GA Document* 64 (March 2001): 10–27.

Giovannini, Joseph. "Renny Saltzman: Complementing Contemporary Volumes in East Hampton." *Architectural Digest* (September 1966): 140–47.

"Hoffman House." *Architecture and Urbanism* (November 1983): 128–33.

"House in East Hampton." *Architecture and Urbanism* (November 1972): 107–14.

"A House that Sets Us Free." *House & Garden* (December 1969): 78–87.

Morgan, James D. "A House That Glows with Crystalline Transparency." *Architectural Record* (April 1972): 97–104.

Muschamp, Herbert. "In City and Suburb, Models for the New Modern Age: Federal Courthouse, Central Islip, N.Y., Richard Meier." *New York Times*, December 31, 2000.

Ouroussoff, Nicolai. "A Hall of Justice That's Actually Sexy." *Los Angeles Times*, December 11, 2000.

Plumb, Barbara. "White on White." *New York Times*, March 23, 1969.

———. *Young Designs in Living*. New York: Viking Press, 1969.

———. *Young Designs in Color*. New York: Viking Press, 1972.

"Record Houses of 1969." *Architectural Record* (mid-March 1969): 76–79.

"Richard Meier on American Architecture." *House Beautiful's Building Manual* 76 (Fall/Winter 1978–79).

Rowe, Colin. *The Mathematics of the Ideal Villa and Other Essays*. Cambridge, MA: M.I.T. Press, 1977.

"A Sculptured Machine for the Living." *House & Garden* (March 1972): 68–77, 115.

"The Space Revolution in Multilevel Houses." *House and Home* (November 1970): 67.

"Top 20 House Designs Emphasize 'Great Spaces.'" *New York Times*, June 22, 1969, sec. 8, p.1.

"Vacation Homes." *House and Home* (February 1965).

"Villa Saltzman." *Progressive Architecture* (April 1970): 100–105.

MIES VAN DER ROHE, LUDWIG

"Callery, Mary." *Current Biography* (July 1955): 19–21.

Cohen, Jean-Louis. *Mies van der Rohe*. Paris: Hazan, 2007.

Cuito, Aurora. *Mies van der Rohe*. Kempen, Germany: teNeues, 2002.

Drexler, Arthur. *Ludwig Mies van der Rohe*. New York: George Braziller, 1960.

Johnson, Philip C. *Mies van der Rohe*. Rev. ed. New York: Museum of Modern Art, 1953.

Lambert, Phyllis, ed. *Mies in America*. New York: Harry N. Abrams, 2001.

Mary Callery: March 14–April 2, 1950. York: Buchholz Gallery, Curt Valentin, 1950.

Mary Callery: March 15–April 9, 1955. New York: Curt Valentin Gallery, 1955.

Riley, Terence, and Barry Bergdoll, eds. *Mies in Berlin*. New York: Museum of Modern Art, 2001.

Schulze, Franz. *Mies van der Rohe: A Critical Biography*. Chicago: University of Chicago Press, 1985.

Society for the Preservation of Long Island Antiquities. "Building-Structure Inventory Form: 19th Century Barn Group." Division for Historic Preservation New York State Parks and Recreation, 1979.

NEUTRA, RICHARD

"Adelphi Uniersity, October 20, 1963, Library Dedicated." *Adelphi Quarterly*, vol. 7, no. 1 (Fall 1964).

"Architect Finds the Light in the Night." *Newsday*, November 23, 1962.

"Architect Richard Neutra: What Will the Neighbors Think?" *Time*, August 15, 1949.

Boesiger, W., ed. *Richard Neutra: Buildings and Projects*. 3 vols. New York: Praeger, 1966.]

Buttrick White & Burtis. "Program Feasibility Study: Existing Conditions Analysis: Swirlbul Library," July 12, 1999. Collection Buttrick White & Burtis, New York.

Drexler, Arthur, and Thomas S. Hines. *The Architecture of Richard Neutra: From International to California Modern*. New York: Museum of Modern Art, 1982.

Gallagher, D. Nora. "Adelphi's Accent on Grace." *Library Journal* 88, no. 21 (December 1, 1963): 4558–61.

Hines, Thomas S. *Richard Neutra and the Search for Modern Architecture: A Biography and History*. Berkeley: University of California Press, 1994.

"Leon Swirlbul, 62, of Grumann Dies." *New York Times*, June 29, 1960.

"Library, Adelphi University, Garden City, Long Island, New York." *Architect and Builder* (November 1964): 8–13.

McCoy, Esther. *Richard Neutra*. New York: George Braziller, 1960.

———. *Vienna to Los Angeles: Two Journeys*. Santa Monica, CA: Arts & Architecture Press, 1979.

Neely, Eugene T. "Adelphi University—Histories of Buildings and their Funding: Swirlbul Library," September

2007. University Archives and Special Collections, Adelphi University.

Neutra, Richard Joseph. *Mysteries and Realities of the Site*. Scarsdale, NY: Morgan and Morgan, 1951.

———. Survival through Design. London and New York: Oxford University Press, 1954.

———. "Centerpiece of a Library." *Library Journal* 89 (December 1, 1964): 4695–99.

Neutra, Richard J., and Robert E. Alexander. "Preliminary Studies for a Masterplan and the Institute of Communication and Performing Arts of Adelphi College," May 24, 1957, June 6, 1957. University Archives and Special Collections, Adelphi University.

"Swirbul Memorial Dedicated; In-Plant Fund Drive Launched." *Grumman Plane News*, September 29, 1961.

PEI, I. M.

"Awesome Mr. Zeckendorf." *Look*, June 11, 1957, 102–8.

DeWan, George. "Breaking the Bank Roth." *Newsday*, November 9, 1999.

Foley, Maurice. "Shopping Centers for Long Island." *New York Times*, December 25, 1955.

Gladwell, Malcolm. "The Terrazzo Jungle." *The New Yorker*, March 15, 2004, 120–27.

Gruen, Victor. *The Heart of Our Cities; The Urban Crisis: Diagnosis and Cure*. New York: Simon & Schuster, 1964.

"Roosevelt Field Shopping Center, Nassau County, Long Island, N.Y." *Progressive Architecture* 36 (September 1955): 90–97.

Wiseman, Carter. *I. M. Pei: A Profile in American Architecture*. New York: Harry N. Abrams, 1990.

Zeckendorf, William, with Edward McCreary. *Zeckendorf: The Autobiography of William Zeckendorf*. New York: Holt, Rinehart, and Winston, 1970.

RAYMOND, ANTONIN, & NOÉMI RAYMOND

"Great Neck, Long Island." In Ford, Katherine Morrow, and Thomas H. Creighton. *The American House Today: 85 Notable Examples Selected and Evaluated*. New York: Reinhold Publishing, 1951: 104–5.

Helfrich, Kurt G. F., and William Whitaker, eds. *Crafting a Modern World: The Architecture and Design of Antonin and Noémi Raymond*. New York: Princeton Architectural Press, 2006.

"House by the Sea." *House & Garden* 85 (April 1944): 58–59.

"A House for Many Ways of Living." *Contract Interiors* 105 (January 1946): 66–68.

"House in New Hope, Pa." *Architectural Forum* 81 (December 1944): 136–37.

"Interiors to Come, Seventh Annual Presentation." *Contract Interiors* 106 (January 1947): 66–117.

Lancaster Clay. *The Japanese Influence in America*. New York: W. H. Rawls, 1963.

Marlin, William. "Thinking about the Past in the Cause of the Future: A Conversation with Ladislav Rado." *Architectural Record* 163, no. 5 (May 1978): 119–24.

"Oriented for Summer." *House Beautiful* 81 (July/August 1939): 22–23, 72.

Oshima, Ken Tadashi. "Designing from the Hearth: The Architecture of Antonin Raymond." *Japan Architect* 33 (Spring 1999).

"Railroad Station, Great River, N.Y." *Progressive Architecture* 29 (November 1948): 68–69.

"Railroad Station—Great River, New York." *Shinkenchiku* 25 (January 1950): 14–15.

Raymond, Antonin. *Architectural Details*. Tokyo: Kokusai Kenchiku Kyôkai, 1938.

———. "Toward True Modernism." *Pencil Points* 23 (August 1942): 76–88.

———. *An Autobiography*. Rutland, VT: Charles E. Tuttle, 1973.

"The Work of Antonin Raymond." *Architectural Design* 31 (February 1961): 79–81.

"The Years Work: Interiors Presents Its Fifth Annual Collection." *Contract Interiors* 105 (August 1945): 57–86.

RUDOLPH, PAUL

De Alba, Roberto. *Paul Rudolph: The Late Work*. New York: Princeton Architectural Press, 2003.

Domin, Christopher, and Joseph King. *Paul Rudolph: The Florida Houses*. New York: Princeton Architectural Press, 2002.

"Fortress for Pharmaceuticals." *Progressive Architecture* 45 (Nov. 1964): 168–73.

Huxtable, Ada Louise. "Design of Garden City Plant Stirs Extreme Reactions." *New York Times*, September 20, 1964.

Israel, Franklin David. "Architecture: Paul Rudolph." *Architectural Digest* 35, no. 5 (June 1978): 90–99.

"Record houses of 1976." *Architectural Record* 159, no. 6 (May 1976): 68–72.

Rudolph, Paul. *Architecture of Paul Rudolph*. London: Thames & Hudson, 1970.

"Sculptured Factory in Suburbia." *Contract Interiors* 124 (Apr. 1965): 118–22.

"Turreted, Castle-Like Structure to Be a Laboratory on Long Island." *New York Times*, November 4, 1962.

Tyler, Jan. "A Village of Treehouses." *Newsday*, May 10, 1998.

SERT, JOSEP LLUÍS

"Architect Gives an Old Barn a New Look." *The Courier-Journal*, November 4, 1956.

Bastlund, Knud. *José Luis Sert: Architecture, City Planning, Urban Design*. New York: Praeger, 1967.

Bentel, Paul, ed. "Monumentality and the City." *Harvard Architecture Review* 4 (Spring 1984).

Blake, Peter. "Sert's Piazza." *Harper's Bazaar* (March 1952).

Borràs, Maria Lluïsa. *Sert: Mediterranean Architecture*. Boston: New York Graphic Society, 1975.

Campbell, Robert. "Harvard Exhibitions Showcase Sert as the Soul of Collaboration." *Boston Sunday Globe*, October 12, 2003, Arts and Entertainment.

Campbell, Robert. "Homage to a Catalonian: A Personal View of AIA Old Medalist Josep Lluis Sert." *Architecture: The AIA Journal* 70, no. 2 (February 1981): 50–53.

Costa, Javier, and Guido Hartray, eds. *Sert: Arquitecto en Nueva York*. Barcelona: Museu d'Art Contemporani de Barcelona, 1997.

Daniels, Mary. "Shaping and Reshaping Latin American Cities: Josep Lluís Sert and Town Planning Associates." *ReVista* (Winter 2003): 17–21.

Davern, Jeanne M. "AIA Medalist, 1981: Josep Lluís Sert, An Interview." *Architectural Record* 169, no. 6 (May 1981): 96–101.

"The Fabled Past: The Lawyers." *The North Shore Journal* 16, no. 2 (May 30, 1985).

Freixa, Jaume. *Josep Ll. Sert*. Barcelona: Editorial Gustavo Gili, 1979.

———. "House of Sert." *ArchitectureWeek* (December 14, 2005): C1.1–2.

Freixa, Jaume, and Antonio Pizza, eds. *J. Ll. Sert and Mediterranean Culture*. Barcelona: Collegi d'Arquitiectes de Catalunya, 1996.

Gray, Christopher. "Streetscapes: A Designer of Lacy Mansions for the City's Eminent." *New York Times*, February 9, 2003.

"House No. 29: How to Remodel and Expand an Old Stable." *House & Garden* (January 1952): 86–89.

Ichinowatari, Katsuhiko. "Josep Lluis Sert: His Work and Ways." *Process Architecture* 34 (December 1982).

Johnson, Marian Willard. "A Commitment to Art." *Chapin School Alumnae Bulletin* (1973): 9–13.

Mackay, David. "Sert for Miró." *Architectural Review* v. 160, n. 953 (July 1976): 34–43.

Mumford, Eric. *Defining Urban Design: CIAM Architects and the Formation of a Discipline, 1937–69.* New Haven: Yale University Press, 2009.

Mumford, Eric, and Hashim Sarkis. *Josep Lluís Sert: The Architect of Urban Design, 1953–1969.* New Haven: Yale University Press, 2008.

Ockman, Joan. "The War Years in America: New York, New Monumentality." In Costa, Xavier, and Guido Hartray, eds. *Sert: Arquitecto en Nueva York.* Barcelona: Museu d'Art Contemporani de Barcelona, 1997.

Oliveras i Samitier, Jordi. "Architecture and Revolution in Catalonia: From the GATCPAC to the SAC." *Lotus International* 23 (November 1979): 41–48.

"Remodeled Diary Building Becomes a Colorful Suburban House." *Architectural Forum* (July 1950).

Rovira, Josep M. *José Luis Sert: 1901–1983.* Milan: Electa Architecture, 2003.

Rovira, Josep, ed. *Sert 1928–1979: Half a Century of Architecture. Complete Work.* Barcelona: Fundació Joan Miró, 2005.

Sert, José Luis. *Can Our Cities Survive? An ABC of Urban Problems, Their Analysis, Their Solutions; Based on the Proposals Formulated by the C. A. M., International Congresses for Modern Architecture, Congrès Internationaux d'Architecture Moderne.* Cambridge, MA: Harvard University Press, 1942.

———. "Centres of Community Life." In Tyrwhitt, J., J. L. Sert, and E. N. Rogers, eds. *The Heart of the City: Towards the Humanisation of Urban Life.* London: Lund, Humphries, 1952.

Sert, José Luis, et al. "Nine Points of Monumentality." *Harvard Architecture Review* 4 (Spring 1984): 62–63.

Society for the Preservation of Long Island Antiquities. "Building-Structure Inventory Form: Guthrie Estate." Albany: Division for Historic Preservation New York State Parks and Recreation, 1978.

"Studio House." *Progressive Architecture* (August 1952): 95–102.

Von Moltke, Willo. "Josep Lluis Sert, 1902–1983." *Progressive Architecture*, no. 6 (1983): 27.

STONE, EDWARD DURELL

Clark, B. "America's Unconventional Master Builder." *Reader's Digest* 86 (February 1965): 192–96.

Doty, Robert, ed. "Anson Conger Goodyear 1877-1964." *Gallery Notes* 26, no. 2 (Spring 1964). Albright Knox Art Gallery.

Goldberger, Paul. "A Wistful Ode to a Museum that Once Was." *New York Times*, June 11, 1989.

Goodyear, A. Conger. A. Conger Goodyear Scrapbooks, 1929–1940. The Museum of Modern Art Archives, New York.

———. *The Museum of Modern Art: The First Ten Years.* New York: Goodyear, 1943.

———. "A Buffalonian Collects the Fine Arts." *Niagara Frontier* 4, no. 3 (Autumn 1957): 12–22.

———. Sidelights. New York: Goodyear, 1960.

Goodyear, George F. *Goodyear Family History.* Buffalo: Goodyear, 1976.

Gray, Christopher. "Streetscapes: 1939 Arrival that Made Its Neighbors Old-Fashioned." *New York Times*, July 27, 1997.

"Home Is Where You Hang Your Mortgage: Points Out Conservatism of Most Prospective Owners." *Architectural Forum* 82 (April 1945): 91–99.

"House Designed to Warm the Winter Scene." *Architectural Record* 115 (May 1954): 154–57.

Hunting, Mary Anne. "The Richard H. Mandel House in Bedford Hills, New York." *The Magazine Antiques* 160, no. 1 (July 1, 2001): 72–83.

———. "Edward Durell Stone, Perception and Criticism." PhD diss., Graduate Center, City University of New York, 2007.

Huntington, Richard. "The Albright-Knox's 'A. Conger Goodyear Collection': One Patron's Vision of the Future." *Buffalo News*, August 4, 1996.

Hylton, Morris. Modernism at Risk: 5 Case Studies. New York: World Monuments Fund, 2010.

Iovine, Julie V. "Modern Long Island Icon Is on the 'Endangered' List." *New York Times*, October 15, 2001.

McAndrew, John. "The 1939 Sculpture Garden." *MoMA: A Publication for Members of the Museum of Modern Art*, Summer 1975.

"Modern Gets a Break: Its Lack of Tradition and Conventionality Make This the Most Promising Style for These Times." *House & Garden* (September 1941): 26–27.

"New Goodyear Fund Climaxes 50 Years of Art Aid by General." *Buffalo Evening News*, January 16, 1964.

"Recent Work by Edward D. Stone." *Architectural Forum* (July 1941): 13–30.

Reeves, Jean. "Gallery to Show Gratitude for Gen. Goodyear's Gifts." *Buffalo Evening News*, 1962.

———. "A. Conger Goodyear Fund Set Up at Albright-Knox." *Buffalo Evening News*, January 16, 1964.

Ricciotti, Dominic. "The 1939 Building of the Museum of Modern Art: The Goodwin-Stone Collaboration." *American Art Journal* 17, no. 3 (Summer 1985): 50–76.

———. "Edward Durell Stone and the International Style in America: Houses of the 1930s." *American Art Journal* 20, no. 3 (1988): 48–73.

Shaman, Diana. "Unloved Masterpieces." *New York Times*, March 4, 2001.

Stone, Edward Durell. *The Evolution of an Architect.* New York: Horizon Press, 1962.

"Three Well-Detailed Small Buildings." *Architectural Record* 143, no.7 (June 1968): 135–42.

Unger, Craig. "The Scent of Money." *Vanity Fair* 53, no. 1 (January 1990): 88–93, 146–51.

Wallach, Amei. "From Austerity to Opulence." *Newsday*, August 8, 1978.

Yan, Ellen. "Designer Buys the Goodyear House." *Newsday*, June 25, 2007.

Zaleski, Caroline. "A. Conger Goodyear House: Rescuing American Modernism." New York: World Monuments Fund, 2001.

Zaleski, Caroline Rob, and James Warren. "National Register of Historic Places: A. Conger Goodyear House." United States Department of the Interior National Park Service, 2003.

THE ARCHITECTS COLLABORATIVE (TAC)

"The Architects' Collaborative." *Arts & Architecture* 53 (August 1946): 28–29.

"Bank for the Suburbs." *Architectural Forum* 117, (August 1962): 126–[129].

"Best Building Ideas of Our Time." *House & Garden* (February 1956): 67–78.

Buck, Susan L. "A Material Evaluation of the Gropius House: Planning to Preserve a Modern Masterpiece." *APT Bulletin: The Journal for Preservation Technology* 28, no. 4 (1997): 29–35.

Burns, Carol, and Norman C. Fletcher. "Masterpieces." *ArchitectureBoston* 1, no. 1 (1998): 26.

"Case a Six Moon Hill, Lincoln [sic]." *Domus*, no. 275 (November 1952): 4–6.

"A Challenging Collaboration for TAC." *Architectural Record* 142, no. 3 (September 1967): 159–64.

"Chase Manhattan Bank, Great Neck, Long Island." *Baumeister* 61 (May 1964): 488–91.

"Chase Manhattan Builds Again: A Pavilion Bank." *Progressive Architecture* 42, (November 1961): 57.

Doran, Valerie C. "Resonance and Consonance: A Profile of Mary Griggs Burke." *Orientations* 31, no. 4 (April 2000).

Gropius, Ise, et al. "The Architects Collaborative: The

Heritage of Walter Gropius." *Process: Architecture*, no. 19 (1980): 1–163.

Gropius, Walter, ed. *The Architects Collaborative, 1945–1965.* New York: Architectural Book Pub. Co., 1966.

Hadley, James. "From Moon Hill to Macallen: Searching for Purpose in the New Modernism." *ArchitectureBoston* 11, no. 3 (May/June 2008): 64–68.

Ichinowaturi, Katsuhiko, ed. TAC: The Heritage of Walter Gropius. Tokyo: Process Architecture Publishing, 1980.

"Informal Landscaping Keynotes a New House [Oyster Bay, Long Island, N.Y.]." *Architectural Record* 120 (August 1956): 154–60.

"Jackson Burke 1908–1975." Memorial booklet, June 11, 1975.

Japanese American National Museum. "Shogo Myaida." http:// www.discovernikkei.org/en/nikkeialbum/items/1647/, March 30, 2011.

"Japanese Treasures: The Collection of Mrs. Jackson Burke." *North Shore* (Fall 1994): 116–20.

"The Last Work of Walter Gropius." *Architectural Record* 146, no. 3 (September 1969): 131–50.

Nerdinger, Winfried. W*alter Gropius: 1883–1969*. Milan: Electa, 2005.

Oshima, Ken Tadashi. "The Modern House in Postwar Period, Part 3: Building Utopia at Six Moon Hill: the Fletcher House." *Architecture and Urbanism*, no. 6 (June 1997): 3–9.

"The Plan of This Cape Cod Summer House Reverses Traditional Procedure to Get Privacy and a View." *House & Home* (August 1952): 94–95.

"TAC, The Architects' Collaborative." *Architectural Record* 125 (April 1959): 147–62.

Taniguchi, Christeen. "Historical Narrative of Shofuso." Philadelphia: Friends of the Japanese House and Garden, www.shofuso.com, Oct 24, 2009.

Teague, Edward H. *The Architects Collaborative: A Bibliography of Books and Articles 1945–1983*. Monticello, IL: Vance Bibliographies, 1984.

Thompson, Jane, and Alexandra Lange. *Design Research: The Store That Brought Modern Living to American Homes.* San Francisco: Chronicle Books, 2010.

WRIGHT, FRANK LLOYD

"The Frank Lloyd Wright Foundation Survey: Rebhuhn Estate." Scottsdale, AZ: Frank Lloyd Wright Foundation, 1967.

Rebhuhn, Ronald, interviewed by George M. Goodwin, Providence RI., July 10, 1994. Scottsdale, AZ: Frank Lloyd Wright Foundation.

Reisley, Roland. *Usonia, New York: Building a Community with Frank Lloyd Wright*. New York: Princeton Architectural Press, 2001.

Scarlett, Rolph. *The Baroness, the Mogul, and the Forgotten History of the First Guggenheim Museum: As Told by One Who Was There*. New York: Midmarch Arts Press, 2003.

Silverman, Jill. "'Humble Yet Grand,' Wright House Leaves Its Mark on L.I." *New York Times*, December 5, 1982.

Storrer, William Allin. *The Frank Lloyd Wright Companion*. Chicago: University of Chicago Press, 2006.

Tafel, Edgar. *Years with Frank Lloyd Wright: Apprentice to Genius*. New York: Dover Publications, 1985.

———. "A Quick Remembrance of the Background of the Ann and Ben Rebhuhn House, Great Neck, NY." Scottsdale, AZ: Frank Lloyd Wright Foundation. 1993. .

Wright, Frank Lloyd. *The Natural House*. New York: Horizon Press, 1954.

———. *The Master Architect: Conversations with Frank Lloyd Wright*. Edited by Patrick J. Meehan. New York: Wiley, 1984.

YU, JANE

Gatje, Robert F. *Marcel Breuer: A Memoir.* New York: Monacelli Press, 2000.

PHOTO CREDITS

T= top
B= bottom
L= left
R= right

From *The American House Today* (Reinhold Publishing, 1951): 61

Esto: Ezra Stoller © Esto: coverjacket front, title page, 9T, 9B, 12T, 12B, 14T, 14B, 15, 20B, 20–21, 24B, 27, 59, 71, 72, 73, 74, 75, 77, 80T, 80B, 81, 113, 114, 115, 116, 118T, 119, 124, 125, 127, 131, 132, 133, 134T, 134B, 135T, 135B, 136–37, 141, 146, 147, 148–49, 149, 150, 151, 169, 170, 171, 195, 197, 198TL, 198TR, 198B, 199, 200, 201TL, 201BL, 201TR, 201BR, 202, 203, 207T, 208, 209, 210–11, 212, 213, 225, 228–29, 230–31, 235, 236, 242–43, 245, 247, 248, 249, 251, 301, 303, 304T, 304B, 305, 306, 307T, 307B, 308–9, 310T, 310B, 311T, 311B, 312; © Scott Frances/Esto: 313

Ann Abeles Collection: 205; Drawing by George Nelson and Gordon Chadwick: 206

Adelphi University Archives and Special Collections: George Meyer, photographer: 175; Hugh Rogers, photographer: 179

Gil Amiaga, photographer: 174, 215T, 215BL, 215BR

Earl Anderson Collection: 284B

From *Architectural Forum*, November 19, 1947: 101

Courtesy Adam Bartos: 217, 219, 221, 222

Courtesy Beth Bogie: 49T, 50, 51

From *Marcel Breuer: Buildings and Projects 1921–1961* (Praeger, 1962): 76

Courtesy Center for Creative Photography, University of Arizona ©1991 Hans Namuth Estate: 223

Avery Architectural and Fine Arts Library, Columbia University: 153, 155T, 155B, 156, 159, 160T, 160B, 161T, 161B, 162, 163, 260T, 269; Katrina Thomas, photographer: 35; John Veltri, photographer: 271, 272T, 272B, 273T, 273B, 274T, 274B, 275

Bryant Conant, photographer: 22T

House & Garden / Condé Nast Archive. Copyright © Condé Nast: 207B

Lionel Freedman, photographer: 244

R. Buckminster Fuller, Dymaxion Bathroom, Patent No. 2,220,482: 167

Gordon Parks/Time & Life Pictures/Getty Images: 218

© Paul Getty Trust. Used with permission. Julius Shulman Photography Archive, Research Library at the Getty Research Institute (2004.R.10): 177

Hanson Family Collection: 78T

Frances Loeb Library, Harvard Graduate School of Design: 103T, 103B, 123

Gift of Francis and Gloria Massimo, Japanese American National Museum (97.77.1): 122

Miani Johnson Collection: 100; Rolf Tietgens, photographer: 99

A. Lawrence Kocher Collection, John D. Rockefeller, Jr. Library, Colonial Williamsburg Foundation: 42, 43

Krakauer Family Collection: 62T, 62B, 63T, 63B

Courtesy David Leavitt, architect: 65, 68T, 68B, 69T, 69B

Douglas Libby, photographer: 16T

Library of Congress: Gottscho-Schleisner Collection: 104T, 104B, 105, 128B, 129, 143; New York World Telegram & Sun Newspaper Photograph Collection: 237, 239, 240, 241; The Paul Rudolph Archive: 282, 284T, 284M; Robert Perron, photographer: 283

From *Long Island: The Sunrise Homeland*, sponsored by the Long Island Association for the 1939 New York State World's Fair: 10–11.

B. Davis Schwartz Memorial Library, Long Island University: 120–21

Donald Luckenbill, Architect: 24T, 289, 290, 291

The MIT Museum: 16B, 117, 118B

Joe Molitor, photographer, courtesy William Landsberg, architect: 87, 88, 92, 93T, 93B

Wurts Brothers Photography Collection, National Building Museum: 28, 297T, 297B

Permissions courtesy Dion Neutra, architect:

Robert Evans Alexander Papers Cornell University Manuscript Collections: 18, 172, 173; © Photography by Erik Gould, courtesy of the Museum of Art, Rhode Island School of Design, Providence: 17T, 17B; Richard and Dion Neutra Papers, Department of Special Collections, Charles E. Young Research Library, University of California, Los Angeles: 18–19, 165, 168

New York State Division of Housing: 187, 190T, 190BL, 190BR

Fay S. Lincoln Photograph Collection, Historical Collections and Labor Archives, Special Collections Library, The Pennsylvania State University, University Park, PA: 40, 41, 45, 46, 47, 48

Courtesy Jan Hird Pokorny Architects and Planners: 255; David Hirsch, photographer: 256, 257BL, 257BR; Norman McGrath, photographer: 258.

Ronald Rebhuhn Collection: 55, 56, 57

Courtesy Ken Resen, photographer unknown: 250

Cervin Robinson, photographer: 22B, 23, 285, 287

Courtesy Paul Rudolph Foundation: 276–77, 279, 280; Robert Perron, photographer: 278, 281

Ben Schnall, photographer: Courtesy William Landsberg, architect: 89, 90–91; Courtesy Antony Herrey: 107, 109, 110, 111T, 111B; Marcel Breuer Papers, Archives of American Art, Smithsonian Institution, Hanson House, 1950: 78B

Ernest M. Silva, photographer: 66, 67T, 67B

Courtesy Hamilton Smith: 97

Collection of the Society for the Preservation of Long Island Antiquities: 130T, 294; Bob Zucker, photographer: 13T, 13B

Courtesy State University of New York College at Old Westbury: 270

John W. Stedman, Jr. Collection: 293, 295, 296

Special Collections, Stony Brook University Libraries: 253, 257T, 259, 260B, 261, 263, 264T, 264B, 265, 266, 267T, 267B.

Special Collections Research Center, Syracuse University Library:

Marcel Breuer Papers: 79; Pierre Bourdelle Papers: 130B; William Lescaze Papers: 180–81, 183, 184, 185T, 185B, 186, 188, 189, 192, 193

Katrina Thomas, photographer: 29, 30, 31, 32, 33T, 33BL, 33BR, 34

Special Collections, University of Arkansas Libraries, Fayetteville: Janney Residence, Edward Durell Stone Papers, MC 340, Box 104, Folder 11: 138, 139; Wohl Residence, Edward Durell Stone Papers, MC 340, Box 121, Folder 15: 140, 142

Thomas D. Church Collection (1997–91), Environmental Design Archives, University of California, Berkeley: 299T, 299B

Courtesy Edwina von Gal: 95

Courtesy Tom Walton: 214

Paul Warchol Photography: 83, 84, 85

Courtesy Farley Welch: 144

© Frank Lloyd Wright Foundation, Scottsdale, AZ: 53, 54

Caroline Rob Zaleski photographer: 20T, 39, 49B, 128T, 204, 288, 298

INDEX

Page numbers in *italic* refer to captions.

A

Aalto, Alvar, 100, 133, 167, *171*
Abeles, Anne, 203, 204
Abeles, Julius, 203, 204
Abeles House (Roslyn), *20*, 195, 203–6
Abramovitz, Max, 26, 82
Addams, Charles, 191–93
Adelphi University, *18*, 89, 164–65, 171–78, *179*
Adinolfi, Anthony, 254
Aferiat, Paul, 304
Ain, Gregory, 196
Albers, Anni, 100
Albers, Josef, 100, 243, 248
Alcoa Building (Pittsburgh, Pennsylvania), 218
Alexander, Robert, 165, 174, 178
Allied Architects, 26
Allied Arts and Building Products Exhibition (New York, 1931), 27–29, 38
Aluminaire House, 27–29, 38, 154, 166
Anderson, Earl, 286
Anderson, George, 176
Angeli, Carlo Frua de, 217
Archigram, 272
Architectural Forum, 101–2, 194, 196, 277–78
Architectural Record, 36, 38, 40, 47, 108, 122, 254
Architecural League, 38
Arp, Jean, 31, 34
Arts and Crafts movement, 226, 285–86
Astor Foundation, 265
Atterbury, Grosvenor, 44

B

Bacon, Edmund, 262
Bancroft, Anne, 302
Barnet, Howard, 278, 280
Barnet, Saretta, 280
Barr, Alfred, 218, 295
Bartos, Armand, *219*, 223
Bartos, Celeste, *219*, 223
Batchker House (Long Beach), *153*, 154
Bauhaus, 36–38, 70–71, 219
Becket, Welton, 92
Beckhard, Herbert, 79, 85
Belluschi, Pietro, 227
Bemelmans, Ludwig, 193
Benjamin Thompson & Associates, 124
Bennett, Ward, 282
Bindrim, Theodore, 177, 223
Blake, Peter, 105, 219, 277–78
Bliss, Cornelius, 126, 128, 129
Bliss, Zaidee, 126
Bloomingdale's stores, 146
Bogie, Beth, 39, *49*, 50
Bogie, Betty, 48
Bogie, William P., 38, 48, 49–51
Bogie House, *39*, 48–51
Bourdelle, Pierre, 129, *130*
Box Kite House, 67–68
Braude House (Amagansett), 163
Brazilian modernist design, 102
Breen, Harold, 250
Breuer, Marcel, 9, 37, 70–81, 82, 86, 87–88, 90, 94, 178, 196, 227, 233, 242, 271, 276, 277, 302, 303
Bridge House, 232
Briggs, Charles, *12*, 37, 59
Briggs Carrerá House, *12*, 59–60
Bristol-Myers Squibb, 283
Brooks, Mel, 302
Brower, Ann, 233
Brower, Peter, 233
Brower, Prentice, 228
Brown, Anne, 166, 167, 168
Brown, Carter, 167
Brown, Denise Scott, 278
Brown, John Nicholas, 166, 167–68
Bunshaft, Gordon, 86, 90
Burke, Jackson, *16*, 116
Burroughs Wellcome Company Corporate Headquarters (Research Triangle, North Carolina), *284*, 286
Burrows, John Shober, Jr., 178

C

Calder, Alexander, 34, 73, 154, 218
Calderone, Frank, 180, 182
Calderone, Mary, 182
Calderone, Salvatore, 182
Calderone Theatre (Hempstead), 180, *181*, 182–87
Callender, John Hancock, 44, 45–46, 47, 48, 50–51, 297
Callery, Mary, 177, 216–19, 230, 233
Callery barn renovation (Huntington), 216, 219–23
Canvas Weekend House, 38, 39–43, 44
Carrerá, Raoul, *12*, 37, 59
Cassini, Oleg, 193
Castiglioni, Achille, *81*
Castiglioni, Pier, *81*
CBS studios, 180, 182
Chadwick, Gordon, 20, 194, 195, 196. *See also* George Nelson and Gordon Chadwick Architects
Chamberlain House (Wayland, Massachusetts), 227
Chase Manhattan Bank (Great Neck), 124
Chatham Towers (New York City), 263
Chermayeff, Serge, 182
Chester, Hyland, 191, 193
Christ-Janer, Victor, 268, 270–71, 273, 274
Church, Thomas, 143, 299
Clark, Ambrose, 270
Coates, Wells, 182
Cobb, Henry, 244, 254
Colen, H. Arthur, 156, 157
Communitas (Goodman and Goodman), 152
Community Service Homes, 154
Conant, Bryant, *277*, 283
Concerned Citizens of Montauk, 215
Condon, William, 176
Congregation B'nai Israel (Millburn, New Jersey), 158
Congrès International d'Architecture Modern, 99, 100
Coolidge Shepley Bulfinch and Abbot, 293
Cooper, Dan, 133
Copeland, Aaron, 106
Costa, Lucio, 102
Cotton Textile Institute, 38, 39
Coudert, Frederic, Jr., 217
Craftsman Farms, 226
Crapster, Thaddeus, 29, 30

D

D'Amato United States Courthouse and Federal Building (Central Islip), 313
Damaz, Paul, 255–56
Damaz, Pokorny & Weigel, 254, 255–56, 258, 261–62
Davis, Brody and Wisniewski, 302
Davison, Constance, 45
Davison, Patsy, *50*
Davison, Robert L., 38, 43–44, 46–47, 203
Davison House, 43–47
Deane, Barbara, 283
Deane, Maurice, 278, 280, 283
Deane House (Kings Point), *23*, 283–88
DePace, Anthony J., 146
DePaoli Mosaic Company, 186
DePree, D. J., 196
Design Laboratory, 154
Design Research, 113, 119, 124
Diamond, Harold, 34, 223
Diamond, Hester, 34, 223
Dietrich, Paul, 123, 124
Dragon Rock (Garrison, New York), 59, 67
Dudley, George, 253–54, 255, 270
Dudok, Willem, 137
Dumper, Henry Alfred, Jr., 188
Dune Deck Hotel (Westhampton Beach), 191–93
DuPont de Nemours, 283
Dymaxion House, 167

E

Eames, Charles, 203, 232
Eames, Ray, 203
Eddy, Paul Dawson, 171, 176
Eisenman, Peter, 301
El Panama Hotel (Panama City, Panama), 143
Emery Roth & Sons, 266

Empire State Plaza (Albany, New York), 26
Endo Laboratories, *23*, 250, *277*, 278–83
Engelman, Anita Davison, 45
Engineered Dwelling, The (Davison), 44, 46
Engle, Claude R., 191

F

Fairchild, Sherman, 196
Faison, Lane, 214
Fallingwater, 52, 55, 205
Farney, Eugene, 226
Farney, Margaret, 226
Farney House (Sagaponack), *20*, 226–27
Farnsworth, Edith, 220
Farnsworth House, 220
Feininger, Lyonel, 100
Fennebresque, Frances, 298
Fennebresque, John, 298
Fennebresque House (Cove Neck), 298–99
Fitzgerald, F. Scott, 60
Foley, Mary Mix, 42
Ford, James, 44
Foster, Richard, 82, 233, 234
Franklin National Bank building (East Garden City), 244–45, 250–51
Frey, Albert, 29, 38, 39–43, 154, 187
Friedberg, M. Paul, 95, *257*, 265–66
Friedman Lodge (Pecos, New Mexico), 214
Fuller, Buckminster, 146, 154, 167

G

Galantay, Ervin, 255–56, 258–61, 262
Garden City movement, 152, 156–57, 191
Geller, Andrew, 208
Geller, Bert, 70, 79, 82
Geller, Joe, 73
Geller, Michael, 75, 77
Geller, Phyllis, 73, 79, 82
Geller House I (Lawrence), *9*, 70–77
Geller House II (Lawrence), 79–81
Geller House III (Lawrence), 82–85
geodesic domes, 270
George Nelson and Gordon Chadwick Architects, 194–215
Getty Center (Los Angeles), 301
Gettysburg Cyclorama Center, 176
Giedion, Sigfried, 100, 104–5, 261
Gilbert, C. P. H., 98
Gilbert, Cass, 58
Glasser, David, 256, 262
Goldberg, Bertrand, 266, *267*
Goldstein, Walter, 193
Goodhue, Bertram, 228
Goodman, Joel, 163
Goodman, Naomi, 163
Goodman, Paul, 152
Goodman, Percival, 152–63, 302
Goodrich, E. P., 44
Goodwin, Philip, 128
Goodyear, A. Conger, 126–27, 128
Goodyear House (Old Westbury), 126, *127*, 128–37
Gordon, Murray, 146
Gordon House (Hewlett Bay Park), 146, *149*
Gores, Landis, 225, 227
Gould, Samuel B., 268
Graves, Michael, 301
Great Gatsby, The, 60
Great Neck Synagogue, 162
Greene & Greene, 139
Greuel, Louise, 108
Griggs, Mary, 112, 113–14, 116–17
Griggs Burke House (Centre Island), 114–24
Gropius, Walter, 36–37, 44, 47–48, 70, 71, 100, 107, 112, 116, 122, 143, 144, 154, 157, 225, 242, 246, 247, 271, 276, 277
Gross, Chaim, 290
Gruen, Victor, 241
Gruppe Junger Architekten, 107
Gruzen, B. Sumner, 262
Gruzen, Jordan, 262, 265
Gruzen & Partners, 254, 262–65
Guggenheim Museum, 56, 234
Guide to Modern Architecture: Northeast States, 41, 47
Guthrie, William, 98
Gwathmey, Charles, 300

334

H

Hamby, William, 196
Hannity, Sean, 171
Hanson, Bea, 79
Hanson, John, 79
Hanson House (Lloyd Harbor), 78, 79, 86
Harbor Hill Houses (Port Washington), 188–91
Harris, Eleanore Potter Ayer, 138
Harris House (Locust Valley), 138–39
Harrison, Ellen, 26, 30, 31, 32, 33, 34, 217, 218–19, 230
Harrison, Sarah, 29, 30
Harrison, Wallace K., 26–34, 35, 82, 217, 218, 254, 255, 271
Harrison & Abramovitz, 293
Harrison House, 26–34, 38, 216
Hauer, Erwin, 280, 282
Heald, Henry T., 253
Hejduk, John, 301
Hempstead State Park Homes, 152, 154–57
Herrey, Hermann, 102, 106–10
Hitchcock, Henry-Russell, 29, 44, 181, 187
Hoffman, Anita, 303, 304
Hoffman, David, 303
Hoffman House (East Hampton), 301, 303–4
Holabird & Roche, 165
Holiday House (Quogue), 195, 196–203
Holiday magazine, 196
Horizon Press, 56
Hotz, Lila, 294
Howe, George, 181, 187
Hudnut, Joseph, 37
Huntington, Long Island, 26
Huxtable, Ada Louise, 233, 234, 237

I

IBM, 247
Idlewild Airport, 26
Imperial Hotel (Tokyo), 37, 58
International Basic Economy Corporation, 230, 254
International Cottage Style, 295
International Style, 37, 38, 41, 138, 156, 165, 166, 181, 187, 300–301

J

Jackson, Huson, 50, 51, 100
Jacobs House (Madison, Wisconsin), 54
Janney, Helen James, 139
Janney House (Cold Spring), 138, 139–40
Janniot, Alfred, 32
Japanese style, 58, 61–62, 64, 66–67, 116–17, 122–23, 143, 144–45, 169, 206
Jewish Museum, 157–58, 302
Joel, Billy, 299
Johansen, John, 268, 270–75
Johnson, Dan, 98, 99
Johnson, Danna, 99
Johnson, Miani, 99
Johnson, Philip, 20, 29, 44, 82, 181, 187, 219, 222, 223, 224–37, 250, 286
Johnson, Richard, 213–14, 215
Johnson, Theodate, 226
Johnson House (Montauk), 195, 213–15
Johnson Wax Company, 52, 55
Jones, Helen Swift, 172
Jordy, William, 181
Joseph, Mildred, 87–88
Joseph, Rudolph, 87–88
Joseph Houses (Freeport), 87–88

K

Kabaski, Jasuo, 119
Kahn, Louis, 263, 273
Kahn & Jacobs, 92
Kallmann McKinnell & Knowles, 261, 273
Karlin House, 163
Katsura Imperial Villa, 144
Kelly & Gruzen, 174, 262
Kennedy Airport (New York), 26
Kennedy Center for the Performing Arts (Washington, D.C.), 146
Kepes, György, 94
Kepes, Juliet, 94
Kerr House (Oregon), 227
Kessler, William, 266
Kiesler, Frederick, 223

Klee, Paul, 100
Klein, David, 278
Kocher, A. Lawrence, 29, 36–47, 48–51, 154
Kocher, A. Lawrence, Jr., 50
Kocher, Margaret, 38–39
Kouzmanoff, Alexander, 268, 270–75
Krakauer, Dan, 61
Krakauer, Rose, 61
Krakauer House (Great Neck), 13, 37, 61–62
Krasner, Lee, 163

L

Lagerwall, Gabriele, 149
Lagerwall House (Lloyd Harbor), 14, 146–50
LaGuardia Airport, 26
Lambert, Saul, 302
Lambert House (Fire Island), 302
Lambrecht, Barbara, 166
Landsberg, Muriel, 87
Landsberg, William, 86–92
Landsberg House (Port Washington), 86–87
Langer von Langendorff, Walter, 149
Larsen, Jack Lenor, 295
Lauren, Ralph, 60
Lauren, Ricky, 60
Leavitt, David L., 59, 64–68
Leavitt, Henshell and Kawai, 64
Le Corbusier, 38, 41, 99, 100, 137, 156, 157, 227, 235, 261, 277, 280, 281, 300–301, 305, 306
Léger, Fernand, 34, 35, 100, 217, 218, 219
Leonhardt, Clifton, 230, 232, 233
Leonhardt, Mary, 228, 230
Leonhardt, Robert, 228
Leonhardt House (Lloyd Neck), 20, 227–33
Lescaze, William, 180–93
Leski, Tadeusz, 31
Letz, Paul, 295
Levitt, William J., 145, 164
Levitt and Sons Executive Office Building, 14, 145–46
Levittown, 60–61, 145, 164, 172, 173
Levy, Matthys, 95
LeWitt, Sol, 242–43
Lincoln Center (New York City), 26, 82, 218
Lindbergh, Charles, 238
Lindsay, John V., 295–96
Lindsay, Mary, 296
Lindsay, Robert, 295–96
Lindsay House (Cold Spring Harbor), 295–97
Linen, James A., 173
Linn, Karl, 209
Lippold, Richard, 108
Lipschitz, Jacques, 244–45
Lloyd-Smith, Wilton, 228
Locust Valley Music Festival, 107, 108
Loewy, Janet, 158
Loewy, Raymond, 208
Long Island, New York, 10–11, 150, 154, 172, 239–40
Longstreth, Thaddeus, 164
Loren, Sophia, 228
Lovell, Philip, 166
Lovell House (Hollywood Hills), 166
Low House (Bristol, Rhode Island), 207, 208–9
Lubin, Ira, 158
Luce, Henry, 196, 294, 295
Luce, Margaret, 293–94
Luce, Peter, 293–94
Luce House (Cove Neck), 293–95
Luckenbill, Donald, 285, 291
Lustig Cohen, Elaine, 302

M

Maduro House (Great Neck), 143–44
Maidman, Dagny, 312
Maidman, Richard, 311
Maidman House (Kings Point), 24, 311–12
Maillol, Aristide, 130, 137
Makowsky, Jacques, 139
Makowsky, Theres, 139
Makowsky House (Great Neck), 139
Malino, Emily, 178
Mandel, Richard, 128
Marx, Lora, 219, 220
Marx, Roberto Burle, 280
Matisse, Henri, 219

Mautner, Robert, 108
Mautner House (Massapequa), 108–10, 111
Maybeck, Bernard, 139
McCrary, Tex, 173
McGrath, Raymond, 182
McIntyre, Angus, 88–89, 90
McIntyre, Helen, 90
McIntyre, Randall, 88–89, 90
McIntyre Houses (Deer Park), 90–92, 93
McKim, Mead & White, 172, 208–9
McNamara, John J., 246
Meier, Richard, 24, 300–313
Melville, Ward, 254
Mendelsohn, Erich, 182
Merrick Reform Congregation (West Hempstead), 158
Merriweather Post, Marjorie, 123
Metropolitan Museum of Art, 218
Metropolitan Realty Associates, 283
Meudon, 16, 98, 100. see also Johnson House
Microporite, 44
Mies van der Rohe, 37, 89, 108, 127, 137, 216, 219–23, 226, 232, 246, 250–51, 302
Miller, Bill, 64, 68
Miller, Herman, 194, 196
Miller House (Fire Island), 67–68
Millers, Dudley, 296
Mizner, Addison, 122
Modern Architecture: An International Exhibition, 29, 225
Moltke, Willo von, 262
Moore, A. Preston, 246
Morgenthau, Alma, 102, 106–7
Morgenthau, Henry, Sr., 106
Morgenthau House (Locust Valley), 106–7, 108
Moses, Robert, 32, 35, 154, 215, 234, 237, 239, 245–46, 283
Mumford, Lewis, 239
Mummers Theater (Oklahoma City, Oklahoma), 272
Murase, Miyeko, 119
Museum of Modern Art, 39, 41, 64, 78–79, 86, 127, 128, 156, 166, 181, 187, 206, 218, 219, 225, 226, 230, 234, 250, 254
Myaida, Shogo, 113, 119–23

N

Nakashimia, George, 13, 145
Nassau Community Temple (West Hempstead), 158
Nelson, George, 20, 193, 194, 195–96. see also George Nelson and Gordon Chadwick Architects
Neski, Barbara, 300
Neski, Julian, 300
Neutra, Dion, 176, 178
Neutra, Richard, 17, 18, 89, 164–78, 306
Nevelson, Louise, 281
New Day association, 154
New Hope Workshop (Pennsylvania), 12, 13, 37, 59
Newman, Barnett, 302
New York City Landmarks Preservation Commission, 255
New York University, 82, 94
Nicholas, John, 17
Niemeyer, Oscar, 102
Nivola, Constantino, 80
Noguchi, Isamu, 31, 62, 133, 137
Norman, Dorothy, 182
Novick, Leo, 191
Noyes, Eliot, 247

O

O.E. McIntyre Plant (Westbury), 88–90
O'Hara, John, 193
Ohlhausen, Rolf, 256, 262
Okamoto, Miyoshi, 288
Omni storage system, 213
O'Neill, Abby Rockefeller Milton, 29, 30, 299
Oud, J. J. P., 127
Ozenfant, Amédée, 218

P

Page, Don, 242, 247–48, 251
Paley Park (New York City), 250
Pei, I. M., 167, 238–51, 262

Pei Cobb Freed & Partners, 244
Pencil Points, 196
Pfisterer, Henry, 282
Philadelphia City Planning Commission, 262
Philadelphia Savings Fund Society, 180, 181
Picasso, Pablo, 217–18
Pierce Foundation, 44, 46, 203
Plumb, Barbara, 302, 303, 304
Poelzig, Hans, 107
Pokorny, Jan, 254–55. *see also* Damaz, Pokorny & Weigel
Polimeni Enterprises, 251
Pollock, Jackson, 75–77
Pope-Leighey House (Falls Church, Virginia), 196, 197
Port Morris Tile and Marble Shop, 236
Price, Alice, 169
Price, Lorin, 164, 168–69
Price House (Bayport), 168–71

R
Radio City Music Hall, 128
Rado, Ladislav, 60
Raeburn, Ben, 56
Raymond, Antonin, 37, 58–62, 64
Raymond, Noémi Pernessin, *12*, 37, 58, 60, 62, 64
Raymond, Olga, 214
Rebay, Hilla, 56
Rebhuhn, Anne, 52–54, *55*
Rebhuhn, Ben, 52–54, 56
Rebhuhn, Ronald, 54
Rebhuhn House (Great Neck), 52–56
Reich, Lilly, *222*
Remie, Maurice, 295
Research Institute of Economic Housing, 44
Resen, Ken, 243
Resor, Helen, 226
Resor House (Jackson Hole, Wyoming), 226, 302
Richard Foster Architects, 224
Richardson, Donald, 250
Richardson, Henry Hobson, 208, 293
Riis House (New York City), 265
Rockefeller, Abigail, 26–27
Rockefeller, John D., 230
Rockefeller, Nelson, 30, 32, 34, 219, 230, 234, 241, 252–54, 268, 270–71
Rockefeller Center (New York City), 26, 29, 128, 138, 252
Rohde, Gilbert, 203
Roosevelt Field Shopping Center (East Garden City), 238–50, 251
Rose, Daniel, 144
Rose, James, 61
Rosen, Sidney, 60–61
Rosen House (Great Neck), 37, 61–62
Ross, Arthur, 251
Roth, Richard, Jr., 266
Rudolph, Paul, *23*, *24*, 235, 250, 276–91

S
Saarinen, Eero, 232
Sadi, Subhi M., 38, 47–48
Sadi House (Fort Salonga), 47–48
Saint John's Abbey (Collegeville, Minnesota), 94
Saltzman, Ellin, 304, 306
Saltzman, Renny, 304, 305, 306
Saltzman House (East Hampton), 304–6
Sandburg, Carl, *186*, 187
Savadove, Pat Davison, 45
Schmidt, Elena, 33
Schulze, Franz, 219
Scully, Vincent, 208–9
Scutt, Der, 291
Seagram Building (New York City), 89, 209, 250
Seike, Kiyoshi, 122
Serchuck, Jerome, 278
Sert, Jackson & Associates, 100
Sert, Josep Lluís, 16, 90, 98–105
Sert, Josep Maria, 100
Sert, Misia, 100
Sert, Moncha, 98, 105
Sert House (Locust Valley), 98, 102–5
Severud, Fred, 183

Shahn, Ben, 62
Shaping Modernity: Design 1880–1980, 39
Shapiro, Morris, 191
Shingle Style, *207*, 208–9
Siegel, Daniel, 288
Siegel, Jeff, 283
Siegel Beach House (Westhampton Beach), *24*, 288–91
Significance for A&P Parking Lots, or Learning from Vegas (Brown and Venturi), 278
Silva, Arlene, 64–67
Silva, Ernest, 64–67
Silva House (Lloyd Neck), 64–67
Sitte, Camillo, 273
Skidmore, Owings and Merrill, 86, 246, 302
Slums and Housing (Ford), 44
Smith, Hamilton, 94–96
Smith, Mrs. Irwin, 241
Smith House (Springs), 94–96
Society for the Preservation of Long Island Antiquities, 126
Socony-Mobil building, 26
Southern State Parkway, 154
Spaeth, Eloise, 206–8, 214
Spaeth, Otto, 206
Spaeth, Otto, Jr., 208
Spaeth House (East Hampton), 195, 206–13, 304
Spector, Michael Harris, 310
Spinney Hill Houses (Manhasset), 187–91
Spivak, Max, 184, 185
Stamberg, Peter, 304
Starrett-Lehigh House, 50–51
State University of New York
  Old Westbury campus, 254, 268–75
  origins and development, 252–54, 266, 268–69
  Stony Brook campus, *253*, 254–66, *267*
Statue of Liberty, 250
Stedman, John W., Jr., 292–99
Stedman House (Laurel Hollow), 292
Steichen, Edward, 182, *186*, 187
Steichen, Lilian, 187
Stein, Ed, 83
Stein, Joseph, 70
Steinberg, Saul, 105
Stella, Frank, 302
Stickley, Gustav, 226
Stillman, Leslie, 94
Stillman, Rufus, 94
Stoller, Ezra, 233, 301
Stone, Edward, Jr., 146
Stone, Edward Durell, *14*, 90, 92, 126–50, 218, 254, 280, 294
Stone, Maria, 145
Stronach-Buschel, B. Tina, 163
Stroock, Alan, 157–58
Structural Study Associates, 154
Survival Through Design (Neutra), 166
Sweeney, James Johnson, 220
Swirbul, Jake, 176
Swissair North American Headquarters (Melville), 313

T
TAC. *see* The Architects' Collaborative
Tafel, Edgar, 52–53, 55–56
Taylor, Barbara, *50*
Taylor, Margaret, 38
Temple Beth Sholom (Roslyn Heights), 158, *160*, *161*, 162
The Architects' Collaborative, *16*, 108, 112, 114, 115, 116, 122, 123, 124, 177
Thompson, Benjamin, *16*, 112, 114, 119, 122, 124
Tiffany, Louis Comfort, 287, 296
Time & Life building, 26
Toll, John, 254, 262, 263
Tomorrow's House (Nelson and Wright), 196
Tompkins House (Hewlett Harbor), 76, 77–78
Tomson House (Kings Point), 143
Touster, Irwin, 158
Town Planning Associates, 98, 100

U
Ultrasuede, 288

Union Reform Temple (Freeport), 158, *163*
United Nations, 26, 252, 255, 271, 293
Urbahn, Brayton & Burrows, 174
U.S. Embassy in India, 145
Ushkow, David, 278
Usonia, 56
Usonian houses, 54, 64, 170, 196, 197, 204

V
van de Bovenkamp, Gerrit and Hans, 146
Venturi, Robert, 278
Villa Rielle. *See* Lagerwall House
Villa Savoye, 41, 137
Vita, Larry, 51
Voorhees, Walker, Smith, Smith & Haines, 254

W
Waldorf-Astoria Hotel, 127–28
Walker, Stanley, *41*
Walter Kidde Constructors, 282
Wang, Chiu-Hwa, 158
Warburg, Felix, 157–58
Warburg, Frieda, 157–58
Warhol, Andy, 233, 237
Wassily chair, 71
Watzek House (Portland, Oregon), 227
Webb & Knapp, 242, 244
Weekes, Billy, 294, 298
Wegner, Hans, *13*
Weidlinger Associates, 95
Weigel, H. Bourke, 255. *see also* Damaz, Pokorny & Weigel
Weiner, Paul Lester, 102
Weinstein, Alvin, 306
Weinstein, Joan, 306
Weinstein House (Old Westbury), 306–10
Weiss, Naftaly, 96
Welch, Barrett, 145
Welch, Mary Scott, 145
Welch House (Oyster Bay), 144–45
Wexler, Barbara, 313
Wexler, Leonard, 313
White, Stanford, 208
Whitney, David, 226
Whitney Museum of American Art, 94
Wiener, Paul Lester, 90, 106
Willard, Marian, 98, *99*, 100
Willard Johnson House (Locust Valley), *16*, 98, 101–2
Williams, Thorndike, 299
Williamsburg, Virginia, 39, 194
Williamsburg Houses (Brooklyn, New York), 180, 181, 187
Windshield House (Fishers Island), *17*, 165, 166–68
Witalis House (Kings Point), 86
Wofford, Harris L., 268–69
Wohl, Joseph S., 140–43
Wohl House (Lawrence), 140–43
Wong, Kellogg, 246
Wong, Pershing, 246
World Monuments Fund, 126
World's Fair (Brussels, 1958), 218
World's Fair (New York, 1939), 26, 30, 123, 181
World's Fair (New York, 1964), 26–27, 224, 233–37
Wright, Frank Lloyd, 31, 37, 52–56, 58, 64, 119, 138, 156, 166, 170, 196, 204, 205, 214, 234, 277, 286–87
Wright, Henry, 44, 196
Wright, Russel, 59, 67
Wurlitzer, Rudolf, 226

Y
Yeon, John, 227
Yoshimura, Junzo, 59, 116–17
Yu, Jane, 82–85

Z
Zalewski, Joseph, 100
Zeckendorf, William, 173, 238–39, 240, 241, 243–46, 251, 262
Zetlin, Lev, 235
Zion, Robert, 243, 248–50, 251, 286
Zion and Breen, 266, 280
Zweigenthal, Hermann, 107